Environment in the Balance

Environment in the Balance

The Green Movement and the Supreme Court

JONATHAN Z. CANNON

Harvard University Press

Cambridge, Massachusetts

London, England

2015

Library of Congress Cataloging-in-Publication Data

Cannon, Jonathan Z., author.
  Environment in the balance : the green movement and the Supreme Court / Jonathan
Z. Cannon.
      pages   cm
  Includes bibliographical references and index.
  ISBN 978-0-674-73678-8 (alk. paper)
   1. Environmental law—United States—History.   2. United States. Supreme Court.
 3. Environmentalism—United States.   4. Environmental policy—United States.   I. Title.
   KF3775.C365 2015
   344.7304'6—dc23

                                                                2014037110

For Alice

Contents

The views of nature held by any people determine all their institutions.
—RALPH WALDO EMERSON

All human knowledge, if it can be justified, must take on no
other form than interpretation.
—WALTER BENJAMIN

Introduction

THIS IS THE STORY of the modern environmental movement's encounters with the United States Supreme Court. It is a story of the movement's efforts to transform the culture of the country and, particularly, the law culture embodied by the Court. The results of these efforts are recorded in hundreds of the Court's decisions in environmental cases over the last four decades but are most vividly revealed in a smaller set of decisions that have special cultural resonance as well as legal significance. These cases show how environmentalism has in important ways affected the Court's deliberations and been affected by them.

Although diverse, the modern environmental movement has cohered around a discrete set of beliefs about the way the world is and how we should value it. Environmentalists embrace an ecological model of the world—one in which human and natural systems are closely interconnected and human actions affecting one part of a system are likely to have harmful effects that may be widespread in place and time. Environmentalists typically assign special value to the environment, view the threats to it as grave, and argue that efforts to protect it are entitled to high priority among competing concerns. They often express a sense of crisis and urgent need for action. Substantial protective measures must be taken, and quickly, often in the form of regulations that limit individual choice, use of technology, and economic growth. At their most ambitious, environmentalists seek not only protective policies but also a transformation of societal institutions and practices to reflect their beliefs and values. Values dominant in the national culture, such as individualism, technological mastery, and commitment to economic growth, resist that ambition.

What follows is a perspective on the success of this transformational enterprise through the lens of the Supreme Court, using its environmental decisions to probe the cultural sources of our resistance as well as our receptivity to environmentalism. In diverse cases over the last four decades, advocates have pressed the Court to shape the law to accommodate environmentalist tenets. Their arguments and the Court's response to them are framed in the specialized language of legal discourse. But a careful reading of these cases shows that the justices' deliberations reflect deep-seated, extralegal beliefs and values, both for and against environmentalist claims.

In a number of these cases, a majority of Supreme Court justices have been receptive to environmentalist beliefs and values. Indeed, in the early years of the environmental movement, the Court seemed to embrace the mood of the movement and to support its goals. But that early embrace was short-lived, and the Court has since distanced itself and adopted a more neutral and often even skeptical stance in its environmental decisions. The legal system over which the Court presides is rich with elements—including protection of private property rights, limited government, and freedom to pursue individual interest within a laissez-faire system—that may work against environmentalist goals. The Court in many cases has rejected environmentalist arguments that challenge these features of the legal system and has retained and sometimes strengthened judicial doctrines that support them. Increasingly in recent years, the Court has shown a propensity to reject environmentalists' claims in favor of industry or government positions. That trend is tempered by the Court's landmark decision in 2007 establishing regulatory authority over anthropogenic greenhouse gas emissions and a handful of other recent "proenvironmental" rulings. Overall, however, environmentalists have lost as much or more than they have won before the Court.

Opinions in these cases reveal sharply divergent views among the justices at the level of cultural as well as purely legal debate. For example, differences among the justices on legal issues such as standing, federalism, landowners' rights, and the scope of regulatory authority in environmental cases often reflect different levels of acceptance of the environmentalists' ecological model and the values associated with it. Similarly, varying degrees of sympathy with claims for the special importance of environmental concerns color the justices' interpretations of institutional orderings and legislative priorities. These persistent divisions among the justices are consistent with other evidence that the environmental movement has yet to achieve its transformative aspirations. Opposing cultural elements have endured and remain deeply embedded in our institutions and practices. This unresolved cultural conflict has produced a stalemate in which the movement has been largely successful in maintaining its historic gains but has struggled to make progress on the issues that remain.

What might this stalemate mean for the future of environmentalism, at a time when the movement is undergoing critical self-analysis and facing environmental challenges, such as climate change, of breathtaking scope and complexity? One choice for environmentalists is to double down on the cultural commitments that have brought them this far. The movement has already succeeded in changing political institutions, including monumental legislative enactments in the 1960s, 1970s, and 1980s, and might make further inroads as circumstances change: for example, improved scientific understanding and public acceptance of the causes and risks of global climate change. But the abiding resistance to environmentalist claims among a number of the justices illustrates the difficulty of simply overwhelming the cultural divisions that limit the movement's success. A second choice is to neutralize the cultural divide by broadening the movement's cultural appeal, through such means as increased reliance on markets and emphasis on economic growth, transformative technologies, and active management of natural systems. These and other innovations offer the movement risks as well as rewards—indeed, they may sever the movement from the very connectedness to nature that has powered it in the past. The book encourages a cultural pragmatism that can engage a range of perspectives in the search for beneficial outcomes while staying connected to ideas about the place of humans in nature that have been crucial to the movement's energy and purpose.

CHAPTER ONE

Environmentalism

EARTH DAY, April 22, 1970, is celebrated as the "day environmentalism in the United States began to emerge as a mass social and cultural movement." Phillip Shabecoff, a former *New York Times* reporter who became a historian and voice of the movement, captured the moment: millions of people in places across the country and around the world staged "varied and often highly inventive happenings"—from students riding horses down a freeway in Tacoma to protest automobile pollution and holding up dead fish along New York's Fifth Avenue to dramatize pollution of the Hudson River to more sedate activities such as planting trees in vacant lots or picking up plastic bottles and beer cans along local streams. They were ordinary people who harbored environmental concerns and nursed private resentments against those they identified as agents of environmental degradation—the sulfur dioxide–spewing power plant that polluted the air along the path by a river or the developer that remade rolling farmland into a shopping center. Earth Day helped turn those millions of private grievances into a powerful social and political force.[1]

Although April 22, 1970, was crucial to the emergence of the movement, environmentalism did not spring forth fully formed that day. Its foundations were laid years—indeed, in some respects, generations—earlier. These include the writings of Henry David Thoreau, George Perkins Marsh, John Muir, Aldo Leopold, Rene Dubos, and Rachel Carson. They include the conservation movement, which fostered a public discourse on the importance of protecting environmental amenities and natural resources and oversaw the birth of public agencies such as the National Forest Service and National Park System and advocacy groups such as the Wilderness Society and Sierra Club. These institutions survived the transition to the modern environmental era and indeed helped drive that transition. The roots of modern environmentalism also include other social movements of the time—civil rights, antiwar, and feminist. These movements provided organizational models for environmental activists and contributed an underlying theme of the need for social change. The late 1960s and early 1970s in the United States were swirling with protest and discontent with the status quo, and it was in this ferment that environmentalism found a new and powerful voice that was to change the nation's institutions and practices—the law perhaps most prominently.

Like its sister movements, modern environmentalism in the United States sought a transformation of the national culture. I use "culture" here to mean the basic beliefs, values, and practices shared by a group of people.[2] This includes symbolic meanings generated by cultural practices, such as law, that confirm, advance, or contest prevailing beliefs and values.[3] Culture is heterogeneous and dynamic, particularly in a postindustrial pluralistic society like the United States.[4] Groups with differing beliefs and values mobilize into opposing cultural factions. Insurgent groups challenge the dominant culture, and institutions and practices resist, adapt, or disappear, to be replaced by others. In this ferment, law and other societal institutions have a role not only in expressing and reproducing cultural norms but also in contesting and mediating among them.

Environmentalism sounds at this level of foundational conflict. It manifests itself in arguments and policies regarding a myriad of particular issues—for example, whether to build a new highway, open a section of national forest for logging, or require reductions in greenhouse gas emissions affecting climate change. But the movement ultimately is about change at a deeper level—that of our beliefs about how nature works and how people relate to it. In 1970, the year that the first Earth Day brought the movement into broad public awareness, Michael McCloskey, executive director of the Sierra Club, wrote that "a revolution is truly needed—in our values, outlook and economic organization."[5] I offer a perspective on whether and to what extent that revolution has occurred in the forty years since McCloskey wrote those words.

Although the accomplishments of the movement have been impressive, by most accounts they have fallen short of the revolution that McCloskey and other activists envisioned. Perhaps some environmentalists are content with less, but others lament the movement's failure to achieve its revolutionary aims and continue to press for cultural transformation as the ultimate measure of success. Shabecoff wrote in 2003 that environmentalists "will lose—unless there are fundamental changes in the nation's economics, its politics, the way it deploys science and technology, and the understanding and actions of its citizens."[6]

The Tenets of Environmentalism

People calling themselves environmentalists hold divergent beliefs and values, often strongly disagreeing about what environmentalism is and how to advance it. Nevertheless, it is possible to identify a set of tenets that within a manageable range of variation have characterized modern environmentalism and shaped the environmental concerns of the American public. These tenets appear in the work of social scientists who have studied the movement as well as in the sayings and writings of modern environmentalism's progenitors and exponents—from Thoreau and Marsh to Carson and McKibben.

The Social Science: Environmentalism and Cultural Contest

Social scientists have spent decades exploring whether environmental concerns can be reduced to "a single underlying social construct" supporting environmental protection and what the elements of that construct might be.[7] Among the first and most prominent efforts to isolate factors underlying environmentalist attitudes was a 1978 study by sociologists Riley E. Dunlap and Kent D. Van Liere. Their study detected an emerging "worldview," which they called the "new environmental paradigm" (NEP).[8] The major elements of the NEP were recognizing the "limits to growth," preserving the "balance of nature," and rejecting "the anthropocentric notion that nature exists solely for human use." In 2000, these researchers added two additional elements to the NEP: the rejection of human "exemptionalism" (that humans are not subject to natural constraints) and the potential for catastrophic environmental change, or "ecocrises."[9] To similar effect, in the mid-1990s three anthropologists—Willett Kempton, James S. Boster, and Jennifer A. Hartley—distilled an interconnected set of values and beliefs identified with American environmentalism. This included beliefs that nature is a limited resource on which humans depend; human-natural systems are interdependent, complex, and balanced; and nature is to be valued for its own sake. Kempton and his colleagues also determined that American environmentalism, as they measured it, was a "consensus view" among the U.S. public.[10] Although this conclusion was disputed, Dunlap and Aaron McCright recently came to a similar result using a different method: environmentalism in the United States is a "consensus movement" with a relatively stable and persistent presence.[11] In any event, these and similar studies offer evidence that attitudes, beliefs, and values associated with environmentalism are measurably present and durable among the American public.

The NEP opposes what Dunlap and Van Liere call the dominant social paradigm, or DSP—the collection of shared beliefs and values that form "the core of [the] society's cultural heritage."[12] Although the DSP is not necessarily endorsed by society as a whole, or even by a majority, it is held by dominant groups and perpetuated by prevailing institutions. Dunlap and Van Liere concluded generally that commitment to the DSP is "a *major factor* influencing environmental concern." Political scientist and environmental scholar Lester Milbrath used a military metaphor: the NEP as a vanguard, struggling to overcome the rearguard DSP.[13]

In the world of law and policy, this conflict is waged on familiar terms. The beliefs and values of the DSP cash out as faith in material abundance and support for private property rights, a laissez-faire economy, and limited governmental regulation—all negatively correlated with environmental concern. By contrast, holders of the NEP value material restraint and support protective regulation, including limits on private property rights and economic activity—all consistent with protecting environmental public goods. Environmentalists tend to be concerned about unintentional systemic effects of economic activity; those following the DSP tend to disbelieve that such effects will occur or will be serious if they do.[14]

ENVIRONMENTALISM AND BASIC CULTURAL VALUES

The NEP maps onto generic value matrices that social scientists have developed to explain what lies behind very different human responses to life's risks and challenges—including environmental risks. Prominent among these matrices is a values typology developed by anthropologist Mary Douglas and used in her work with Aaron Wildavsky on a cultural theory of risk.[15] Douglas and Wildavsky's theory holds that people assess the risks of everything from guns to premarital sex to nanotechnology in ways that advance the cultural values they hold. More recently, Dan Kahan and others have expanded on that work to claim that these values—"ways of life" or "cultural worldviews"—lead people not only to assess risks differently but also to screen information about risks selectively in ways that support their views.[16]

Douglas's theory assigns values along two scales: "grid" and "group," as shown in Figure 1.1. The grid measures values along a dimension keyed to the assignment of power, status, and other resources in society; the group,

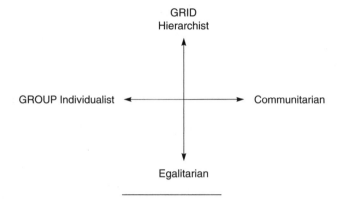

Figure 1.1
Douglas's Culture Typology (From Dan M. Kahan and Donald
Brahman, "Cultural Cognition and Public Policy," *Yale Law and
Policy Review* 24, no. 1 (2006): 151)

along a scale of individual versus group interests. Per Kahan, the contrasting
grid values are hierarchy ("pervasive and stratified 'role differentiation,'"
distribution of resources based on "explicit public social classifications")
and egalitarianism ("egalitarian worldview," resources distributed without
regard to social characteristics). The contrasting group values are individualism (competition, individuals act without collective assistance or constraint) and community (mutual dependency, society secures collective
needs).[17]

These general values preferences are predictive of environmental concern.
Kahan and his colleagues found that people with a hierarchical-individualistic
worldview can be "expected to be skeptical of claims of environmental and
technological risks." They will understand intuitively that crediting these
risks would invite "restrictions on commerce and industry, forms of behavior that Hierarchical Individualists value."[18] People with an egalitarian-
communitarian worldview will likely show greater concern about the same
risks. Their heightened sensitivity stems from suspicions of "commerce and
industry, which [egalitarian-communitarians] see as the source of unjust disparities in wealth and power" and assertive use of environmental resources.
Environmentalists are gathered largely in the lower-right quadrant of the
group-grid framework—the home of what Douglas and Wildavsky called
"sectarians," fighting from the "border" of society against a complacent
"center."

A recent study by Kahan and others on climate change illustrates how
groups with opposing cultural outlooks form contrasting assessments of
environmental risks. Using assessment of the risks of climate change,

researchers compared the views of subjects subscribing to a "hierarchical individualist" worldview with those subscribing to an "egalitarian-communitarian" worldview characteristic of environmentalists. The hierarchical individualists "rated climate change risks significantly lower" than the egalitarian-communitarians. Moreover, this difference between the groups only *increased* with greater scientific knowledge and technical reasoning capacity.[19]

Researchers have detected similar correlations between attitudes toward climate change and ideological orientation (conservative-liberal) and political party (Republican-Democrat).[20] But Kahan and his colleagues found that Douglas's cultural values scales were better predictors of views on environmental and other policy issues than were ideology or party affiliation.[21] My analysis of the cases features this values framework because it incorporates the concepts that environmentalists themselves have used to define their own and opposing worldviews and because it gives a more nuanced analysis than do terms with less specific values content such as conservative-liberal and Democrat-Republican, although I sometimes use those labels too.

Elements of the NEP also accord with the moral foundations theory of Jonathan Haidt and others, which links attitudes on issues such as the environment with activation of distinct moral domains. Haidt identifies six of these domains, each identified with an adaptive challenge that humans faced in their evolutionary history and a virtue developed to meet that challenge. These domains include "care-harm," which when activated evokes compassion in response to others' harm, and "sanctity-degradation," which produces disgust in response to perceived impurity. The NEP suggests that environmentalism is rooted in the care-harm domain, with its urgent concerns about environmental injury ("ecocrisis"). A recent survey of print and video media by Matthew Feinberg and Robb Willer found that harm- and care-based morality predominates over other moral domains in discourse on the environment.[22]

Political liberals are more likely to draw on care-harm than are conservatives, making them more inclined to see the environment as a moral issue. Sanctity-degradation, which conservatives are more partial to than are liberals, is a separate source of potential environmental concern, but it is much less prominent in the environmental discourse. Feinberg and Willer have shown that switching the routes of moral appeal can increase environmental responsiveness among conservatives. In their study, proenvironmental messages calculated to trigger the sanctity-degradation response (e.g., how polluted and contaminated the environment has become) produced a level of concern among conservatives comparable to that of liberals.[23] This finding has promise in addressing the current polarization on environmental issues.

Cross-cultural studies have shown that values and beliefs associated with the DSP are particularly strong in the United States. In a comparative study covering the United States, Canada, Spain, and a number of Latin American countries, Wesley Schultz and Lynnette Zelezny found that "U.S. respondents scored lower on the New Environmental Paradigm than respondents from all countries except the Dominican Republic, Ecuador, and Peru." Lester Milbrath faults the United States for lagging behind other developed countries in recognizing the gravity of global environmental problems and taking action on them and believes that may have much to do with the way Americans see and value their world. If modern environmentalism was born in the United States, as Bill McKibben claims, it picked a particularly challenging setting.[24]

Environmental Literature: The Culture from Inside

The U.S. environmental movement draws on a literature that spans centuries and includes writers as diverse as literary iconoclast Edward Abbey, marine biologist and nature writer Rachel Carson, and American monk and theologian Thomas Berry. Although I cannot do justice here to the richness and variety of this literature, a brief survey will help round out the portrait of environmentalism that will be useful in the analysis of the Supreme Court's decisions.

INTERDEPENDENCE: THE ECOLOGICAL PARADIGM

Environmentalists share a belief about the way the world is: that humans and the rest of nature are closely interconnected and that human intervention affecting one part of a human-natural system can be expected to have deleterious, if unintended, effects on other aspects of the system. This is the "interdependence" or "ecological" model. It stands in opposition to atomistic or disaggregated approaches that focus on substances, events, and causalities as individual and isolated.

The idea of interdependence so central to environmentalism has origins in the science of ecology. Ecology studies the interactions among life forms and physical matter in particular settings or systems. It is inevitably about relationships between and among things. Rene Dubos, an influential environmental thinker who first achieved distinction as a Nobel Prize–winning microbiologist, argued in the 1960s that science in the industrial age had been primarily concerned with "atomistic descriptions of substances and phenomena." What society needed, as the adverse effects of technological development on the environment and civilization became insupportable, was an integrated, ecological approach that could comprehend the complex interplay between technological man and nature. "A sophisticated ecology" would complement the atomism and reductionism of traditional science.[25] Ecology's holistic perspective led to its embrace by environmentalists as a "subversive" science that challenged the "assumptions and practices accepted by modern societies."[26] My analysis of the Court's environmental cases will show this subversiveness at work in a range of settings—from statutory interpretation to constitutional doctrine on judicial access, federalism, and property rights.

The litany of interdependence cascades through the environmental literature. Often accorded the distinction of the first environmentalist, George Perkins Marsh wrote one of the early works of ecology, *Man and Nature,* in 1864 before the term had been coined. His densely documented account showed "how human agencies acted in and reacted on the whole web of soil and water, plants and animals." In Paris's Jardin des Plantes, Ralph Waldo Emerson marveled at the "close and compact web of mutual relations and dependence" among objects of nature, felt the "centipede in me," and vowed to "be a naturalist." Wilderness enthusiast and advocate John Muir wrote, "When we try to pick out anything by itself, we find it hitched to everything else in the universe." Aldo Leopold envisioned a complexly interdependent "land organism" or "biotic community," which included humans as well as nonhuman nature. In *Silent Spring,* Rachel Carson described diverse harms to humans and wildlife from chemical poisons as "a problem of ecology, of interrelationships, of interdependence." David Brower, perhaps the most prominent leader of the nascent environmental movement in the 1960s and 1970s, preached Muir's "gospel" of interconnectedness to groups around the country.[27]

The interdependence or ecological model is associated with the belief that human intervention in the environment is likely to have broad-ranging effects that are serious and may be irreversible. In *Man and Nature,* Marsh identified humans as "everywhere a disturbing agent," upsetting the harmonious balances of natural systems. Natural systems were not inexhaustible or endlessly self-renewing. Epic damage could be done, as in the desertification of once-fruitful landscapes in Greece, Syria, and North Africa. And that damage might be beyond repair.[28]

Marsh's themes of limits and of the vulnerability of natural systems to the enormous destructive capacities of *Homo sapiens* echo throughout the early environmental literature and into the present. But it was Rachel Carson's *Silent Spring* that struck a peculiarly modern variation on those themes: the "evil spell," as Carson called it, the specter of environmental apocalypse. Carson's book begins with "A Fable for Tomorrow." She asks her readers to imagine a harmonious setting, a small town in rural

America—prosperous farms, foxes, and deer in the countryside, clear streams full of trout, a place "famous for the abundance and variety of its bird life." Then enters a "strange blight" encompassing the entire landscape: illness and death among humans and livestock and an eerie, shocking stillness—spring without the song of birds. This "fable," Carson wrote, might easily become reality, the result of the widespread release of man-made chemical contaminants into the environment. With this fable and the scientific but vividly written exposition that supported her dire claim, Carson installed crisis and urgency in the modern environmentalist lexicon.[29]

Carson's second major contribution in *Silent Spring* was her focus on the potential for hazards to human life and health from environmental contamination as well as harm to natural systems. Previously, environmental health concerns had focused on contaminants such as human waste and heavy industrial emissions or chemical poisons that could cause immediate discomfort, hospitalization, or death.[30] Carson identified more subtle but no less serious health threats posed by agricultural chemicals that were becoming ubiquitous in the environment and that had "immense power not merely to poison but to enter into the most vital processes of the body and change them in sinister and often deadly ways."[31] The sinister changes included a compromised immune system and the hidden and lengthy chain of cellular mutations leading to cancer. Carson's image of the human body as a complex system vulnerable to insidious threats from human agents mirrored the ecological model of interdependent and vulnerable nature and ushered in a new era of public fears over chemicals in the environment.

Silent Spring was assailed by critics as overwrought, but it set the tone for many environmentalists who followed with warnings of impending disastrous consequences of human action in an interconnected world.[32] This "doomsayer" strain of environmentalism has spawned its own cadre of skeptics seeking to undermine the environmentalists' predictions. Self-styled "ecopragmatist" Gregg Easterbrook argued in *A Moment on Earth* that nature is not fragile, as environmentalists believe, but "close to indestructible." Easterbrook acknowledged that *Silent Spring*'s predictions of ecological harm would have come to pass if reforms had not been enacted in response to Carson's warning. But he nevertheless criticized Carson's book for the practice of "selective doomsdaying," which he believed was common among environmentalists—emphasizing reasons to be afraid that adverse consequences will occur while failing to cite countervailing reasons to believe they won't.[33] In the same vein, Danish statistician Bjorn Lomborg's *The Skeptical Environmentalist*, first published in English in 2001, accused environmental groups of overstating the seriousness and extent of environmental problems and sought systematically to disprove "our doomsday conceptions."[34] For their part, environmentalists have shown no inclination to abandon the belief that the world is facing serious risks that demand strong action, as illustrated most recently by dire warnings on the dangers of climate change. For many of them, at least, environmental crisis remains "a moral master narrative of modern life," although communications experts caution that audiences may react to apocalyptic language with feelings of helplessness or despair, or they may be pushed to disbelief.[35]

In *Discordant Harmonies,* ecologist Daniel Botkin sought to dispel the notion that there is an inherent equilibrium or stability in natural systems that should be protected from human disturbance. Modern ecological science shows that nature is constantly changing and in ways that cannot be entirely predicted. There is no natural "order" or ideal steady state that can be used as an obvious benchmark for limiting human interference with nature. As Botkin has acknowledged, *Discordant Harmonies* notwithstanding, the "grand idea of a balance of nature" remains deeply entrenched in our culture and among environmentalists particularly.[36] But assertions of the absence of a naturally ordained benchmark have stoked recent efforts to reform the movement.

The interdependence model not only embodies a belief about the way the world works, it is also associated with a sense of community with nonhuman nature and collective responsibility to care for the environment. Published after his death in 1949, Aldo Leopold's "The Land Ethic" argued for extending moral consideration to an expanded "community" that includes both humans and nonhuman nature. Leopold believed that this "extension of ethics" would take root as society came to understand its essential dependency on an increasingly beleaguered land organism. "All ethics . . . rest upon a single premise: that the individual is a member of a community of interdependent parts." In his influential history of the environmental movement, Shabecoff quoted this sentence from Leopold with the comment that "almost all else in environmentalism proceeds from that premise."[37]

VALUES

The environmental literature confirms the values account of Kahan and his colleagues, particularly the emphasis that environmentalists place on egalitarian and communitarian values. (I will often refer to the latter as "collectivism.") As in Kahan's account, these values are balanced by a set of competing values—individualism and hierarchy. Also prominent in the environmental literature is a third value dimension—mastery-harmony—which aligns with the hierarchy-egalitarianism axis in Douglas's typology. Mastery-harmony contrasts a hierarchical view of humans in relation to nature (humans as "conquerors" of nature) with one of equality (humans as "mere citizens" in community with nature). This extension of the hierarchy-egalitarian value opposition to relations between humans and nature distinguishes environmentalism from other modern social movements that share similar values but limit their concerns to status among humans. At its extreme, the harmony value manifests as the "biospheric egalitarianism" of the deep ecologists, but it also has more moderate expressions in environmentalist thought and practice.[38] (I will use the terms "hierarchy" and "egalitarian" to refer to relationships among humans but "harmony" and "mastery" to denote comparable values applied to relationships between humans and nature.)

Harmony and mastery.   More than a century before the first Earth Day, Henry David Thoreau planted the seeds of the harmony-mastery opposition that was to become central to twentieth-century environmentalism. For Thoreau nature was not the "other"; it was his community, it was himself. In *Walden,* he celebrated the "sweet and beneficent society in nature" and asked, "Shall I not have intelligence with the earth? Am I not partly leaves and vegetable mould myself?" Later, in his essay "Walking," he argued even more provocatively for a notion of humans as "a part and parcel of Nature, rather than a member of society." This accompanied a distaste for "man's improvements, so called"—"the building of houses and the cutting down of the forest and of all large trees, simply deform the landscape, and make it more and more tame and cheap."[39]

Aldo Leopold recast Thoreau's intuitions in ecological terms, with a strongly ethical thrust. His idea of the biotic community incorporated the value of living harmoniously with nature and contrasted that with the drive to conquer, master, or dominate it. The land ethic, Leopold maintained, "changes the role of *Homo sapiens* from conqueror of the land-community to plain member and citizen of it." The progress is a moral one, from mastery to harmony. In delineating the "ecological conscience," Leopold made this explicit: "conservation is a state of harmony between men and land."[40]

Leopold's successors assured the centrality of the harmony-mastery opposition as the environmental movement emerged. In *Silent Spring,* Rachel Carson's idyll is town life lived "in harmony with its surroundings." The atavistic drive to mastery is the despoiler: "the 'control of nature' is a phrase conceived in arrogance, born of the Neanderthal age of biology and philosophy, when it was supposed that nature exists for the convenience of man." In *So Human an Animal,* Rene Dubos wrote, echoing Leopold, that what we needed was a "new social ethic—almost a new social religion." The essence of that religion would be "harmony with nature as well as man, instead of the drive for mastery." The rejection of humans-over-nature unites many strains of modern environmentalism.[41]

Mastery values emphasize getting ahead through assertive use of the natural environment. They are associated with economic growth and material abundance and are closely linked to American individualism. But mastery values may be pursued through group action as well as individual initiative, by governmental as well as private initiatives. Some of the environmental literature's most vivid evocations of mastery values have concerned governmental undertakings.

For example, John McPhee's *Encounters with the Archdruid,* which came out in 1971 just as the movement was gaining broad momentum, recorded a classic clash between harmony and mastery values in the persons of David Brower, the "archdruid" himself, and Floyd Dominy, director of the Bureau of Reclamation in the U.S. Department of the Interior and lifelong builder of dams. The debate was over the Bureau's construction, with authorization from Congress, of the giant Glen Canyon Dam on the Colorado River. The dam flooded the canyon to create Lake Powell. Brower had belatedly opposed the construction of the dam; Dominy had pushed the dam through. By Dominy's lights, the dam had improved the river, putting it to work for humans—for water supply, electricity, recreation. For Brower, the scenic features and wilderness values of the river that were destroyed far exceeded in significance and value anything the dam offered in return. He likened the event to flooding the Sistine Chapel.[42]

Cloaked in the language of judicial deliberation, versions of this dispute inform a number of the cases, such as *Citizens to Preserve Overton Park, Inc. v. Volpe* (routing an interstate highway through a city park with old-growth forest) and *Robertson v. Methow Valley Citizens Council* (siting a luxury ski resort in a national forest).[43]

Collectivism and autonomy. The master narrative of the American dream stresses personal autonomy—the desirability of expressing and pursing one's own interests as well as the freedom to do so. The aspect of autonomy most relevant to environmental concerns focuses on the manipulation of nature to advance one's self-interest, and like mastery it is strongly associated in the United States with the laissez-faire economy and material abundance. (I will use "autonomy" in this sense interchangeably with "individualism" in the Douglas-Wildavsky-Kahan framework.) This autonomy may be in conflict with group interest and opposed to collective measures to secure that interest.[44]

In his 1968 essay, "The Tragedy of the Commons," American ecologist Garrett Hardin argued that individual self-interest, rationally pursued, leads to overuse of the environmental commons and other shared resources. Hardin asks us to imagine a grazing commons, to which herdsmen enjoy unfettered access to graze their cattle. Initially, open access might not threaten

the productivity of the commons: the pressure represented by those par-
taking would be below the carrying capacity of the land. But in time, as
each herdsman grazed as many cattle as possible to maximize his returns,
the commons would reach a point of collapse, leaving all the herdsman
worse off than they would have been had they limited their grazing. The
"tragedy" occurs because in deciding whether to graze additional animals,
each herdsman fully takes into account his own benefits from the sale of
his animals and largely ignores costs to others from destruction of the commons. Although rational from the perspective of each autonomous herdsman,
the result can be collectively disastrous.[45]

Hardin's immediate concern in his essay was overpopulation, but his metaphor applies to a wide range of abuses involving both taking too much out
of the environment (using the environment as raw material for wealth
creation) and putting too much into it (using the environment as a sink for
the by-products of wealth creation). Garrett's prescription for the problem
of overuse was collective restraint: "mutual coercion mutually agreed to
by a majority of those affected." Mutual coercion to temper the abuse of
the commons might take several forms, including the assignment of property rights in the resource. Hardin's own preferred solution was "administrative law"—that is, regulation. This solution to the tragedy was in tension with autonomy in the assertive use of the environment for economic
gain. That tension is important in environmental cases concerning not only
property rights but also issues of citizens' access to the courts and the regulatory scope of federal environmental statutes.

Although Hardin's essay has been criticized in a number of its particulars, it enjoys canonical status as a conceptual foundation of modern environmental policy and law. In particular, it serves as a theoretical basis of
environmental regulation, consistent with the communitarian or collectivist
values shared by most environmentalists and antithetical to the competing
autonomy values. But Hardin's parable also has hidden within it the seeds
of an economic approach to environmental policy, which many environmentalists resist: for them, the issue is not securing the optimal use of the
commons but recognizing moral obligations to the commons itself as well
as to other herdsmen.

Many environmentalists are uneasy with what they see as the valoriza-
tion of the autonomous individual in American culture. Writing in the 1960s,
not long after the publication of *Silent Spring,* environmental policy pioneer
and public official Steward Udall blamed the "extreme individualism" associated with a frontier mentality for the nineteenth-century destruction of
the great buffalo herds and the passenger pigeons and blamed a kind of
"laissez-faire individualism" for the destructive practices of hydraulic miners
and loggers. Unchecked individualism led to reckless exploitation of re-

sources that ignored sound practice and cheated future generations. Udall argued that from this sad history, we learned the importance of government action to protect the environmental commons.[46]

More recently, writer and activist Bill McKibben has called for deemphasizing individualism in protecting our common interest in the environment. In his book *Deep Economy*, he writes that we have pursued "more" at the expense of "better." "Our exaltation of the individual, which was the key to more, has passed the point of diminishing returns." Indeed, he argues, we have passed from individualism to "hyper-individualism" and produced an economy that while enhancing monetary wealth is degrading the environment for future generations. The antidote is not socialism, McKibben writes, but a new emphasis on community.[47]

At the heart of the tension between autonomy, on the one hand, and community solidarity and collective restraint, on the other, are competing notions of liberty. A landowner unchecked by regulation has broad latitude in deciding what to do with the resources on his land—sometimes called negative liberty. But his exercise of that liberty may limit the choices available to others. He may use his land in a way that involuntarily burdens neighboring landowners, thus reducing their liberty. Holding the landowner exempt from government constraints also limits the positive liberty we associate with collective self-determination—the freedom to define our community through majoritarian processes rather than have it defined through the choices of individuals acting on their own. The autonomy values associated with individualism stress the liberty of the landowner at the expense of these competing forms of liberty. Most environmentalists instead stress the value of a collective restraint that is capable of binding everyone in the interests of the common good.[48]

Egalitarianism and hierarchy.   Egalitarianism, which emphasizes equality, is broadly opposed to hierarchy, which accepts the legitimacy of an unequal allocation of social roles and resources. Hierarchy is linked to both mastery and autonomy because aggressive use of the natural environment, whether by individuals or groups, may generate unequal allocations of resources and power. Environmentalists vilify the powerful elites they see as having caused or sanctioned environmental harm. In *Silent Spring*, Carson traced environmental threats to the powerful chemical pesticide industry, which drove the development, distribution, and use of its products and turned a blind eye to their destructiveness. In addition to powerful corporate interests, environmentalists also implicate governmental officials and private developers as suspect elites.

The movement's narratives often take the form of the David and Goliath tale. Environmentalists celebrate the struggle of Lois Gibbs, an ordinary housewife in the blue collar community of Love Canal in Niagara Falls, New York, who fought the chemical industry and the government to protect her family from the effects of a toxic waste dump. Versions of this story appear in such cases as *Solid Waste Agency of Northern Cook County v. U.S. Army Corps of Engineers* (local activists resisting siting of a solid waste facility by a public agency) and *Friends of the Earth, Inc. v. Laidlaw Environmental Services (TOC), Inc.* (local citizens and environmental groups protesting pollution of their watershed by a hazardous waste facility owned by a large multinational corporation). Sometimes the narrative line flips, however: in *Rapanos v. United States* and *Lucas v. South Carolina Coastal Council,* landowner-developers took on the role of David against the regulatory state's Goliath.[49]

Commentators such as social critic Murray Bookchin have pressed to have egalitarian values play an even more fundamental role in the movement. Environmentalism, he argues, should be understood as a social movement; "ecology . . . has always meant *social* ecology." In this view, environmental crises are merely symptoms of the prevalent sensibility of domination, the hierarchical institutions, and the exploitative strategies of the mainstream culture. Environmentalism cannot succeed in its aims unless it addresses classism, racism, sexism, and other systemic inequalities. Bookchin's environmentalism is thus of a piece with other social justice movements that emerged in the twentieth century. His social radicalism rests uneasily at the movement's margins, but it is the model for a recent critique by prominent environmentalist Gus Speth, who contends that a progressive revolution is necessary for environmentalism's ultimate success.[50]

Emerging in the late 1970s and 1980s, the environmental justice movement generated an egalitarian critique of mainstream environmentalism itself. In 1990, UCLA sociologist Robert Bullard published *Dumping in Dixie: Race, Class, and Environmental Quality,* in which he argued that African Americans, lower-income groups, and working-class people had suffered disproportionately from environmental harms and that these same groups were poorly represented in and by the environmental movement. Rather than seek redress for these groups, environmentalists redirected resources away from the concerns of the disadvantaged (e.g., toxic waste, industrial siting, housing quality) toward the priorities of the well-off (e.g., preservation, outdoor recreation, regulatory stringency). Bullard advocated a more radical social justice–based movement patterned closely on the civil rights movement, one that could correct for the lack of political and economic power among communities of color and the poor.[51]

Despite disputes over the strength of the data supporting its claims of disproportionate risk, the environmental justice movement has achieved social and institutional recognition. It exists now both outside mainstream environmentalism, as a critique of the movement, and within it, as a component of mainstream efforts and governmental programs. Its theme of unequal environmental burdens on the disadvantaged has broad resonance, as in *Lyng v. Northwest Indian Cemetery Protective Association* (a road-building project on federal lands threatening Indian tribes' ceremonial use of sacred lands).[52]

THE ETHICS OF THE ENVIRONMENT: LEOPOLD'S ECOCENTRISM

The ecological model and its associated harmony values support a unique and deeply radical feature of environmentalist thought: that nature has value in itself, apart from its ability to serve human needs or preferences. This idea of nonanthropocentric moral value has numerous versions but can be roughly divided under the rubrics of "biocentrism" (which locates value in individual plants or animals) and "ecocentrism" (which locates value in aggregations such as species and ecosystems). It is opposed to "anthropocentrism," the notion that nature has no value apart from its usefulness or appeal to human beings. Nonanthropocentric approaches argue for an extension of moral consideration to nonhuman nature as the next step in the historical expansion of the moral universe from the more immediate and familiar to the more remote and foreign.

Leopold begins "The Land Ethic" with godlike Odysseus's return from Troy, at which moment he reclaimed his wife and home and "hanged all on one rope a dozen slave-girls of his household whom he suspected of misbehavior during his absence." By the lights of his time, Odysseus was entitled to do this because the slave-girls were his property, governed by expediency only, and not part of an ethical community. In the 3,000 years since, however, the ethical community has expanded, as sheer expediency has been replaced "by cooperative mechanisms with an ethical content." The next and now ecologically necessary step is an ethical relation to the land community based on "love, respect and admiration for land, and a high regard for its value." Leopold distills the new ethical obligation thusly: "A thing is right when it tends to preserve the integrity, stability, and beauty of the biotic community. It is wrong when it tends otherwise."[53]

Leopold was not a philosopher. His ethical precept raises interpretative, practical, and philosophical questions that he made no effort to answer. Yet commentators return again and again to these words because Leopold's influence makes them impossible to ignore for anyone advancing or opposing the independent moral status of the biotic community. His land ethic is the fountainhead of modern ecocentrism as well as a mandatory reference point for competing or emerging theories of environmental ethics.

Despite the contests over its meaning, or because of them, it offers a useful touchstone for how egalitarian-communitarians might think about the environment.[54]

Leopold saw moral value in the biotic community as a whole and did not advance the notion of rights for individual organisms. Although he did refer in passing to the "right to continued existence" of the biotic community, he did not develop the concept.[55] But rights-talk moved front and center in environmentalist discourse with legal philosopher Christopher Stone's much-publicized essay, "Should Trees Have Standing?" Stone's article was written to influence the Supreme Court's deliberations in *Sierra Club v. Morton,* a case brought to protect Mineral King, a glacial valley in California, from development as a ski resort. Although the case is nowhere mentioned in the piece, Stone argued that things in nature—"forests, . . . rivers and other so-called 'natural objects' "—should be accorded some legal rights, including the right to seek legal redress on their own behalf. Stone analogized his innovation to the expansion of rights to children, women, blacks, and Indians. Extending rights to natural objects would be consistent with the "history of man's moral development [as] a continual extension . . . of [man's] 'social instincts and sympathies.' " Stone's argument was similar to Leopold's in its extension of moral consideration to the land community, but Stone went a step further by expressing the moral development in institutional terms—the language of legal rights. Although Stone's article was not published in time for the oral argument in *Sierra Club,* it did influence the Court's deliberations. Along with Justice Douglas's dissent in that case, it enjoys canonical status in the literature of the environment.[56]

There are much-debated differences among nonanthropocentrists about whether the moral value in nature should attach to individual animals, species, ecosystems, or some other unit of nature and whether it should be expressed as rights, obligations, virtues, or something else. But the common notion of extending moral significance beyond ourselves gives these diverse strains of nonanthropocentrism a place of importance in the environmental movement that transcends their differences. As its advocates recognize, the notion is revolutionary: if taken seriously, it would require a thorough restructuring of our policies, priorities, and institutions. And it is correspondingly strange. Bill McKibben observed: "the idea that the rest of creation might count for as much as we do is spectacularly foreign, even to most environmentalists."[57]

But perhaps not so foreign as it might seem. Ecocentrism is most closely associated with strong versions of environmentalism, such as deep ecology or animal rights, and radical groups, such as Earth First! and the Animal Liberation Front. However, it may also have broader social currency. Anthropologist Willett Kempton and colleagues surveyed individuals from five groups: Earth First!, Sierra Club, dry cleaners, sawmill workers, and the general public. To each group they offered the proposition that "our obligation to preserve nature isn't just a responsibility to other people but to the environment itself." Predictably, large majorities of the environmental groups agreed, but so did substantial majorities of the other groups.[58] Comparable majorities of each group also agreed with an alternative justice-based formulation: "Justice is not just for human beings. We need to be as fair to plants and animals as we are towards people." This suggests that environmentalism's most challenging idea may already be planted in the culture, although it is unclear how deeply or to what effect. Ecocentrism's cultural standing is implicated in *Sierra Club* and other cases in which the Court has held the fate of a species or a landscape in its hands.

Environmentalists also include anthropocentrists, who base the imperative for environmental protection on the importance of healthy natural systems to human well-being. These environmentalists don't accept the intellectual basis or wisdom of the nonanthropocentric accounts but may otherwise share key tenets of the movement—for example, living in harmony with nature (because it is good for humans) or collectivist regard for group welfare. They distinguish themselves from nonenvironmentalists as progressives who value the aesthetic and recreational benefits of nature, the conservation of resources for future generations, and strong protections for human life and health. Environmentalists may hold both anthropocentric and nonanthropocentric views in a kind of ethical pluralism. E. O. Wilson, who argues for an ethic of biodiversity preservation based on the genetic unity of life, also argues for species preservation based on human benefits such as medicinal uses, ecosystem services, and aesthetic appeal. Perhaps because they have wider or more intense public appeal, anthropocentric arguments are vastly predominant in policy debates on environmental issues; ecocentric views remain an important subtext for many environmentalists but are increasingly under fire from reformists within the movement.[59]

ENVIRONMENTALISM AND RELIGION

Environmentalism and religion have had a fraught relationship, beginning with a provocative and influential essay written by historian Lynn White in 1967. White claimed that in its Western form, "Christianity is the most anthropocentric religion the world has seen." His essay also put environmentalism in direct opposition to the nation's predominant religion. Christianity was to blame, White argued, for draining the natural world of spiritual significance and sanctioning the human dominance over nature that had brought us environmental crisis. But he also identified a minority strain of Christianity, based on the teachings of St. Francis, who "tried to depose man from his monarchy over creation and set up a democracy of all God's creatures"—much as Leopold and other secular environmentalists attempted to do in their upending of the mastery narrative.[60]

While many religionists rejected White's argument as an unjustified attack on the faith, others accepted his assumption about the centrality of religion and urged changes in religious practice or doctrine to promote the cultural change necessary to meet the environmental challenge. These changes rippled through established religions. In 1979, a little more than a decade after White's essay, Pope John Paul II designated St. Francis as the patron saint of "caretakers of ecology." In 1990, he issued a message, "Peace with All Creation," in which he endorsed the "new ecological awareness. . . . Theology, philosophy and science all speak of a harmonious universe, of a 'cosmos' endowed with its own integrity. . . . *This order must be respected.* The human race is called to explore this order . . . and to make use of it while safeguarding its integrity." Here were shades of Leopold's land ethic. Then-senator and environmentalist Al Gore, a Baptist, applauded the pope's statement and urged a revival of the stewardship duties of the Judeo-Christian tradition.[61]

In his *The Dream of the Earth,* American monk and ecotheologian Thomas Berry argued for new spiritual practices for the modern ecological age. The first step must be to restore what Western Christianity took away, as Lynn White had it: our "sense of the sacred character of the natural world as our primary revelation of the divine." Like others seeking expression of their environmentalism in spiritual terms, Berry looked to the American Indian as a model for this essential reconnection. "The Indian peoples of America have their own special form of mysticism. Awareness of a numinous presence throughout the entire cosmic order establishes among these peoples one of the most integral forms of spirituality known to us." This was dangerously close to pantheism, of which White was also accused, but for Berry and others it was a tradition of broad significance to the whole human community in the cultural moment in which it found itself.[62]

Environmentalism may be a religion of its own. Environmentalists themselves have sometimes described their ventures as religious or having religious overtones. John Muir wrote of the threatened Yosemite Park's Hetch-Hetchy Valley that "no holier temple has ever been consecrated by the heart of man." "Instead of lifting their eyes to the God of the mountains," he charged, proponents of damming the valley "lift them to the Almighty Dollar." National parks advocate Joseph Sax pictured himself and his fellow advocates as "secular prophets, preaching a message of secular salvation." After writing "The Trouble with Wilderness," a controversial essay that criticized the wilderness concept, environmental historian William Cronon sought the understanding of angry fellow environmentalists by acknowledging that he too was among "those who worship at the altar of wilderness" and was only trying to reveal the problems in "[his] own" religion. David Brower, who was as crucial as anyone to the emergence of the modern movement, regularly delivered his "sermon" to the environmental faithful. Chronicler John McPhee indelibly linked Brower's nature mysticism to the pre-Christian druids of Europe. *Lyng v. Northwest Indian Cemetery Protective Association* offers a glimpse of what environmentalism-as-religion might mean in practice.[63]

Contemporary environmental leaders have been hesitant to advance the movement as a religion. To the extent that environmentalists do experience their beliefs as a kind of religion, that experience is largely submerged or disguised in the public discourse. Like ecocentrism, to which it is closely related, environmentalism-as-religion has a cultural strangeness that may cause unnecessary resistance among those whom environmentalists would persuade. It is a target for criticism from at least two sides: traditionalists, who see it as a false religion, worshipping nature over God and upsetting the divinely ordained relationship between humans and the rest of creation, and rationalists, who see in its devotion to nature a mysticism divorced from fact and reason. Nevertheless, if cultural critic Robert Nelson is right, "American environmental groups derive much of their moral energy, their funding, their sense of purpose, and their crusading drive from an 'environmental fundamentalism'" that has grown out of "religious awakening."[64] In Chapter 10, I explore what role, if any, such a fundamentalism might play in the future of a diverse and changing movement.

PRIORITIES: ENTER THE DISMAL SCIENCE

Environmentalists believe that the threats that concern them are urgent. In part this urgency is driven by the sense that humans have created environmental crises requiring immediate attention. But even in the absence of a crisis, environmentalists believe that the things they seek to protect—natural systems, human life, and health—are of special value and that addressing threats to these things deserves priority over competing claims for public attention and resources. These claims may be supported by diverse arguments—ethical, economic, scientific—but collectively they form perhaps the most universal feature of the movement. They figure prominently in public debates on policy choices about whether and how much to require protection of environmental goods, and they are reflected in the Court's decisions on issues from preservation of biodiversity to protection of human health.

While environmentalists were developing their vision of a new relationship with nature based on harmony, equality, and community, welfare economists were advancing their own view of the human-natural relationship. That view was thoroughly anthropocentric and accorded only as much value to things in nature as the aggregate preferences of affected human individuals justified. It had roots in the Progressive Era's commitment to scientific management for the efficient use of natural resources under Teddy Roosevelt and Gifford Pinchot. J. H. Dales offered a version of this view in his 1968 classic, *Pollution, Property and Prices*. Others such as William F. Baxter followed with simplified accounts, making the welfare economists' take on environmental issues broadly accessible. In his widely read and influential *People or Penguins*, first published in 1974, Baxter posed the question of whether humans should act to halt the use of DDT in the environment to preserve the penguin population. His answer: we should give up DDT but only if and to the extent that "the well-being of people would be less impaired by halting use of DDT than by giving up penguins."[65]

Contrary to many environmentalists, Baxter and his fellow economists rejected the notion of a "right" or "morally correct" state of nature or level of pollution apart from overall human well-being. The notion of an "ought" extending beyond the human community made no sense, they argued: nature can have no rights. Also, in the welfare economist's world, everyone's preferences counted the same—no person's preferences were given more weight than another's because he or she was thought to be morally superior. There was no moral high ground in the welfare calculus.[66]

For Baxter and other economists, finding the "optimal" or "efficient" level of pollution or environmental harm was a matter of balancing human preferences for the environmental good that is threatened against preferences for the goods that would be forsaken to avoid that threat. The method that welfare economists have developed for deciding the optimal level of an environmental good, such as penguins, is cost-benefit analysis (CBA), a matter of intense cultural and methodological debate. Environmentalists and other health and safety advocates argue that CBA ignores the moral importance of environmental protection and other public goods; is relentlessly antienvironmental in its design and implementation; privileges the cultural status quo; and impoverishes the political discourse.[67] On the other side, proponents of CBA argue that it is essential for balanced, welfare-enhancing regulatory decisions; is neutral as between pro- and antienvironmental outcomes; and contributes to transparency and informed political discussion.[68] This debate extends beyond the environment to other regulatory policy arenas, such as worker and consumer health and safety.

Although legal scholar and former regulatory czar Cass Sunstein has argued that the dawning of the "cost-benefit state" is at hand, most environmentalists continue to resist CBA as systematically undervaluing their concerns and as blind to the expansion of moral community that they seek. Robert Nelson, who was himself trained as an economist, sees this conflict between economics and environmentalism in theological terms. In *The New Holy Wars,* he argues that economics, like environmentalism, is a religion in disguise, offering a progressive gospel in which efficiency is the salvation of mankind.[69] Because environmentalism has defined itself largely against this gospel, he concludes that an epochal struggle between the two is unavoidable. I test this proposition in my analysis of the cases on economic approaches and their implications for environmentalism's future.

PRECAUTION: ENVIRONMENTALIST ANTIDOTE
TO THE EFFICIENCY PARADIGM

In lieu of efficiency, environmentalists offer precaution. The precautionary principle derives from the German *Vorsorgeprinzip,* "which translates literally as the 'principle of prior care and worry.'" The precautionary approach has weaker and stronger forms. Weaker forms, such as the 1992 Rio Declaration on Environment and Development, counsel simply that measures to combat substantial environmental threats not be rejected because of a lack of scientific certainty surrounding those threats. Stronger, more controversial forms create a presumption of regulation in the face of uncertain threats.[70] The Court has dealt with statutes embodying this principle, perhaps most notably in *Massachusetts v. EPA* (Environmental Protection Agency's authority to regulate greenhouse gas emissions under the Clean Air Act).

Seeing a direct challenge to the efficiency paradigm, CBA proponents have produced a drumbeat of criticism focused particularly on strong forms of the precautionary principle. Cass Sunstein argued that these versions of the precautionary approach provide "no guidance" in making the hard trade-offs that are typical of environmental decisions and risk excessive or counterproductive regulation. To the extent that the principle depends on a concept of benevolent nature—"nature as harmonious or in balance"—it was simply wrong. There is no intrinsic or stable balance in nature, as Botkin taught us. And "what is natural may not be safe at all." For Douglas Kysar and other defenders of the precautionary principle, however, its strength is its relational emphasis, including "notions of 'caring *for* or looking *after,* fretting or worrying *about,* and obtaining provisions, or providing *for*'" that resonate with the values of caring, community, and harmony prevalent among environmentalists. "On the precautionary account, environmental, health, and safety regulation is not merely an opportunity to maximize an existing set of individual preferences or interests, but rather a moment to consider the regulating body's obligations to its present and future members, to other political communities, and to other species."[71]

THERE IS PLENTY that divides environmentalists. Radical factions disdain the accommodationism of reformists; grassroots activists disdain the professionalism and interest group tactics of national organizations; environmental justice advocates separate themselves from white middle-class environmentalism. Ecocentrists argue with anthropocentrists. Environmentalists stressing limits on human action or pessimism about the future are criticized by those urging possibilities and optimism. Those embracing economic instruments and models are criticized by those who reject them. Some of these divisions will play out in the analysis of the cases, and in Chapter 10 they are explored in light of that analysis, to assess the success of the movement and consider its possible futures.[72]

My initial emphasis, however, is on the commonalities. A coherent (though eminently contestable) set of values and beliefs informs the modern environmental movement. The evidence suggests that heightened environmental concern accords generally with a set of beliefs and values with which those calling themselves environmentalists generally identify. This environmentalism is a distinct and persistent feature of modern U.S. culture, is shared to some degree by the majority of Americans, and has proved to be relatively stable over time.

We face a paradox, however. Despite its apparently successful inroads into the culture, environmentalism is perceived widely as having failed in its basic transformative mission and lacking the strength to force further change. In the words of one of its chief expositors, Phillip Shabecoff, "environmentalism has barely scratched the skin of the old order." Environmental preferences among the public, while widespread, do not appear deep. Environmental concern chronically ranks below potentially competing concerns, such as economic progress, in public opinion surveys. In its current balkanized state, the political system is incapable of effectively addressing what environmentalists are convinced are the most critical issues facing the nation's and the world's future.[73]

This book is an effort to understand this paradox through the deliberative institution of the Court. It explores the cultural roots of the paradox in the specialized discourse of law and legal decisions and attempts to understand not only the institutional practices that support environmentalism and the values and worldviews that underpin it but also the practices that oppose it. And finally, it draws out the implications of that paradox for environmentalism's future and for the country's ability to address major environmental challenges such as climate change.

CHAPTER TWO

Environmental Law, the Court, and Interpretation

Fᴿᴏᴍ ᴛʜᴇ ʟᴀᴛᴇ 1960s through the early 1980s, environmentalism generated an astounding wave of new and demanding legislation in the United States at the federal level, with comparable activity in some states. It also gave rise to new institutions, such as the U.S. Environmental Protection Agency (EPA), to implement and enforce these laws. These innovations have proved remarkably durable, despite political efforts to weaken them or wipe them away. Many environmentalists, however, question whether environmental laws have fulfilled their promise. At one level this is a question about whether these laws have achieved sufficient protections and whether those protections can survive in the future under hostile pressure. More deeply, the question is whether these laws advance the cultural change that environmentalists seek or whether they are only marginal adjustments to an essentially unchanged social, economic, and political system. The environmental laws enacted during this period, both in number and content, suggested for many a sea change—a fundamental altering of how people in this country saw themselves in relation to their physical environment and to each other—but the cultural portent of these laws has weakened over time, partly as a result of political and judicial responses that have constrained their expression.

This chapter illustrates the transformational promise of these laws and sets the stage for our examination of the Supreme Court's role in advancing or checking their fulfillment. The Court represents a distinct law culture, but the Court is also shaped by the ambient culture and helps shape it in kind. While purporting to follow neutral principles of legal analysis, the decisions of the Supreme Court—or some of them—reflect the Court's response to conflicts in the ambient culture. In the Court's most culturally salient environmental decisions, the clash of values and beliefs implicit in the cases spills into the judicial opinions, often revealing intense differences in the worldviews of the justices themselves.

Modern Environmental Law: A Brief Portrait

As the modern environmental movement came to prominence, advocates expressed high expectations for the role that law and the courts might play.[1] Claiming parallels between their movement and the civil rights movement, environmentalists sought constitutional-level recognition of environmental rights comparable to the Court's decision barring racial segregation in schools in *Brown v. Board of Education.* In a foreword to the May 1970 issue of the *Cornell Law Review,* Senator Edmund Muskie, a leader of the environmental legislative successes of the early 1970s, put environmental quality on the same footing as other basic human goals: "peace and dignity for all." In that same issue, law professor E. F. Roberts argued that in the absence in the U.S. Constitution of an express right to a clean environment, the Supreme Court should imply one. This "right to an environment fit for human habitation" would sound in the Fifth Amendment's due process clause, embodying the basic guarantees of life and the pursuit of happiness as well as liberty. Much as in *Brown,* Roberts argued, the system was in crisis, the politicians could not be trusted (in this case, because of their entrenched dependence on economic interests), and it was up to the Court—its justices serving as the priestly class, the "enlightened skeleton of society"—to protect basic human values. In his widely read *Defending the Environment,* also published in 1970, environmentalist and law scholar Joseph Sax also argued for a transformative role for the courts. Sax did not urge a constitutional level right to the environment; instead he made the case for judicial expansion of common law nuisance to facilitate the right of citizens to sue for injury to public environmental resources.[2]

The court-made environmental rights so urgently sought in the early days of the movement did not materialize. And the need for them seemed to fade with the wave of federal environmental legislation that soon followed. Rather than play the institutional champions, risking their legitimacy to boldly advance the nascent movement, the courts settled into their more familiar, modest, interstitial role.

This more modest role still leaves plenty of room for the courts to affect the course of environmental law and policy. They interpret constitutional doctrines with an important bearing on whether environmental advocates will be allowed to bring their claims to court and how and where disputes will be resolved. In addition, they interpret the federal environmental statutes and pass on the reasonableness of agency actions to implement them. Finally, they also play a key role in enforcing these laws, often over the opposition of powerful economic interests.

The Constitutional Setting

The U.S. Constitution—the eighteenth-century document establishing the nation's foundational arrangements—is pre-ecological. It makes no provision for environmental rights or authorities. It fairly bristles with elements of the dominant paradigm that sociologists cast as inimical to environmentalism: protection of private property rights, support for limited government, and freedom to pursue individual interests within a laissez-faire system. These are all backed by a thoroughgoing anthropocentrism.

The Constitution's failure to expressly address environmental concerns may be a function of its age, but it makes the United States an outlier internationally. Most of the world's constitutions (all of them younger) establish some form of a right to a healthy environment or a government duty to protect it.[3] There have been numerous suggestions for amending the U.S. Constitution along these lines, and a number of states in this country have adopted such amendments to their constitutions.[4] But this avenue of change is difficult procedurally and of uncertain benefit. The experience of many of the states that have adopted these provisions is that the rights or obligations conferred are weakly enforced.[5]

Although the Constitution lacks any provision specifically for the environment, several generic constitutional doctrines have figured importantly in the Court's environmental cases, mostly to the detriment of environmentalist claims. These include standing, federalism, and protection of private property against governmental takings. The Court has used these doctrines to limit the scope of federal environmental protections and to condition access to the federal courts by citizens seeking to vindicate those protections.

STANDING

The Constitution allocates governmental powers among the three branches of the federal government and between the federal government and the states. The Supreme Court and lower federal courts have the power to hear and decide "cases" and "controversies." The Supreme Court has read this grant of power as limiting access to the federal courts for parties, such as environmental groups, seeking to protect a common good. In *Lujan v. Defenders of Wildlife* (*Lujan II*), decided in 1992, the Court sent a message to environmentalists and other public interest advocates that it would be tougher in policing limits on judicial access than in the past: it denied standing to endangered species advocates for failing to show sufficiently "concrete and particularized" injury from harm to the species of concern. While the Court later moderated the impact of *Lujan II,* its standing doctrine continues to limit judicial access to, among other parties, environmentalists seeking favorable interpretations and enforcement of environmental laws.[6]

FEDERALISM

Federalism concerns the allocation of power between the states and the federal government. Federal law has supremacy over conflicting state law, but the federal government is one of limited powers, as enumerated in the Constitution. Powers not assigned to the federal government or not specifically withheld from the states by the Constitution are reserved to the states. In spelling out the permissible uses of Congress's legislative power, the Constitution makes no specific provision for laws to regulate environmental concerns. Express authorizations for legislation include regulating commerce among the states and with foreign nations, collecting money through taxes and spending it for "the common defense and general welfare," and regulating property owned by the government. In the absence of an "environmental regulation" clause, each federal environmental law must rest on one or more of these enumerated powers; the major environmental statutes rest primarily on the power of Congress to regulate interstate commerce (commerce power). The fit may be awkward, and where it is, the law is exposed to possible invalidation on review by a federal court.[7]

The massive federalization of environmental law that took place in the 1960s and 1970s was followed in the 1990s by a doctrinal shift in the Court that emphasized the limits of federal power. *New York v. United States,* decided in 1992, the first in a line of cases that produced this shift, invalidated a federal statute requiring states to regulate disposal of low-level radioactive waste. The Court followed it with other decisions that limited the use of the commerce power to support federal regulatory legislation. The Court has not invalidated a federal environmental statue as exceeding the commerce power, but it has invoked commerce clause concerns in restrictive interpretations of federal environmental protections. In *Rapanos v. United States,* for example, the Court curtailed regulatory jurisdiction under the Clean Water Act (CWA) to avoid the issue of whether the expansive jurisdiction claimed by federal agencies was supported by the commerce power.[8]

PROPERTY RIGHTS

The Fifth Amendment of the Constitution prohibits governments at all levels from "taking" private property for public purposes without just compensation. In 1922, the Supreme Court held that the Fifth Amendment requires compensation not only where the government appropriates property for its own use but also where government regulation "goes too far." In the decades after Earth Day, ecologically based regulations burgeoned at the state and local levels as well as the federal level. In *Lucas v. South Carolina Coastal Council,* the Court made an example of one of these regulations—a state law to protect a fragile coastal system—and reinvigorated the Fifth Amendment takings doctrine with a new rule that any regulation denying all economic use of land will require compensation. The Court limited *Lucas's* per se takings rule in later cases, but it has continued to show solicitude for landowner-developers subject to environmental restrictions. *Lucas* and other takings cases force legislators and other government officials to balance regulatory effectiveness against the budgetary strains of compensation.[9]

The Federal Environmental Statutes

In the absence of a constitutional recognition of environmental rights or authorities, environmentalists sought federal legislation equal to their transformational goals. And it appeared that they got what they wanted.[10] In his influential history of modern environmental law, scholar and advocate Richard Lazarus gave a detailed account of the "revolution in law" ("dramatic, sweeping, and uncompromising") that took place in the environmental movement's first full decade. He counted no fewer than eighteen federal environmental statutes that were enacted in the 1970s. These include the mainstays of the environmental canon: the National Environmental Policy Act (NEPA), Clean Air Act (CAA), Clean Water Act (CWA), Endangered Species Act (ESA), Federal Insecticide, Fungicide, and Rodenticide Act (FIFRA), Safe Drinking Water Act (SDWA), Resource Conservation and Recovery Act (RCRA), Toxic Substances Control Act (TSCA), National Forest Management Act (NFMA), and Federal Land Policy and Management Act (FLPMA). The Wilderness Act had been enacted a few years before, in 1964. The Comprehensive Environmental Response, Compensation, and Liability Act (CERLCA or Superfund) was enacted in 1980, completing the essential canon.[11]

This wave of environmental legislation suggested a fundamental reordering of societal values and priorities.[12] These statutes were passed by lopsided majorities in Congress.[13] They took seriously the assertions of environmentalists on the urgency, scope, and complexity of environmental problems and institutionalized the beliefs and values that were driving the movement: they adopted the ecological model as a foundation of policy and law; communicated urgency and priority for environmental concerns; made harmony between humans and nature a national policy; and envisioned a

future in which human impact on the environment would be radically minimized. The "field of environmental law" that was created by these statutes
may be defined more by the distinct cultural understandings they reflect than
any uniqueness in the legal principles they embody.[14]

Institutional innovations to implement and enforce these statutes included the creation of the Council on Environmental Quality (CEQ) in the
Executive Office of the President and the EPA, a noncabinet agency within
the executive branch. CEQ came into being on January 1, 1970, with the
signing of NEPA; the council's function was to advise the president on environmental policy and oversee compliance with NEPA.[15] President Richard
Nixon created the EPA by executive order in December 1970. Pieced together from other agencies and departments, the EPA's sole function is environmental protection, and it plays the dominant role within the federal
government in implementing and enforcing environmental regulatory requirements. Responsibilities not assigned to the EPA are parceled out
among other departments and agencies, including the Department of the
Interior, the Department of Labor (Occupational Health and Safety Administration), and the Department of the Army (Corps of Engineers). The Department of the Interior and the Department of Agriculture's Forest Service
have the primary responsibility for administering federal land management
statutes.

Reflecting the magnitude of the regulatory undertaking commenced by
Congress in the 1970s, the EPA has grown to an agency of almost 16,000
employees, with an annual budget of roughly $8 billion. It issues more reg-
ulations than any other department or agency of the federal government.
Major EPA rules issued over the last decade drive expenditures of more than
$30 billion per year, yielding benefits of between $112 billion and $638
billion. The agency's reach is pervasive, touching not only major industrial
and natural resource development operations but also the actions of consumers and small landholders.[16]

The new regulatory statutes imposed environmental controls that typically disregarded compliance costs or considered them only on the question of whether the controls were feasible or practicable. They did not embrace cost-benefit analysis (CBA). Of the major environmental regulatory
statutes enacted during this period, only two clearly authorized the balancing
of costs and benefits for core regulatory actions.[17] The remainder relied on
ambitious harm-based or technology-based approaches that either expressly
excluded cost-benefit balancing or at least did not provide for it. Similarly
these statutes did not expressly allow the use of flexibility devices like plantwide permits or cap-and-trade, although provision for these devices has since
become more common—and acceptable to environmentalists.

Despite their revolutionary cast, political and institutional developments since the 1970s have constrained the implementation of these laws. The U.S. conservative movement with its distinctive antiregulatory cast began in the 1950s and by 1980 had captured the presidency with the election of Ronald Reagan. Prominent among Reagan's deregulatory efforts was a requirement that federal agencies prepare CBAs for all significant regulations unless conducting such analysis was prohibited by law. He gave his Office of Management and Budget (OMB) the job of reviewing all agency rules subject to this requirement before their adoption. Once established, OMB regulatory review became a fixture: it has continued through both Republican and Democratic presidencies into the present. Democratic presidents, ostensibly aligned with environmentalists concerns, as well as Republicans, have relied on the reviewers at the OMB to check the enthusiasm of the EPA and other regulatory agencies. Congress has codified the CBA requirement in the Unfunded Mandates Reform Act.[18]

Federal environmental laws continue to face considerable political and institutional resistance. Partisanship and the increasingly overt resistance to environmental regulation among conservatives and allied economic interests have affected the behavior of all the major institutional players. That resistance not only constrains the laws' implementation but also undermines the sense of a consensus-based, quasi-constitutional reordering that surrounded their enactment. It occurs at the issue level, where interests are opposed, but it also occurs at the values level. Opponents cast environmental regulation generally as inimical to economic freedom, material abundance, or rational resource allocation. In the run-up to the 2011 presidential primaries, Republican candidates attacked the EPA as the poster child of regulation run amok—the "job killing organization of America"—and several urged its abolition.[19]

So far these laws have avoided severe weakening amendments, but their enemies in Congress work to undermine them through proposed repeals, budget riders, and oversight hearings. With Congress in stalemate, there has been no major new environmental legislation for over two decades. A major push in the 111th Congress (2009–2010) to enact comprehensive climate change legislation ended in failure. The EPA continues to work under its existing mandates, but its efforts to advance or strengthen environmental regulation in areas such as climate change, water quality, and clean air face intense political opposition. The overall effect is erosion of the initial promise of the environmental laws, despite the real and remarkable improvements that they have produced over the last four decades. This registers as a loss of confidence that these laws reflect, or are capable of advancing, the fundamental change that environmentalists imagined.

A sampling of a few of the major environmental statutes illustrates both their early promise and the political and institutional forces that have helped produce this flattening.

NATIONAL ENVIRONMENTAL POLICY ACT (NEPA)

Famously dubbed the Magna Carta of environmental protection, NEPA sets forth an environmental policy for the nation. Unlike other statutes discussed, NEPA does not regulate the actions of private parties—at least not directly—but sets policy for agencies that administer federal resources and authorities. The new environmental policy codifies the interrelatedness and vulnerability of the natural environment, the pervasive effects of human action, and the critical need to reverse those effects—all central environmentalist tenets. It is not implausible to read its vision of "man and nature . . . in productive harmony" as a rudimentary recognition of the claims of nature beyond its usefulness to humans—the ecocentrism of Leopold's land ethic. Nor is it implausible to read the responsibilities assigned to federal officials under the act as establishing "a protoconstitutional right to environmental protection."[20]

The Supreme Court has bluntly denied the existence of such a right, although the purpose and text of NEPA could have led to a different result. It has recognized the enforceability of procedures under NEPA that require federal agencies to compile and "consider" information on the impacts of proposed actions and alternatives but has refused to second-guess the agencies' procedural compliance. More generally, the Court has compiled a lopsided record in favor of the government in NEPA cases. Of the seventeen challenges to the federal government's implementation of NEPA decided by the Court on the merits, environmentalists have prevailed in none. Although lower federal courts have enforced the procedural requirements of NEPA, political hostility to these requirements and bureaucratic incentives to shortcut them have limited their influence in the decision process, leading to suggestions that NEPA is not a "Magna Carta" but a "paper tiger."

ENDANGERED SPECIES ACT (ESA)

The ESA aims to protect species that federal agencies have listed as threatened or endangered and the ecosystems on which those species depend. It includes provisions that prevent federal actions that may jeopardize the continued existence of a listed species and that make it unlawful for anyone to kill or harm an endangered animal species. These protections on their face were absolute, at least in the form first enacted. As the Supreme Court held in its celebrated decision in *Tennessee Valley Authority v. Hill* (*TVA v. Hill*), Congress's intent in the ESA was to "halt and reverse the trend toward species extinction, whatever the cost" and to "give endangered species priority over the 'primary missions' of federal agencies." This holding gives credence to E. O. Wilson's characterization of the ESA as a "rudimentary bill of rights for biodiversity."[21]

But *TVA v. Hill* is not a straightforward endorsement of protecting species whatever the cost. Instead, it undercuts its own holding with questions about the wisdom of protecting species with no apparent human use in the face of significant costs. Congress later amended the ESA to provide a limited cost-benefit review for government actions and to allow permits for private actions that involved only unintentional harms. The statute has so far escaped truly debilitating amendments, which have been urged by property rights and wise use advocates and by affected economic interests. It remains a strong tool for species preservation, and it has earned its ecocentric stripes. But it has been hampered in its implementation by continued intense political resistance, particularly in the West, where many listed species live, and its enemies in Congress have succeeded in starving key elements, including the listing process, through budgetary restrictions.

CLEAN WATER ACT (CWA)

Like NEPA and the ESA, the CWA embraced an ecocentric perspective: its objective was to protect and restore "the chemical, physical and biological integrity of the Nation's waters." It announced a policy of eliminating the discharge of pollutants to the nation's waters by 1985, perhaps the boldest undertaking, if it were to be taken seriously, of any environmental law; it added an interim goal of ensuring fishable, swimmable waters by 1983, where attainable. Proponents of the CWA justified the no-discharge policy on ethical grounds: no one has a "right to pollute," and the continued use of the nation's lakes, streams, rivers, and oceans as a waste sink is "unacceptable." They saw the statute as asserting "the primacy of the natural order, on which all, including man, depends," and as making a national commitment to protect that order regardless of cost.[22]

As should have been obvious from the beginning, however, the machinery of the act was not geared to meet the no-discharge goal, or anything close to it; its ability to meet the interim goal remains doubtful. The act provided for demanding national technology-based limitations for industrial and municipal dischargers and for even more demanding limitations for these dischargers where necessary to meet local water quality standards. But it did not regulate runoff pollution from diffuse agricultural and residential sources, which happen to account for most remaining water pollution problems. The Supreme Court further undercut the act's ability to meet its defining commitments with narrow readings of the act's key jurisdictional term, "navigable waters." These jurisdictional constraints prevent federal regulatory actions that, in the view of environmentalists, would be necessary to fully protect the "integrity of the Nation's waters." Agricultural and development interests and their antiregulatory allies have successfully blocked efforts to extend the act's reach.[23]

CLEAN AIR ACT (CAA)

Unlike the ESA and CWA, but like many other modern environmental statutes, the CAA safeguards human health mainly and the nonhuman environment only secondarily. The act's featured purpose is to protect the nation's air quality "so as to promote the public health and welfare and the productive capacity of its population." This suggests an anthropocentric and even utilitarian orientation. But the key regulatory drivers of the act—the primary national ambient air quality standards (NAAQS)—are notoriously cost-blind, expressing the premium environmentalists have placed on protectiveness over economic concerns. In 2001, the Supreme Court in *Whitman v. American Trucking Associations, Inc.,* unanimously upheld the EPA's interpretation that the ambient air quality standards are to be set at levels necessary to protect public health, without regard to the costs of meeting them. In addition to aggressive ambient standards and state-adopted implementation actions, the act imposes demanding technology-based requirements on emissions from automobiles and major new stationary sources, with only limited consideration of costs.[24]

Despite its stringency, the CAA has yielded an outstanding surplus of benefits over costs of implementation. Air quality regulations account for 98 percent to 99 percent of the monetized benefits of major EPA rules. Nevertheless there is strong resistance from antiregulatory groups to further tightening requirements, as may be warranted by the public health standard of the statute, even where justified by CBA. Witness the Obama Administration's withdrawal of the EPA's proposed strengthening of the national air quality standard for ozone pollution in September 2011.[25]

The CAA has moved front and center in the climate change debate. In 2007, a closely divided Court in *Massachusetts v. Environmental Protection Agency* (*MA v. EPA*) held that the EPA had the authority under its existing statute to regulate emissions of greenhouse gases and affirmed that interpretation in more recent cases. In light of these rulings and in the absence of congressional action on the issue, President Obama has made the CAA the main vehicle for his climate change policies, and the EPA has undertaken several rulemakings under the act to control major U.S. greenhouse gas–emitting sectors. That venture faces the volatile politics surrounding climate change as well as the technical, administrative, and legal difficulties of advancing a climate change regulatory program under the existing act.

Common in many of the new environmental laws (e.g., ESA, CWA, CAA) was an innovative feature that seemed to capture their revolutionary thrust—the citizen suit. Under a citizen suit provision, "any person" could sue to enforce legal restrictions against an alleged violator or even sue agencies themselves for failure to take regulatory actions mandated by Congress— they communicated skepticism on Congress's behalf that environmental agencies could be trusted to vigorously carry out their missions in the face of political and economic pressures. Federal courts could grant successful citizen plaintiffs injunctive relief and civil penalties against violators—the same relief available to government enforcers. Plaintiffs could also recoup their attorney's fees and litigation costs. Giving this power to the people would serve as a defense against the impotence of governmental actors or their capture by powerful economic interests. Citizen suits complemented the demanding regulatory requirements of these laws, further signaling the end to business as usual. But the Supreme Court has limited their availability in its standing decisions.[26]

As this account suggests, the effect of the Court's decisions on laws seeking to protect the environment is mixed. The Court has both advanced and limited the broad commitments signaled by the federal environmental statutes as well as state and local measures. In some cases, the Court not only reached "proenvironment" outcomes but also issued opinions that resonated with the beliefs and values that are identified as environmentalist. In other cases, it did the opposite. There is, however, strong agreement among environmental law scholars that the Court has become more resistant to environmentalist claims since the 1970s. In 2000, Richard Lazarus found that "the Court as a whole is steadily becoming less responsive to environmental protection." The Court's general unresponsiveness has continued and perhaps even intensified since then, but with important exceptions, most notably *MA v. EPA*.[27]

In the rest of this chapter, I take a closer look at the law culture of which the Court is a part, the Court's role as cultural arbiter as well as decider of "cases and controversies," and what that role may mean for an interpretation of its environmental decisions that engages both "legal and cultural meanings."[28]

Law, Culture, and the Court

The Court is the exemplar of the law culture, which presents itself as distinct from surrounding culture. From the first day of law school, students are taught to "think like a lawyer," as if that were distinct from other ways of thinking.[29] The law has its own standards for inclusion, its own subject matter and ethics, its own procedural, methodological, and linguistic practices. It also has the ability "by its own operation to produce effects" on the rest of society. In this way, as from its ostensibly autonomous domain, it shapes the surrounding culture. But the larger society "first creates the law" and exerts continuing influence over its practices.[30] Robert Post describes this interaction as the "ceaseless dialectic" between law and culture writ large.[31]

How this dialectic works in the Court's deliberations is a matter of debate. By some accounts, the Court can be expected to take the initiative in advancing cultural change. By others, the Court is more passive, reflecting existing or emerging cultural consensus rather than leading change. Both accounts are explored in more detail below. In either case, however, because of the permeability of the law to the larger culture, the potential for reform is inherent in the Court's deliberations. This potential, as philosopher and legal theorist Paul Kahn has described it, is "an opening within law to developments outside of law, such that the world of law has a self-regulating mechanism that stabilizes law in relation to wider patterns of belief and practice." For the Court, this opening is through the beliefs and values of the justices drawn from the ambient culture and reflected in their legal judgments.[32]

Values Affecting Court Decisions

In his concurring opinion in *James B. Beam Distilling Co. v. Georgia,* Justice Antonin Scalia offered a version of legal interpretation based on the law culture's autonomous system of rules and principles:

> I am not so naive . . . as to be unaware that judges in a real sense "make" law. But they make it as judges make it, which is to say as though they were "finding" it—discerning what the law is, rather than decreeing what it is today changed to, or what it will tomorrow be.

Justice Scalia's metaphor of "finding" the law is opposed to the notion that judges are influenced by nonlegal factors, such as their own value preferences or their sense of changing values within society. But many embrace a contrary view—that nonlegal factors can, and often do, affect judicial decisions. An early and distinguished proponent of this view was Oliver Wendell Holmes, who said that behind the logical form characteristic of judicial decisions "lies a judgment as to the relative worth of and importance of competing legislative grounds, often an inarticulate and unconscious judgment, . . . yet the very root and nerve of the whole proceeding." Modern commentators continue the argument for the pervasive influence of culture in judicial decision making. Even Justice Scalia, Robert Post points out, succumbs to the siren of culture in his own judicial decision making. Post argues that Justice Scalia's "own federalism decisions appeal to . . . ambient values in the context of what might fairly be called a 'cultural war' about the importance of state sovereignty." One might say the same of Justice Scalia's decisions on property rights under the takings clause, in which he has invoked the "constitutional culture" of land ownership.[33]

Decades of empirical studies confirm that a judge's ideology or values preferences can and often do make a difference in how he or she decides cases.[34] This view of how judges work is also widely shared by the American public. Although a majority of the public believes that judges should make decisions based on an impartial reading of the law, a majority also believes that judges are influenced by ideology or partisan affiliation.[35] This same understanding is widespread in the political system and underlies the intense scrutiny of a prospective justice's views on social and political issues as well as her or his "judicial philosophy" seen in the Senate confirmation process.

Ideology matters more in cases that implicate basic values and present novel or undetermined legal issues that may not yield readily to neutral analysis.[36] (I will sometimes refer to these cases as "political.") Because the Supreme Court has discretion in selecting cases for review and tends to select cases that have a high values salience and in which the law is not settled, it has proportionately more of these "political" cases than the lower federal courts. The Court is also less constrained in deciding cases than are the lower courts—for example, it may overrule precedents that it no longer agrees with. From this we can expect that values and beliefs of the surrounding culture will matter more in the Supreme Court's decisions than in the rulings of the lower courts.[37] And we can expect this to hold true not only in constitutional cases but also in statutory cases implicating fundamental values, including a number emerging from the quasi-constitutional environmental law canon.

This is not to say that judicial decisions are culture, or politics, all the way down. As Post puts it, law remains a "relatively autonomous discourse" that seeks to preserve its own distinctness even as it absorbs and reflects the surrounding culture. Justices are subject to the norms of the legal profession and the conventions of adjudication, including adherence to precedent, protocols for the interpretation of legal texts, and acceptance of a limited role for the judiciary in the tripartite system of governance. Justices interpret these conventions differently, and these differences no doubt have something to do with the underlying value preferences of the justices. But some level of adherence to accepted judicial practice is important to the Court's legitimacy, as an unelected body, as well as to the standing of individual justices among their peers, and thus exerts a constraining influence.[38]

A multitude of additional factors may affect a justice's decision. These include a justice's commitment to a particular legal interpretive method (e.g., textualism versus intentionalism); considerations of collegiality and reciprocity among the justices; and differences among justices in personality, experience, and "cognitive style"—how the justice processes information and solves problems. Some even add to the list, not facetiously, "what the judge ate for breakfast," or didn't eat. Although my focus is on the interaction of law and culture, these other factors can also be important to a full understanding of the Court's environmental decisions, and I will note their potential importance at points in the analysis.[39]

The Court as a Reflection of Culture

It is one thing to say that at least in some of their decisions Supreme Court justices reflect values and beliefs drawn from the larger culture; it is another to say that the Court's practice can be expected to offer a meaningful or useful representation of the values dynamics within that culture. Using the Court to illuminate the cultural debate over environmentalism requires closer attention to how the Court, as an institution, operates with respect to social conflict and change.

At the most basic level, there are at least two general schools of thought on how the Court relates to the larger culture. One projects a relatively passive Court (I will call this the "embeddedness model"); the opposing school attributes greater agency to the Court (the "agency model"). In the embeddedness model, the Court is capable of responding to change on an issue of public importance that is occurring broadly in society, but it does not stray very far or for very long from the majority views of the American public. A corollary of this view is that the Court cannot be expected to play the role of "Republican schoolmaster" leading the public to new understandings of what is right and good. In the agency model, by contrast, the Court may go against prevailing public opinion on culturally important issues, as it appears to have done in at least some notable constitutional cases, such as overturning state laws criminalizing flag burning and banning prayer in public schools.[40] Advocates for this model emphasize the ways in which the Court's decisions, or the views of dissenting justices, might influence social change even if they do not directly alter public opinion.[41]

If we embraced the embeddedness model, the Court's strong predisposition to locate itself in the mainstream might give us some confidence that the deliberations of the Court in environmental cases are generally representative of public attitudes affecting important environmental issues. By the same token, we would not expect the Court to play an assertive role in advancing environmentalism against an opposing dominant paradigm. Our confidence in the representativeness of the Court's decisions might be diminished under the agency model. But we might still expect the cases to reflect the key terms of the cultural debate surrounding environmentalism, if not some prevailing or consensus view. And viewing a contested environmentalism through the lens of the Court might in its own way prove useful in assessing the progress of the movement, identifying barriers to its success, and imagining possible futures for the movement.

Political scientist Robert Dahl advanced a version of the embeddedness model in his 1957 discussion of the Supreme Court as "national policymaker": "the policy views dominant on the Court are never for long out of line with the policy views dominant among the lawmaking majorities of the United States." A pattern of consistency with majority views would not be surprising given the Court's institutional setting. While independent in important ways, the Court is vulnerable to attacks from the political branches of government and is dependent on other governmental actors to carry out its judgments. As Justice Sandra Day O'Connor once remarked, "We don't have standing armies to enforce opinions." Sustained defiance of dominant public sentiment could undermine the Court's legitimacy and leave it impotent to effectuate its decisions. The political selection of justices, particularly under conditions of divided government, may also serve to moderate ideological variance.[42]

In Dahl's account, the Court's strong institutional and cultural rootedness also explained its failure to "play the role of Galahad," although he did recognize that the Court has "some bases of power of its own" within the political structure. In his 1991 book, *The Hollow Hope*, political scientist Gerald Rosenberg expanded on the not-Galahad theme, arguing that the "U.S. courts can almost never be effective producers of significant social reform." This is because the courts are subject to, and dependent on, the political branches in ways already discussed and because they lack significant influence over public opinion. Empirical studies since *The Hollow Hope* have found limited public awareness of Supreme Court decisions and lack of a measurable effect on public opinion in the Court's direction, although the question of the Court's impact on the public's views is far from settled. In Rosenberg's view, the Court may contribute to social change, but only if the existing institutional and cultural barriers to change are weak.

Or as another commentator put it, the Supreme Court is "better at 'piling on' than at 'tackling.'"[43]

Prominent legal historians, including Michael Klarman, the preeminent chronicler of the landmark civil rights decision, *Brown v. Board of Education,* offer another source of support for the embeddedness model. In *From Jim Crow to Civil Rights,* Klarman concluded that the Court's civil rights decisions "reflected social attitudes and practices more than they created them." He later extended this view in further examination of *Brown* and another high-profile decision, *Lawrence v. Texas,* in which the Court invalidated a Texas law that imposed criminal penalties on same-sex sodomy. In both cases, Klarman concluded, the movements that the decisions supported "had already acquired significant momentum by the time their grievances had reached the Supreme Court." Both decisions reflected the weight of public opinion on race and homosexuality at the time they were decided, although the decisions were socially divisive. More recently, in his book on the issue of gay marriage in state courts, Klarman acknowledged that courts are more likely to stray far from public opinion (as two state supreme courts did on this issue) than are legislators, but nevertheless reaffirmed public opinion's constraining effect.[44]

Predictably, given his view of the limited role of courts in social reform, Rosenberg argued that the judiciary has done little to advance environmentalism. Environmentalists failed to establish a constitutional right to a clean environment because judges "constrained by precedent and the beliefs of the dominant legal culture" were unlikely to be environmental crusaders. In the wake of the environmental legislation in the 1970s, federal judges acting within their institutional constraints focused on reviewing statutory implementation rather than framing constitutional imperatives. In this more modest role, courts have successfully aided environmental interests where there was substantial political or market support for their decisions. At the same time, they have shown considerable deference to the implementing agencies, both in matters of legal interpretation and on technical and scientific issues, and more generally have shown little inclination to strike out in ways that provoke the political branches. Rosenberg's assessment accords with the general sense among environmental law scholars that overall—with some important exceptions—the Court's decisions have been a disappointment to environmentalists hoping for leadership from the Court.[45]

Proponents of the agency model criticize scholars like Rosenberg and Klarman for spreading an overly thin conception of the law culture that accords "insufficient credit to the law's transformative power." Constitutional law scholar Justin Driver attacked what he called the "consensus constitutionalism" of Klarman and other historians who have closely linked

Supreme Court decisions to prevailing public sentiment. These interpreters are wrong, Driver argued, both because their emphasis on consensus or "emerging" consensus belies the "deep cleavages" in society and because they wrongly assume that Supreme Court justices are "almost inevitably in step with the citizens they help govern." Instead Driver offered "contested constitutionalism," which emphasized the diversity of views within society and granted space for the Court to champion movements such as civil rights or gay rights against majoritarian opposition. But even Driver granted that justices don't exist "in utter isolation from the cultures (legal and otherwise) that produced them and that they in turn produce."[46]

The distance between these two models may be less than it seems. Proponents on both sides agree that the Court is situated in the larger culture. Both agree that the justices are influenced by beliefs and values flowing from that culture, although they differ on the extent of that influence (and perhaps also on its desirability). One model stresses the Court's role in grasping and articulating consensus or emerging consensus. The other stresses its role in selecting a path through the thicket of dissensus. But dissensus and an emerging consensus may be hard to distinguish.

Law's relationship to the larger culture remains elusive.[47] My working understanding is a synthesis of the two models that sees the Court as semi-autonomous. The Court has its own practice and sphere of legitimacy, but it is also linked to a political and cultural context. It "reflects"—in ways that are not easily predictable or straightforward—"mainstream" culture. But along with David Pozen, I understand that "mainstream [to] be a broad current, accompanying a range of controversial viewpoints." Rather than expecting the Court's environmental opinions to reflect consensus on environmentalism's most basic claims, emerging or otherwise, we might look for them instead to bear the marks of cultural conflict and to reflect choices among the justices from a range of politically plausible alternatives. If there is an environmental consensus in this country, it is a fragile and uncertain one and not one that we would necessarily rely on the Court to ascertain or express.[48]

Why Focus on the Court?

This raises the question of what a cultural analysis of the Court's environmental decisions is likely to add to what we could learn from exploring the progress of environmentalism in other venues. We might hope, for example, to get a clearer or more accurate understanding of the environmental debate from a study of practice in other areas that are less specialized or less remote from daily social, political, and economic exchange—for example, lawmaking by Congress, community action, or corporate environmental policy. The Court, however, offers a unique vantage point from which to track cultural conflict through the law and other major institutions for at least two reasons: first, the Court's self-legitimating practice of writing opinions to explain its decisions and, second, its strategic location at the intersection of social, political, and economic systems, all affecting and affected by law.

The Court typically issues a written opinion in each case that explains and justifies the ruling supported by a majority of the justices—the opinion of the Court. And beginning in the 1940s, separate concurring or dissenting opinions have been filed for 60 percent to 80 percent of the cases. These opinions set forth the views of individual or groups of justices that differ from or elaborate on the Court's opinion. William Popkin interprets this proliferation of concurrent and dissenting opinions in modern practice as a tacit acknowledgment that neutral legal principles are not sufficient to decide most cases and that votes are inflected by values that vary among the justices.[49]

In these opinions, justices—whether individually or collectively—attempt to persuade the parties, political actors, the public, and each other that they are right. Although they address legal issues in language peculiar to the law, the opinions often are at pains to explain the significance of rulings in layman's terms; this may be particularly true in political cases in which contested cultural views are implicated. Even opinions that speak in the institutional voice of a unanimous Court, such as the opinion in *Brown v. Board of Education,* have been framed to justify the Court's actions to the public. The persuasive intent of concurrences and dissents is even more apparent, as outlying justices attempt to mobilize constituencies for their views and lay the groundwork for future interpretations or changes in the law in accordance with those views.[50]

The opinions in political cases are where law and culture come together, a place where—in Robert Post's phrase—"public meaning is debated and created." In environmental cases, this juncture offers a vantage point from which to see environmentalist beliefs and values played out in the social, political, and economic systems to which law is linked. Through the lens of the Court, a picture forms of whether and how key institutions and practices are open to changes sought by the environmental movement. That can sharpen our practical understanding of both the acceptance of the movement and the resistance to it. I do not argue that the Court's role is central to the progress of environmentalism, although that may be the case. My claim is simply that the Court is a participant in the cultural debate. And its deliberative habits allow insights into the structure of that debate that are revealing and may be useful in assessing the progress of the movement and considering possible futures.[51]

Interpretation

Reflecting the practical social functions that law serves, legal interpretation is consequentialist, with an emphasis on outcomes and doctrines. It ascertains the meaning of law for purposes of its application to present facts and for the purposes of potential future applications. It frames and resolves disputes and sets the patterns of future expectation so as to extend the power and efficacy of law. These are the primary functions of the Supreme Court's "finding the law" in the cases before it. In environmental cases, the Court's interpretations may have immediate consequences not only for the parties but also for whole programs or economic sectors or geographic domains of environmental policy.

But the Court's rulings not only have practical consequences but also generate social meanings: the Court as "moral symbol," as in *Brown v. Board of Education*.[52] Lawyers are aware of these meanings too, although they may not figure in advice to clients or arguments to courts. This expressive or symbolic dimension exists at the level of cultural beliefs and values, as discussed, and is present in many of the Court's prominent decisions, including the environmental decisions explored in this book. The cultural resonance of these cases may ultimately define what is most distinctive and important about them.

In contrast to a purely consequentialist reading, this interpretative undertaking is intended to elicit the symbolic or cultural significance of these cases. (It is second-order interpretation—an interpretation of the justices' interpretations that aims to unpack the significance of the opinions as cultural texts.) At the same time, the analysis seeks to avoid the "kind of sociological aestheticism" in cultural analysis that Clifford Geertz warned against by keeping in close touch with law's consequentialist aspects. Indeed, the interpretative premise is that the cultural meanings of these cases are not separate from the law but grow from the interplay of legal doctrine and reasoning with the values and beliefs drawn from the larger culture, of consequence with symbol, and of logic with emotion.[53]

The interpretive challenge is that the justices typically do not represent themselves as importing cultural strains from outside the law into their opinions. The metaphor of "finding the law" has a strong hold on all the justices, not just Justice Scalia. While the instrumentalist aspects of the opinions—the holdings, doctrines, and legal reasons supporting them—are developed at length, the cultural dimensions may be largely submerged unless they are directly linked to a relevant legal provision or principle, and even then they may be weakly developed. As Robert Post commented:

> When it comes to deciding cases, courts conceive politics as the medium within which, and out of which, they construct law. The difficulty, however, is that this cannot be frankly acknowledged without simultaneously undermining the Court's ability to speak as the "instrument" of a law that is known and fixed, in which "principle and logic" entirely determine "the decisions of this Court."

Cultural elements that are underdeveloped or hidden in these opinions require the use of tools beyond those of conventional legal analysis to retrieve them.[54]

Interpretive Method

My approach to these opinions is descriptive and interpretive. In addition to the objects of standard legal analysis, the interpretations attend to emotions, values, master narratives, and cosmologies. These elements are important to understanding the cases at a symbolic or cultural level, and to get at them I borrow from basic techniques of literary analysis.[55] Accordingly, the interpretations of the cases pay attention to imagery, tone, story, and connotation as well as the structure and content of legal argument.

The analysis looks to both text and context. The text is the words of an opinion, in both their legal and nonlegal significations. I ascribe those words to the justice who authored the opinion, whose identity is made public except in the relatively rare case of a per curiam opinion (literally "by the court"), and also associate them with other justices who joined the opinion.[56] The analysis treats the text of the opinions broadly as rhetoric, which literature and law scholar Peter Brooks defines as "a system of communication and persuasion, everything we do with words in order to make an argument, win a case, convince a listener."[57] It explores the values implications of the justices' rhetorical choices. It considers individual words not only in their denotative sense, which is the currency of standard legal analysis, but also in their implicit meanings. It looks for "the power of pattern," the assemblage of words to create an image, story, or argument, and what those assemblages suggest. It also looks closely at how the justices present and resolve the conflict that is at the heart of each case—"the way the argument moves—its plot."[58]

Context takes in elements outside the text of the opinions that help place the case in its full cultural as well as legal setting. It includes legal context, such as relevant doctrine and judicial precedent, proceedings in courts below, and factual and legal arguments made by the parties and amicus curiae ("friend of the court") in the case, all of which shape the options available to the Court and their meanings. It may encompass social and political circumstances not mentioned by the parties or the Court, facts outside the judicial record, and other information useful to an understanding of the figurative significance of the parties, their conflict, and the environmental issues at stake. Context may also include events after the decision that put its cultural significance into temporal perspective.

Interpretation is a collective undertaking. All of the cases analyzed have been the subject of many interpretations by legal scholars and practitioners as well as nonlegal commentators. This substantial body of interpretation contributes importantly to understanding both the legal and cultural dimensions of these cases. My analysis will build on these existing interpretations, with an effort to acknowledge key commentators who have gone before.

Finally, consistent with the social science, my analysis assumes that extralegal beliefs and values affect how justices view and decide "political" cases. But my primary claims are interpretive, not causal. The causal claims cannot be more than suggestive, since I consider only a subset of the Court's environmental cases and provide no systematic way of distinguishing the effect of the cultural orientations of the justices relevant to environmental issues from other factors that may also affect their votes.

The Frame of Analysis

The thirty cases featured ("selected cases") are drawn from a group of 150 significant environmental cases decided between 1970 and 2014. (The selected cases are listed in the Appendix.) A number of them are recognized as of special significance by the environmental bar and are also known in environmental circles outside the legal community. Others I have selected for what I judge to be their particular cultural as well as legal significance, with the suggestion that they too might deserve canonical status. A number of these cases have been the occasion for innovations by the Court in constitutional or administrative law, but in others the Court purports simply to be applying the law as it is. Given my interest in mapping the cultural cleavages in the Court's interpretations, the selection favors cases that display disagreements among the justices on the relevance or soundness of environmentalist tenets or their compatibility with existing doctrine. I ask my readers to forgive the omission of cases that they believe, for their own good reasons, also belong in the canon. To guide the analysis, I have schematized potential linkages between law and culture based on the account of the environmental movement in Chapter 1 and the description of environmental law earlier in this chapter.[59]

Figure 2.1 shows the terms of the analysis and their relationships. On the right side of the figure, outside the circle, are the general cultural values associated with environmentalism (egalitarianism, harmony, collectivism [community]). Just inside the circle are elements of the new environmental paradigm (NEP) linked to these values (environmental urgency, interdependence, ecocentrism, resource limits). On the left side are the competing cultural values (autonomy [individualism], mastery, hierarchy) and associated dominant social paradigm (DSP) elements (limited government, property rights, economic growth, material abundance). The figure shows these opposing beliefs and values influencing the Court's interpretations in areas of relevance in environmental cases (federalism, judicial access, property rights, free exercise of religion, and statutory interpretation).

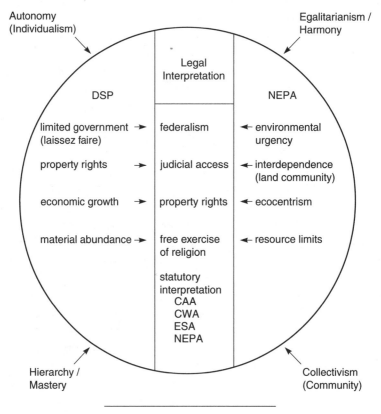

Figure 2.1
Interpretive Guide to the Cases

This matrix offers a general analytical guide—an interpretive compass that serves to orient as the reader navigates the extensive and varied landscape of the selected cases. But the analysis will take each case on its own terms because cultural meanings depend on the specific facts and history of the case, the legal doctrines to be applied, and other contextual elements already mentioned. The analysis will also reflect the irreducible plurality of environmentalist views apparent from the account of the movement in Chapter 1. An individualized account of the cultural meanings of each case is a necessary predicate to any useful observations about the meanings of the cases as a whole.

THE SUPREME COURT'S decisions in culturally salient environmental cases reflect the justices' responses to the beliefs and values of the environmental movement. That reflection is complex, refracted; the Court's written opinions, the artifacts of its deliberations, do not hold a mirror up to culture. But they do offer a unique vantage point from which to see environmentalist beliefs and values played out in practice—not only in the law but also in the social, political, and economic systems to which law is linked. Through these opinions, understood as cultural texts, a picture forms of whether and to what extent key institutions and practices have been open to the environmental movement's transformative efforts. We can also develop a practical understanding of the sources and strength of the cultural resistance to environmentalism and discern possible paths for the movement that would enhance its future success.

The interpretive enterprise is not straightforward. Although the justices' opinions often reflect cultural strains outside the law, the law culture itself encourages submergence of those strains. Because culture operates at unconscious as well as conscious levels, the justices may not even be aware that extralegal beliefs and values are shaping their views of the cases. Making these elements visible requires a combination of traditional legal analysis, keyed to the legal doctrine and rationales offered by the justices, with interpretive techniques designed to get at more suggestive or "literary" aspects of the opinions that contribute to their symbolic meanings. The strategy is to use this broad set of tools to produce an interpretation of each case in which its cultural meanings are fully integrated with its legal and practical dimensions.

This analysis yields complementary insights on the environmental movement and the Court. It comes at a cost, however. The treatment of these two subjects together requires some simplification of both the environmental movement and the Court's opinions. The history of the movement is far richer and more complex than can be shown through a review of the Court's opinions, however detailed. And each of the cases is richer and more complex than will be apparent from my analysis emphasizing cultural themes. The definitive analysis of the Court's environmental cases remains to be written.[60] Meanwhile, I hope this book will show what these cases can tell us about the movement that was, in a quite real sense, the occasion for them.

CHAPTER THREE

Environmental Urgency and Law

ENVIRONMENTALISTS ASSIGN a particular urgency to their concerns—they see environmental threats as serious and demanding a forceful response. This claim of priority has a basis in the ecological worldview—the environment as interdependent, vulnerable to human disruption, and essential to all species' survival. It reflects the sense of community identified with this worldview, which assigns inherent value to the chemical, biological, and physical systems of which humans are a part as well as to the humans themselves. It resists commodification of the health of humans, species, and ecological systems and is suspicious of priorities assigned on the basis of comparisons of costs and benefits.

In this chapter and in Chapters 4 and 5, I explore these dimensions of environmentalism. The cases discussed suggest the operation of deep-rooted beliefs and values among the justices that resist environmentalist priorities as well as others that support them, and they help us begin to understand the tension between environmentalism and values underpinning the nation's foundational institutions.

The urgency that drove environmentalism found expression in federal laws of the 1970s and 1980s that responded to a range of perceived environmental crises. These laws raised the priority given to environmental concerns in governmental decisions, for example, by prohibiting environmentally damaging actions or by limiting considerations of costs or technological feasibility in setting environmental standards. They also shifted decision-making authority from certain institutions to others perceived as more responsive to environmental concerns or more competent to address them—for example, from states to federal authorities or from bureaucracies to courts.

Environmentalists also brought this urgency to actions in the federal courts. Environmental problems required new judicial doctrines or exceptions to existing doctrines that would recognize their special seriousness. Often disappointed with political outcomes under the new generation of laws, environmentalists asked the courts to take an assertive role in policing these laws and to make room for their full expression within the larger institutional framework. The results have been mixed.

In the earliest days of the movement, it appeared that the Supreme Court had internalized environmentalists' sense of urgency. In a decision that predated the first Earth Day, the Court extended the criminal prohibitions of the Rivers and Harbors Act to industrial polluters, citing the water pollution "crisis" as a background condition of its interpretation. In *Citizens to Preserve Overton Park, Inc. v. Volpe,* decided in 1971, the Court expanded judicial scrutiny of informal agency decisions in securing adherence to congressional policy that the Court interpreted as giving "paramount importance" to protecting parkland against "accelerating destruction." Two years later, in *United States v. Students Challenging Regulatory Agency Procedures,* the Court expanded standing to allow student environmentalists to sue against barriers to recycling. These and other decisions at the dawn of the movement encouraged environmentalists to believe that the Court was with them against hostile economic interests and entrenched political forces aligned with those interests. *Overton Park* is revealing of the Court's early receptiveness.[1]

Overton Park: Great Highways versus Green Havens

Authorized in 1956, the National System of Interstate and Defense Highways was touted as "the greatest public-works program in the history of the world." This monumental undertaking expressed mastery values that were ascendant in the rapid economic expansion that followed World War II. The interstate system was to comprise more than 40,000 miles of limited-access highways connecting major U.S. cities at a cost of $33 billion, 90 percent of which would come from federal funds. Although the system advanced important economic and national security interests, it also generated opposition in communities marred by its construction. Sections of interstate highway displaced businesses, disrupted (often poor and minority) neighborhoods, and destroyed green space and historical sites. "Freeway revolts" erupted in cities slated for interstate construction, led variously by environmentalists, preservationists, and civil rights activists as well as business interests.[2]

Responding to constituent anger, Congress conditioned approval of federally funded highway projects. Enacted in 1966, Section 4(f) of the Department of Transportation Act prohibited federal transportation officials from approving projects that ran through a public park unless "there is no feasible or prudent alternative to the use of such land." Section 4(f) also required that "all possible planning" be done to "minimize the harm" to any park. Two years later, in 1968, Congress adopted identical language in Section 318 of the Federal-Aid Highway Act. The meaning of this language is at the heart of *Overton Park.*[3]

Overton Park is a 342-acre park near the center of Memphis, Tennessee. It was laid out in the early 1900s during the City Beautiful Movement, an antecedent of modern environmentalism, by noted landscape architect George Kessler. The park is roughly a mile long and a half-mile wide. As Justice Thurgood Marshall noted in his opinion for the Court in *Overton Park,* it "contains a zoo, a nine-hole municipal golf course, an outdoor theater, nature trails, a bridle path, an art academy, picnic areas, and 170 acres of forest." The forest is old-growth oak-hickory.[4]

Interstate 40 (I-40), as originally conceived, was to be a transcontinental highway that "would cross the Mississippi at Memphis" and would "connect Memphis with Nashville to the northeast and Little Rock, Arkansas, to the southwest." Initial plans were for the portion of I-40 passing through Memphis to go through the middle of Overton Park. The first federal approval of I-40's route came in 1956, the same year Congress established the interstate highway program. However, for the next twelve years that decision remained unsettled, as federal, state, and local officials debated the location. In March 1968, the Memphis City Council voted unanimously to have I-40 routed elsewhere. But a month later, after meeting at the Memphis Airport with the administrator of the Federal Highway Administration, Lowell Bridwell, the city council reversed itself and voted eight to two to approve the route through the park. (This decision came on April 4, only minutes before the tragic assassination of Martin Luther King Jr. at the Lorraine Motel in Memphis.) Advocates against the park route were excluded from the meeting, and despite a promise by Bridwell that the meeting would be recorded, no recording was made, purportedly due to equipment failure. Some would later question whether Bridwell had "extorted the Council's agreement by monetary threats or perhaps misrepresentation."[5]

Two weeks after the council's decision, Bridwell, apparently speaking for his boss, Secretary of Transportation Alan Stephenson Boyd, announced renewed federal approval of the park route, supported by the governor of Tennessee and the U.S. congressman from Memphis. In November 1969, the new secretary of transportation, John Volpe, announced approval of the design of I-40 through the park. As the Court in *Overton Park* would later observe, neither Bridwell's decision of April 1968 nor Volpe's of November 1969 was accompanied by factual findings or an explanation of "why [the secretary] believed there were no feasible and prudent alternative routes or why design changes could not be made to reduce the harm to the park."[6]

Citizens to Preserve Overton Park (CPOP) is a classic grassroots environmental organization, "created in outrage" over actions threatening harm to local populations or resources. Many such groups do not survive past their initial success (or defeat) in preventing the action that galvanized their formation. CPOP, however, still exists, working to protect the park's old-growth forest from nonhighway incursions. Formed in 1957, when the official preference for the I-40 route became clear, CPOP focused on political persuasion for over a decade. But after Volpe's November 1969 decision, and as federal officials prepared to authorize construction through the park, CPOP brought suit in federal district court to stop the project. It was joined by two national environmental groups, the Sierra Club and the National Audubon Society, but CPOP's role as lead plaintiff emphasized the intensely local quality of the conflict and the value to communities of the green spaces that Section 4(f) addressed.[7]

Under the law that existed at the time, plaintiffs had an uphill battle to convince the courts to invalidate federal approvals. Congress had not prescribed procedures for the administrative determinations that they challenged—the finding of "no reasonable and prudent alternative" and "all possible planning" to minimize impacts. Federal courts reviewed such determinations, if they reviewed them at all, under an undemanding "arbitrary and capricious standard" that carried a strong presumption of regularity.[8]

It was not surprising then that CPOP failed to persuade the federal district court or the Court of Appeals for the Sixth Circuit to set aside the federal approvals of the park route. Both courts accorded the secretary of transportation broad discretion under the highway statutes. The district court decided against CPOP on the basis of affidavits and exhibits submitted by the parties and without allowing CPOP to examine federal officials on the reasons for their decisions. It concluded that no trial was necessary, because it "could never find in this case that . . . such determinations are so wrong as to be arbitrary and capricious." The court of appeals agreed that the secretary of transportation had made the required determinations and that those determinations were not "arbitrary or capricious." The only real dispute in the case, the court believed, was the wisdom of the decisions, and that was not for the courts to second-guess. In a dissenting opinion that foreshadowed the Supreme Court's review, Circuit Judge Anthony Celebrezze argued that the lack of an explanation by the secretary prevented meaningful judicial review of compliance with the statutory requirements and that plaintiffs should be granted a trial to explore the issues.[9]

The Supreme Court granted a stay to CPOP, which stopped the project while the Court considered the case on the merits and was an early sign that the government might be vulnerable. CPOP argued to the Court that the findings required by Section 4(f) had not been made and that, if they had, they were "infirm or legally invalid." The government countered that it was clear that the findings had been made and that the statutes gave wide latitude to the secretary in making them. In particular, the government argued that Section 4(f)'s requirement of "no other feasible and prudent alternative" gave discretion to the secretary to balance competing interests in exercising his "good judgment" about the location and design of interstate routes through parks. The statute required no findings. But in case the record left any doubt that the secretary had decided appropriately in the matter of Overton Park, the government produced two new affidavits ("certificates") from former and present secretaries of transportation saying that they had understood and complied with the requirements of the highway statutes in approving the park route. The Court would hold that these last-minute affidavits were insufficient for judicial review.[10]

In a memorandum that he wrote to himself on the case, included in papers made public after his death, Justice Harry Blackmun expressed no great enthusiasm for reversing the court of appeals and remanding the case for further proceedings. "This . . . is a messed up case," he wrote, but "remand[ing] for adherence to some of the formalities" would not change the outcome; the road would be built through the park, he was certain. He quoted a comment to similar effect by Justice Marshall in the postargument conference among the justices: "if we remand we will get only a snow job and nothing more." Despite his misgivings, Blackmun ended up voting with the other justices to reverse the court of appeals. Marshall was assigned to write the opinion for the Court.[11]

If some of the justices seemed lukewarm about the case in their deliberations, the Court's opinion remanding the case to district court for further review of the secretary's decision was not. Authored by Justice Marshall, it began not with procedure but with substance: the meaning of Section 4(f), which governed the federal actions in the case. The first sentence of the opinion signaled the Court's view of the importance of this provision and what lay behind it:

> The growing public concern about the quality of our natural environment has prompted Congress in recent years to enact legislation designed to curb the accelerating destruction of our country's natural beauty.

With remarkable economy, this opening captured the environmentalist narrative of decline and the urgent need for corrective measures: the public's concern is "growing," the destruction of the country's natural beauty is "accelerating." It is left to Congress to check the downward slide.[12]

This sense of parkland protection as a pressing priority carried into the Court's interpretation of Section 4(f). The government's argument focused on the meaning of "prudent" in the phrase "feasible and prudent" and used the dictionary definition of "exercising good judgment and common sense," which gave the secretary broad latitude to weigh competing considerations to reach a sound result. But in the Court's analysis, Section 4(f) could not be read consistent with its purpose as a simple directive that highway officials balance parkland loss against competing concerns such as cost and community disruption. Highways will almost always be less costly and disruptive if they can be built through parks. If Congress had intended for these competing concerns to be on an equal footing with threats to parkland, there would be no reason for Section 4(f). Rather, the Court concluded,

> the very existence of the statutes indicates that protection of parkland was to be given paramount importance. The few green havens that are public parks were not to be lost unless there were truly unusual factors present in a particular case or the cost or community disruption resulting from alternative routes reached extraordinary magnitudes. If the statutes are to have any meaning, the Secretary cannot approve the destruction of parkland unless he finds that alternative routes present unique problems.[13]

"Few green havens"—the Court's words, not Congress's—gave rhetorical support to the Court's contention that Congress intended park preservation to be accorded the highest priority and signaled the Court's subjective alignment with the policy. "Haven" is literally "harbor," from the Old English, with derivative meanings of a place of safety or refuge. In this context, "green havens" suggests city parks as places of retreat from the stresses of urban life. This celebration of the restorative quality of natural settings, as an antidote to the burdens of civilization, goes back to Thoreau and other writers in the pastoralist tradition. In his essay "Huckleberries," Thoreau argued that every "town should have a park, or rather a primitive forest, of five hundred or a thousand acres, . . . where a stick should never be cut for fuel—nor for the navy, nor to make wagons, but stand and decay for higher uses—a common possession forever, for instruction and recreation." (The 340 acres of Overton Park, with its expanse of old-growth forest, came close to meeting Thoreau's specifications.)[14]

Having set a demanding decision standard for the secretary—no federally funded highways through parklands in the absence of "truly unusual factors"—and understanding that it would not be met if the usual forces bearing on his decisions went unchecked, the Court considered how it would hold the secretary accountable. It agreed with the government that the "arbitrary and capricious" standard of judicial review was appropriate for actions of this sort. But in Justice Marshall's opinion, "arbitrary and capricious" took on a new toughness. It required the "reviewing court to engage in a substantial inquiry." The customary "presumption of regularity" did not "shield [the secretary's] action from a thorough, probing, in-depth review." Courts were to search the facts to ensure that the secretary had a reasonable basis for believing that the statutory standard was met, that the secretary considered the relevant factors, and that there had not been a clear error in judgment.[15]

The Court combined this newly assertive rendition of the arbitrary and capricious standard with two further innovations in judicial review of informal agency action: review would be based on the administrative record that was before the secretary when he made his decision (not on affidavits and exhibits selectively offered by the parties, as in this case), and the reviewing court could require the secretary to explain his decision to ensure consistency with Section 4(f). Although he may have privately expected a "snow job" on remand, Marshall's opinion seemed designed—both in tone and substance—to materially advance the urgent priority for parkland protection that it read Section 4(f) to require.

A separate opinion by Justice Hugo Black, joined by Justice William Brennan, was even more demanding. It argued that the government should not be given the chance to rehabilitate its case in the district court; instead, the case should be remanded to the secretary for hearings and findings "in full good-faith obedience to the Act of Congress. That Act was obviously passed to protect our public parks from forays by road builders except in the most extraordinary and imperative circumstances."[16]

One effect of *Overton Park* was to shift at least some control of the siting of I-40 through Memphis from the political arena, where it had been for more than a decade, into the judicial arena. Peter Strauss, administrative law scholar and leading commentator on the history of *Overton Park*, is critical of this move. He argues that there was little evidence in the legislative history or language of Section 4(f) of what Congress intended the decision criteria to be. The government's interpretation of "prudent" was at least as plausible as the Court's. Moreover, there was no evidence that Congress intended that the courts be the final arbiters of disputes surrounding interstate routes through parkland rather than the political and bureaucratic institutions that traditionally controlled these decisions. The Court was merely substituting one political judgment for another—its own.[17]

Of course, the Court in *Overton Park* did not present itself as deciding the question of the I-40 route alignment through Memphis or as displacing the political process by which that issue would be decided. It pictured itself instead as placing constraints on the political process in accordance with Congress's purposes in enacting Section 4(f). The Court interpreted those purposes in light of the broad "public concern" reflected in the nascent environmental movement, captured so succinctly in the opening sentence of its opinion. Its objective was to discourage the marginalization of those purposes by highway politics as usual. In this, the Court might be accused of substituting its own preferences for those of the dominant political players in the Memphis controversy, but those preferences were not formed in a vacuum; they were informed by the Court's understanding of shifts in the larger political and cultural context in which Congress had acted.

For environmentalists, the decision was a high-water mark. The Court's openness to the urgent need for protective measures, combined with a willingness to shape legal doctrine to meet that need, promised the sort of sea change environmentalists sought: the Court would help rearrange the institutional landscape to advance environmentalism's fragile enterprise against entrenched political and economic interests. Of course, this hopeful vision assumed a Court attuned to the environmentalist vision and not subject to the same cultural currents that threatened the advance of environmentalism in other venues.

In the years after *Overton Park*, it became clear that this assumption was unwarranted: there would be no sea change, at least not with the Court as its catalyst. The Court became less open to environmentalist claims, and later decisions limited the expansive role for the Court suggested by *Overton Park*. In *Chevron v. Natural Resources Defense Council, Inc.*, the Court held that reviewing courts should defer to reasonable agency interpretations of ambiguous statutes rather than supply their own preferred interpretations. *Vermont Yankee* forbid reviewing courts from imposing procedures on agencies not otherwise required by law. Nevertheless, in its framing of the standards for judicial review, *Overton Park* remains one of the most influential administrative law decisions of the twentieth century, as well as an environmentalist icon. And recent cases such as *Massachusetts v. EPA* show that the Court is still willing, in the right settings, to align itself with the most pressing priorities of the environmental community and to make institutional adjustments to ensure expression of those priorities.

Massachusetts v. EPA: Some Call It Pollution

In April 2007, the Supreme Court handed down its decision in *Massachusetts v. Environmental Protection Agency* (*MA v. EPA*), its first case dealing with climate change. The Court's decision established climate change regulation as within the existing authority of the Environmental Protection Agency (EPA) and set limits on the agency's discretion in deciding whether and on what terms to exercise that authority. It was an enormous, if narrow (the justices split five to four), victory for environmentalists: it legitimized their fears about global warming and their claims that the administration of George W. Bush was not doing what it should to address it. In its opinion, the Court showed a sympathy for environmentalist concerns that it had not shown since the early 1970s. Commentators described it as "truly remarkable," "a breathtaking result for [the] greens," "a highly consequential environmental law case," and an "indisputably . . . major political event." Others criticized it as a legally tortured indulgence of the majority justices' political inclinations.[18]

Science, Opinion, and Law

The years preceding the Court's 2007 decision saw a marked increase in scientific understanding of the global warming trend, the human contribution, and the risks of serious consequences if the trend continued—from rising sea levels to more intense tropical storms to more damaging patterns of drought and flood. The first comprehensive synthesis of the scientific evidence on climate change came in 1990 with the First Assessment Report of the Intergovernmental Panel on Climate Change (IPCC), a United Nations–affiliated scientific body whose purpose is to depict the current state of knowledge about climate change and its impacts. The IPCC issued updated assessment reports in 1995, 2001, and 2007 that made increasingly confident pronouncements that global surface temperatures are rising and that this warming is due primarily to anthropogenic greenhouse gas concentrations. The 2007 IPCC report's Summary for Policymakers stated that the warming of Earth is "unequivocal" and that it is "very likely" (greater than 90 percent probability) that recent warming is primarily due to anthropogenic greenhouse gas concentrations. This well-publicized summary came out in February 2007 as the justices entered their final deliberations in *MA v. EPA*.[19]

Global warming was on the public's mind in the years leading up to the Court's decision. The press reported widely on climate change matters during this period. Al Gore's documentary, *An Inconvenient Truth*, debuted in 2006 and became one of the highest grossing documentary films. Opinion polls from around the time of the Court's decision showed that over 60 percent of the U.S. public believed that recent global warming was caused primarily by human activities and over half considered it a very serious problem warranting highest priority attention from government officials. Widespread scientific and popular concern over climate change was an important feature of the cultural setting in which the Court addressed the legal issues in *MA v. EPA*. But just as important was that public opinion about climate change was divided along ideological lines.[20]

The events leading to *MA v. EPA* began obscurely at a March 1998 hearing before the House Appropriations Committee. Referring to an EPA study of the agency's authority to regulate emissions of four pollutants of concern from electric power plants, Congressman Tom DeLay, then House majority whip, asked EPA administrator Carol Browner whether she believed that the Clean Air Act (CAA) allowed the EPA to regulate emissions of carbon dioxide (CO_2). Browner answered yes and agreed to provide a legal opinion on that point. The upshot was an April 1998 opinion by the EPA's General Counsel, concluding that the EPA did have authority to regulate emissions of CO_2 and other greenhouse gases under the existing CAA. This question became the threshold issue on the merits in *MA v. EPA*.[21]

Generally, the CAA authorizes the EPA to regulate a substance if it is an "air pollutant" and if the administrator finds that emissions of it endanger public health or welfare. The CAA defines "air pollutant" as "any air pollution agent or combination of such agents, including any physical, chemical, biological, radioactive . . . substance or matter which is emitted into or otherwise enters the ambient air." The April 1998 legal opinion was based on this text. Because CO_2 and other greenhouse gases fell into the very broad class of substances indicated by "any physical, chemical . . . substance or matter," they qualified as air pollutants when emitted into the air. The 1998 opinion was clear, however, that although greenhouse gas emissions were within the scope of the CAA, the EPA's authority to regulate them required an endangerment finding, which the agency had not made.[22]

There was mixed public reaction to the potential regulation of CO_2 and other greenhouse gas emissions as air pollutants. Environmentalists were delighted that without further action by a reluctant Congress, the EPA could begin to attack what they considered the most urgent environmental problem in a generation. Industry groups and conservative politicians, however, heaped scorn on the notion that "air pollutants" would be stretched to cover benign, life-supporting gases such as CO_2. In May 2006, as *MA v. EPA* was moving through the courts, the Competitive Enterprise Institute, a conservative think tank, ran two television ads in fourteen U.S. cities extolling

CO_2's life-enhancing virtues and disputing its characterization as a pollutant. Both ads ended with a young girl in a bucolic setting blowing seeds from a dandelion head (with innocent breath that viewers would understand contained CO_2). The voiceover said, "Carbon dioxide. Some call it pollution. We call it life."[23]

The Origins of the Case

In 1999, relying on the agency's we-call-it-pollution legal opinion, a coalition of environmental groups filed a rulemaking petition with the EPA asking the agency to regulate greenhouse gas emissions from new motor vehicles under Section 202 of the CAA. Section 202(a) provides that the EPA administrator "shall" issue regulations prescribing standards for emissions of "any air pollutant" from new motor vehicles "which in his judgment cause, or contribute to, air pollution which may reasonably be anticipated to endanger public health or welfare."[24]

After George W. Bush assumed the presidency, a new EPA general counsel reversed the 1998 legal opinion, concluding that the agency did *not* have the authority to regulate greenhouse gas emissions for their effect on climate change. And soon after that, the EPA denied the rulemaking petition on the grounds (1) that it lacked the necessary regulatory authority and (2) that, even if it had the authority, regulating greenhouse gas emissions from motor vehicles would not be "effective or appropriate . . . at this time." On this latter point, the agency invoked a range of considerations, including the comparative advantages of the administration's "comprehensive [and nonregulatory] approach" to climate change, the adverse effect of unilateral regulation on convincing developing countries to control emissions, and uncertainty about the causes and future extent of climate change.[25]

As scientific authority for its uncertainty claims, the EPA drew extensively on a 2001 report that the National Academy of Sciences (NAS) had developed at the request of the White House: *Climate Change Science: An Analysis of Some Key Questions*. In an amicus curiae brief later submitted to the Court, contesting the agency's claims, eighteen climate scientists, including several who had helped write the NAS report, stated that the EPA had "misrepresented the findings of [the report] by selectively quoting statements about uncertainty while ignoring statements of certainty and near-certainty, thus giving the appearance of far more fundamental uncertainty than stated in the NAS/NRC report." In oral argument before the Court in *MA v. EPA*, Justice John Paul Stevens would use these scientists' allegations to press government counsel on the EPA's "selective quotations, [leaving] out parts that indicated there was far less uncertainty than the agency purported to find."[26]

Twelve states, three cities, and a host of environmental groups petitioned the Court of Appeals for the District of Columbia Circuit for review of the agency's decision declining to make the endangerment finding. A fractured three-judge panel of that court upheld the decision. Judge Arthur Randolph wrote to deny the petitions for review on their merits: in his view, even with the assumption that the EPA had the legal authority to regulate greenhouse gas emissions, it had properly declined to exercise that authority. Judge Sentelle believed that the petitions should be dismissed for lack of standing but joined Randolph in denying the petitions for review. In a dissent that foreshadowed the majority's opinion in the Supreme Court, Judge Tatel found that the petitioners had standing and that the EPA had erred both in denying its legal authority and in failing to explain its refusal to make the endangerment finding on the terms required by the statute. It was clear to him that the EPA had cherry-picked the 2001 NAS report to support its claims of uncertainty. Indeed, Tatel ventured his own view that it would be very difficult *not* to conclude on the basis of the 2001 report taken as a whole that global warming meets the endangerment standard of Section 202.[27]

In making their case to the Supreme Court, the environmental petitioners faced a tactical question of how to present the connection between their legal claims and the seriousness of the climate change issue that was their reason for being in court. According to Lisa Heinzerling, an environmental law scholar who served as one of their lead attorneys, the petitioners considered "situat[ing] the legal issues explicitly within the context of the problem of climate change, and . . . us[ing] the urgency and importance of this issue to set the tone for our legal arguments." But they chose instead to present the case as "an ordinary administrative and statutory case." This choice was driven by a hope that justices who might be indifferent or even hostile to the issue of climate change might still be convinced to side with petitioners on issues of statutory interpretation or agency discretion. As it turned out, however, the Court took the case because of "the unusual importance of the underlying issue," and the justices' different views on the legal issues were colored by their sense of the seriousness of climate change and the role its seriousness should play in the Court's deliberations. As Heinzerling has written, while victorious, petitioners "failed miserably in [their] effort to disguise this breakthrough case about climate change as an ordinary administrative and statutory matter. No one, apparently, was fooled."[28]

The issue of the seriousness of climate change that petitioners sought to downplay erupted early in the oral argument in a revealing comment by

Justice Scalia, who is notable among the justices for his antipathy to the environmentalist paradigm, including its stress on systemic fragility and harm. It might have been expected that he would resist environmental petitioners' concerns about climate change. He did, and quickly. Counsel for Massachusetts and other environmental petitioners, James Milkey, had barely finished his opening statement that this was primarily a case about "statutory interpretation and administrative law" and not about climate change, when Scalia interjected: "I thought that the standing requires imminent harm. . . . Is this harm imminent?" Intent on pressing his point, Scalia brushed past Milkey's response—that harm was already occurring with rising sea levels—to ask: "When? I mean, when is the predicted cataclysm?" The justice went on to offer his own understanding of the science: "there's something of a consensus on warming, but not a consensus on how much of that is attributable to human activity." He developed this thread further in his written dissent with a sympathetic portrayal of the EPA's review of the science.[29]

Dan Kahan and his colleagues wrote that the main reason people disagree about climate change science and the risks it conveys is that "positions on climate change convey values—communal concern versus individual self-reliance; . . . humility versus ingenuity; harmony with nature versus mastery over it."[30] Justice Scalia's skepticism was consistent with Kahan's observation that cultural values not only predict our assessment of climate change risk but also serve as a screen in the processing of information on the issue. "When is the predicted cataclysm?" carried the suggestion that petitioners' concerns were animated by phantom "sky-is-falling" fears, a common claim among environmentalism's critics. His recitation of the view that "we don't know what's causing warming" sought to undercut the heightened sensitivity to systemic risk that supported those fears. In his dissent on the merits, Scalia attributed the majority's receptivity to petitioners' legal arguments to their "alarm" over the risks of human-caused climate change and, by implication, the egalitarian-communitarian values that amplified those risks. But his resistance to the same arguments might just as easily be explained by his hierarchical individualist's discounting of those same risks.[31]

The Court's Opinion

Justice Stevens delivered the opinion of the Court, speaking for a bare majority that included Justices Anthony Kennedy, David Souter, Ruth Bader Ginsburg, and Stephen Breyer. The Court concluded that at least one of the environmental petitioners, the state of Massachusetts, had standing. On the merits, it held that the EPA had the statutory authority to regulate CO_2 and other greenhouse gases and that, in declining to regulate, the agency had based its decision on reasons that were improper under the endangerment standard. Chief Justice John Roberts and Justices Antonin Scalia, Clarence Thomas, and Samuel Alito joined in a pair of dissenting opinions, one on standing authored by Roberts and one on the merits authored by Scalia.

The Court's opinion began, in striking fashion, with this assertion: "a well-documented rise in global temperatures has coincided with a signifi-cant increase in the concentration of carbon dioxide in the atmosphere. Respected scientists believe the two trends are related." These two sentences established the main factual premise for the rest of the opinion. The Court then quoted environmental petitioners' claim that global warming is "the most pressing environmental challenge of our time." The prominent place-ment of the quote so early in the opinion left little doubt that the Court agreed with it.[32]

Assuming that the Court uses the opening passages of an opinion to signal what is most important about the case, the most important thing in *MA v. EPA* was that anthropogenic climate change is real and very serious. The Court reinforced this message with a rehearsal of the emerging climate sci-ence, including the 1990 and 1995 IPCC reports, and of international ef-forts to address climate change. It also cited the 2001 NAS report that the EPA had relied on for its own assessment of the science and that Justice Stevens, during oral argument, had suggested had been the victim of "se-lective quotations" by the agency. In an implicit rebuke of the agency's char-acterization of the science, Justice Stevens's opinion for the Court quoted the first sentences of that report, which the agency had failed to note in its review, confirming the scientific basis for anthropogenic climate change: "greenhouse gases are accumulating in Earth's atmosphere as a result of human activities, causing surface air temperatures and subsurface ocean tem-peratures to rise. Temperatures are, in fact, rising."[33]

Both merits issues turned on the degree of discretion the Court was willing to grant the agency. The deputy solicitor general argued for broad agency discretion on both issues. The Court owed deference to the EPA's interpretation of its statutory authority under *Chevron v. Natural Resources Defense Council,* which recognized the primacy of an agency's interpreta-tion of its statute in cases where Congress had not spoken clearly to the question. It also owed the agency particularly broad deference in its review of the denial of the environmentalists' petition because decisions not to reg-ulate may be based on "discretionary considerations unrelated to the agen-cy's legal authority to act."[34]

The Court rejected both arguments in limiting the EPA's options under Section 202. On the first merits issue, the Court gave no deference to the agency's legal interpretation because it was precluded by the text of the statute. Greenhouse gas emissions fall clearly within the statute's definition of "air pollutant" because they are "without a doubt 'physical [and] chemical . . . substance[s] which [are] emitted into . . . the ambient air.' The statute is unambiguous." The Court rationalized the statute's broad reach—embracing "all airborne compounds of whatever stripe—with the observation that without sufficient flexibility, new problems, such as climate change, would render the statute obsolete and inadequate. Congress may not have had climate change specifically in mind when it enacted Section 202, but it gave the EPA authority to address emerging serious problems of precisely this kind.[35]

On the second issue, the Court gave the EPA only a narrow choice under Section 202's endangerment standard. The statute, it concluded, requires the EPA to determine either that CO_2 emissions from automobiles pose a danger or that they do not, or that the scientific uncertainty is so profound that the EPA cannot reach a reasoned decision on the question. The Court found that the EPA did neither here. The "laundry list" of reasons the agency offered for not regulating were not to the point. Although uncertainty in the climate science would be relevant to the question of "whether sufficient information exists to make an endangerment finding," the agency had not directed its consideration of uncertainty to that question. Because the EPA had offered no reasonable explanation related to the statutory standard, the Court found that its action on the petition was arbitrary and capricious and remanded the case for further proceedings.[36]

As with *Overton Park,* the effect of *MA v. EPA* was to shift control from the executive branch to the judiciary in correcting a failure to protect environmental values. And as in the earlier case, the result in *MA v. EPA* required a doctrinal advance. It was not clear going into the case that agency decisions declining to initiate rulemakings were judicially reviewable at all. Although some lower federal courts had determined that they were, on an extremely deferential standard, the Court had not stated its view. *MA v. EPA* was the first time the Court held that denials of this sort were reviewable. And although it applied the usually undemanding arbitrary and capricious standard, it used Section 202's endangerment standard to rein in the agency's discretion.[37]

Administrative law scholar Ronald Cass suggests that Al Gore's documentary and the climate crisis fatally infected the Court's thinking on this and other issues in the case and caused the Court to trespass onto territory reserved for politically accountable actors. Decisions not to begin rulemakings, he observes, "are generally regarded as beyond judicial ken absent an unequivocal legal command removing administrative discretion," and in this case nothing in the statute required the EPA to make an endangerment finding. Other commentators have been kinder to the Court on this question. Jody Freeman and Adrian Vermeule offer a sympathetic view of the ruling as encouraging agencies to regulate on the basis of expertise and statutory design rather than the private preferences of political actors.[38]

The Court stopped short of dictating a final outcome. It did not require that the EPA find endangerment, and unlike Judge Tatel, Justice Stevens's opinion for the Court did not say that a fair reading of the evidence compelled an endangerment finding. But the Court's characterization of the science left the clear implication that an endangerment finding would be warranted. The opinion was critical, at times even dismissive, of the agency's legal efforts to avoid making a finding. Just below the surface was a sense that the agency contorted the statute and misrepresented the science to reach the administration's politically preferred result. The Court barely disguised its frustration with an agency that refused to address a serious risk under a precautionary statutory provision.[39]

The decision has been criticized as sacrificing neutral legal principles to the value preferences of the majority of the justices. The Court showed its colors in *MA v. EPA,* and its colors were green. But that remarkable feature may add to the decision's symbolic power, rather than detract from it. The Court risked some of its precious legitimacy in stretching the membrane that separates neutral analysis from engagement. Its willingness to do so signaled its own sense of the urgency of the crisis to which it saw itself responding. As Freeman and Vermeule capture it, the decision "communicated to the public something on the order of: *even the Supreme Court thinks something must be done.*" I'm not aware of evidence that this message moved the public on climate change one way or the other, but it is significant that the Court believed the situation merited a message being sent and ventured to send it.[40]

Perhaps, as in *Overton Park,* the Court in *MA v. EPA* saw itself not as the crusader but simply as the handmaiden of congressional purpose. According to former Stevens law clerk and administrative law scholar Kathryn Watts, Justice Stevens's customary approach to statutory interpretation paid "particularly close attention to Congress's own protective and remedial purposes." She sees this approach at work in many of his opinions that read remedial statutes liberally to advance their beneficial purposes. In *MA v. EPA,* Watts suggests, Stevens refused to defer to the EPA's narrow reading of the statute not because he believed that a pressing social issue such as climate change warranted more assertive judicial intervention but because that reading would be contrary to the protective purpose of the statute.[41]

To say that Stevens's interpretive approach in *MA v. EPA* was purposive, however, does not resolve the role of climate change in the Court's decision. Like all interpretive approaches, purposivism suffers from some indeterminacy.[42] Which purposes are to be advanced, and how far? In the end, it is hard *not* to read the Court's opinion in *MA v. EPA* as inflected by the majority's views on climate change risks and the egalitarian-communitarian values supporting those views. The Court took the case expressly because of the importance of the climate issue and featured the supporting science in its opinion. It packed its opinion with language on the imminence and seriousness of the climate change threat. It did this notwithstanding the tactical decision of the environmental petitioners to downplay the threat. And it innovated to bring about a favorable outcome for petitioners. Without climate change as context, it seems unlikely that Stevens or others in the majority would have seen a threat to the protective purpose of the statue that warranted their intervention or would have gone to such lengths to vindicate it.

Justice Scalia's Dissent

Scalia also saw the Court's frustration, born of its sense of urgency, as driving its decision, and that urgency became the target of his dissent on the merits. He found sufficient ambiguity in the definition of "air pollutant" to warrant deference to the agency's interpretation. The text, he argued, requires that any "air pollutant" must also be an "air pollution agent." The agency reasonably concluded that greenhouse gas emissions are not agents of "air pollution" because they are not pollution (they don't render the air "impure or unclean") and because they are not in the air (they reside instead in the "upper reaches of the atmosphere" and not in the "ambient air"). Scalia's division of the affected resource (air) into discrete units (air at ground level and air in the upper atmosphere) as a way of limiting regulatory authority is an interpretive approach that he has applied to similar effect in other environmental cases.[43]

Scalia's segmenting of the "air" had both symbolic and legal implications. His resort to the dictionary definition of "pollute" ("to make or render impure or unclean") evoked the word's moral dimensions. "Pollute" connects to Jonathan Haidt's "care-harm" domain (compassion in response to threats of harm from impurity or uncleanness) and also the "sanctity-degradation" domain (disgust in response to perceived impurity). As discussed in Chapter 1, much environmental concern flows from care-harm, to which liberals are partial. But sanctity-degradation favored by conservatives can also generate concern if the environment is understood to be sullied. Acknowledging greenhouse gas emissions as "pollutants," as the Court's opinion did, opens both these potential values pathways in response to climate change. By limiting pollution to defilement of the ambient air, Scalia would not only achieve a contrary legal outcome but also dampen the ethical connotations of the climate debate. This is a repetition, in the judicial setting, of the "some call it pollution" values message in the political campaign against regulation of greenhouse gas emissions.[44]

Scalia also concluded that nothing in the statute's language requires the administrator to make a judgment about endangerment or limits what the EPA may consider in deciding to defer making a judgment. The factors the EPA cited in deciding that it would not be wise to grant the petition at this time were reasonable and proper. Such decisions were traditionally within the broad prerogative of the executive branch, without close checking by the courts, and were best left so.[45]

Scalia ended his dissent with a coda that captured the tension between environmentalism and institutional restraint that pervaded the case:

> The Court's alarm over global warming may or may not be justified, but it ought not distort the outcome of this litigation. This is a straightforward administrative-law case, in which Congress has passed a malleable statute giving broad discretion, not to us but to an executive agency. No matter how important the underlying policy issues at stake, this Court has no business substituting its own desired outcome for the reasoned judgment of the responsible agency.

In the context of Scalia's discounting of climate change risks, however, judicial restraint took on a values hue of its own.[46]

Affirming *MA v. EPA: American Electric Power Corp. v. Connecticut* and *Utility Air Regulatory Group v. EPA*

Two recent cases have bolstered *MA v. EPA*'s core ruling of the CAA's authority over greenhouse gas emissions while moderating the tone and reach of the decision. In *American Electric Power Corp. v. Connecticut (AEP)*, the Court concluded that the CAA, as interpreted by *MA v. EPA* to cover emissions of CO_2, displaced federal common law actions on climate change. The vote was eight to zero, although two of the four dissenters in *MA v. EPA*, Justices Thomas and Alito, issued a short concurrence indicating their continued disagreement with the merits holding in *MA v. EPA*.[47]

AEP affirmed *MA v. EPA*'s interpretation of the EPA's authority to regulate greenhouse gas emissions by making it integral to the Court's holding, and *AEP* made it clear that this authority reached to stationary as well as mobile sources. But the Court's opinion by Justice Ginsburg lacked *MA v. EPA*'s extravagant rehearsal of the science and risks of climate change; its tone was comparatively subdued. Ginsburg did summarize the finding of endangerment by the EPA that came in the wake of *MA v. EPA*, including the agency's conclusion that " 'compelling' evidence supported the 'attribution of observed climate change to anthropogenic' emissions of greenhouse gases." But attached to her summary was the following footnote: "The Court, we caution, endorses no particular view of the complicated issues related to carbon-dioxide emissions and climate change." The Court gave no reason for this cautionary note; it may simply have been demanded by one of the *MA v. EPA* dissenters as the price for unanimity. In any event, its effect was to draw the Court to a more modest stance after its bold gesture in *MA v. EPA*.[48]

In *Utility Air Regulatory Group v. EPA (UARG)*, decided in 2014, Justices Thomas and Alito continued to argue that *MA v. EPA* was wrongly decided. The rest of the justices acknowledged the EPA's authority to regulate greenhouse gas emissions under the CAA. But an opinion for the Court by Justice Scalia qualified that authority, leaving it open to dispute in future cases and reanimating the cultural conflict that seethed in *MA v. EPA*. At issue was the EPA's authority to require permitting of new and modified stationary sources of greenhouse gas emissions under CAA provisions applicable to sources emitting "air pollutants" in amounts above specified thresholds (100 or 250 tons per year).[49]

With Chief Justice Roberts and Justices Scalia, Kennedy, Thomas, and Alito in the majority, the Court rebuffed the EPA's effort to regulate sources due solely to their greenhouse gas emissions. *MA v. EPA* rejected a reading of "air pollutant" that categorically excluded greenhouse gas emissions, Scalia wrote for the Court, but it did not require that the term be read to include greenhouse gases in every regulatory setting under the CAA. In this setting, the EPA's reading of "air pollutant" to include greenhouse gas emissions was unreasonable because it would require burdensome permitting of small and medium sources that Congress did not intend to cover and that would not be covered if only conventional pollutants (typically emitted in much lower volumes) were considered. The EPA's attempt to avoid this overreach by adopting generous alternatives to the statutory thresholds for greenhouse gases (e.g., 100,000 tons per year) was "well beyond the 'bounds of its statutory authority.' "[50]

Also at issue was the EPA's authority under a related provision to require best available control technology (BACT) for greenhouse gas emissions from sources that would be subject to permitting in any case because their emissions of nongreenhouse "air pollutants" were above the statutory thresholds ("anyway sources"). By a vote of seven to two, the Court upheld the application of BACT for greenhouse gas emissions from "anyway sources," arguing that differences in the triggering language and modest incremental burdens warranted a different outcome. As Justice Scalia's opinion for the Court acknowledged, BACT regulation for anyway sources would cover 83 percent of the greenhouse gas emissions projected from new or modified stationary sources, only 3 percent less than the EPA had sought to regulate under its more aggressive interpretation.

Although the ruling was essentially a win for the EPA, the Court's rationale and rhetoric harbored unsettling portents. The opinion destabilized the definition of "air pollutant" established by *MA v. EPA* and opened an avenue of attack against the EPA's regulation of greenhouse gas emissions under other CAA provisions, such as the EPA's proposed rule for emissions from existing power plants. The Court's castigation of the EPA for attempting "an enormous and transformative expansion of [its] regulatory authority without clear congressional authority" also cast doubt on the force of *MA v. EPA* in future expansions of greenhouse gas regulation. Ominously, the Court declared its skepticism of "agency claims to discover in a long-extant statute an unheralded power to regulate 'a significant portion of the American economy' "—exactly the kinds of claims that the ruling in *MA v. EPA* foreshadowed.[51]

In his partial concurrence and dissent, joined by Justices Ginsburg, Sotomayor, and Kagan, Justice Breyer argued that the accommodation reached by the Court could just as easily have been achieved by finding flexibility in the definition of "source" rather than "air pollutant." The majority's choice instead to create a special greenhouse gas exception to "air pollutant"—the CAA's pivotal jurisdictional phrase—"chip[ped] away at our decision in Massachusetts." Thus, even though a substantial majority of the Court in *UARG* accepted the core ruling of *MA v. EPA*, aftershocks from the confrontation in the earlier case continued to reverberate within the Court with potential but largely unpredictable consequences for future climate change initiatives under the CAA.[52]

The Legacy of *MA v. EPA*

MA v. EPA leaves both a practical and a symbolic legacy. Practically, it set the EPA, and the nation, on a pathway of regulation to reduce greenhouse gas emissions. In December 2009, under the new Obama administration, the EPA made the endangerment finding for greenhouse gas emissions under Section 202, triggering the adoption of vehicle emission standards. In May 2010, acting jointly with the National Highway Traffic Safety Administration, it issued those standards for passenger cars and other light-duty vehicles, limiting the amount of greenhouse gases vehicles emitted per mile and establishing corresponding fuel economy requirements. The EPA has also adopted rules for greenhouse gas emission controls for major new stationary sources. With President Obama embracing climate as a legacy issue, the agency has also commenced rulemakings to limit emissions from new and existing power plants, representing about 40 percent of U.S. emissions.[53]

The symbolic significance of *MA v. EPA,* still largely intact after *AEP* and *UARG,* exceeds its so far modest practical impact. The Court accepted the environmentalists' view of climate change as the issue "of our time." It legitimized the environmentalists' concerns against the efforts of an antagonistic administration to discredit and put them aside. It developed legal doctrine to ensure that the protective purposes of the statute, as the Court read it, were not undermined by political convenience. It provided a rallying point for climate change advocates and a touchstone for the public on climate change. *MA v. EPA* does not rise to the level of cultural significance of *Brown v. Board of Education,* but in environmental law, it may prove to be as close as we will come.

The situation is hardly stable. There is widespread acknowledgment that the CAA is not the optimal vehicle for climate change regulation, and the EPA itself has said it would prefer comprehensive climate change legislation. But Congress has not enacted that legislation. Instead, it has threatened repeatedly to strip the EPA of its existing CAA authority over greenhouse gas emissions. Agency efforts to carry out that authority face political and litigation risks, as *UARG* intimates. Nevertheless, the first steps have been taken, the status quo is no longer to do nothing to mitigate climate change, and the burden is on Congress to realign the current regulatory trajectory.

New York v. United States: The Crisis of the Day

Opposed to decisions like *Overton Park* and *MA v. EPA* are Court decisions that dismiss the urgency and priority of environmentalist claims. These are not cases in which the Court reframes legal doctrine to advance environmental degradation. Rather, the opposites of *Overton Park* and *MA v. EPA* are cases in which the Court, while giving some acknowledgment to environmental concerns, subordinates those concerns to other values. The message of these decisions is *yes, we all want to protect the environment, but other values rightly limit how we can or should go about that.* These

other values include autonomy, mastery, and hierarchy values that have animated a number of the Court's decisions on federalism, property rights, and
judicial access over the last three decades. These values are in tension with
core environmentalist values, and the decisions they drive typically produce
an "antienvironment" result.

The year 1992 was a watershed for environmental decisions by the
Rehnquist Court. William Rehnquist had become chief justice in 1986, but
it was not until Justice Thomas joined the Court in late 1991 that the conservatives secured a relatively firm majority. The next year, the Court issued decisions in three environmental cases that signaled the extension or
revitalization of doctrines in federalism, takings, and standing, all in a conservative direction and all with strong cultural overtones inimical to environmentalism. I will address two of these cases in later chapters, but I focus
here on the federalism case, *New York v. United States*.[54]

Commentators debate how conservative or "activist" the Rehnquist Court
turned out to be. However, they generally agree that the Rehnquist Court
saw a revolution in the law of federalism, as the Court drew new limits on
federal powers vis-à-vis the states or revived limits that had been thought
dead.[55] From early in his tenure on the Court, Rehnquist made no secret of
his desire to reshape post–New Deal judicial doctrine to assert constitutional limits on federal power. Thomas's appointment secured a majority
in support of this reshaping, and with the Court's 1992 decision in *New
York v. United States*, the reshaping began. The case made "legal history . . .
as the New Federalism's Tenth Amendment anti-commandeering doctrine
was born." *New York v. United States* tested the relative strength of pressures, on the one hand, to address an imminent environmental crisis and,
on the other, to establish and defend a preferred institutional arrangement—
in this case, "the constitutional structure underlying and limiting [federal]
authority" with respect to the states. The federalism claim won out over
the environmental one, giving a new majority on the Court an occasion to
put environmental concerns in their place relative to what they believed were
more important public concerns, although this drew vigorous dissent.[56]

The environmental problem in *New York v. United States* was the threatened lack of disposal capacity for low-level radioactive waste (LLRW).
LLRW is hazardous, and at least some of it is produced in every state by
a range of enterprises—hospitals, research facilities, and a variety of
industries—in addition to nuclear power plants. Although we all benefit
from these essential activities, there are risks associated with the disposal
of the wastes that are born primarily by people living near disposal sites.
As the Court summarized it, "Most citizens recognize the need for radioactive waste disposal sites, but few want sites near their homes." This imbal-

ance in the distribution of costs and benefits complicated the supply of safe disposal capacity.[57]

The disposal problem had the classic form of Hardin's tragedy of the commons among the states. States choosing to allow LLRW disposal capacity (sited states) incurred all the costs of hosting the facilities but enjoyed only some of the benefits they provided. Because the Constitution's dormant commerce clause forbids states from discriminating against interstate commerce, sited states were obligated to receive waste from nonsited states for disposal on the same terms as their own waste. Unsited states had a place to send their waste and avoided the costs of having their own facility. Sited states could lawfully avoid being taken advantage of only by limiting access to their disposal facilities to all users, including their own LLRW sources, or closing the facilities entirely. Hardin's model foretold a collapse of the disposal commons as each state sought strategically to better its position vis-à-vis other states at the expense of meeting the common need.

Events leading up to *New York v. United States* fit the collapse scenario. By the Court's own account, the number of LLRW disposal sites in the United States shrank from six in the early 1970s to three in 1979. Of these three sites, two—located in Washington state and Nevada—were shut down temporarily, leaving all the nation's LLRW to be disposed of in the one remaining site, in Barnwell, South Carolina. "The Governor of South Carolina, understandably perturbed, ordered a 50% reduction in the quantity of waste accepted at The Barnwell site. The Governors of Washington and Nevada announced plans to shut their sites permanently." And the country faced a crisis—the real possibility that there would be insufficient disposal capacity and that the public would face increased risks as LLRW sources were left to store or dispose of their wastes without proper management.[58]

The Low-Level Radioactive Waste Policy Act of 1985 (LRWPA) codified an agreement worked out among the states under the auspices of the National Governor's Association. Like an earlier unsuccessful federal law dealing with the problem, it hewed to a state-based approach, with federal enforcement as backup, rather than direct federal control of the management of LLRW. The LRWPA reaffirmed the responsibility of each state, either alone or together with other states, to provide for disposal of the LLRW generated within its boundaries. It added timelines for progress by unsited states toward disposal self-sufficiency and imposed consequences for failure to meet those timelines. The consequences came through a combination of measures. Compact regions with disposal facilities could exclude waste from outside beginning in 1992. In the meantime, they could impose a surcharge on that outside waste. A portion of the surcharges were to go to the secretary of energy for use in rewarding unsited states for meeting the self-sufficiency milestones; unsited states that failed to meet the milestones were subject to an even higher surcharge. Finally, the LRWPA required states that did not provide disposal capacity by 1996, either on their own or through a compact, to take title to and possession of LLRW produced within their boundaries and to be liable for all damages suffered by waste generators if they failed to do so. It was this last measure—the "take title" provision—that the Court would find constitutionally defective.[59]

New York took part in the negotiations leading to the legislation. An official of the state's energy office testified before Congress in favor of it. The state's senior senator, Daniel Moynihan, urged its passage on the Senate floor, and all of New York's congressional delegation supported it. After enactment, however, as it moved to implement the LRWPA, the state met fierce political resistance from communities near potential disposal sites that included public demonstrations and civil disobedience. In another setting, these local activists might have played the part of environmentalist heroes, but within the framework of the case they figured as NIMBY obstructionists and eventually drew the state into that role. The state joined two protesting counties in a suit against the United States in federal court, claiming that the LWRPA violated the Constitution's Tenth and Eleventh Amendments, the Fifth Amendment's due process clause, and the guarantee clause of the Article IV. The district court dismissed all these claims, and the court of appeals affirmed. The Supreme Court took review on the Tenth Amendment and the guarantee clause claims, but in oral argument all the Court's attention was on the Tenth Amendment claim.[60]

The Tenth Amendment says nothing on its face about federal use of states as instruments of regulation. It reads in its entirety: "The powers not delegated to the United States by the Constitution, nor prohibited by it to the States, are reserved to the States respectively, or to the people." As the Court's opinion would acknowledge, this is a tautology: the states keep what they have not given up. And for decades preceding *New York v. United States,* the Court had done little with it. In a 1976 opinion by Justice Rehnquist in *National League of Cities v. Usery,* a closely divided Court struck down an extension of federal minimum wage requirements to state and local governments because the restrictions encroached on the "traditional governmental functions" of states. But nine years later, the Court overruled *National League of Cities* in *Garcia v. San Antonio Metropolitan Transit Authority.* State sovereignty was better protected through the political process than through judicial oversight. Justices Rehnquist and Justice O'Connor dissented in *Garcia,* complaining that the Court abdicated its proper role in policing the limits of federal power, and Rehnquist predicted that a later Court would overrule it.[61]

Justice Blackmun's notes of the conference after the oral argument in *New York v. United States* reveal that feelings against the "take title" provision ran high among the justices who would eventually join Justice Sandra Day O'Connor's opinion for the Court. O'Connor herself called the provision "'a frightening result' from the perspective of the Tenth Amendment. Scalia described the statute as 'pure punishment,' while Kennedy characterized it as 'very dangerous.'" For his part, Blackmun, who would join Justice Byron White's dissenting opinion, considered *New York v. United States* "a political case taken here to reconsider *Garcia*." He believed that the federal interest in environmental protection, as in this case, was even greater than in wage and hour regulation, which had been the issue in *Garcia*.[62]

O'Connor's opinion for the Court was joined by Chief Justice Rehnquist and Justices Scalia, Kennedy, Souter, and Thomas. The relevant question, as the Court put it, was the extent to which the Tenth Amendment empowered Congress to use states "as implements of regulation." After a lengthy review of constitutional history and precedent and despite the vagaries of Tenth Amendment jurisprudence up to that point, the Court concluded, "We have always understood that even where Congress has the authority under the Constitution to pass laws requiring or prohibiting certain acts, it lacks the power directly to compel the States to require or prohibit those acts." The take title provision of the LRWPA ran afoul of this understanding by forcing the states to choose between regulating as Congress directed (providing disposal capacity) or assuming title to and liability for wastes generated within their jurisdiction. Because either alternative by itself would be an impermissible intrusion on state sovereignty, the Court reasoned, the choice was also unconstitutional.[63]

The Court's opinion recognized other, constitutionally permissible means by which Congress could encourage the states to site disposal capacity. These included options under the spending clause (e.g., giving states a choice to regulate according to conditions placed on the availability of federal funds or to forego the funds) and the commerce clause (e.g., giving the states the choice to regulate under federal standards or to have their citizens subjected to direct federal regulation). This recognition left the Court open to the charge that this application of the Tenth Amendment represented a hollow formalism. But the Court argued that the take title provision's "commandeering" of state institutions undermined political accountability in a way that the permissible options did not. If the federal government directs the states to regulate, rather than gives them a "choice," citizens may blame state officials for unpopular policies for which federal officials are responsible. "Accountability is thus diminished when, due to federal coercion, elected state officials cannot regulate in accordance with the views of the local electorate."[64]

Constitutional law scholar Herman Schwartz calls the Court's accountability argument "patent nonsense." It was at least an unconvincing makeweight. As Schwartz points out, those involved in the LLRW disposal business knew "who has set which rules." More to the point, so did the two New York counties that joined the state in suing the federal government, expressing the not-in-my-backyard sentiments of their constituents.[65]

The Court's real rationale surfaced in its explanation of why it invalidated the take title provision even though New York initially concurred in the arrangement. The Tenth Amendment's prohibition was not negotiable, it wrote. "The Constitution does not protect the sovereignty of states for the benefit of the States . . . [but] for the protection of individuals. . . . 'Federalism secures to citizens the liberties that derive from the diffusion of sovereign power.' " In this rendering, the rationale for federalism sounds in a desire to check governmental authority at all levels, state and federal; "therefore, the departure from the constitutional plan cannot be ratified by the 'consent' of state officials."[66]

Schwartz finds that "the logic of this is baffling," because "political liberty is the freedom to participate in the community's political life and thereby influence public policy."[67] But the kind of liberty that the Court had in mind was not freedom to participate in collective decisions but freedom from overburdening collective constraints. It was the autonomous individual's freedom from governmental "tyranny." This liberty opposes the collectivist values behind environmental and other ameliorative social legislation and energizes the antiregulatory thrust of contemporary conservatism. Its invocation in *New York v. United States* made plain that the new federalism would be less about reasserting state sovereignty than about recovering individual autonomy lost under the weight of modern government.

In the opening sentence of its opinion, the Court set up a tension between "one of our Nation's newest problems of public policy and perhaps our oldest question of constitutional law." It returned at the end to resolve that tension, and the resolution was straightforward. "The shortage of disposal sites for radioactive waste is a pressing national problem," but it is only the "crisis of the day." "The Constitution protects us from our own best intentions" by enabling us to "resist the temptation to concentrate power . . . as an expedient solution to [such] cris[es]." The hierarchy was clear: Environmental concern was a policy fashion that for our own good must be subordinated to the institutional ecosystem ordered by the Constitution to uphold autonomy values. We should not expect the Court to alter that system to accommodate environmental "crises," no matter how urgent.[68]

In dissent, Justice White, joined by Blackmun and Stevens, argued that the Court's analysis "undervalued the effect the seriousness of this [LLRW] public policy problem should have on the constitutionality of the take title provision." This public policy problem was "a crisis" whose "imminence . . . cannot be overstated." Under the pressure of this crisis, sited and unsited states had reached a compromise that Congress enacted, "acced[ing] to the wishes of the States by permitting local decisionmaking rather than imposing a solution from Washington." New York should be stopped from complaining about this agreement, having obtained the benefit of concessions from other states in the negotiations. Alternatively, the LRWPA should be upheld as constitutional, as White found no principle of federalism to prevent "the National Government from acting as referee among the States to prohibit one from bullying another." The states sought to solve their disposal commons problem in the manner Hardin had suggested—through mutual coercion mutually agreed to—with the federal government in the indispensable role of enforcer.[69]

The principal difference between White's approach and the Court's was his integration of the LLRW "problem" into his search for an appropriate legal outcome. O'Connor's opinion for the Court rhetorically minimized the problem ("crisis of the day") by cordoning it off from its constitutional analysis, which was crisis-proof by design. White invoked the problem repeatedly and with intensity ("crisis" whose "imminence . . . cannot be overstated," "very serious danger," "problem of grave import"). The problem was driving the central events of the LRWPA story; it was a major actor, and the law could not be ascertained without it. In White's view, it was the function of law to foster and support a collective solution to this urgent problem, against the abstract claims of an institutional design. His emphasis on collectivist values in construing law opposed the Court's focus on autonomy.[70]

As in *Overton Park* and *MA v. EPA,* the Court's doctrinal shift in *New York v. United States* moved control over public policy from a political branch, in this case Congress, to the judiciary. Here, however, the shift came through constitutional, not administrative, law and with a different implication for the political process. The Court in *New York v. United States* did not purport to uphold legislated values against the vagaries of executive branch implementation, as it had in *Overton Park* and *MA v. EPA.* Instead it rebuked Congress itself for failing to honor values it found implicit in the constitutional structure. On the cultural battlefield that the Supreme Court sometimes is, the Constitution offers the ultimate trump to justices seeking to advance their value preferences.

Justice Kennedy has described the anticommandeering decisions as establishing "the etiquette of federalism." In *New York v. United States,* the

Court offered limits on federal power as a figure for individual liberty—against the weight of too much government. It would soon extend this theme in path-breaking federalism decisions under the commerce clause. For a time, despite its symbolic importance as the annunciator of the Court's liberty-themed federalism revolution, *New York v. United States* seemed of limited practical effect. Few federal enactments were found to violate the anti-commandeering doctrine, suggesting that states were able, as *Garcia* presumed, to protect their institutional integrity in the political process.[71] In *National Federation of Independent Business v. Sebelius* (decided in 2012), however, the Court gave new life to the earlier case. Seven of the justices agreed that the withholding of all Medicaid funds from states refusing to expand their coverage as required by the Affordable Care Act exceeded Congress's power under the spending clause and ran afoul of the Tenth Amendment's anticommandeering principle under *New York v. United States*.[72]

THIS CHAPTER'S CASES REVEAL some important features of the relationship between environmentalist values and the dominant culture. In *Overton Park* and *MA v. EPA*, environmentalist values carried the day. The Court spoke, in Richard Lazarus's phrase, with an "environmental voice." In both cases the Court advanced legal interpretations and doctrinal innovations that gave practical expression to those values. Given its norms of neutrality and restraint, the Court's opinions in these cases represented an extraordinary affirmation of the environmentalist perspective. However, the strong countercurrent of Justice Scalia's dissent in *MA v. EPA*, which he rechanneled in his opinion for the Court in *UARG*, prefigures the cultural battles in cases discussed in chapters to come, in a number of which Scalia's voice is decisive. The ringing affirmation of environmentalist values in the Court's opinions in *Overton Park* and *MA v. EPA* proves to be the exception rather than the rule in the Court's environmental cases.

New York v. United States illustrates a subtler side of the cultural oppositions in the Court's environmental cases. Justice O'Connor's opinion for the Court was mildly dismissive of environmentalist concerns, but it was not exactly antienvironmentalist. It acknowledged radioactive waste disposal as a "pressing national problem" and outlined constitutionally permissible alternatives for regulating it. The choice for the Court seemed a matter of emphasis. It found an opposing value in the case—"liberty"—more compelling than the environmental concerns and used the case to announce a new era of liberty-protecting federalism doctrine. O'Connor herself did not seem to harbor antienvironmentalist hostility. In her environmental votes, as in other areas, she was the median justice during her time on the

Court. And she wrote sympathetically on environmental issues in other cases.[73]

This reminds us that the values we have identified with environmentalism and the opposing values of the dominant culture are a matter of degree. Society contains all the values we have identified. What defines the dominant culture is the relative emphasis that the nation places on these values. It is possible, as others have suggested, that environmentalism's influence in the United States is very wide but not very deep. While a great majority of the public may be sympathetic to environmentalism, the culture's dominant value set may nevertheless regularly produce antienvironmental outcomes. This underlying structure of resistance to environmentalism may be largely invisible, like an iceberg mostly underwater, and its solidity may therefore be easy to underestimate. In our navigation of the Court's environmental cases, however, its looming presence is unmistakable.

CHAPTER FOUR

Law for the Environmental Other

ENVIRONMENTALISTS often embrace ecocentric values or religious or spiritual regard for nature. In his 1972 classic, *Should Trees Have Standing?*, philosopher and legal scholar Christopher Stone imagined a legal system that would integrate ecocentric values. There were three key features, he concluded. For a thing in nature—such as an animal species—to have legal rights, the law would have to (1) allow suit be to be brought in the species' own interests (not in humans' interests in the species), (2) base judgment on harms to the species (not on economic or other impacts to humans), and (3) provide redress for the benefit of the species (not for its human benefactors).[1]

Measured against Stone's criteria, the legal system shows limited recognition of the rights of nature. Congress has made no express provision for the representation in legal proceedings of the interests of the environment, as distinct from the interests of its human users and appreciators. In a handful of statutes it has established strong entitlements to protection for things in nature and redress for harms to them. In the Endangered Species Act (ESA) and the Marine Mammal Protection Act, for example, the legal protections that Congress created for species are to a great extent without regard to the effects of those protections on economic or other human interests. In Superfund, Congress established strict liability for harm to natural resources from chemical contaminants. Damages recovered are for restoration or replacement of the resources that have been injured or destroyed. Even these statutes are underlain by human utilitarian rationales, however, and openly ecocentric arguments are muted in the public debate that surrounds their continuation.

For its part, the Supreme Court has done little to incorporate ecocentrism in its legal doctrines and interpretations. In the cases that follow, I explore diverse sources of respect for the environmental other, as well its cultural antithesis, and outline the limits of ecocentrism's influence on institutional practice. In these cases, the Court has resisted arguments from ecocentric perspectives, including that nonhumans are entitled to representation of their own legal interests or rights. These decisions endorse the dominant culture's anthropocentrism and the marginalization of ecocentric views in the public discourse. In contemplating whether things in nature should be given legal recognition, Stone asked himself whether he had thought the unthinkable. In mainstream political and legal discourse, ecocentrism remains largely invisible, if not unthinkable, a fact that points to the immense difficulty of the transformation environmentalists envisioned in the early days of the movement. Nevertheless, minority views in two of these cases express sympathy for ecocentric views and suggest the potential for further incorporation in institutional practice.

Sierra Club v. Morton: Standing for Trees

In *Sierra Club v. Morton,* the Sierra Club opposed the federal government's approval of construction of a ski resort in the remote Mineral King Valley of California, then a national game refuge adjacent to Sequoia National Park. The Sierra Club's 1990 book, *Wild by Law,* begins with this paean to the case and the club's role in it:

> In 1956, the Sierra Club made Walt Disney an honorary life member in gratitude for his films on wildlife, which enthralled a generation of Americans. A dozen years later, the Sierra Club launched its first major environmental lawsuit, to block the filmmaker's bid to build a gigantic ski resort in a remote valley in the Sierra Nevada of California. The ensuing contest would lead to one of the most important Supreme Court decisions ever rendered on environmental matters. It would also launch environmental organizations in a whole new direction—toward the courthouses of the United States.[2]

The Court denied standing to the Sierra Club but mapped a route by which the club (and any other public interest plaintiff) might successfully claim standing. Sierra Club took that route on remand in the district court. Under the pressure of continued litigation and political opposition, official support for the ski resort collapsed, and Disney withdrew. The legal and political importance of the Court's decision in *Sierra Club v. Morton,* however, is overshadowed by the fame of Justice Douglas's lone dissent in the

case. It is the best-known environmental statement by a Supreme Court justice and enjoys iconic status in the literature of environmentalism, if not in
law.

Mineral King Valley lies in the southern Sierra Nevada Mountains, whose
natural and spiritual values John Muir celebrated in his writings. Congress
created Sequoia National Park in 1890 and expanded it in 1926 to protect
the central and southern Sierras. Mineral King Valley, however, was left out
of the park and was instead made into a national game refuge with fewer
protections. The valley could not claim the pristine wilderness status of
areas included in the park because of silver mining that had occurred there
in the 1870s as well as more recent development. In defending its approval
of the ski resort before the Court, the government stressed that the valley
was "not a wilderness area"—that it already had development, including
an old access road, a hydroelectric facility, and some summer cabins. This
characterization did not persuade the Court, however. In the opening paragraph of its opinion, the Court described the valley as "an area of great
natural beauty" whose inaccessibility had preserved its "quality as a quasi-
wilderness area largely uncluttered by the products of civilization."[3]

In the late 1940s the U.S. Forest Service, the land management agency
for the valley, began to explore use of Mineral King as a ski resort. Initially
the Sierra Club had no objection to "winter sports development" in the
valley, but as the plans evolved, the club's concerns grew. With the Forest
Service's encouragement, Walt Disney Enterprises (Disney) developed a proposal for a resort that included ski-lift capacity of 11,400 per hour, motels,
restaurants, parking for 3,600 cars, and a twenty-mile access road, part of
which would go through Sequoia National Park itself. The club tried political means to head off the final approvals of the project by senior federal
officials, to no avail. In December 1968 the Sierra Club's board of directors authorized legal action to stop the development, and in June 1969 its
lawyers filed suit in federal district court in San Francisco.[4]

The filing of the suit reflected a shift toward a more adversarial stance
by the Sierra Club and a new emphasis on litigation. Cofounded by John
Muir in 1892, the Sierra Club was a prominent force in the preservationist
movement that was a precursor to modern environmentalism. But litigation was "a relatively new tactic by Sierra Club." In 1969, the same year
that the Sierra Club filed its suit, Michael McCloskey replaced the legendary
David Brower as the club's executive director. Formerly the club's conservation director, McCloskey had been plotting legal strategy in Mineral King
for more than a year before the case was brought. His elevation to executive director signaled not only the importance of the Mineral King litigation to the club but also the increased reliance on litigation within the na-

scent environmental movement. As environmental historian Susan Schrepfer wrote, "the club's ideological shift and dramatic growth in the 1950s and 1960s impelled its leadership into the role of private attorney general." Before the fight over Mineral King was over, the club assembled its own legal strike force, the Sierra Club Legal Defense Fund, now Earthjustice, which grew to be a major public interest law firm representing environmental clients in hundreds of cases.[5]

In its suit, the Sierra Club claimed that the Forest Service and Department of the Interior had acted unlawfully in approving the resort development and the highway through the national park. Although not a defendant in the case, Disney stood in the background as the party that had the most to gain from the development of Mineral King. This seemed an anomalous role: in the 1950s and 1960s Walt Disney Productions had made the True-Life Adventure series, an award-winning series of documentary films that celebrated the mystery and beauty of wild nature. Audubon Society chairman Ludlow Griscom praised these films for "open[ing] the eyes of young and old to the beauties of the outdoor world and arous[ing] their desire to conserve priceless natural assets." But later these films were criticized as having staged or manipulated scenes in nature for dramatic effect. Justice Douglas himself, in his 1974 autobiography *Go East, Young Man,* asserted that "Walt Disney did more than anyone to distort and deprecate our wildlife." In his view, the Disney enterprise was symptomatic of the retreat of modern humans into "a shell of artificial, mechanical insulation." The transformation of Mineral King Valley into a luxury ski resort could be seen as simply another manifestation of that insulation—an assertion of mastery values over harmony values that would argue for a less invasive human presence or none at all.[6]

Sierra Club based its standing to sue on Section 10 of the Administrative Procedure Act, which entitles a person "adversely affected or aggrieved by agency action" to judicial review. Noting its interests in the conservation of parks, forests, and refuges, particularly in the Sierra Nevada Mountains, the club alleged that those interests would be "vitally affected" and "aggrieved" by the federal agencies' unlawful actions. The district court held that this allegation was sufficient to give standing and issued a preliminary injunction against the agencies until it could decide Sierra Club's claims. The Court of Appeals for the Ninth Circuit reversed because the Sierra Club failed to allege any injury to itself or its members beyond the affront to its general interest in protecting the wildlands of the Sierra Nevada. At the club's behest, the Supreme Court agreed to review the Ninth Circuit's decision.[7]

In two cases decided two years before *Sierra Club,* the Supreme Court had outlined requirements for parties to obtain standing under Section 10 for review of agency actions. In *Data Processing Service v. Camp*, the Court volunteered that for Section 10 standing purposes, the interest harmed "may reflect 'aesthetic, conservational, and recreational' as well as economic values." This observation was not essential to either *Data Processing* or its companion case; the plaintiffs in both cases had economic interests at stake. But in its opinion in *Sierra Club*, the Court reaffirmed this broad reading, bringing Sierra Club's noneconomic interests in protecting the Sierra Nevada within the permissible range for standing. This by itself was an important step forward for environmentalists seeking to attack government policies in court. The question that remained, as the Court put it, was "what must be alleged by persons who claim injury of a noneconomic nature to interests that are widely shared."[8]

In their arguments to the Court on standing, lawyers for the Sierra Club hewed to the line they had taken in the earlier rounds of the case. The club had a longtime interest in protecting "scenic and recreational resources" and a "special interest" in conserving the natural resources of the Sierra Nevada Mountains; the Disney project and related development would injure those interests. There was no allegation that the Sierra Club or any of its members used the Mineral King Valley for aesthetic or recreational purposes, although they certainly did so. As the Court observed, the club simply refused "to rely on its individualized interest, as a basis for standing." Instead, the club claimed that it represented the "public interest" at stake in Mineral King, and it was well qualified to do so.[9]

The club's refusal was deliberate and strategic. In an interview a decade after the case, Michael McCloskey said that the Sierra Club had wanted to establish that "intellectual" or "vicarious interests in the enjoyment of wilderness [were] as important as the practical enjoyment of it." Many of the club's members and other environmentalists might never travel to the Mineral King Valley, but they still wanted it protected. McCloskey believed that injury to their "intellectual interest in nature ought to suffice for the public interest movement to have access to the courts." The goal of the club's suit was twofold: save Mineral King Valley and open courts to representation of environmental and other public interests by worthy "private attorneys general."[10]

While the Court considered the case, law professor Christopher Stone worked feverishly on an even more radical, though complementary theory of standing that he hoped would influence the Court's deliberations. As discussed in Chapter 1, Stone's concept rested on ecocentric views pioneered by Aldo Leopold and others. His innovation was to outline changes to the legal system to accommodate a nature-oriented concept of rights, including a new doctrine of standing that was of particular relevance to *Sierra Club*.

Stone argued that things in nature (a lake, a forest, a species) were entitled to standing in their own right. Because they could not speak for themselves, they would be represented by guardians appointed by the courts, as was already done for humans who were deemed legally incompetent. On Stone's list of environmental organizations that would be qualified to serve as guardians, Sierra Club was at the top. Although the article was not published in time for the oral argument in *Sierra Club,* a draft of Stone's manuscript was in Justice Douglas's hands in December 1971, months before the Court handed down its decision, providing the grist for his famous dissent.[11]

In conference after the argument, a majority of the seven justices participating in the case were inclined to affirm the Ninth Circuit. Notes of the conference show that Chief Justice Burger did not want to let Sierra Club "go into everything, for government would be immobilized." Justice White was of the view that "everyone in the [United States] is not a private Attorney General." Justices Brennan and Blackmun were in a minority, voting for reversal. Blackmun noted candidly, "I may be reaching for a position I emotionally desire enough . . . to sustain [Sierra Club's] standing"; his emotionally charged view of the case would carry through in his dissent. Uncertain about whether to recuse himself because of his prior service on the Sierra Club's board of directors, Justice Douglas had nothing to say about the case.[12]

In an opinion by Justice Stewart, joined by Chief Justice Burger and Justices White and Marshall, the Court ruled that the Sierra Club had not alleged the necessary injury for standing under the statute. The club could rely on injury to aesthetic and conservation interests, but to obtain Section 10 review it had to show in effect that the club or its members used or intended to use the Mineral King Valley in a way that would leave them worse off as a result of the development. Once that showing was made, the club could represent the public interest in preserving Mineral King Valley, but it was the threshold to get in the courthouse door. It was necessary, the Court believed, to prevent an unmanageable flood of judicial review actions by individuals as well as groups like the Sierra Club and to put litigation "in the hands of those who have a direct stake in the outcome" rather than those seeking only to "vindicate their own value preferences." The direct stake of Mineral King Valley itself in the outcome was not material.[13]

The Sierra Club would follow the Court's invitation to amend its complaint in the district court to keep the case alive. But the private-attorney-general theory of standing was dead.

In his classic dissent, Justice Douglas argued that standing should be conferred on the environment itself, where injury to the environment was shown.[14] Apart from its substance, the dissent is unusual among judicial opinions because of its direct, personal, emotional tone; vivid imagery; and sweeping scope. Douglas was a judicial activist, particularly when it came to the protection of civil liberties and minority rights.[15] He was also an avowed environmentalist, who saw environmentalists as a threatened minority. In his 1965 book *A Wilderness Bill of Rights*, he argued for laws to protect the "minority rights" of passionate wilderness lovers and the "large areas of the original America" that they love. In that same book, Douglas advocated for a "conservation land ethic," quoting Aldo Leopold's *Sand County Almanac* on the ethical claims of the biotic community and the need to change the role of humans "from conqueror of the land-community to plain member and citizen of it." In his autobiography, *Go East, Young Man,* Douglas reflected that Leopold's statement of the need for a land ethic presented "a challenge that consumed much of my energies in the latter part of my life." In his *Sierra Club* dissent, Douglas's judicial activism and environmental passion came together in a statement of deep cultural resonance, if not legal influence.[16]

The logic of the dissent was straightforward. The natural world is under siege from development pressures; agencies charged with protecting that world operate under vague "public interest" mandates and are subject to capture by economic interests; therefore, we must give nature ("the inanimate object") a voice in court proceedings affecting it. Groups with established interests in the affected environment would have leave to speak on the environment's behalf, but the interests they represented and the harms they sought to redress would be those of the environment itself. Citing Stone, Douglas drew support for this innovation from "contemporary public concern for protecting nature's ecological equilibrium" and from precedents in corporate and maritime law for inanimate beings as parties in litigation. At the close of his opinion, he quoted Leopold on the land ethic, affirming the ecocentric pedigree of his argument.[17]

The dissent built a vivid urgency in support of standing for the environmental other. Things in nature are threatened with being "despoiled, defaced, or invaded by roads and bulldozers . . . subject to public outrage"; "priceless bits of Americana . . . are forever lost or are so transformed as to be reduced to the eventual rubble of our urban environment"; and "the bulldozers of 'progress' [are poised to] plow under all the aesthetic wonders of this beautiful land." This image, recurrent in the dissent, also appears in Douglas's nonjudicial writings. In response to this environmental apocalypse, the community most deeply and directly affected—"the pileated woodpecker as well as the coyote and bear, the lemmings as well as the trout in the streams"—must have a voice. The dissent closed with a tableau of all these creatures "stand[ing] before the court," represented by their human surrogates.[18]

While rhetorically powerful, Douglas's dissent offers little in the way of a blueprint for importing ecocentric intuitions into legal institutions. In his largely sympathetic account of Douglas's contributions to environmental jurisprudence, law professor Peter Manus observed that "when read from the perspective of a jurist looking for law on which to rely, [the] dissent offers so little that today's Court could point to it as evidence that law is uniquely *unsuited* to environmental concerns." A host of unanswered questions clouds the crucial guardianship concept: Which things in nature would be represented, how would we divine their interests, and who would represent them?[19]

On the first question, is the proper plaintiff the Mineral King Valley, the plants and animals in the valley, the mountain ecosystem of which the valley is a part, or something else? Douglas suggested "the river . . . [as] the living symbol of all the life it sustains or nourishes [from aquatic insects to bears to humans]. The river as plaintiff speaks for the ecological unit of life that is part of it." But why the river and not the watershed or the ecosystem of which the river is a part? And is the river the exclusive voice of "the ecological unit of life" that is a part of it, or does each unit have potential standing in its own right? These questions are crucial to determining what interests and injuries count, but Douglas offered no real criteria for answering them.[20]

Similarly, Douglas did not address how we are to understand the wants or interests of the natural plaintiffs once we have decided what they are. Are their interests to avoid pain, achieve a life goal, or maintain "balance," "stability," or "integrity" at a species, ecosystem, or landscape level? Without that understanding, we cannot know whether the plaintiff has been injured or harmed. Also, without some way to assess the interests of the natural plaintiffs, courts might have difficulty taking steps beyond standing to address the merits of nature's claims and provide redress.

On the question of the qualifications of the guardian-representative for the natural plaintiff, Douglas's guidance created as much ambiguity as it resolved. Qualified as guardians were those who have "a meaningful relation" with the natural plaintiff—"a fisherman, a canoeist, a zoologist, or a logger." These were users, in the broadest sense: "those who hike it, fish it, hunt it, camp in it, frequent it, or visit it merely to sit in solitude and wonderment are legitimate spokesmen for it." Not qualified as guardians were "those who merely are caught up in environmental news or propaganda and flock to defend these waters or areas." This preference for users in determining who may represent nature had an ironic twist. As Manus pointed out, if the dissent is "simply a call for standing for persons who establish a personal stake in connection with a particular threat to an element of nature, . . . Justice Douglas's thesis [was] no more than a poetic reiteration of the majority opinion." This was the reading of Douglas's opinion that Blackmun's law clerk presented in his memo to his justice on the case. Carefully read, the law clerk wrote, the thrust of Douglas's dissent was not that "somebody ought to start appointing guardians ad litem for trees" but instead that "those with the closest connection" should have standing.[21]

Also, by listing such a diversity of users among his potential guardian class, Douglas created uncertainty about the nature of the qualifying relationship to the resource. Did he mean to suggest that a logger that makes a living cutting down old-growth forest would be an appropriate representative of that forest? If he meant the focus to be on the logger's intimate knowledge of the forest gained working in it day to day, how is that knowledge separable from the economic interest? These questions go again to the issue of which interests or values are to be represented and how that can be determined objectively for a nonhuman subject.

Douglas was aware of the vagueness of his opinion on the guardianship concept but rejected the suggestions of his law clerk to correct it. Perhaps, as Manus suggests, he was hesitant to invest too heavily in Stone's guardianship model or was unsure that the time had come for full-fledged development of an ecocentric legal model. Perhaps he was not writing for a legal audience but for the public. He may have intended that his dissent make its mark primarily as a symbolic statement rather than a legal document. Having made the bold move to recognize the "rights of nature," however, his failure to provide the gloss necessary for the actualization of those rights increased the risk that the opinion would become legally marginalized, an artifact with little perceived relevance for the evolution of institutions and practice. For Manus, despite his criticisms, the dissent is a "monument to the possibility that the law could embrace the increasingly biocentric perspective of an evolving U.S. culture." But that possibility lies largely dormant.[22]

Decades after *Sierra Club v. Morton*, Stone canvassed lower federal court cases to determine what effect, if any, Justice Douglas's dissent or his article had had in practice. He found that although a few cases have been brought in the name of things in nature, "the sum of cases is insubstantial and the substance unclear." In many of these cases, counsel have hedged their bets by also including conventional plaintiffs—individuals or organizations—to ensure standing. The most colorful of these cases is *Palila v. Hawaii Department of Land and Natural Resources*. There the Court of Appeals for the Ninth Circuit wrote: "As an endangered species . . . the [palila] bird . . . also has legal status and wings its way into federal court as a plaintiff in its own right. The Palila (which has earned the right to be capitalized since it is a party to this proceeding) is represented by attorneys for the Sierra Club, Audubon Society, and other environmental parties." Although the court didn't mention the Douglas dissent in *Sierra Club v. Morton,* its rhetoric invoked an ecocentric theory of standing of the sort Douglas argued for. But there were other, human plaintiffs in *Palila,* both individuals and organizations, and the bird's inclusion was unopposed. In cases where defendants have challenged the inclusion of nonhuman plaintiffs, the courts have excluded the nonhumans. Bringing a case in the name of a species or river may have symbolic appeal for humans. But prevailing judicial doctrine, certainly so far as it pertains to access to courts, remains anthropocentric.[23]

Justice Blackmun's dissent was joined in part by Justice Brennan and also by Justice Douglas. Blackmun's opinion stated his admiration for the eloquence and imagination of the Douglas dissent, which he read narrowly—per his law clerk's interpretation—as simply adding to the usual criteria for standing the requirement that "the litigant be one who speaks knowingly for the environmental values he asserts." But the Douglas dissent was "too personal"—and perhaps too radical—for him to join. Blackmun advocated a seemingly more modest doctrinal change to recognize organizational standing for groups like Sierra Club that could establish their environmental bona fides, an expansion of standing consistent with what some lower federal courts had already done.[24]

Blackmun's dissent outed his environmentalist sympathies. "The case poses—if only we choose to acknowledge and reach them—significant aspects of a wide, growing, and disturbing problem, that is, the Nation's and the world's deteriorating environment with its resulting ecological disturbances." This sense of urgency, similar to that animating the Court's doctrinal innovations in *Citizens to Preserve Overton Park, Inc. v. Volpe* and *MA v. EPA,* led Blackmun to look for an alternative to "existing methods" that would allow the Court to reach the merits right away. Failure to change standing doctrine, he feared, would allow the transformation of Mineral King Valley to proceed, "and sadly so." His emotional identification with Mineral King Valley was clear, and it drove the need he felt to reach the merits. In a note to Supreme Court historian Scot Powe after the decision, he wrote: "I am concerned about ecological problems, and I fear that my concern may have been much too apparent." Blackmun's dissent won him a literal pat on the back from Douglas, whose contempt he had felt in the past. Although never the demonstrative environmentalist that Douglas was, Blackmun would be a voice for environmentalist perspectives in future cases.[25]

The legacy of *Sierra Club v. Morton* is complex. While refusing to accept organizational or ecocentric standing, the Court did affirm injury to aesthetic and conservation interests as a basis for standing. Somewhat perversely, this opening of the field of environmental standing reduced the practical need for more radical alternative theories for access to the courts on behalf of an environmental other.[26] Douglas's dissent, seemingly transparent to the deeply held environmentalist views of its author, is ultimately enigmatic. Interpretations of it range from a bold step toward the eventual establishment of ecocentric legal doctrine to a poetic repackaging of homocentric views. If the former, the dissent's failure to offer specifications for an ecocentric jurisprudence undermines its own viability. If the latter, one wonders why all the fuss.

The Douglas dissent's continued fascination for environmentalists, notwithstanding its lack of influence on the law, is emblematic of the disjunction between environmentalist aspirations and mainstream institutional practice. Yet the dissent has a kind of shadow life in the law: it is mentioned sporadically by lower federal lower courts and commented on by legal scholars. Emboldened by it, a Palila bird occasionally flies into court unopposed. Taken in the most positive light for environmentalists, the dissent is a marker for work still to be done in adjusting institutions to reflect new understandings about nature and ourselves and about the connections, moral as well as material, between the two.

Tennessee Valley Authority v. Hill: Fish over People?

Sierra Club v. Morton dealt with the threshold question of standing for the environmental other. Decided six years later, *Tennessee Valley Authority v. Hill* (*TVA v. Hill*) dealt with the substantive "rights" of things in nature and the vindication of those rights through legal remedies, the second and third features of an ecocentric legal system envisioned by Stone. In *TVA v. Hill,* the rights were in the form of statutory prohibitions, particularly those of Section 7 of the ESA, protecting species from human intrusions that threatened their existence. The Court construed those prohibitions to give the species an entitlement to be free of those intrusions and used its power to enforce that entitlement. But the ironic tone of the Court's opinion conveyed skepticism about the categorical protection for species that undercut the ruling.

Section 7 of the ESA directs federal agencies such as the TVA to "insure that any action authorized, funded, or carried out by [them] is not likely to jeopardize the continued existence" of a threatened or endangered species or "result in the destruction or adverse modification of habitat of such species." The justifications that Congress gave for enacting the ESA are largely anthropocentric. Endangered and threatened species "are of esthetic, ecological, educational, historical, recreational, and scientific value to the Nation and its people"; preserving these species is "for the benefit of all citizens." But the regulatory provisions of the act have an ecocentric cast. For example, as interpreted by the Court in *TVA v. Hill*, Section 7 creates an entitlement on the part of species to be free of any government action that is likely to jeopardize their existence, including degradation of habitat critical to their survival. This entitlement suggests a value in the continuation of species that is distinct from human welfare concerns, but there was considerable ambivalence about this interpretation among the justices as well as in the larger culture.[27]

Dams, People, and a Little Fish

Perhaps the "best-known case in environmental law," *TVA v. Hill* applied Section 7 to prohibit completion and operation of the TVA's Tellico Dam, a monument to mastery values on the Little Tennessee River.[28] Congress created the TVA in the 1930s as a government-owned public corporation whose purpose was to foster development of the natural resources of the Tennessee Valley for the economic and social benefit of the people of the region. After developing a number of hydroelectric dams on the main stream of the Tennessee River, the TVA looked to the tributaries for further dam-building ventures. Unlike the main stream dams, the tributary dams would not offer significant power generation; the TVA would justify them instead for their regional development potential. In 1960, the TVA's board of directors approved the Tellico dam on the Little Tennessee River as its first "large tributary project." The dam would flood the lower thirty-three miles of the Little Tennessee River, which the Court described as "clear, free-flowing waters [moving] through an area of great natural beauty."[29]

The proposed dam fired opposition among diverse interests—farmers whose lands the TVA would take to make room for the reservoir and the economic development that the agency had built into its plans for the project; fly fishermen who prized the river for "its teeming aquatic insect life and broad shoals and riffles"; historians and archaeologists who esteemed the valley's long history of continuous human habitation; and the Eastern Band of Cherokee, for whom the valley was an ancestral and religious homeland. The opponents campaigned to stop the dam, and that campaign included appearances before congressional appropriators whose approval was necessary for the project. They "argued forcefully that economic development without a dam would be practical and far more beneficial." But they were no match politically for the powerful TVA and its allies among development interests and the region's congressional delegation. With funds appropriated by Congress, the TVA began construction of the Tellico dam in 1967.[30]

Outgunned politically, opponents turned to the courts. A suit under the newly enacted National Environmental Policy Act (NEPA) halted construction for almost two years. In 1973, as the TVA completed the environmental impact statement required by NEPA, new developments conspired against the dam's completion. Congress passed the ESA, and a University of Tennessee ichthyologist named David Etnier discovered a new fish species, the snail darter, inhabiting a portion of the Little Tennessee River that would be flooded by the dam. The federal court lifted its NEPA injunction against the project in October 1973, but by then opponents of the dam were developing a new legal strategy.[31]

Spurred by Etnier's discovery, University of Tennessee law student Hiram Hill and his professor Zygmunt Plater developed a legal theory to stop the dam under Section 7, based on the dam's likely effect on the snail darter's continued existence. With the endorsement of a remnant group of the dam's opponents, Plater worked with Etnier to take the first step in executing this theory—a petition to the Department of the Interior to list the snail darter as an endangered species. Interior listed the fish in October 1975 and months later designated the area that would be affected by the dam as critical habitat for the species. Meanwhile, the TVA "continued building at a frenetic pace," refusing to be deterred by Interior's actions to protect the snail darter or the prospect of judicial reversal.[32]

With Plater and Hill among the named plaintiffs, opponents of the dam sued the TVA in federal district court, claiming that the authority's determination to go forward with the dam violated Section 7 and seeking an injunction against final completion and operation of the dam. The district court concluded that the completion of the dam and the filling of the reservoir would adversely modify the snail darter's critical habitat and jeopardize the continued existence of the species. But the court declined to enjoin further work on the dam, which was now 80 percent complete and represented over $50 million in sunk costs. Sitting as "a court of equity," the district court fixed on the disproportionate costs of protecting the snail darter under the circumstances and the "unreasonable result" that would flow from applying a "statute enacted long after inception of the project." The Court of Appeals for the Sixth Circuit reversed, holding that the district court abused its discretion in not enjoining the statutory violation, and the TVA sought review by the Court.[33]

The Court came close to deciding the case without oral argument and in the TVA's favor. In the justices' initial conference, there was sentiment among five of them for summary reversal of the Sixth Circuit. This unusual disposition would have required a sixth vote, however, and the justices favoring summary reversal could not agree on a rationale. Two justices opposed to it circulated draft dissenting opinions for use if the case was not set for briefing and argument, including a fiery indictment by Justice Stevens concluding that the proposed reversal would be "lawless." The Court granted review and set the case for oral argument.[34]

In written communications with his fellow justices during this initial skirmishing, Chief Justice Burger derisively referred to the ESA as the "Snail Darter Act." In a typed memo to Justice Powell, he argued that the appropriations acts that funded the Tellico Dam should be read as amending the ESA to allow the project: "The 'rabbit' capacity of the perch species to launch a new species 'in even numbered years' shows how absurd it would be to ignore the *positive* Act of Congress in Appropriations Acts, subsequent to the 'Snail Darter Act.'" One of the mysteries of *TVA v. Hill* is how a justice so dismissive of the claims made for the snail darter came to write one of the Court's opinions most venerated among environmentalists.[35]

U.S. Attorney General Griffin Bell argued the case for the TVA. Bell told the Court that there were 130 varieties of darters, with eleven varieties in the Little Tennessee River alone. Not only were there many kinds of darters but also the number of darter species was growing rapidly. Experts had identified eight to ten new species of darters in the last ten years. In the most vivid moment of his argument, Bell showed the Court an exhibit from the trial in the district court—a dead snail darter in a clear vial. There was some joking between Bell and the justices as to whether the fish was actually dead. Bell told the Court he was not arguing that some species were less valuable than others; all listed species were equal under the ESA. But his visual worked to solidify an impression of the snail darter as an insignificant and not particularly appealing species.[36]

Against this indifferent-looking fish with no economic value was the dam, which Bell argued promised multiple benefits for the region and now represented $110 million in public funds already spent. The dam was "finished for all intents and purposes"—all that remained was to close the gates and let the reservoir fill. The advanced stage of the dam's completion meant that there was no "action" left to be taken within the meaning of Section 7 and therefore no violation. But even if completing the dam would be "an action," it should not be enjoined because of equitable factors such as the level of completion of the dam.[37]

Arguing on behalf of the dam's opponents, Plater urged the Court to affirm the Sixth Circuit's ruling. His legal argument was straightforward. Section 7's prohibition was mandatory; it contained no exception for projects that had commenced prior to the ESA's enactment, where "actions," such as closing the gates of the Tellico dam, remained to be taken. Congressional appropriations contained no express exception to the ESA for the dam, and they should not be read as de facto amendments to the act. This legal argument would prove to carry the day.

Plater, however, understood that his persuasive task was a broader one—to "pull together economic as well as ecological themes into a commanding case for the darter." To counter the degrading image of the snail darter offered by Bell's dead fish in a vial, he offered a color lithograph of two snail darters alive in "the crystal clear beauty of the river shoals." He worked to connect the fish with the riverine system threatened by the dam. When Justice Powell asked him what purpose there was, if any, for the "little darters," Plater associated the snail darter with the vanishingly rare "clean, clear, cool flowing rivers" of the Tennessee Basin on which it depended for survival. The snail darter's vulnerability was an indicator of the broader threats to ecology and human welfare from the impoundment of the "TVA river system." But Plater was unable to fully dispel the irreverent tone that infected the Court's discussion of the "little fish." Powell followed up with a question about whether the snail darter was "suitable for bait."[38]

Plater also sought to impugn the economic benefits that the TVA had claimed to justify the dam. He cited a recent Government Accountability Office study commissioned by Congress that found that the cost studies supporting the dam were "highly unreliable" and that other alternatives were more beneficial than the dam. He stressed that the project was not for hydropower but for "industrially subsidized lots and more recreation in an area where you have already got 22 recreational lakes within 60 miles." But Justice Marshall questioned whether these arguments were based in the record before the Court, and they would have little impact on the Court's deliberations.[39]

In the conference after oral argument, Chief Justice Burger and Justice White passed in the voting on the case. Justices Marshall, Brennan, Stevens, and Stewart voted to affirm the Sixth Circuit, and Justices Powell, Blackmun, and Rehnquist voted to reverse. Among those voting to affirm, however, there was grumbling about the ESA. Marshall complained that "Congress can be a jackass," and he "hope[d] Congress will do something about it." Even Stevens, who had been so intense in his opposition to summary reversal of the Sixth Circuit, called the statute "stupid" while expecting that Congress would enact a sensible rule. None of the justices questioned the wisdom of the dam. A few days later, White voted to affirm, making a majority to uphold the Sixth Circuit. Burger then also voted to affirm, putting himself in the majority, and assigned himself to write the opinion.[40]

The Court's Opinion: A Study in Ambivalence

Chief Justice Burger's opinion for the Court addressed whether the completion of the Tellico Dam would violate Section 7 and, if so, whether the Court retained equitable discretion not to issue an injunction. In answering yes to the first question, the Court cited congressional testimony and reports that stressed the rapid decline in species resulting from disruption of habitats, the irreversible impact of this loss on potential future uses of genetic information and on the planetary ecosystem, and the "quite literally, incalculable" value of these genetic resources. The 1973 ESA was a response to the real and immediate threat of incalculable loss that had been conveyed to Congress and internalized by it in the legislative process. The language of Section 7, the Court found, admitted no exception, framing an absolute prohibition against federal actions that put endangered species in jeopardy of extinction or that destroyed the species' critical habitat. The Court concluded that Congress's intent was to "halt and reverse the trend toward species extinction, whatever the cost" and to "give endangered species priority over the 'primary missions' of federal agencies."[41]

Acknowledging that "in this case the burden on the public through the loss of millions of unrecoverable dollars [might be argued to] greatly outweigh the loss of the snail darter," the Court insisted nevertheless that Congress had not authorized it to make "such fine utilitarian calculations." Further, even if Congress had left room for "a weighing process," the Court would hardly know where to begin, given that one side of the cost-benefit equation, the value of a species, had already been determined by Congress to be "incalculable."[42]

Having decided the merits in favor of the snail darter, the Court turned to the question of whether to enjoin the operation of the dam. In exercising their equitable power, federal courts typically undertake a "balancing of the utilities" in deciding whether injunctive relief is warranted.[43] In *TVA*, this equity tradition of judicial balancing to determine the overall public interest was in tension with a congressional directive for the protection of endangered species. The Court resolved the tension in favor of the species. When it came to balancing under the ESA, the Court wrote, Congress itself had ordered the priorities, "making it abundantly clear that the balance has been struck in favor of affording endangered species the highest of priorities." Here again, the Court's hands were tied by Congress.[44]

TVA v. Hill can be—and typically is—understood as a ringing endorsement of the preeminent importance of species preservation: "Chief Justice Burger's stentorian declaration repeatedly echoed in successive endangered species cases." But the meaning of the case is more complex. The chief's last-minute vote raises the suspicion that he added himself to the majority for the purpose of writing an opinion that undercut the result. But others in the majority shared the reservations that surface in his opinion for the Court.[45]

The opinion reveals a deep ambivalence, mixing a ringing declaration of legal protection for the snail darter with pervasive skepticism about the fish's importance. The opening lines of the analysis set the tone: "it may seem curious to some that the survival of a relatively small number of three-inch fish among all the countless millions of species extant would require the permanent halting of a virtually completed dam for which Congress has expended more than $100 million." "It may seem curious" mimicked the ironic phrasing of Abraham Lincoln's Second Inaugural Address: "It may seem strange that any men should dare to ask a just God's assistance in wringing their bread from the sweat of other men's faces. But let us judge not that we be not judged." This rhetorical echo made the irony of the Court's opinion unmistakable.[46]

Reflecting points made by Attorney General Bell in oral argument, the opinion further trivialized the snail darter with a footnote stating that there are upward of one hundred species of darters in Tennessee, new species of darters are constantly being discovered, and it is hard even for experts to tell the species apart. A second footnote emphasized the enormous reach of the ESA's protections as extending to "every animal and plant species, subspecies, and population in the world needing protection" and covering as many as 200,000 species or "three to five times that number" if subspecies were counted. The origin of these footnotes makes clear their negative implications for the unqualified protections written into the ESA and the effort to save the snail darter. Chief Justice Burger lifted both of them, essentially verbatim, from a draft dissent that Justice Powell had circulated to the Court. When they showed up in the next draft of the majority opinion, Powell was taken aback. Powell biographer John Jeffries recounted: "Thinking there had been a mistake, Powell's clerk went to Burger's clerk, who said that the Chief felt entitled to take from a dissent any material that he thought belonged in the majority opinion."[47]

There are several remarkable aspects of this exchange, but most remarkable for interpretive purposes is that Burger thought these footnotes belonged in his opinion for the Court. Powell drafted them to support his argument that the literal application of Section 7 to save an inconspicuous species such as the snail darter from an essentially completed dam was "absurd." The footnotes carried the sense of absurdity into the Court's opinion upholding that literal application.

The Court called the sacrifice of so large a project for so small a fish "a paradox," but it was a paradox that the Court never really tried to resolve. It was simply, the Court said, the result required by congressional enactment. Unlike *Overton Park* or *MA v. EPA,* the Court's opinion provided no cues that it was in sympathy with this priority or with the protection afforded the snail darter in this case. Its whole emphasis was on finding and enforcing "the law" and maintaining appropriate institutional roles as between the courts and Congress.

This sense of distance from the policy of the statute gathered at the end of the opinion and revived the skepticism expressed at the beginning. The Court quoted a passage from Robert Bolt's play about Sir Thomas More, which turned on a metaphor of the law as a forested landscape in which the devil is hiding. "What would you do?" More asked. "Cut a great road through the law to get after the Devil?" And he gave his own answer, arguing that because the trees protect him as well as the devil, "I'd give the Devil benefit of law, for my own safety's sake." Here, by the metaphor's logic, the devil was the "paradox" of sacrificing a completed dam for an inconsequential species. This logic carried into the final words of the opinion: "In our constitutional system the commitment to separation of powers is too fundamental for us to preempt congressional action by judicially decreeing what accords with 'common sense and the public weal.'" The result here might be a bad one, the Court suggested, contrary to "common sense and the public weal," but to ignore congressional edict would be worse.[48]

The Dissents: Reason over Absolutism

The undercurrent of skepticism puts the Court's opinion much closer to the two dissenting opinions than might first appear. Joined by Justice Blackmun, Justice Powell argued that it was unreasonable to believe that Congress could have intended the "absurd result" in this case and predicted that Congress would amend the act "to prevent the grave consequences made possible by today's decision." In a separate dissent, Justice Rehnquist argued that Section 7 did not clearly constrain the Court's equitable discretion and that the district court had therefore appropriately declined to issue an injunction because of the harm to the public interest that would flow from it.[49]

The doubts about the wisdom of stopping the project that to one degree or another pervaded all the opinions in *TVA* were expressed with Congress in mind: in an internal memo to the justices, Burger wrote that in his opinion he intended to "serve notice on Congress that it should take care of its own 'chestnuts.'" Congress answered by amending the ESA to empower a cabinet-level committee to grant exceptions from the act based on a limited cost-benefit evaluation. The committee's first case for review was the Tellico Dam. Ironically, however, given the tacit assumption by the Court that "utilitarian balancing" would favor the project, the committee unanimously denied an exemption for the dam. Committee member Charles Shultze, then chairman of the President's Council of Economic Advisors, made the most damning observation: "The interesting phenomenon is that here is a project that is 95 percent complete, and if one takes just the cost of finishing it against the total benefits and does it properly, it doesn't pay, which says something about the original design!"[50]

It took a late-night appropriations rider specifically mandating completion of the dam to fulfill Justice Powell's prophecy and salvage the project. So in the end, David succumbed to Goliath, although relict populations of snail darters have since been found outside the area of the dam. One might congratulate the Supreme Court for taking David's part, but it did so with its fingers crossed.[51]

Revisiting *TVA v. Hill*

Thirty years later, the Court in *National Association of Homebuilders v. Defenders of Wildlife* undercut the preeminence it had given Section 7 in *TVA v. Hill*. *NAHB v. Defenders* dealt with whether Section 7 required the EPA to make a no-jeopardy finding before transferring water discharge–permitting authority to the state of Arizona under the Clean Water Act (CWA). Resolving that issue required the Court, in its words, "to mediate a clash of seemingly categorical—and, at first glance, irreconcilable—legislative commands." The ESA's Section 7 directs all federal agencies to consult and avoid actions ("shall insure") that are "likely to jeopardize listed species." The CWA directs the EPA to transfer water-permitting authority to states ("shall approve") if nine criteria specified in the statute are met, none of which involve species protection. Neither directive admits of qualification on its face.[52]

The federal fish and wildlife agencies charged with implementing the ESA interpreted Section 7 as applying only to "discretionary" agency actions. Using this interpretation, the EPA argued that because its transfer of water-permitting authority to Arizona was not discretionary, where the state met all nine criteria, its action did not require a no-jeopardy determination. In an opinion by Justice Alito, joined by Chief Justice Roberts and Justices Scalia, Thomas, and Kennedy, the Court upheld the agencies' interpretation as a reasonable resolution of the ambiguity created by the clash of "shalls." While not overtly disowning *TVA v. Hill,* the Court in *NAHB v.*

Defenders was plainly intent on cutting Section 7 down to size. It expressed concern that reading Section 7 "for all that it might be worth" would cut a swath through "every federal statute mandating agency action," of which presumably there were many. To avoid this, the Court reversed the presumptive status of Section 7 in cases of mandatory authority from controlling to subordinate. The effect was to eliminate any aura of legal super status still clinging to the ESA after *TVA v. Hill.*[53]

Justice Stevens's dissent, joined by Justices Souter, Ginsburg, and Breyer, argued that the Court's ruling was contrary to the Court's "unequivocal holding in *Hill* that the ESA "has 'first priority' over all other federal action." More than just the particular issue at hand involving CWA permitting programs, what was lost was the ability to "tilt the balance of legal interpretation in favor of the ESA's central goal of species protection." Somewhat ironically, given the anti–snail darter valence that the quote carried in its use by Chief Justice Burger in *TVA v. Hill,* Stevens closed with the same extended quote from Sir Thomas More. Here, of course, its implication was quite different: that the Court was sacrificing law to indulge its own assessment of the perils of an overly restrictive ESA.[54]

Shifting Assessments

TVA v. Hill's bold vindication of the protections written into the ESA is rightly honored among environmentalists. The decision has served as a legal and political touchstone for environmental advocates in continuing battles over protection of species and the ecosystems on which they depend. It has given hope to the ecocentric enterprise, endowing species with "a legal status above and beyond that of mere object."[55]

Yet the legal and political ground has shifted under it. ESA scholar J. B. Ruhl argued that the decision has become an "extreme outlier" in the Court's ESA cases, the pro-species high point in an "arc of . . . decisions" that culminates with its subtle repudiation in *NAHB v. Defenders of Wildlife.* Since *TVA v. Hill,* the ESA has also become embattled politically. Every Congress debates further weakening amendments and project exemptions, although the act's core protections have survived intact. Inadequate appropriation of funds for implementation, foot-dragging by action agencies, and political pressure from the hinterland to moderate enforcement all undermine the implementation of the act. The ESA may still be the "'pit bull' of environmental laws" as some have called it, but it is a pit bull that must fight every day for its life.[56]

Paradoxically, *TVA v. Hill* anticipated and may have even aided these developments: it contained the seeds of its own negation. The human protagonist of *TVA v. Hill,* Zygmunt Plater, has lamented that the "warped mischaracterization" of ESA cases, including the snail darter, have helped

> shift endangered species from a position of broad instinctive public support to a targeted wedge issue that often can be framed so as to invite trivialization and disrespect. The way our story was presented to the public—a silly, non-economic little fish blocking a huge, important hydroelectric dam (never mind that that was factually completely incorrect)—evoked an immediate bemused response from American public opinion: "Maybe this ESA goes too far."

As seen earlier, however, the Court in *TVA v. Hill* was complicit in this "trivialization." It might have embraced the harmony values at the heart of Section 7's prohibitions; it might have accepted Plater's invitation to see the snail darter as an integral part of a clear, free-flowing river ecosystem threatened by improvident human development. Instead, it chose as its subtext: "Maybe this ESA goes too far." This sense of the case resides within the Court today: in comments at the 2008 oral argument in another environmental case, Justice Scalia used "snail darter" dismissively as a synecdoche for inconsequential species.[57]

In his recent engaging book-length account of the case, Plater seeks to change this cultural narrative by stressing the economic foolishness of the project, the ecological and human richness of the valley it inundated, and the political machinations of the TVA and its allies in pushing the project through. His book effectively reargues the case in the court of public opinion. But the now iconic judicial text that memorializes Plater's astonishing legal victory resists efforts to shift the meaning of the case.[58]

Lyng v. Northwest Indian Cemetery Protective Association: Property over Ecoreligions

As imagined by Christopher Stone, the institutionalization of ecocentric values would focus on development of legal rights for things in nature. Another way to imagine this project, however, would be to focus on the irreducible human element of ecocentrism. Ecocentric values may attach to the environmental other, but they are human in the sense that they are held and exercised by human beings. Rather than grant legal rights to things in nature, we might instead grant them to those who claim a moral community with nature or revere nature as sacred. This focus on the rights of ecocentrists rather than the rights of nature may have been what Justice Douglas had in mind when he argued for the "minority rights" of wilderness lovers to protect the unspoiled nature that was the object of their passion.

The Constitution offers no obvious place for locating rights of ecocentrists, but the First Amendment's free exercise clause offers at least a possibility for groups claiming a "religion" whose practice depends on particular natural settings or features. American Indian tribes with traditional earth-centered religions are prominent among such groups. Commentators liken the views of modern ecocentrists to traditional Native American spiritual practice. Justice Douglas, for example, equated Aldo Leopold's land ethic—the enlargement of the moral community to include nonhuman nature—with the traditional teaching of the Sioux Indians: "'With all beings and all things we shall be as relatives.'" While cautioning against overgeneralization, Indian law scholar Kristen Carpenter observed that "indigenous peoples have a common and central concept of 'respect' for the 'inherent . . . value which something has insofar as it inheres in, or belongs to, the natural world.' . . . These values—of relatedness, moral obligation, and respect—often guide indigenous approaches to resource management, economic development, and religious practice."[59]

In *Lyng v. Northwest Indian Cemetery Protective Association,* the Supreme Court considered First Amendment protections for an earth-centered Native American religion, with disappointing results for the Indians. *Lyng* is typically classified as a religious rights case, not an environmental one, but it addresses ecocentric strains that modern environmentalism shares with some religious traditions. Like *TVA v. Hill, Lyng* reflected the conflict between mastery and harmony values in government-sponsored land development, but its cultural significance has the added dimension of the conflict between the dominant culture and a historically abused minority with very different ideas of the human-natural relationship. In his dissent from the Court's decision rejecting the tribes' free exercise claims in *Lyng,* Justice Brennan wrote that the ruling privileged "the dominant Western culture, which views land in terms of ownership and use," over "that of Native Americans, in which concepts of private property are not only alien, but contrary to a belief system that holds land sacred." *Lyng* was an environmental justice case too.[60]

The controversy in *Lyng* was over decisions by the Forest Service to construct a road and allow timber harvesting in the relatively undisturbed "high country" of the Six Rivers National Forest in the northwestern corner of California.[61] The high country was an area of rocky outcrops and peaks rising more than 7,000 feet above the Klamath River. The Yurok, Karuk, and Tolowa tribes believed that the area was sacred—"so sacred that humans could not interfere with the creator's natural intention or use it for any other purpose than gathering medicine, preparing for ceremonies, and training Indian doctors." The high country was indispensable to the tribes' religious practice: "the medicine and communication with the sacred—could only be accomplished by a doctor visiting the High Country in its pristine condition."[62]

In 1977 the Forest Service proposed to complete a logging road through Six Rivers National Forest that would connect the towns of Gasquet and Orleans (the G-O road). The final six-mile segment of the G-O road would bisect the high country held sacred by the tribes. In response to concerns about the impact on Indian religious sites, the Forest Service commissioned a study that was completed in 1979 and known by the name of its lead author: the Theodoratus report. The 450-page report found that the tribes' religious "use of the high country is dependent upon and facilitated by certain qualities of the physical environment, the most important of which are privacy, silence, and an undisturbed natural setting." The report concluded that completion of the G-O road would directly impact "this sacred area" and would be "potentially destructive of the very core of [the tribes'] religious beliefs and practices." It recommended against completion of the G-O road in any of its alternative forms.[63]

The Forest Service rejected the recommendations of its consultants and determined to go forward with the road. Opponents filed suit in federal district court to enjoin the project. Plaintiffs included the Northwest Indian Cemetery Protective Association, originally created to protect Indian graves from being robbed for artifacts; environmental groups including the Sierra Club and the Wilderness Society; and individual tribal members and environmentalists. The state of California, acting through its Native American Heritage Commission, filed a second suit, which was consolidated with the first. Both suits asserted violations of the Indians' First Amendment free exercise rights along with more than a half dozen other claims. The free exercise claims were the focus of Supreme Court's deliberations.

The Court's free exercise doctrine was unsettled going into *Lyng*. The First Amendment says that "Congress shall make no law . . . prohibiting the free exercise" of religion. One line of cases interpreting this language was promising for the Indians' efforts to protect their religious practice from the incidental burden of the government's G-O road. In *Sherbert v. Verner*, the Court held that a Seventh Day Adventist could not be denied state unemployment benefits where her inability to hold or find a job was due to religious scruples against working on Saturday. In *Wisconsin v. Yoder*, it held that Wisconsin could not enforce its compulsory education law against Old Order Amish whose religious beliefs dictated that children not be sent to school after eighth grade. In both cases, while neutral to religion on its face, the offending laws penalized free exercise in a way that could only be justified by a compelling governmental interest, which the Court found lacking.[64]

In tension with these decisions, however, was the Court's more recent decision in *Bowen v. Roy.* The plaintiffs in that case were parents of a two-year old child, Little Bird of the Snow. Federal law required that the parents furnish a social security number for their daughter as a condition of federal welfare benefits for which the family had applied. The child's father, Stephen Roy, argued that the assignment and use of a social security number for his daughter would violate his "recently developed" native religious belief by robbing her of her spirit. Rejecting the parents' claim, the Court wrote that while the free exercise clause afforded protection against compulsion, it did not give individuals the right "to require the Government to conduct its own internal affairs" to accord with the religious beliefs of its citizens.[65]

But *Roy,* like *Sherbert,* was a case in which government benefits turned on actions subject to a religious prohibition: What was the relevant difference? Was it, as the Court suggested, the breadth and need for administrative uniformity in the federal aid programs in *Roy* and how that distinction would apply in future cases? Was it the relative insubstantiality of *Roy's* religious beliefs or the limited government intrusion on them? Or did *Roy* signal the Court's broader disaffection with the *Sherbert-Yoder* line of cases? These uncertainties about the direction of the Court's free exercise jurisprudence loomed over the proceedings in *Lyng*—the Court's first free exercise case featuring a clash between Native American religious practices and government land use policy.[66]

After a two-week trial, federal district court judge Stanley Weigel held for the plaintiffs on their free exercise claims (as well as several others) and permanently enjoined construction of the last segment of the G-O road and related harvesting of timber. He found that the high country was "'central and indispensable' to the Indian plaintiffs' religion" and, citing the Theodoratus report, determined that the disturbance of the high country would be "'potentially destructive of the very core of Northwest [Indian] religious beliefs.'" Relying on *Sherbert* and *Yoder,* he concluded that the Forest Service's actions unlawfully burdened the Indians' free exercise of religion in the absence of a compelling government interest. A divided panel of the Ninth Circuit upheld the district court's judgment on the free exercise claim. In a partial dissent that introduced a theme later developed by the Supreme Court, Judge Beezer emphasized the government's ownership of the lands the Indians sought to protect and its "substantial, perhaps even compelling, interest in using its land to achieve economic benefits."[67]

From its opening brief, the government worked to elevate the prerogatives of federal land ownership over Indian religious practice.[68] *Roy*, not *Sherbert* and its progeny, applied to the free exercise claims in *Lyng* because the tribes were seeking to direct the internal affairs of the government (*Roy*) in management of its land rather than avoiding a religious penalty (*Sherbert*). If the tribes succeeded, the government painted the prospect of "limitless expansion in the types of government action subject to free exercise scrutiny." The potential for mischief was particularly great in the use of public lands, the government argued, because the "natural environment is often an important element in Indian religious belief." And the government's exposure did not end with the Indians. Because protected religious beliefs need not be traditional or longstanding, any individual could develop religious affinity for any feature or quality of the vast domain of federal lands and coerce land use concessions. The Court was left to imagine as among the potential claimants non-Indian environmentalists who came to consider nature, or parts of it, sacred or holy.[69]

The government hammered these themes even more boldly in its reply brief and in oral argument. "The unique nature of land and the weight accorded to the government's interest as a property owner require a different constitutional standard" than other governmental decisions. Success by the Indians would "work [a] dramatic, dramatic effect upon the Government's authority to regulate and control its own land."[70]

The Indians worked to keep the case on the *Sherbert-Yoder* track followed by the Ninth Circuit and discourage the Court from throwing the switch that would send the case down the *Roy* track instead. They argued that completion of the G-O road was like the compulsory school attendance law in *Yoder* because it would compel abandonment of traditional religious practices. In distinguishing *Roy*, the Indians stressed that the G-O road's intrusion was physical (not internal or subjective) and that it struck at the core of the Indians' ability to practice their religion (not peripheral concerns). But it was clear in oral argument that the government's "slippery slope" claim and emphasis on government property rights were succeeding with some members of the Court. Counsel for the Indians spent most of her time answering pointed questions about the restrictions she would impose "in favor of religion on what the government can do with its property."[71]

Justice Kennedy did not participate in the case. Justice Blackmun's notes of conference showed a vote of five to three against the Indians and in favor of reversal. Those favoring reversal believed *Roy* should control. Among them, Chief Justice Rehnquist characterized the Indian's demands as "religious servitude." Justice White said the "U.S. can manage its land."[72]

Justice O'Connor wrote the opinion for the Court reversing the Ninth Circuit, joined by Chief Justice Rehnquist and Justices White, Scalia, and

Stevens; Justices Marshall and Blackmun joined Brennan's dissent. The Court did not dispute that "the logging and road-building projects at issue in [the] case could have devastating effects on traditional Indian religious practices." But it argued that even if the Supreme Court assumed, as the Ninth Circuit did, the G-O road would "virtually destroy the . . . Indians' ability to practice their religion," the road did not violate the Indians' free exercise rights. Strongly influenced by the government's arguments, the Court's analysis began with a restrictive reading of the constitutional text ("Congress shall make no law . . . *prohibiting* the free exercise [of religion]"). The Court refused to consider the destruction of the Indians' religion as the legal equivalent of compulsion under *Sherbert* or *Yoder*, as the Indians had urged, and instead equated the government's property management decisions with conduct of the government's "internal affairs" not directed at religion, as in *Roy*. It also refused to draw a line between government actions that would cut to the core of religious practice and those that offered only minor subjective interference, as in *Roy*. That would cast the Court in an obtrusive arbiter's role—"a role that we were never intended to play."[73]

In sending the case down the *Roy* track, the Court gave center stage to the interests of the government as a property owner and to the effect that recognition of the Indians' claims would have on those interests. Using Chief Justice Rehnquist's characterization of the Indians as wanting to impose a "religious servitude" on national forestlands, the Court wrote that their "beliefs could easily require de facto beneficial ownership of some rather spacious tracts of public property." The Court was particularly upset by the prospect of a lockup of substantial portions of federal lands otherwise available for development (e.g., construction of roads and timbering). "Whatever rights the Indians may have to the use of the area, . . . those rights do not divest the Government of its right to use what is, after all, *its* land." Because this was publicly owned property, impacts on the personal autonomy of the landowner were not at issue, but mastery values, inherent in the government's right to use and develop "*its* land," certainly were. The claims of the Indians in *Lyng* threatened those values by creating competing rights in sacred sites or entire landscapes that could stifle use and development reflecting majority wishes.[74]

For Justice Brennan, this opposition between the culture of the Indians and the dominant culture was at the core of the case, and the Court's refusal to mediate it was the chief failing of its decision. He elaborated in his dissent: "The site-specific nature of Indian religious practice derives from the Native American perception that land is itself a sacred, living being." For the California tribes, the high country, including the Chimney Rock area, was "the most sacred of lands," and as district judge Weigel had found, its disturbance by the road building and timbering would "virtually destroy the . . .

Indians' ability to practice their religion." To give full meaning to the free exercise clause required the Court to give controlling weight to the impact of government action, not its form. The alternative led in this case to the "cruelly surreal result" that "governmental action that will virtually destroy a religion is nevertheless deemed not to 'burden' that religion." Therefore, the G-O road should be completed only if justified by compelling governmental interests, of which there were none.[75]

It is possible to understand *Lyng* as simply a link in the progression of the Court's free exercise jurisprudence toward greater reluctance to intervene in cases of religiously neutral government actions that incidentally impact religion. This progression may have been driven mainly, as Justice O'Connor suggests in *Lyng*, by the Court's growing institutional discomfort in refereeing intense cultural disputes surrounding a myriad of government programs. It culminated after *Lyng* in *Employment Division v. Smith*, which also dealt with Native American religious practices (sacramental use of peyote) but not the protection of sacred lands. *Smith* generally did away with strict scrutiny for neutral state or federal laws that happened to affect religion and left *Sherbert* and *Yoder* as clear outliers in a new doctrinal order.[76]

For this analysis, however, *Lyng*'s importance lies less in its doctrinal significance than in its cultural revelations. Commentators Amy Bowers and Kristen Carpenter asked the question: "How can one read the *Lyng* opinion as anything other than the Supreme Court trying to hammer . . . the final nail in the coffin of Indian conquest?" The theme of conquest that their question suggests is of obvious and major significance to Native Americans, but it is also important to environmentalists who see affinities with Indians in their beliefs and values and their cultural estrangement.[77]

The conquest motif in *Lyng* develops along at least three related dimensions—people, land, and religion. First, *Lyng* symbolically rehearses the European settlers' conquest of the Indians by emphasizing the prerogatives of public ownership over lands once owned by the Indians and by subordinating Indian religious beliefs and practices to views identified with Western religions. This figurative reconquest of the Indians advances not only mastery but also hierarchy values, as it upholds the legitimacy of the dominant culture and its institutions of public land management at the expense of the minority culture. While Justice O'Connor acknowledged the adverse effect on the Indians, she was comfortable enforcing the hierarchy's claim. The dissent, by contrast, while not arguing that the Indians' claims should necessarily prevail, would have created a space for judicial deliberation in which they might be credited. This egalitarian strain reinforces the harmony values in the dissent and resonates against the backdrop of the historical abuse of Indians at the hands of the dominant culture.

Second, *Lyng* recapitulates the United States' appropriation of Indian lands, the high country in particular. Bowers and Carpenter pointed out the irony in the Court's solicitude for the government's property ("its right to use what, after all, is *its* land"): the high country was ancestral Indian land that had been unilaterally converted to the U.S. public domain by Congress in 1853. The Court may have missed this irony or simply preferred to ignore it. In any event, it ruled out, with a rhetorical wave of its hand, the possibility that the Indians might have rights in the land, including rights as nonowners.[78]

Finally, while paying surface respect to the Indians' religion, *Lyng* also subordinates that religion to competing values conveyed through Western religious tradition. In the nineteenth century, the U.S. government sought to suppress Indian religion and replace it with Christianity.[79] Those efforts ceased long ago, but the religious conflict they represented was subtly present in *Lyng*. In Lynn White's account, Christianity made clear to its followers that humans and nature are different from each other, "and man is the master." It also enforced the distinction between the secular and the sacred, between earth and heaven. "The whole concept of the sacred grove is alien to Christianity and to the ethos of the West." The high country was the California Indians' sacred grove. Ostensibly at least, the Court in *Lyng* was not thinking of the G-O road as a competing religious expression. But White's point is that having internalized these elements of Christian doctrine, Western culture has ceased to think of them as religious at all. *Lyng*, White might suggest, was simply moving one religion aside for another.[80]

The cultural reverberations of *Lyng* extend beyond traditional Native American religions. Lawyer and scholar of religion Brian Brown pointed out that the Court in *Lyng* "abandoned First Amendment protection . . . to . . . any sincerely held religious convictions . . . that revere the land as holy." Religionists such as Thomas Berry proposed emulating Indian religions in the broad restoration of the pre-Christian "sense of the sacred character of the natural world as our primary revelation of the divine." As discussed in Chapter 1, this impulse has spawned new thinking in established denominations as well as more radical earth-based alternatives, such as the "new ecologically-sensitive harmony-oriented wild-minded scientific-spiritual culture" of poet and Zen Buddhist Gary Snyder. Brown imagined all religious traditions as "responding to the plight and plunder of the natural world by . . . evoking a transformed human consciousness of the earth as numinous." Nothing in *Lyng* would prevent this broader recognition of the numinous in nature, but the decision resists it by privileging the mastery values of a public land management hierarchy.[81]

The G-O road was never built. Political efforts by the Indians and their environmental allies after the decision brought Congress to add the G-O road corridor to an existing wilderness area, preventing further road construction. This reminds us that, *Lyng* notwithstanding, there remain political avenues for expression of the sacred in nature, for example, through designation of wilderness areas and national parks and monuments. Presidents from Ronald Reagan to George H. W. Bush have described the giant sequoia and redwood groves as "cathedrals" and as having "a grandeur beyond our power to equal." These and other places like them offer a vestige of a different way of responding to the land. But the "Presidents have limited their nature-as-holy talk to unique or unusual natural landmarks—the Grand Canyon, the giant sequoia groves, the Everglades—and wilderness areas." They provide "rhetorical justification for leaving these places untouched, while not undermining the general proposition" of *Lyng* that earth is given to us, or taken by us, "for our use and benefit."[82]

Each of these cases, in its own way, marginalized the claims of the environmental other and its human surrogates. The Court rejected ecocentric perspectives, as in *Sierra Club v. Morton* and *Lyng,* or belittled them while upholding laws advancing them, as in *TVA v. Hill.* Still not content, in *NAHB* it qualified the legal preeminence that *TVA v. Hill* had reluctantly accorded those perspectives. The views of the majority of the justices in these cases reflect the prevailing public discourse, which remains oriented around human utility.

Yet aspects of these cases represent the potential of ecocentric views to enter cultural discourse and practice. Justice Douglas's dissent in *Sierra Club v. Morton,* while of negligible influence in law, has become a classic of environmental literature. It keeps alive for environmentalists the aspiration of moderating the thoroughgoing anthropocentrism of mainstream institutions. Even the majority in *Sierra Club* was not entirely hostile to this enterprise: it provided a path for indirect expression of ecocentric views through the aesthetic and conservation interests of environmental litigants. Despite its strong undercurrent of skepticism over sacrificing a dam to save a little fish, the Court in *TVA v. Hill* hewed to the letter of a law that it believed required just that result—a ruling that retains wide sway despite *NAHB.* Justice Brennan's dissent in *Lyng* was a classic brief for ecocentric perspectives in the law, arguing for recognition of Native American religious beliefs and practices against the instrumentalist claims of the dominant culture. In sum, despite their anthropocentric cast, all these cases offer contributions to an ongoing process of deliberation, as Douglas Kysar described it, to reconsider "humanity's relation to the rest of the natural world and to imbue that relation with a renewed sense of responsibility."[83]

CHAPTER FIVE

Efficiency

ECONOMIC APPROACHES to environmental policy have stressed the role of efficiency in selecting regulatory instruments and goals. Broad resistance to these approaches was a defining feature of environmentalism in the 1970s and early 1980s. Environmentalists rejected them on the belief that they undermined the priority of environmental concerns, failed to condemn environmental degradation as a moral bad that should be avoided wherever possible, and anchored policies in the status quo of private human preferences rather than in the potential for increased public acceptance of the urgency of environmental issues.

This chapter analyzes the Supreme Court's efforts to navigate the divide between efficiency and environmentalist concerns and uses the cases to tease out the cultural dimensions of that divide, which may be less sharply drawn than those we encounter on other issues, such as property rights or judicial access—perhaps attributable as much to historical contingency as to deep-seated values oppositions. Many environmentalists still register strong disapproval of economic approaches, but others have embraced at least some applications as supportive of their goals. Understanding the cultural underpinnings of the arguments on both sides may help us determine whether the divide is inevitable or whether, as some argue, it can be bridged to the movement's benefit.

The first part of the chapter deals with the selection of tools by which environmental goals—however determined—are to be implemented. It tracks the Court's responses to flexibility devices that allow the selection of the most cost-effective (and therefore efficient) path to meeting whatever goals have been set. The second part addresses efficiency (as welfare maximization) in the selection of the goals themselves. It uses the Court's decisions to explore diverse cultural views on modern welfare economics and the practice of cost-benefit analysis (CBA).

Flexibility Devices: Cost-Effectiveness and Market Mechanisms

The early emphasis in the implementation of environmental law was on prescriptive measures, sometimes called "command-and-control," which specified how environmental goals—for example, a level of emissions reduction or a limit on development—were to be met. In response to criticisms that these measures were too rigid and unnecessarily expensive, policymakers considered an array of flexibility tools that could allow regulated entities to choose more cost-effective modes of compliance. These tools included relatively simple devices, such as the plantwide bubble in *Chevron v. Natural Resources Defense Council, Inc.,* as well as sophisticated market mechanisms such as pollution taxes or cap-and-trade programs.

Market mechanisms allow each pollution source to decide how much it will reduce pollution based on its reduction costs. Under cap-and-trade programs, for example, a cap sets the total emissions allowed for an area (e.g., state or region), emissions allowances are assigned to sources within the area consistent with the cap, and those sources are allowed to buy and sell emission allowances at a price established by an allowance market. In such a system, sources for which pollution reduction is relatively inexpensive will reduce more than will sources for which it is relatively expensive. In theory at least, flexibility devices such as this produce the most cost-effective allocation of reductions for any reduction goal.

Chevron: Of Plantwide Bubbles (and, Yes, Agency Discretion)

In her account of *Chevron v. Natural Resources Defense Council, Inc.* as an environmental law story, Jody Freeman wrote that *Chevron* "was the first . . . Supreme Court case to memorialize the turn toward market mechanisms in environmental regulation." This by itself is enough to give *Chevron* a place in the "environmental law pantheon." But the main reason for the case's fame rests on its signal contribution to administrative law: the definition of the role of courts in interpreting statutes carried out by agencies such as the Environmental Protection Agency (EPA). In a parallel account of the case from the administrative law perspective, Thomas Merrill calls *Chevron* "the most frequently cited case in administrative law," perhaps on its way to be the most cited case of all time. Understanding *Chevron* requires grasping how a case about the legality of the EPA's use of the "bubble" concept under the Clean Air Act (CAA) provoked what turned out to be the Court's most influential pronouncement on the relationship between the courts, Congress, and the administrative state.[1]

The plantwide bubble in *Chevron* was a rudimentary form of cap-and-trade. It authorized regulators to cap air emissions for an entire plant (which may have included hundreds of separate stacks and other emission points) at existing levels and allow the plant to avoid additional controls as long as any increases in emissions were offset by reductions elsewhere in the plant. Because the emissions trades were made within a single entity, the plant owner, rather than between different entities, there were no market transactions. But the expected effect was similar to allowance trading under more developed versions of cap-and-trade: the bubble would allow the plant manager to select the lowest-cost pollution control scenario under the no-net-increase cap.

In 1981, the same year that the EPA adopted the bubble that led to *Chevron,* political scientist Steven Kelman published a book that explored the "philosophical" or "ideological" objections that environmentalists might have to market mechanisms—objections "relating to the kind of society we ought to create." Kelman's critique assumed that market mechanisms produced the efficiency gains claimed by economists but probed the concerns that remained notwithstanding these acknowledged gains. As a basis for his critique, Kelman surveyed environmentalists, congressional staffers involved in environmental policy, and industry groups. Among the first two sets, two concerns about market mechanisms dominated: First, respondents felt that they granted "a license to pollute," effectively condoning environmentally harmful behaviors that should be avoided wherever possible; permitting people to pollute for a price instead suggested a "right to pollute." The second objection was that market mechanisms put a monetary value on environmental goods that had not previously been priced or traded. This monetization also threatened to devalue those goods even as it seemed to heighten their vulnerability: "Rivers are treasures," one of the respondents offered, "and not fair game."[2]

THE MODIFICATION ISSUE UNDER THE CLEAN AIR ACT

The bubble in *Chevron* addressed the "modification issue"—the question of when an existing stationary source of air emissions would be subject to more stringent limits as a modified source. The question arises under three separate but related CAA provisions for regulating emissions from new or modified stationary sources—a statutory scheme that the Court described with some restraint as "technical and complex." New Source Performance Standards (NSPS) under Section 111 of the act apply to categories of new or modified stationary sources for which the EPA has adopted emission standards. The act also provides for regulation of new or modified stationary sources on a case-by-case basis, placing more stringent requirements on sources in areas that are not attaining air quality standards than on those in areas that are. This is known as New Source Review (NSR). Under each of these provisions, the "modification issue" is whether an existing facility will be allowed to escape regulation as a modified source by offsetting emissions increases in one aspect of its operations with decreases in another.[3]

In the years leading up to *Chevron,* the EPA's efforts to resolve this issue produced a pair of legally and culturally fraught decisions by the Court of Appeals for the District of Columbia Circuit. In 1975, the agency adopted a bubble approach for NSPS by defining "stationary source" as an entire plant, for the purpose of determining whether physical or operational changes in existing equipment qualified as a "modification." On review in *Asarco v. EPA,* the District of Columbia Circuit invalidated the EPA's definition as inconsistent with both the language and the purpose of Section 111, which defines "stationary source" as "any building, structure, facility, or installation which emits or may emit any air pollutant." "Modification" is "any physical change in, or change in the method of operation of, a stationary source which increases the amount of any air pollutant emitted by such source." The court held that in defining a source as the entire plant, the EPA had "attempted to change the basic unit to which the NSPSs apply from a single building, structure, facility, or installation the unit prescribed in the statute to a combination of such units." The court also held that the bubble approach was contrary to the purpose of the NSPS: because it allowed existing sources to put off installing new emission reduction technology by offsetting emissions increases, it avoided changes that would otherwise qualify as modifications and trigger the NSPS.[4]

In 1978, the EPA tried the bubble approach again, this time in the setting of NSR in attainment areas, which Congress had added to the statute the year before. In its review of this attempt in *Alabama Power Co. v. Costle,* the District of Columbia Circuit was much kinder than it had been in *Asarco,* finding room for the bubble in the same language of Section 111 that the court in *Asarco* had not. It also concluded that the bubble was consistent with the purpose of NSR provisions for attainment areas, which was to maintain air quality rather than improve it. Indeed, the court suggested that it would be inconsistent with these provisions *not* to apply a bubble because requiring review of every in-plant change necessary "to keep pace with technological advances, or to respond to changing consumer demands . . . was never intended by Congress." Echoing the economists, the court celebrated bubbles as "precisely suited to preserve air quality within a framework that allows cost-efficient, flexible planning for industrial expansion and improvement."[5]

Although *Alabama Power* took pains to reconcile its holding with *Asarco*, the opinions were in tension legally and at opposite poles culturally: the District of Columbia Circuit split the values baby in half. In Thomas Merrill's account, Judge Skelly Wright's opinion in *Asarco* "portrayed the controversy as one in which the EPA, faced with a concerted lobbying campaign by one industry, had caved in and adopted a position that it knew to be 'contrary to both the language and the basic purpose of the Act.'" The bubble concept was an impediment to the spread of advanced controls and a servant of values inimical to environmental progress. By contrast, Judge Malcolm Wilkey, writing for the court in *Alabama Power,* praised the bubble for advancing values of efficiency, growth, and material improvement. This ideological contrast was underscored, as Merrill pointed out, by the political orientations of the authors: Judge Wright, "a staunch liberal," and Judge Wilkey, "one of the court's more conservative and pro-business members." One might have expected that this cultural standoff would also animate the Supreme Court's consideration of the bubble that was to come in *Chevron.* But that did not happen, for reasons to be explored; instead the Court distanced itself from the bubble debates and created a new doctrine to account for its disengagement.[6]

THE PRELUDE: CULTURAL CONTEST AND LEGAL CONFUSION

In October 1981, after the Reagan administration took office with a goal of reducing regulatory burdens, the EPA put out a new rule allowing states to use a plantwide definition of "source" for NSR in nonattainment as well as attainment areas. Predictably, the District of Columbia Circuit held that the rule ran afoul of the "bright line test" in *Asarco* and *Alabama Power* that prohibited the bubble in CAA programs to improve air quality. In its opening brief to the Supreme Court on review, the EPA slammed the circuit court's decision as "unwarranted usurpation" of policy-making authority reserved to agencies such as the EPA. The lower court's "bright line test," the government argued, was policy disguised as law. The statutory language and legislative history were not clear on the issue of the bubble, as the District of Columbia Circuit itself had acknowledged. The CAA's NSR provisions had multiple, competing purposes, including economic development as well as environmental protection. In the absence of specific direction from Congress, the EPA had the discretion to balance those competing purposes. The bubble was a reasonable interpretation of a complex act.[7]

In making its case for the reasonableness of what it had done, the EPA urged the virtues of the bubble on the Court. Through a Brookings

Institution study, it introduced the bubble as a "first attempt" in making "'the profit and cost incentives that work so well in the marketplace work for pollution control.'" The bubble, the economists taught, allowed pollution control to be achieved "more quickly and cheaply." Moreover, the EPA argued, the bubble as applied to NSR could lead to fewer emissions than the point-source alternative. Modifications that could lead to net reductions in emissions under the bubble might not make economic sense under a point-source approach due to the added expense and delay of NSR; discouraging these modifications would cement the status quo both environmentally and economically. In oral argument, Deputy Solicitor General Paul Bator, appearing for the EPA, came back to these same themes of efficiency, industrial renewal, and real rather than theoretical emissions reductions in his last words to the Court.[8]

In his arguments to the Court, the Natural Resources Defense Council's (NRDC) David Doniger focused on the language and legislative history and purposes of Section 111 and the NSR provisions and was less overtly concerned with the policy considerations featured by the EPA. But NRDC countered the EPA's normative claims for the bubble in its analysis of the purposes of the NSR requirements. These purposes included technology-forcing and reducing pollution to the maximum extent feasible. The aggressive control technology required for sources by nonattainment NSR was a legal embodiment of the moral imperative often invoked by critics of market-based mechanisms to do all that we can to avoid environmental harm. The bubble was antithetical to that imperative.[9]

Both the oral argument and the conference afterward were marked by confusion among the justices and uncertainty about the outcome. Justices Marshall and Rehnquist did not participate in the case, and Justice O'Connor would later recuse herself before the decision came down. The vote in the conference following the argument was split four to three for reversal, sanctioning the EPA's use of the bubble. But Justice Blackmun's notes of the conference show ambivalence on the part of all the justices except Justice Brennan, who seemed strongly for affirmance, although he later switched his vote. There was some discussion of the merits of the bubble, but the focus was on the statute, its legislative history, and the District of Columbia Circuit's prior rulings. At least some of the hesitancy in the Court's deliberations seemed due to the complexity of the statute, and at least two of the justices—Justices Powell and Stevens—suggested that complexity argued in favor of the agency. Stevens, who would write the opinion for what turned out to be a unanimous Court, described a key legislative report as "confusing," and added, "When I am so confused, I go with the agency." Out of this confusion came an opinion that redefined the interpretive roles of federal courts and administrative agencies.[10]

In his opinion for the Court reversing the District of Columbia Circuit, Justice Stevens set out the now famous two-step formula for judicial review of an agency's interpretation of a statute that the agency has responsibility for implementing. At step one, the reviewing court uses "traditional tools of statutory construction" to decide whether Congress addressed the issue before it. "If the intent of Congress is clear, that is the end of the matter." The court must give effect to that intent. But if Congress did not address the issue, or if its intent is unclear, the reviewing court moves to step two, where it decides whether the agency's interpretation was a "permissible" or "reasonable" construction of the statute. If the interpretation meets this standard, the court must uphold it.[11]

In this case, the Court found, Congress had not spoken to the plantwide definition of "source" under NSR, and the EPA's bubble approach was a reasonable interpretation. The Court disagreed with NRDC that the definition of "stationary source" in Section 111 ruled out the bubble. The definition could be read either as applying to the separate parts of a plant or to the plant as a whole, and there was nothing else in the statute or the legislative history that made clear that Congress intended one reading over the other. The statute, which was technical and complex, had multiple and competing purposes, as the EPA had argued. The agency's bubble was a reasonable accommodation of these conflicting policies, the Court concluded, on an issue that Congress had left to the agency's discretion. The Court was obliged to uphold it.[12]

Although *Chevron* became the Court's landmark statement on judicial review of agency interpretations, it was also a statement about the bubble—conditionally favorable and ultimately noncommittal but signaling the acceptability of the bubble and, by extension, an assortment of market mechanisms waiting in the wings. The Court approved the agency's rationale for choosing the bubble, quoting from the same study that the EPA had cited in its brief extolling the virtues of "economic incentives" over "the cumbersome administrative-legal framework" and announcing the bubble as a first step in making regulation more efficient. The Court also gave credence to the EPA's claim that the bubble was environmentally beneficial, quoting a comment from the New York State Department of Environmental Conservation (also cited in the EPA's brief) that point-source review encouraged continued use of "old, more polluting sources."[13]

Nothing in the opinion, however, suggested that the bubble commanded the Court's allegiance as it had the circuit court's in *Alabama Power*. The Court buried these quotes in favor of the bubble in footnotes and summarized them perfunctorily in the text. Its perspective was at a remove from the bubbles' merits, a distance that seemed compelled by the framework of review that it adopted.

Several factors may have led the Court to frame the case as one of agency "flexibility" rather than to stretch the search for a definitive answer in the statute, as the District of Columbia Circuit had done. Perhaps, just as the Court's opinion said, all six voting justices were really convinced that the statute gave no answer, although there seemed a lot of uncertainty on that score in their early deliberations. The Court's opinion also suggested that it was influenced in finding agency discretion by the technical complexity of the statute and the regulatory arena in which the EPA operated. "Confusion"—to use Justice Stevens's term—over the statute or the policy or both may have encouraged the Court's detachment. Finally, perhaps the justices believed that the bubble was a policy tool that deserved a chance, which could be accomplished in this case with a minimalist approach. In any event, although the Court's affirmation of the bubble was muted, it was unanimous; there was no surrogate for Judge Wright on the Court. The ideological debate that roiled the surface in *Asarco* and *Alabama Power* was absent, consigned at least ostensibly to the realms of politics and administration.

The Court's ruling anticipated the broad acceptance of the bubble and its relatives. In the wake of the decision, environmental programs have made increasing use of flexibility devices in the search for efficient implementation. Major environmental nongovernmental organizations such as Environmental Defense Fund (EDF) and World Resources Institute have made market approaches a centerpiece of their strategies. Prominent environmentalist and author Gustave Speth laments environmentalists' early opposition to market mechanisms and economic incentives. "We paid scant attention to them because we saw pollution charges, for example, as allowing companies to buy the right to pollute, ... but I do wish we had started earlier with market mechanisms. They would have led to earlier and better integration of environmental objectives into business planning and would have forged a stronger alliance between environmentalists and economists." Speth's view is increasingly accepted among environmentalists, although the embrace is not universal.[14]

EPA v. EME Homer: The Triumph of Efficiency in Implementation

This cultural progression was manifest in a sequel to *Chevron, EPA v. EME Homer City Generation, L.P.,* decided in 2014. Like *Chevron, EME Homer* addressed the lawfulness of a bubble approach in CAA implementation, albeit at a much grander scale. Rather than the plantwide bubble in *Chevron,* the bubble in *EME Homer* encompassed air emissions from power plants in a twenty-seven-state region in the eastern United States. And rather than rely on a plant manager to efficiently allocate reductions among emission points, it featured the assignment of cost-effective emission reduction targets among the states by the EPA and an allowance trading regime to further enhance the efficient allocation of reductions. As in *Chevron,* the Court approved the bubble as a reasonable interpretation of an ambiguous statutory provision for dealing with interstate pollution, and it emphasized, more openly than it had in *Chevron,* the "good sense" of cost-effective implementation.[15]

The EPA adopted the Cross-State Air Pollution Rule (Transport Rule) under the Good Neighbor Provision of the CAA, which requires states to prohibit in-state sources "from emitting any air pollutant in amounts which will . . . contribute significantly to" failure of downwind states to attain a national air quality standard, or will interfere with their maintenance of a standard. The rule set reduction budgets for emissions of sulfur dioxide and oxides of nitrogen for states whose emissions were determined to materially contribute to nonattainment in one or more downwind states. The EPA used an analysis of cost-effective reductions available in each state to set the budgets. A collection of industry interests, labor groups, and states sought review, arguing that the EPA's rule impermissibly considered costs in implementing a provision that spoke only of "amounts" of pollutants contributing to downwind pollution. The District of Columbia Circuit agreed, holding that Section 110(a)(2)(D) required each upwind state to reduce in a manner that was physically proportional to its contribution to nonattainment in downwind states, without consideration of relative costs.[16]

The Supreme Court reversed, six to two (Justice Alito abstaining), in an opinion by Justice Ginsburg in which Chief Justice Roberts and Justices Kennedy, Breyer, Sotomayor, and Kagan concurred. The statutory language that the District of Columbia Circuit found to be unambiguous on its face, the Court found to be unclear in the realities of its application and therefore appropriate for agency interpretation. "Most upwind states contribute pollution to multiple downwind states in varying amounts," the Court determined. Literally applied, the circuit court's proportionality rule in these circumstances would result in "costly overregulation," clearly not the intent of the Good Neighbor Provision. Thus it was permissible, indeed necessary, for the EPA to consider factors other than proportionality, and its choice to be guided by relative costs of reduction was a reasonable one. But the Court went beyond a bare finding of reasonableness in affirming the "good sense" of the agency's path:

Eliminating those amounts that can cost-effectively be reduced is an efficient and equitable solution to the allocation problem the Good Neighbor Provision requires the Agency to address. Efficient because EPA can achieve the levels of attainment . . . the proportional approach aims to achieve, but at a much lower overall cost. Equitable because, by imposing uniform cost thresholds on regulated states, EPA's rule subjects to stricter regulation those States that have done relatively less in the past to control their pollution.

The tone of approbation was clear.[17]

The Court's opinion drew a dissent from Justice Scalia, concurred in by Justice Thomas, based on a textualist parsing of "amounts" of pollutants. The meaning of that dissent was complicated, however, by an apparent conflation of efficiency in implementation (cost-effectiveness) with efficiency in goal setting (CBA), as I discuss at the end of the chapter.

EME Homer was a ringing confirmation of the march of flexibility devices into the mainstream of environmental thought and practice. The decision drew significant support from both conservatives and liberals on the Court. Environmentalists overwhelmingly supported the rule. Having opposed the bubble in *Chevron,* the NRDC along with EDF, Sierra Club, and other major environmental groups joined the EPA as petitioners before the Court. Energy companies and the Chamber of Commerce opposed the rule because they wanted to delay stronger clean air controls, not because they opposed the principle of cost-effective implementation. The broad support for market mechanisms among environmentalists and those of other cultural persuasions reflected in *EME Homer* carries into efforts to address even more daunting challenges such as climate change, as discussed in Chapter 10.

Cost-Benefit Analysis, Environmentalist Priorities, and Institutional Practice

Although it passes under the guise of a technocratic exercise overseen by economists, CBA is about values. It is about what (or whose) values are considered and how those values are weighted and ranked. CBA draws special attention from environmentalists because it goes to the heart of policy—what levels of environmental harm should we consider acceptable?—and because many environmentalists believe that it systematically devalues the environment.

In a progression of decisions from 1972 to 2007, the Supreme Court resisted calls for the balancing of costs and benefits under environmental and worker safety statutes. The statutes demanded higher priority for environmental and safety concerns than cost-benefit balancing would provide, or at least federal agencies were entitled to so conclude. In its 2009 decision in *Entergy v. Riverkeeper*, however, a majority of the Court shifted from skepticism to a modest embrace of CBA. Although *Entergy* interpreted a relatively narrow provision of the Clean Water Act (CWA), with immediate application only to water intake structures for electric power plants, it marked a shift in the Court's posture in the CBA culture wars.

The CBA Values Debate

Formal CBA as practiced in the United States is both "commensuralist" and "welfarist"—that is, it describes the effects of policy options, both pro and con, on a single monetary scale, and its use is to maximize overall well-being. Its measure of well-being is individual preferences, usually expressed in willingness to pay, summed across the affected population. It strongly encourages (if not categorically demands) that nonmarket goods such as environmental quality be given a monetary value to facilitate comparison of pros and cons. And it carries a presumption against regulatory options whose costs exceed their benefits. Some (but not all) CBA proponents, however, agree that even a well-conducted CBA is not necessarily decisive and that decisionmakers may take account of other morally relevant considerations.[18]

For many environmentalists, CBA's welfarist goal and its commitment to monetization undercut the broad goals of the movement. Environmentalists reject the welfarist premise of CBA in favor of approaches based on duties to avoid harm to the living environment or to other humans, including future generations. They also criticize monetization as skewing CBA against protective options because of the relative ease of measuring monetary costs of regulation compared with measuring prospective benefits, monetary or otherwise. Decisionmakers will instinctively give more weight to what can be quantified than to what can only be described qualitatively. More fundamentally, environmentalists argue, placing a monetary value on human life, healthy ecosystems, and other environmental goods that are normally not traded in markets ignores that they belong to "the realm of specially valued things." Concerns about monetization also link back to concerns about the hegemony of welfarism—the squeezing out of nonwelfarist considerations that are not, and cannot be, quantitatively valued. This anticommodification strain has its roots deep in the history of environmental thought, beginning with Marsh and Muir and running through Leopold: all of them fought the notion that regard for nature should be based solely or even primarily on economic value.[19]

The problem with CBA for many environmentalists and others interested in social change is its rootedness in the status quo—in existing preferences, existing market conditions, existing institutional arrangements. In *Regulating from Nowhere,* Douglas Kysar argues that CBA shuts down our collective openness to new possibilities of the sort that environmentalism urges. Because CBA is based on existing individual preferences, reliance on it limits the ability of deliberative processes to enlarge the social importance of environmental concerns beyond what "they attract under current market and political equilibria." It exerts a conservative social and cultural bias, with unfortunate consequences for transformational movements such as environmentalism.[20]

A number of CBA's defenders, including some who would consider themselves environmentalists, agree that CBA methodology is not perfect and should be improved. But, they argue, CBA is much more likely to produce a welfare-enhancing result than approaches that ignore welfare considerations entirely in favor of nonwelfarist rights or duties, such as protecting the intrinsic rights of species or ecosystems. Human well-being may not be the only morally relevant consideration, but it is certainly an important one. Moreover, the absolutist rhetoric of some environmentalists notwithstanding, trade-offs are unavoidable; balancing costs against benefits is something we do instinctively in making choices. CBA provides a systematic way of making those trade-offs and avoiding harmful misallocations of limited societal resources. Through their Institute for Policy Integrity, Richard Revesz and Michael Livermore have encouraged methodological changes to eliminate antiregulatory bias in CBA and urged environmental and other public interest groups to use CBA in their advocacy.[21]

A weak form of CBA, which is simply a weighing of all the desirable effects of a proposed action against all the undesirable effects, avoids some of the criticisms aimed at CBA proper (the "strong form"). The weak form shares neither the commensuralist nor the welfarist features of the strong form. Pros and cons need not be converted to a common metric, such as dollars; anticipated benefits of regulation may be considered in their natural units, such as lives saved, acres of habitat protected, or species restored. The weak form of CBA is not tied to an optimizing goal, such as welfare maximization. It operates instead to weed out regulatory alternatives that may be perceived as absurd, irrational, or otherwise not in accord with common sense, as where an option's costs are grossly disproportionate to its benefits. This distinction between reasonableness (in the sense of avoiding grossly disproportionate outcomes) and efficiency (welfare maximization) becomes important in my analysis of the Supreme Court's ventures into the disputed territory of cost-benefit balancing.[22]

Institutional Practice and the Court: The CBA Paradox

The efficiency goal and its handmaiden CBA are as much in dispute at the level of institutional practice as at the level of theory. Congress's approach in environmental statutes has been mixed: it has sometimes expressly provided for the use of CBA, sometimes forbidden its use, and sometimes been silent or ambiguous on the issue. Most of the major environmental regulatory statutes enacted in the 1970s and 1980s rely mainly on harm-based or technology-based approaches that either expressly exclude cost-benefit balancing or do not expressly provide for it. By contrast, from the 1980s onward, where the law permits, the executive branch has required federal agencies to conduct CBA for all "significant" federal regulations and to propose and adopt only those regulations whose benefits justify their costs.[23]

This divergence in institutional practice has left the federal courts to navigate between the two politically accountable branches of government on the use of CBA. The courts' role is interpretative, not constitutive, but the line between the two is often blurred, as we have seen. Commentators offer competing suggestions for how courts should interpret environmental and other regulatory statutes to determine whether agencies may use CBA or are required to use it. Should courts put a thumb on the scale for or against the use of CBA as a policy guide, and if so, on which side, and with what force?

Legal scholars have offered an array of interpretive presumptions, or "default rules," which would answer these questions. These range from a pro-CBA presumption, which would favor agency use of CBA where the authorizing statute is silent or unclear, to an anti-CBA rule, which would disfavor the use of CBA in cases of statutory silence or ambiguity. Dan Farber proposes a middle ground, a "hybrid" canon under which ambiguous statutes would be construed to permit a weak form of CBA—a rough weighing of costs and benefits without the requirement that all benefits be monetized. The justices have flirted with some form of all of these presumptions.[24]

Four Cases in Search of a Presumption

Four pre-*Entergy* Supreme Court decisions offer insights into the possibility of a judicial presumption on CBA. They also provide a background against which the innovation of *Entergy* is clear. Each of them addressed the priority to be accorded environmental or worker health concerns and the consideration of costs or weighing of costs and benefits as affecting that priority. Among the majorities in these cases, there is no apparent urge to establish a presumption in favor of CBA; indeed, there is some inclination toward a contrary presumption in the absence of express authorization for CBA. Concurring and dissenting justices in these cases, however, associate balancing costs and benefits with avoiding irrational or absurd results in a way that would support a presumption in favor of at least a weak form of CBA in cases of ambiguity or silence.

CITIZENS TO PRESERVE OVERTON PARK, INC. V. VOLPE

As discussed in Chapter 3, the Court in *Overton Park* rejected the Department of Transportation's interpretation of Section 4(f) of the Department of Transportation Act as allowing the Secretary to balance competing interests in deciding to route a highway through a public park. It read the language of Section 4(f)—"no feasible and prudent alternative"—in light of its purpose to give parkland protection "paramount importance." Balancing parkland against routine concerns such as the additional costs of alternative locations and community disruption was inconsistent with this purpose because highways would almost always be less costly and disruptive when built through parks. Public parks were to be sacrificed only if there were "truly unusual factors present" or if "community disruption resulting from alternative routes reached extraordinary magnitudes."[25]

Overton Park offers an early example of the Court's perception of the urgency of environmental protection as overriding the claimed need for "prudential" balancing of costs and benefits. Congress did not intend the secretary to strike his own balance of costs and benefits in deciding whether to protect our "last green havens." Congress had already struck the balance in favor of park protection. Consideration of costs and benefits, conventionally understood, would systematically undermine that policy preference.

TENNESSEE VALLEY AUTHORITY V. HILL

As discussed in Chapter 4, in *Tennessee Valley Authority v. Hill* (*TVA v. Hill*) the Court interpreted Section 7 of the Endangered Species Act as preventing the completion of TVA's Tellico Dam to protect the endangered snail darter. Although the Court wrote that "in this case the burden on the public through the loss of millions of unrecoverable dollars [might be argued to] greatly outweigh the loss of the snail darter," it concluded that Congress had not authorized the courts to balance costs and benefits. There is no evidence in the opinion that the Court's reading of the statute was animated by a presumption against the cost-benefit balancing that it excluded. To the contrary, the opinion implicitly questions the wisdom of Congress's unyielding preference for species protection.[26]

Justice Powell, joined by Justice Blackmun in dissent, chose not to be passive in the face of the statute's formidable language and legislative history on this issue. Arguing that Congress should not be presumed to have intended the "absurd result" in this case, he worked to find room in the statute for the kind of balancing the Court precluded. His approach rested on a presumption in favor of weighing costs and benefits, at least as necessary to weed out cases in which costs are grossly disproportionate to benefits. This presumption rested on the absurd results doctrine, which allows courts to construe congressional directives to avoid obviously irrational outcomes. Powell used the presumption to generate ambiguity in a key statutory term ("action") that the majority concluded was clear and to construe the term to avoid what he considered an irrational outcome. In this he laid the groundwork on which Justices Breyer and Scalia would build in *Entergy*. Justice Rehnquist's dissent similarly presumed in favor of the Court's traditional balancing of the equities in selecting a remedy.[27]

AMERICAN TEXTILE MANUFACTURERS INSTITUTE, INC. V. DONOVAN

Here the Court addressed whether the Occupational Safety and Health Administration (OSHA) was required to apply a quantitative CBA in adopting a workplace standard for cotton dust and to ensure that the costs of the standard bore a reasonable relationship to its benefits. Section 6(b)(5) of the Occupational Safety and Health Act requires the agency to set "the standard which most adequately assures, to the extent feasible, . . . that no employee will suffer material impairment of health or functional capacity." Reading "feasible" to mean "capable of being done, executed, or effected," a majority of the justices concluded that OSHA was justified in rejecting the use of CBA: "Congress itself defined the basic relationship between costs and benefits, by placing the 'benefit' of worker health above all other considerations save those making attainment of this 'benefit' unachievable."[28]

Justice Brennan's opinion for the Court can be read to reflect a presumption against the use of CBA in the absence of express statutory authorization. The Court offered a blanket observation, apparently encompassing all federal statutes: "when Congress has intended that an agency engage in cost-benefit analysis, it has clearly indicated such intent on the face of the statute." "Feasibility," as the Court construed it, did not convey that intent. The logical inference is that Congress did not intend that OSHA engage in CBA under Section 6(b)(5). The Court concluded that, consistent with this inference, CBA by OSHA "is not required by the statute because feasibility analysis is."[29]

The papers of Justice Marshall made public years after the decision, however, suggest that this inference was not, after all, what the Court intended. An initial draft of Justice Brennan's opinion circulated among his fellow justices stated that the statute "precluded" CBA. The Court was not required to go this far in its holding: OSHA in this case had rejected CBA and therefore all that was necessary was a ruling that the rejection was permissible. But Brennan believed that the statute should be read to prohibit CBA and that it was in everyone's interest for the Court to make that clear. Justice Stevens, who represented the fifth vote necessary for a majority upholding OSHA, persuaded Brennan that "an advisory opinion" on this issue would be ill-advised. In the final opinion, "precluded" became "not required."[30]

In his dissent, Justice Rehnquist capitalized on the substitute language without, of course, revealing the internal exchanges that produced it. While he agreed that "feasibility" is the crucial statutory term, he argued that its meaning is indeterminate and read the Court's conclusion that CBA is not "required" as implying that it is permitted at the agency's option. In *Entergy*, Justice Scalia adopted this reading of *American Textile* in sanctioning the EPA's use of CBA.[31]

Taken as a whole, the Court's opinion in *American Textile* remains unclear on this issue, perhaps because it was written originally to make a definitive pronouncement against use of CBA, and portions of the final opinion still point in that direction. CBA proponent Cass Sunstein, among others, read *American Textile* as prohibiting OSHA from balancing costs and benefits, and he branded it a poor decision for that reason. In *Industrial Union Department, AFL-CIO v. American Petroleum Institute,* also decided under the Occupational Health and Safety Act, the Court had held that the act required OSHA to document a significant risk before regulating a toxic substance. Putting the two holdings together, Sunstein lamented "the basic irrationality of a system in which OSHA is required to find a significant risk, but is prohibited from undertaking cost-benefit analysis. . . . A rational system of regulation looks not at the magnitude of the risk alone, but assesses the risk in comparison to the costs." The holding in *Entergy*, with Justice Scalia's Rehnquist-inspired reading of *American Textile,* was to answer Sunstein's critique.[32]

WHITMAN V. AMERICAN TRUCKING ASSOCIATIONS, INC. (ATA)

The Court decided unanimously that Section 109 of the CAA precluded consideration of the costs of implementation in setting national ambient air quality standards (NAAQS) for ozone and particulate matter. Section 109 requires the EPA to set NAAQS at a level "requisite to protect the public health" with "an adequate margin of safety." Justice Scalia's opinion for the Court considered industry's arguments that the words of Section 109—"public health," "requisite," "adequate"—were sufficiently flexible to accommodate consideration of the costs, as well as the health benefits, of a new or revised NAAQS. But Congress had made specific reference to costs in related provisions of the CAA, and consideration of costs in setting the NAAQS was too important, the Court concluded, to be authorized "in vague terms or ancillary provisions": Congress "does not, one might say, hide elephants in mouseholes." The burden was on industry to "show a [clear] textual commitment of authority to the EPA to consider costs in setting NAAQS," and industry failed to carry that burden. In the absence of such a commitment, the EPA had no authority to do so. The Court's formulation echoed the presumption-suggesting language of *American Textile*: when Congress intends an agency to balance economic costs against environmental benefits, it makes that clear in the statute.[33]

The Court's opinion was a vindication of the priority for environmental health concerns that the EPA had been claiming in its NAAQS decisions for decades. The tone of the opinion was neutral: it evinced no particular sympathy for the path that Congress laid down. But given the antienvironmentalist reputation of its author and the vehemence of his resistance to environmental regulation in other contexts, such as *MA v. EPA*, it is striking that Justice Scalia sided with the EPA on this important issue. Scalia's methodological commitment to the plain meaning of statutory text and structure may simply have compelled this result. It may also have mattered to Scalia that *ATA* addressed public health concerns from exposure to emissions rather than dealing primarily with ecological harm.[34]

Public health protection has a long tradition in common law tort actions (e.g., public nuisance) and local and state regulation (e.g., antismoke ordinances), whereas protection of ecosystems with no immediate impact on human health or welfare is an innovation of modern environmentalism. For a traditionalist like Justice Scalia, an environmental regulatory statute giving priority to public health concerns would have a cultural plausibility that a statute giving priority to protection of natural resources following the modern ecological model would not. *City of Chicago v. Environmental Defense Fund*, an earlier case in which Scalia wrote for the Court, requiring the EPA to apply strict regulatory requirements to ash generated by municipal waste combustors, supports the importance of this distinction. As in *ATA*, the statute in *City of Chicago* addressed threats to human health from direct exposure to environmental contaminants—the nuisance paradigm. *ATA* and *City of Chicago* presented "pollution" in its conventional sense, with values connotations of harm and impurity, in a way that *MA v. EPA* did not.[35]

The sweep of Justice Scalia's opinion in *ATA* remained unclear. Was the requirement that there be "a clear textual commitment" to authorize agency consideration of costs limited to the NAAQS provisions of the CAA, or did it have broader applicability? If the former, it would not qualify as a presumption but simply an interpretive gloss of the text and structure of the statute at issue. If the latter, it could have broad implications for the interpretation of regulatory legislation on this crucial issue of costs.

Concern over the latter possibility sparked a separate concurrence by Justice Breyer, in which he stressed the dangers of a presumption against the consideration of the costs along with the benefits of environmental regulation. Breyer's scholarly and judicial writings led him inevitably to this stance. In his 1993 book, *Breaking the Vicious Circle,* he had attacked what he called the "tunnel vision" problem of regulation. His premise was that the incremental costs of protection will increase with stringency; for example, removing the last 10 percent of a toxic chemical from the environment is likely to cost many times more than removing the first 10 percent. Regulators in single-minded pursuit of a toxics-free environment may seek removal of the last 10 percent, even though the incremental costs could dwarf the incremental benefits. The result is irrational policy. This analysis fits with a more general pattern in Breyer's judging and writing of using rough cost-benefit balancing to detect irrationality. This pattern was evident in his *ATA* concurrence and surfaced decisively again in his concurrence in *Entergy.*[36]

If followed generally, Justice Breyer argued in his *ATA* concurrence, a presumption against consideration of costs would produce irrational results. Regulators often must consider "all of a proposed regulation's adverse [as well as beneficial] effects, at least where those adverse effects clearly threaten serious and disproportionate public harm. Hence, "we should read silences or ambiguities in the language of regulatory statutes as permitting, not forbidding, this type of rational regulation." Breyer was able to subscribe to the Court's interpretation of Section 109 only by persuading himself that the EPA had "sufficient flexibility [in mechanisms for implementing NAAQS] to avoid setting ambient air quality standards ruinous to industry." But in concluding that the NAAQS scheme need not "lead to deindustrialization," he made his cautionary meaning clear: "Preindustrial society was not a very healthy society; hence a standard demanding the return of the Stone Age would not prove 'requisite to protect the public health.'" His images of a "preindustrial society" and a "return of the Stone Age" starkly depicted the risks of overzealous pursuit of environmental goals. The latter phrase echoed the title of Edgar Rice Burroughs's 1937 classic, "Back to the Stone Age," which depicts its hero's adventures in a savage world of extreme material and cultural deprivation.[37]

ATA's rejection of cost considerations in the CAA's core policy choice has stood as a major triumph for environmentalists, affirming the paramount importance of protecting human health from pollution risks. CBA advocates Michael Livermore and Richard Revesz, however, have sought to invert the meaning of *ATA*—from a signal environmentalist victory to a decision that sanctions less than optimal protections. By forbidding any consideration of costs, they argue, the Court's opinion may be read to foreclose selection of a cost-benefit justified standard that is more protective than a health-based alternative. Although all the parties and the justices in *ATA* assumed that a balancing of costs and benefits would lead to a less stringent standard, the CBA for fine particulate matter—prepared to meet OMB requirements but not considered by the EPA administrator in her decision—showed that the standard for fine particulate matter selected as "requisite to protect human health" was *less stringent* than an alternative that arguably would have maximized net benefits (i.e., the efficient choice). Livermore and Revesz show that in a number of other NAAQS rulemakings, the efficient alternative would also have been more protective than the alternative selected by the EPA. They conclude that *ATA* should be interpreted narrowly to permit relitigation on the question of whether the EPA may consider costs in selecting standards based on CBA that are more stringent than are harm-based alternatives. The courts may or may not permit this relitigation. Considered purely as a symbolic gesture, however, Livermore and Revesz's shot at the *ATA* sacred cow boldly challenges environmentalist opposition to CBA.[38]

Making Sense of *Entergy*'s Precursors

These pre-*Entergy* cases gave contrary indications. On one hand, in three of them, a majority held that the statute precluded the balancing of costs against benefits in agency or judicial determinations. In the fourth, *American Textile*, the Court came close to doing so, and its opinion remained ambiguous on this point. In two of the rulings—*Overton Park* and *TVA v. Hill*—the Court expressly concluded that CBA was inimical to the statute's protective purpose. And in two others—*American Textile* and *ATA*—it feinted in the direction of a presumption that would preclude or limit consideration of costs in the absence of express authorization. In the end, however, it was not clear whether any of these anti-CBA rulings would transcend the particulars of the statutes to which they applied to establish a broader norm.

On the other hand, dissents and concurrences in three of the cases resisted the anti-CBA interpretations of their colleagues. Justice Powell in *TVA v. Hill* and Justice Breyer in *ATA* connected the balancing of costs and benefits with the basic rationality necessary to avoid "absurd" decisions or gross misallocations of societal resources. Breyer ultimately acquiesced in the Court's interpretation in *ATA,* but he made clear his predisposition to read regulatory statues as permitting comparison of costs and benefits unless they expressly forbade it: a pro-CBA presumption, cutting against the anti-CBA thrust of *American Textile.* Although Breyer was a lone voice in *ATA,* his views would catch the imagination of his more conservative colleagues in *Entergy.*

The Decision in *Entergy*

With these precedents as prologue, the Supreme Court decided *Entergy Corp. v. Riverkeeper, Inc.,* upholding the EPA's use of CBA in regulating cooling intake structures for existing electric power plants under Section 316(b) of the CWA, a relatively minor provision. Unlike the act's major provisions, which regulate the discharge of pollutants into the nation's waters, Section 316(b) regulates the way in which one sector—the electric utility industry—extracts water for cooling purposes. Yet it shares textual features with these more prominent provisions, and the Court's treatment of the issue in *Entergy* suggested a new openness to the use of CBA generally.[39]

Cooling intake structures at power plants kill large numbers of fish, shellfish, and other organisms by squeezing them against the intake screens ("impingement") or sucking them into the cooling system ("entrainment"). Section 316(b) requires the EPA to set cooling water intake standards for these plants that "reflect the best technology available [BTA] for minimizing adverse environmental impact," but it does not specify the factors that the EPA is to consider in determining BTA. For new power plants, the EPA mandated a level of reduction in fish and shellfish mortality that could be achieved by closed-cycle systems, which sharply limit the amount of water that must be withdrawn for cooling. For existing large power plants (more than 550 nationwide), the EPA imposed less demanding standards based on a combination of less-expensive technologies. These regulations also provided for facility-specific variances from the standards whereby the facility could demonstrate that the costs of compliance would be "significantly greater" than the benefits. Known as the "Phase II standards," these regulations were the subject of the *Entergy* litigation.[40]

Although the EPA's rationale for adopting the Phase II standards was less than clear, at least one consideration was the "national cost of those technologies in comparison to the national benefits." The EPA estimated that the operation of the cooling water intake structures covered by its Phase II rule killed more than 3.4 billion fish and shellfish each year. The closed-cycle cooling water system rejected by the EPA could have reduced these deaths by up to 98 percent. The EPA anticipated that, as applied across the universe of Phase II cooling water systems, its standards based on the less expensive technologies would reduce fish mortality by only about 40 percent (1.4 billion fish per year). But although the closed-cycle cooling system would have achieved greater reductions in fish and shellfish deaths, it would have cost much more than the alternative technologies the EPA selected ($3.5 billion per year versus $389 million per year).[41]

In this cost-benefit study, the EPA calculated the benefits of the Phase II rule based solely on the "use value" of fish and shellfish harvested by commercial or recreational fisheries—less than 2 percent of the total aquatic life at risk. On this basis, the EPA set the benefits of the rule at roughly $83 million. It recognized that fish and other organisms affected by the rule offered a variety of nonuse "ecological and public services" (e.g., sustaining the food web, maintaining biodiversity, and satisfying human preferences for a healthy ecosystem), but it abandoned efforts to monetize these services. That meant that the value of the lives of billions of creatures was not captured at all in the quantified comparison of costs and benefits; the loss was represented qualitatively.[42]

The EPA was clear that the benefits were "incomplete," but it nevertheless compared them with the full costs of the rule. The comparison showed that the costs of the Phase II standards exceeded their monetized benefits by a factor of five ($389 million in costs/$83 million in benefits)—a meager .21 cost-benefit ratio. The costs of a closed-cycle cooling system would have been even more disproportionate to the monetized benefits, even assuming total elimination of water intake deaths ($3.5 billion in costs/$212 million in benefits). The agency concluded that the Phase II rule "approach[ed] the performance" of the closed-cycle system at substantially less cost.[43]

Riverkeeper, an environmental watchdog for the Hudson River and its tributaries, and other environmental groups petitioned for review of the EPA's Phase II rule in the U.S. Court of Appeals for the Second Circuit. They argued that the EPA had erred in failing to set more stringent controls, particularly the closed-cycle cooling systems that the EPA had rejected in part on cost-benefit grounds. Joining them were a half dozen states, including Connecticut, New York, Massachusetts, and New Jersey. Industry interests, including Entergy, a large owner and operator of electric power plants in the South, challenged the rule from the other side, complaining that it overreached agency authority.

The Second Circuit concluded that Section 316(b) precluded cost-benefit balancing in determining BTA. It rested its interpretation on three grounds: the structure of the CWA, Section 316(b)'s plain meaning, and the anti-CBA presumption suggested by *American Textile*. The court's statutory structure rationale was that BTA should be interpreted similarly to "best technology" standards elsewhere in the act that did not provide for comparing costs and benefits. In addition, the Second Circuit read the language of Section 316(b) itself ("best technology available for minimizing adverse environmental impact") as plainly requiring the most effective ("best") technology for reducing the impact on aquatic life to the maximum extent ("minimizing . . . environmental impact") technologically and economically feasible ("available"). Finally, the Second Circuit read *American Textile* as supplying an anti-CBA default rule—prohibiting the weighing of costs and benefits in regulatory decisions in the absence of express permission from Congress.[44]

The Supreme Court granted review solely on the question of whether Section 316(b) authorizes the EPA "to compare costs with benefits in determining 'the best technology available for minimizing adverse environmental impact' at cooling water intake structures." In their opening briefs, industry petitioners and the EPA (which was defending its rule) sought quickly to demolish the Second Circuit's default rule precluding CBA unless expressly authorized. This point was crucial: if the Court were to take this clear statement rule at face value, the likelihood of a reversal would plummet. *American Textile* had not intended such a presumption, the industry and the EPA argued, and even if it had, the presumption would be inconsistent with the later-decided *Chevron*, emphasizing the interpretive discretion of agencies in the face of statutory silence or ambiguity. Entergy asserted that CBA "is nothing more than common sense—the imperative of basic rationality to ensure that actions do more good than harm." CBA analysis should be "*favored* by the law, not disfavored," the "opposite of the [presumption] employed by the Second Circuit." To similar effect, the EPA argued that the appropriate presumption was Justice Breyer's in his *ATA* concurrence, reading "silences or ambiguities in the language of regulatory statutes as permitting, not forbidding, this type of rational regulation."[45]

With the default rule (they hoped) disposed of, the EPA and the industry petitioners worked to open room in the language of Section 316(b) for their preferred reading. Section 316(b) made no mention of costs and benefits; indeed it did not specify any factors that the EPA was or was not to consider in setting BTA. A close parsing of the key statutory terms—"best," "available," "minimize," and "adverse environmental impact"—showed that Section 316(b) was best read (or at least could reasonably be read) as authorizing the EPA to balance costs and benefits to ensure an acceptable, desirable, or satisfactory level of reduction in aquatic impacts, not necessarily the lowest possible level. The analogous best technology provisions did not, as the Second Circuit had concluded, foreclose CBA, and even if they did, the provisions were different in language and purpose and therefore did not control the meaning of Section 316(b). The EPA's interpretation was a permissible, if not mandatory, reading of Section 316(b), which *Chevron* required that the courts uphold. The Second Circuit's contrary reading was "absurd," Entergy argued.[46]

In its arguments to the Court on the merits, Riverkeeper pointedly disclaimed reliance on the anti-CBA plain statement rule that the Second Circuit used. Riverkeeper's lead counsel, environmental law scholar and Supreme Court advocate Richard Lazarus, believed that *American Textile* would carry little weight with the justices that he needed most to convince— particularly Kennedy and Breyer. Instead, using arguments similar to the textual and structural analysis in the Second Circuit opinion, Lazarus contended that Section 316(b) clearly evidenced Congress's intent to preclude CBA and that the EPA's interpretation therefore failed at Chevron step one.[47]

Riverkeeper worked to debunk the notion that without CBA, Section 316(b) would lead to irrational excess. "Nor is there any merit to the absurd result most often repeated by petitioners and their amici: the specter of industry paying billions of dollars to save one fish (or trillions to save one hapless individual plankton). Although the meaning of 'minimizing' is plainly not merely to reduce, it is also just as plainly not so constricted as to require the EPA to require industry petitioners to spend billions to save one more fish or plankton." The EPA had flexibility to decide at what point impacts had been minimized. This move gave Riverkeeper some protection against the absurdity argument, but other questions remained: If the EPA had flexibility in deciding how stringently to regulate, how was it to exercise that flexibility? If not allowed to consider the costs and benefits of regulatory options, how would it decide whether it had minimized enough? At oral argument, Justice Souter wondered aloud whether Riverkeeper's reading to avoid the most extreme outcomes was just "a kind of smoke and mirrors way [to] take cost-benefit analysis into consideration sub rosa."[48]

Most of the questions at oral argument came from Justices Scalia and Breyer, and most of their questions were for Riverkeeper's Lazarus. Scalia dealt mostly with the text and structure of the statute, but at one point he seemed to tip his hand on the value dimensions of the case. Commenting on Congress's explicit authorization of CBA in other areas of the CWA, Scalia stated, "it seems ridiculous to allow it, and indeed require it in effluent situations where human health is at stake, and yet to forbid it in this intake situation when you were just talking about the snail darter." His use of the "snail darter" as a synecdoche for aquatic species with little apparent connection to human welfare recalled the skepticism of *TVA v. Hill* and implied the wastefulness of strict controls imposed without consideration of the relative insignificance of the resource protected. With this comment, Scalia signaled that although in *ATA* he had hewed the line against consideration of costs in setting air standards to protect human health, he would not be inclined to rule against balancing of costs and benefits where the beneficiaries of regulation were largely economically insignificant aquatic creatures—continuing a pattern of hostility to regulation to protect ecological resources. Lazarus adroitly addressed the legal premise of Scalia's comment, but the disparaging tone of it was telling.[49]

Justice Breyer pressed Lazarus on the irrationality, in his view, of making policy without some consideration of benefits in relation to costs. Lazarus agreed that "available" in Section 316(b) permitted the agency to consider costs, as economic feasibility, but disagreed that the agency could balance those costs against the benefits. "But how is it . . . feasible if it has no benefits at all," Breyer responded. "Then we are going to reach our insane results." He came back to the point twice during Lazarus's argument.[50]

Justice Breyer's questions throughout oral argument searched for support for a weak form of cost-benefit comparison—a "reasonableness standard" to avoid "absurd results" or a "vague, grossly disproportionate test" rather than a more precise determination of efficiency. In an exchange with Lazarus, he hypothesized: "Don't do a formal cost-benefit analysis; don't try to evaluate the paramecium. . . . Do 'grossly' or 'wholly' or something." Justice Scalia too seemed intent on validating a weak form of CBA—one that minimized aquatic impacts "to the maximum extent reasonably possible" or avoided "wholly disproportionate" results. Taking these cues, counsel for the EPA argued in rebuttal that what the EPA had done here "was not among the most robust forms of cost-benefit analysis." The agency had only done a rough weighing to determine whether costs were "significantly greater than the benefits." It had kept "an obvious thumb on the environmental side of the scales." It hadn't tried "to assign artificial monetary values to everything." In short, it had done precisely what Scalia and Breyer seemed most comfortable with. In amicus briefs filed with the Court, anti-CBA groups had argued that the EPA had in fact used formal CBA to select among regulatory options and to identify "allocatively efficient regulation." But Scalia and Breyer accepted the EPA's contrary characterization of what it had done as CBA in its weak form—a characterization that was likely crucial to the case's outcome.[51]

In his opinion for the Court, Justice Scalia, joined by Chief Justice Roberts and Justices Thomas, Kennedy, and Alito, concluded that the statute was sufficiently ambiguous to permit the EPA's balancing of costs and benefits and reversed the lower court. A separate opinion by Justice Breyer, concurring in part and dissenting in part, largely agreed with the Court's views. A dissent by Justice Stevens, joined by Justices Souter and Ginsburg, argued that the statute precluded CBA. All three opinions turned at least in part on presumptions about the use of CBA and associated decision criteria (such as "reasonableness" and "efficiency") in regulatory policy making. These presumptions formed around competing views of CBA that reflected the public debates about efficiency and the role of economic methodologies in setting environmental goals. Although none of the opinions in *Entergy* spoke of "default rules" or "canons" or otherwise made these presumptions explicit, one can see evidence of them at work in shaping the conclusions in this case.[52]

JUSTICE BREYER'S PARTIAL CONCURRENCE

In his partial concurrence, Justice Breyer expanded on his performance in *ATA,* blending proregulatory sympathies with an economist's instinct for balance. The opinion provides a useful point of entry because it is transparent about the justice's views of the pros and cons of CBA and their effects on the interpretive enterprise and because those views reflect serious engagement with these issues in prior judicial opinions and academic writings. In largely siding with the majority, Breyer acknowledged that Congress had reason to limit reliance on CBA: CBA may unduly delay the regulatory process, underemphasize factors less susceptible to quantification (e.g., the value of preserving nonmarketable fish and shellfish), and reduce incentives for the development of advanced treatment technologies that might, "whatever the initial inefficiencies, . . . eventually mean cheaper, more effective cleanup." Breyer tabbed these criticisms to comments in the legislative history, but they echoed common proregulatory views.[53]

On the other side, true to his views at oral argument, Justice Breyer offered two reasons why Congress might not have wanted to forbid CBA entirely. A prohibition on CBA would be hard to enforce because every "real choice" requires such a comparison; furthermore, "an absolute prohibition would bring about irrational results." Breyer did not key these observations on the need for CBA to the legislative history; these pro-CBA arguments were his own, although he related the latter argument to Riverkeeper's concession in its brief that the statute does not require "spend[ing] billions [of dollars] to save one more fish." These were both powerful contentions, which, if true, would seem to compel some sort of cost-benefit comparison, not merely tolerate it. In *Entergy,* however, Breyer was content to use these pro-CBA arguments toward a more modest end.[54]

Justice Breyer concluded that the "statute does not require the Agency to compare costs with benefits when determining 'best available technology,' but neither does it expressly forbid such a comparison." He took on the strongest piece of legislative history against that conclusion—a written statement by Senator Muskie, the principal sponsor of the act—and determined after painstaking analysis that it gave the EPA the option of "a test of reasonableness." This test was the weak form of CBA that the EPA claimed to have used in its Phase II rule: presenting environmental benefits in nonmonetized terms and avoiding "results that are absurd or unreasonable in light of extreme disparities" while taking into account "Congress' technology-forcing objectives." To read Senator Muskie's statement and the statute differently, Breyer wrote, would "[threaten] to impose massive costs far in excess of any benefit." The "last ten percent" paradigm from Breyer's scholarly writing was not far below the surface.[55]

Extrastatutory precepts were at work in Justice Breyer's analysis. The reasons he offered for limiting CBA were largely imported from the legislative record, but his reasons for not prohibiting CBA were based on his own understanding of established norms or practices of rational decision making. The resulting pro-CBA presumption was a modest one. Breyer made clear in his concurrence that he was inviting the EPA not to recalibrate the technology-forcing policy that animates Section 316(b) but merely to temper that policy at the margins. His concern to limit the use of cost-benefit comparisons under Section 316(b) also appeared in the dissenting part of his opinion, in which he questioned the portion of the EPA's rule allowing variances from the national standard where the agency determined that a facility's costs would be "significantly greater than the benefits of complying." He would have remanded the case to the EPA either to affirm its traditional "wholly disproportionate" standard for case-by-case determinations or to better explain why it changed to the "significantly greater" formulation.[56]

JUSTICE SCALIA'S OPINION FOR THE COURT

In its selective treatment of the language and structure of the CWA and its limiting use of precedent, Justice Scalia's opinion for the Court reached a similar result by a different interpretive route. It reflected an unspoken preference in favor of the weak form of CBA used by the EPA—an extratextual preference, like Justice Breyer's, rooted in a concept of rational governance.

The Court framed its analysis under *Chevron*, which, as it explained, allowed the EPA's view of Section 316(b) to "[govern] if it is a reasonable interpretation of the statute—not necessarily the only possible interpretation, nor even the interpretation deemed most reasonable by the courts." As in his opinions in other cases in which the agency's interpretation has a regulation-limiting thrust, Justice Scalia's opinion for the Court used textualist tools to open the possibilities for language to make room for the interpretation, not foreclose it. Building on the arguments of industry and the EPA, the Court found ample support for the reasonableness of the EPA's interpretation in the CWA's language and structure. "Best technology available for minimizing adverse environmental impact" does not necessarily mean most stringent pollution-reducing technology; it could also mean most efficient. The modifying phrase "minimizing adverse environmental impact" does not necessarily preclude that meaning because "minimize" does not specify any particular degree of reduction. Therefore, Section 316(b) "does not unambiguously preclude cost-benefit analysis."[57]

The Court offered a similarly deferential analysis of Section 316(b)'s statutory context. Recall that in *ATA,* dealing with similar questions of statutory context, Scalia's opinion for the Court read other provisions of the CAA expressly authorizing consideration of costs as evidence that the NAAQS provision, which contained no such authorization, did not. The CWA offers a similar pattern. Statutory factors for some treatment standards specifically include comparison of costs and benefits but do not for "best technology" standards such as Section 316's BTA. But in *Entergy,* Scalia's opinion for the Court brushed aside arguments based on *ATA* that Section 316's silence on the question meant that CBA was foreclosed. Silence here seemed neutral, at best. It was not clear that the other "best technology" provisions precluded CBA, the Court argued, and even if they did, BTA had more modest environmental objectives and therefore "need not be interpreted to permit only what those other . . . tests permit." Moreover, "if silence . . . implies prohibition, then the EPA could not consider *any* factors in implementing [Section 316(b)]," because the provision lists no factors for consideration.[58]

But Justice Scalia's opinion for the Court halted the march of its own logic short of full endorsement of CBA by suggesting that statutory context may limit the kind of CBA available under Section 316(b). Having read silence as authorizing the use of CBA in this case, the Court commented that "other arguments may be available to preclude . . . a rigorous form of cost-benefit analysis." It is not clear why the Court bothered to make this observation; as it was quick to note in the opinion, it was not necessary. Because in the Court's view the EPA didn't undertake a "rigorous form" of CBA in its Phase II standard-setting, there was no need to opine on whether the EPA had the authority to do so. The exact rationale for this addendum was equally mysterious. The Court didn't specify the "other arguments" that might be available but simply referred to the portion of the opinion on related provisions.[59]

The reason for this unexplained and analytically dubious move to suggest preclusion of "rigorous" CBA is unclear. It may have been to hold Justice

Kennedy with the majority. Riverkeeper's counsel Richard Lazarus noted that at oral argument Kennedy "seemed to grasp the difference between weak and strong CBA . . . and seemed inclined to support a position that drew such a distinction or at least left the door open." A second explanation is that the Court's concession was to acknowledge Justice Breyer's complementary position. Certainly its effect was to move the Court's opinion closer to Breyer's, despite their differences in interpretive approach.[60]

A third explanation is that the Court's caveat mirrored the extralegal views of its author on the limits of CBA. In a 1987 lecture delivered at the University of Houston, Justice Scalia described a broad concept of cost-benefit balancing as "a weighing of all the desirable effects of a proposed action against all the undesirable effects, whether or not they are susceptible of being expressed in economic terms." He distinguished this concept from CBA "in the narrow sense . . . of quantifying all the pro and con effects of a proposed action in dollar and cents terms." CBA in this narrow sense, he said, "is feasible, and usually determinative, if the pros and cons are purely economic ones." CBA in the broader sense, however, is appropriate for "weighing the impact of the proposed action upon two quite different social values—for example . . . aesthetic values versus full employment, or minor health risk versus low consumer prices." This earlier, broader CBA "has *always* been . . . part of rational administration," while the rigorous form of CBA is new and narrowly applicable. This distinction prefigures the line that Scalia's opinion for the Court in *Entergy* suggests between the CBA it sanctions in the silence of Section 316(b) and the "rigorous form" of CBA that it does not.[61]

In addition to its proagency gloss on the language and structure of Section 316(b), the Court interpreted prior decisions to make room for CBA in a statute's silence. It limited *ATA* to its unique statutory circumstances and foreclosed the potential reading of the Court's opinion in that case as establishing a general presumption against considering costs against environmental benefits in cases of silence or ambiguity. In effect, eight years after the fact, the Court responded to Justice Breyer's concerns about the broad inferences that might be drawn from *ATA* by cutting those inferences off. Similarly, it neutralized *American Textile,* reading the case as permitting while not requiring CBA. In doing so, it elevated Justice Rehnquist's characterization of the Court's holding in that case, rejecting the anti-CBA presumption that the Second Circuit in *Entergy* drew from that case. That move alone represented an important, deliberate evolution in the Court's position.[62]

In the face of a statute that was arguably but not clearly ambiguous on the issue, the preference of both Justice Scalia, writing for the Court, and Justice Breyer was to allow, but not require, a rough weighing of costs and benefits in setting technology-based standards. This preference was shaped by background understandings—explicit in Breyer's opinion, implicit in Scalia's—about the social value of this intuitive form of CBA and its established (Scalia's "we have always done it") or inevitable (Breyer's "we cannot avoid it") use in decision making. This preference was not raised to the level of a formal presumption, default rule, or canon. Its influence in the interpretive enterprise was more subtle, but palpable nonetheless.

JUSTICE STEVENS'S DISSENT

Based on skepticism of CBA that has both statutory and extrastatutory sources, Justice Stevens's dissent concludes that Congress intended to preclude use of CBA. The dissent largely talks past the Court's and Breyer's opinions by focusing its attack on the strong form of CBA—CBA as "typically performed by the EPA" requiring monetization of costs and benefits and maximization of net benefits—not the weak form sanctioned by the Court. In a footnote near its end, the dissent acknowledges the EPA's reliance on "a mild variant of cost-benefit analysis" but cryptically declares that fact "irrelevant" to the legal conclusion.[63]

Having established its target, the dissent offers two objections to CBA drawn from the common pool of such objections: the comparative difficulty of quantifying environmental benefits and the tendency of CBA, "often, if not always," to favor results that do "not maximize environmental protection." These criticisms directly support the dissent's conclusion that CBA "fundamentally weakens" Section 316(b)'s ambitious environmental "mandate" and therefore Congress meant to preclude it. Although these criticisms are also among the reasons for limiting CBA that Justice Breyer mentions in his opinion, the dissent does not balance them with pro-CBA considerations and thus gives them unqualified sway.[64]

In the silence of Section 316(b) on the CBA issue, Justice Stevens found support for his conclusion in the structure and legislative history of the CWA. Far from being agnostic, Congress in the CWA viewed CBA with even more than the usual suspicion ("special skepticism") and "controlled its use accordingly," limiting it to a transitional role in the regulatory suite. Justice Stevens anchored his legal argument in the presumption-suggesting language in *American Textile* and in the interpretive formula of *ATA,* turning Justice Scalia's own elephants-in-mouseholes trope squarely against him. "We should not treat a provision's silence as an implicit source of cost-benefit authority, particularly when such authority is elsewhere expressly granted and it has the potential to fundamentally alter an agency's approach to regulation." Because CBA would undermine Section 316(b)'s ambitious environmental protection mandate with "tangential economic efficiency concerns," *ATA* requires that Section 316(b)'s silence be read as prohibition.[65]

The skepticism about CBA that animated the dissent, particularly the assumption that CBA is inimical to robust environmental regulation, reflects a view that is still widespread among environmentalists. But because the dissent focused on the strong form of CBA and assumed that the weak form is objectionable on the same grounds, it did not fully engage the Court's opinion and Justice Breyer's concurrence. It closed ranks against any form of balancing that might compromise the strong harm-avoidance norm the dissenters find implicit in Section 316(b)'s technology standard.

Entergy marked a shift in the Court's orientation toward cost-benefit balancing in environmental and related safety regulation. Abandoning the seeds of an anti-CBA canon in *American Textile* and also the preclusive thrust of the no-elephants-in-mouseholes rationale of *ATA*, the *Entergy* Court countenanced an agency's use of CBA in the face of the statutory silence on the issue. Perhaps an anti-CBA presumption based on *American Textile* was, as Richard Lazarus believed, "the stuff of enviro[nmentalist] dreams, and their academic cheerleaders" without convincing support in the language and holding of that case. But *American Textile* would have given the Court much to work with, if it had been so inclined. The case was reduced instead to an arguing point for the dissenters. So too did the Court retreat from *ATA*, limiting it to its particular statutory context.[66]

Reduced to its basic cultural elements, the decision in *Entergy* represented the elevation of mastery values over harmony values. Electric generating plants are a collective technological undertaking to power an advanced industrial civilization. This undertaking drives the displacement and appropriation of vast amounts of natural resources, including the aquatic species and ecosystems harmed by the water cooling systems in *Entergy*. Instead of reading the statute as requiring us to do all we feasibly can to protect these species and ecosystems, the Court read it to allow us to do less where regulation would impose substantial costs and bring scant quantifiable use benefits. For Justice Scalia, the ecological assets were relegated to "snail darter" status. The difference between the actual snail darter case, *TVA v. Hill*, and *Entergy*, was that in *TVA v. Hill* Justice Powell's interpretative bid to avoid "absurd results" attracted only one other justice. In *Entergy*, a majority of the Court found a way to let agency "rationality" reign. The finding of statutory ambiguity sufficient to accommodate the agency's interpretation in *Entergy* was less strained than Powell's interpretative effort to avoid "absurd results" in *TVA v. Hill*. But the Court's opinion and Justice Breyer's concurrence both had to stretch to find that ambiguity.

For environmentalists, the pro-CBA leaning of *Entergy* threatens the urgency and priority of their concerns. The threat seems strongest in ecological protection, where the problem of quantifying the benefits of protective measures is pervasive and ecological harms risk invisibility; *Entergy* offers a poster child for arguments that monetization skews results against elements, like the nonuse values of aquatic systems, which cannot readily be monetized. But the threat extends on a different level to the protection of human health as well. The deeper objection of environmentalists is to the balancing of environmental harms against the costs of preventing them to produce an "optimal" outcome. That decision process ignores the pricelessness, nonfungibility, or irreplaceability of life, human or nonhuman. By contrast, as Douglas Kysar puts it, all-we-can-feasibly-do standards of the sort environmentalists argued for in *Entergy*, refuse "to deny the irreplaceability of life or to embrace the utilitarian notion that an 'optimal' amount of death ever can be identified." This preferred regulatory approach perfectly captures environmentalism's transformative aspiration.[67]

Even if read as falling short of an endorsement of efficiency-seeking CBA, *Entergy* challenges this aspiration. Like its stricter cousin, the weak form of CBA associated with basic rationality is rooted in prevailing notions of what people value and what trade-offs make sense. It encourages us to reject harm-avoiding options, like the closed-circuit cooling systems in *Entergy*, which are economically and technologically doable, because they offend conventional judgments about the worth of anonymous creatures (even billions of them) that may lie in the path of progress. It thus has the potential to check movement toward a more open and generous stance on our obligations to the environmental other as well as to our fellow humans.[68]

The cultural appeal of this basic rationality check is strong, however, as suggested by the joint embrace of conservative justice Scalia and progressive justice Breyer. Rejection of it risks having environmentalists and the laws that they have secured seen as "selfish" or "extreme." Riverkeeper was sensitive to this risk in *Entergy*, agreeing that the command to "minimize" did not require the EPA "to spend billions to save one more fish or plankton." But by relegating balancing to the margins of policy, the concession also expressed the fear widespread among environmentalists that broad consideration of costs and benefits would lead to wholesale discounting of their concerns.

The legacy of *Entergy* was complicated by Justice Scalia's dissent in *EME Homer*, which conflated consideration of cost-effectiveness in implementation with CBA in the setting of goals. Scalia accused the majority of forcing "cost-benefit analysis" on a textually resistant statute, although *EME Homer* was not about balancing costs and benefits. Consistent with this view of the key issue in the case as well as his preferred result, the touchstone of his analysis was *ATA* (consideration of costs in goal setting) rather than *Chevron* (cost-effective implementation). He made no mention at all of *Entergy*, in which the agency had argued for CBA in the context of a similarly complex statute, and in which he had written for the Court in agreement.[69]

It is not clear whether Justice Scalia's dissent reflected a deeper disaffection with cost-benefit balancing or cost considerations generally. He may simply have been acting as the honest textualist in his interpretation of the CAA's Good Neighbor Provision, helped by his revival of *ATA*'s presumption against consideration of costs. Or he may have oriented to the fact that in *EME Homer*, unlike *Chevron*, *ATA*, or *Entergy*, it was industry, not the environmentalists, which sought to keep efficiency out. Three times in the opinion, he characterized the EPA's approach, which puts more of the burden of reductions on states with less strict controls, using a close variant of the Marxist phrase "from each according to his abilities." As Dan Farber pointed out, the characterization seemed silly, because industry should benefit from reduced compliance costs. But it inevitably conveyed the sense of egalitarianism on the march.[70]

THESE "EFFICIENCY" cases show the Court's comfort with market-based approaches in environmental settings and its increasing receptivity to cost-benefit balancing. The Court has not adopted a strong pro-CBA presumption, but in *Entergy* it moved in that direction. CBA advocates Livermore and Revesz press for more generous recognition, including reinterpretation of the classic environmentalist win in *ATA* to permit CBA where it would support a more protective outcome. Meanwhile, the persistent and pervasive use of CBA within the executive branch suggests that, notwithstanding the objections of environmentalists and other health and safety advocates, CBA has become the dominant policy discourse.

Since *Chevron*, acceptance of market mechanisms has become widespread (though not universal) among environmentalists, as reflected in the alignments of *EME v. Homer*. Some groups have also shown the willingness and capacity to use CBA as an advocacy tool, but resistance within the environmental community remains strong. Environmentalists object not only to the lax policy outcomes they expect from CBA (the target of Livermore and Revesz's revisionist interpretation of *ATA*) but also to the values choices they see embedded in the methodology (e.g., CBA's rejection of duties to avoid harm; reduction of value to market equivalents). Against this resistance, Revesz and Livermore argue that CBA offers environmentalists a policy tool that they can use to their advantage and that their very use of it will help ensure it does not give too little weight to their concerns. To succeed in their mission, Revesz and Livermore will likely have to convince environmentalists that CBA is or can be consistent with their values as well as conducive to the outcomes they seek.

CHAPTER SIX

Standing

A S WE SAW IN CHAPTER I, environmentalists subscribe to the ecological model—the idea that nature is fragile and interdependent; human disturbances are likely to have broad, harmful consequences; and those consequences can be distant in place and time. In the absence of conclusive evidence of harmful effects, environmentalists are inclined to presume them. The ecological model is associated with the cultural values of collectivism and harmony. Aldo Leopold and others have linked this model directly to a responsibility to care for the "biotic community" or "the land organism": understanding the close interdependencies within the biotic community, they argue, supports the extension of ethical consideration to that community— Leopold's "land ethic." Environmentalists often use the rhetoric of altruism, stressing action for the "common good" or moral regard for the environmental "other," in arguing for public constraints on private interests to protect vulnerable, interconnected natural systems.[1]

The alternative model is atomistic. It projects a world of discrete features and events, contained within a narrow physical or temporal sphere, with largely individual or local significance. It assumes the natural world is resilient rather than fragile. Environmental disturbances are not expected to radiate broadly through a larger system. Proponents of this model emphasize boundaries, distances, and distinctions among components of natural systems and the actions of their human inhabitants. The atomistic model too is associated with a set of cultural values, but these values stress human agency. Those resisting collective intervention to protect natural systems often use the language of individualism, stressing the merits of autonomous choice, pursuit of self-interest, and active self-assertion within a rights-based system. These voices also emphasize the hierarchical claims of humans in the appropriation of resources (e.g., "people before fish"). They may even acknowledge, at some level, the systemic nature of environmental problems but resist the regulation urged by environmentalists as inimical to autonomy-mastery values.[2]

The ecological/interdependence model has potentially sweeping implications for law. It is more likely to assume that there are secondary effects or externalities from environmental disturbances, even though they may be difficult to predict or measure, and it supports measures to control those externalities. Supreme Court justices who have shown some sympathy for this worldview (including Justices Stevens, Blackmun, Souter, Ginsburg, Breyer, and sometimes Kennedy) tend to favor more open access to the courts, a broad scope of federal regulatory power, public limitations on private property rights, and generous interpretations of environmental regulatory authority. Justices who have resisted the ecological model (for example, Chief Justice Roberts and Justices Scalia, Thomas, Alito, and sometimes Kennedy) show contrary tendencies on these issues. Against the claims of environmentalists, they promote limits on judicial access and federal power, protection of property rights, and narrow constructions of regulatory authority.

The opposing atomistic model is associated with pre-ecological common law notions of injury, private causes of action, and property rights. Common law actions such as negligence, nuisance, and trespass traditionally involved immediate and obvious injuries such as bodily trauma or property damage. These harms were limited in space and time and did not depend on complicated causal relationships. Environmentalists argue that the new ecological model requires a subtler, more extensive and systemic view of injury. They accuse justices that draw on common law traditions in addressing issues arising under modern environmental laws not only of rejecting an ecological worldview supported by modern science but also of using a relict atomism to protect and foster values opposed to environmentalism.

In this chapter and in Chapters 7 and 8, I trace the contest between these models in cases on standing, federalism, and property rights.

Standing

Federal law gives environmentalists two broad judicial avenues for challenging actions that may damage the environment. Any person who is "adversely affected" or "aggrieved" may seek judicial review of federal agency actions under the Administrative Procedure Act, which authorizes federal courts to set aside agency actions they find unreasonable or unlawful. Under the citizen suit provisions in most federal environmental statutes, "any person" or "any citizen" may also bring an action to compel a federal official to perform a mandatory duty or to enforce the statute against a violator. Citizen suits were among the institutional innovations of environmental legislation and were included to ensure that the executive branch would scrupulously implement and enforce the legislation as Congress intended.[3]

A plaintiff's allegation of unlawful action, however, is not enough to give that plaintiff access to a federal court. The plaintiff must also have "standing"—historically, the qualification of a party literally to stand before the court to present its case. The Court bases its modern standing requirement on the Constitution's limitation of the federal judicial power to "cases" and "controversies." The specifics of the Court's reading of this limitation have evolved in decisions beginning in the 1920s. The Court's recent formulations, as a constitutional minimum, require that parties bringing claims in federal court show a concrete injury-in-fact that is caused by the illegality complained of and able to be redressed by judicial action—in short: injury, causation, and redressability. In addition, the Court has required as a prudential matter that claims be within the zone of interests protected by the statue under which the claim is brought.[4]

This three-pronged test has been stable for several decades; it has also been controversial. Commentators have accused it—with particular emphasis on the "injury-in-fact" requirement—of improperly injecting "common law conceptions of harm into the Constitution" and of inviting normative judgments about what actions are worthy of going forward under the guise of an objective standard. Moreover, although giving the outward appearance of precision, the standing test has shown a high degree of indeterminacy as applied by the justices. Repeatedly, justices come to markedly different conclusions about whether the standing requirement has been met, a pattern of divergence that feeds the suspicion that "value-laden judgments" are at work. Environmental cases seem especially susceptible to culturally inflected standing decisions, for reasons discussed below.[5]

The Court's rationale for its standing requirement is at least threefold. First, the requirement limits the matters coming before the federal courts, which struggle to manage their caseload with existing resources. Second, the requirement of concrete injury helps shape matters in a way that is suited to effective judicial resolution. "This requirement . . . preserves the vitality of the adversarial process by assuring both that the parties before the court have an actual, as opposed to professed, stake in the outcome, and that 'The legal questions presented . . . will be resolved, not in the rarefied atmosphere of a debating society, but in a concrete factual context conducive to a realistic appreciation of the consequences of judicial action.'"[6]

Third, the standing requirement helps maintain the separation of powers among branches of the federal government by confining "the Judicial Branch to its proper, limited role in the constitutional framework of Government." In its 1968 opinion in *Flast v. Cohen,* the Court wrote that standing did not raise separation-of-powers concerns; its only purpose was to ensure the suitability of disputes for judicial resolution, as above.[7] Soon afterward, however, the Court reconsidered, recognizing a connection between standing and separation of powers that it continues periodically to endorse.[8] For some justices, led by Justice Scalia, the separation-of-powers rationale for standing is paramount, with direct implications for the viability of suits to enforce ameliorative public legislation, such as the federal environmental statutes.

Justice Scalia made standing and separation of powers a signature theme even before he joined the court. In 1983, while still a judge on the Court of Appeals for the District of Columbia Circuit, he published an article in the *Suffolk University Law Review* titled "The Doctrine of Standing as an Essential Element of the Separation of Powers." The article claimed that standing was "a crucial and inseparable element" of the separation of powers, "whose disregard will inevitably produce—as it has during the past few decades—an overjudicialization of the processes of self-governance." By "overjudicialization" he meant the courts' taking on cases brought by the beneficiaries of "a general program (such as environmental protection) which will enhance the welfare of many individuals." The role of the courts, he maintained, was "protecting individuals and minorities against impositions of the majority," not enforcing such impositions at the behest of the majority, the general beneficiaries who he presumed would have effective recourse through the political branches. The implementation and enforcement of federal public interest legislation was primarily the job of the executive branch, not the courts, even where Congress has specified a judicial role for citizen enforcement, as in the citizen suit provisions of environmental statutes.[9]

Then-judge Scalia concluded with a remark that has etched itself indelibly in standing lore: "Does what I have said mean that, so long as no minority interests are affected, 'important legislative purposes . . . [can be] lost or misdirected in the vast hallways of the federal bureaucracy?' Of course it does—and a good thing, too." Observing that "yesterday's herald is today's bore," Scalia argued that the executive branch's discretion to lose or misdirect "once-heralded programs" in light of changing political circumstances was progressive—"one of the prime engines of social change."[10]

Whether this misdirection of legislative purposes is a "good thing" is much debated. Executive branch nonimplementation may be objectionable under a competing separation-of-powers rationale, as Cass Sunstein has written.

It is Congress's power to write the laws; the president's Article II obligation to "take care that the Laws be faithfully executed" includes the power to temper legislative enactments but not to rewrite them. Sunstein also questioned the political process assumptions on which Scalia's "good thing" argument rested. Executive agencies that lose or misdirect congressional policies may be reflecting the influence of special interests (e.g., regulated parties), not majority sentiment. And diffuse beneficiaries may have difficulty in organizing to express their interests in the political system. Congress had such political process failures in mind when it added the citizen suit provisions, assigning a corrective function to the courts.[11]

Merits aside, the antiregulatory thrust of Scalia's comment was clear. He did not say that "less regulation is better," but he did stack the deck against environmentalists and others seeking to advance congressionally enacted regulatory policies.[12] Those subject to regulation in the public interest presumptively have standing as being among the "individuals and minorities" entitled to protection by the courts; the beneficiaries of regulation do not, unless they can claim "minority" status by showing some particularized injury not shared by other beneficiaries. The courts are to guard against overenforcement by government officials; underenforcement is generally a matter for the political branches. "Asymmetry on this point [threatens to] translate judicial antipathy to regulation into administrative law."[13]

The future justice's provocative pronouncement prefigured his Court opinions in *Lujan v. Defenders of Wildlife II* and *Bennett v. Spear,* which I analyze in this chapter. It also revealed the values that would animate his views in the Court's standing decisions. It elevated autonomy (individual rights) over collectivism (public goods). To the extent that it would narrow judicial access to environmentalists seeking to stop development, whether by private or public entities, it also privileged mastery over harmony values. Justices receptive to opposing values reflected in public legislation would resist Scalia's campaign, supporting a more active role for the federal courts in vindicating protective legislative policies.[14]

Environmental standing cases have proved particularly troublesome and divisive for the Court because the ecological model that modern environmental statutes reflect does not fit easily with the Court's traditional injury-based test. These statutes often address systemic harms with attenuated lines of causation that differ from the direct injuries typical of common law litigation. They are more difficult to reduce to the required concrete injury-in-fact suffered by an individual plaintiff as the result of a specific action or actions by the defendant. Also, as environmental law pioneer Joseph Sax pointed out, the requirement that environmental claims be presented through individuals with an immediate and personal relationship to an affected resource seems out of keeping with the ecological thrust of these laws. In the wake of the Court's decision in *Sierra Club,* he wrote:

> The Court majority seems oblivious to the central message of the current environmental literature—that the issues to engage our serious attention are risks of long-term, large scale, practically irreversible disruptions of ecosystems. By denying to persons who wish to assert those issues the right to come into court, and granting standing *only* to one who has a stake in his own present use and enjoyment, the Court reveals how little it appreciated the real meaning of the test case it had before it.

The important risks at stake were systemic risks, not personal risks. By forcing standing into a narrowly instrumentalist frame, the Court mistook the environmentalist enterprise.[15]

The Court's standing doctrine and its environmental jurisprudence have evolved in a kind of dynamic tension over the last forty years. Many if not most of the Court's important standing decisions during this period have come in environmental cases, several of them in citizen suits. Because of the pervasive role of competing cultural values and concepts of governance, these standing cases have high symbolic content. They have been particularly revealing of the underlying views of the justices not only on the proper role of the judiciary but also on the urgency of environmental issues, the importance of the regulatory statutes that address them, and the salience of the ecological model on which those statutes are based.[16]

Sierra Club: A Standing Classic Revisited

Sierra Club was an early test of ecocentrism's ability to penetrate the ingrained anthropocentrism of legal institutions. Viewed more conventionally, the decision was also one of several environmental standing cases in the early days of the movement that signaled ready access to the courts. Although the Court required injury as a condition of standing, all that was required was a showing that a member of the Sierra Club used the area near the proposed ski resort for recreational, aesthetic, or other purposes. Sierra Club was easily able to meet this modest demand on its return to the district court.

The case remained something of a disappointment to environmentalists, however, both because it failed to embrace the ecocentric standing posed by Justice Douglas and because, for the reasons above, its consideration of standing seemed insensitive to the systemic nature of the risks to the valley. Justice Blackmun's dissent addressed this second shortcoming. Although he proposed a seemingly more modest doctrinal change than did Justice Douglas in that visionary dissent, Blackmun was more radically aligned with the notion of interdependence. Douglas argued that guardians representing the interests of a place or thing in nature should come with close personal experience of that place or thing—a qualification that put his opinion quite close, in practice if not in theory, to the majority's requirement of injury based on actual use of the resource. Justice Blackmun would have required no such personal connection. The litigant needed only be one "who speaks knowingly for the environmental values he asserts," not necessarily a present user of the resource. Limiting standing to "the real 'user,'" he believed, would tend to select for those with an economic stake in development, who would be unlikely to take the long view in protecting the whole. He ended his opinion with the "particularly pertinent observation and warning of John Donne":

> No man is an Iland, intire of itself; every man is a peece of the Continent, a part of the maine; if a Clod bee washed away by the Sea, Europe is the lesse, as well as if a Promontorie were, as well as if a Mannor of thy friends or of thine owne were; any man's death diminishes me, because I am involved in Mankinde; And therefore never send to know for whom the bell tolls; It tolls for thee.

This passage by the eighteenth-century poet and divine uses the connectedness of the natural landscape as a metaphor for relationships among humans, but the image of pervasive interdependence anticipates the modern ecological worldview. Justice Blackmun would continue to advocate for imaginative restructuring of legal arrangements consistent with this worldview in future environmental standing and property rights cases.[17]

SCRAP: Standing for All Who Breathe

In 1973, a year after *Sierra Club,* the Court rendered perhaps its most liberal version of standing in *United States v. Students Challenging Regulatory Agency Procedures (SCRAP)*. In that case, a group of law students sought review of the refusal by the Interstate Commerce Commission (ICC) to prepare an environmental impact statement before allowing a nationwide railroad freight rate surcharge to take effect. The students alleged that they "'[u]se[d] the forests, rivers, streams, mountains, and other resources surrounding the Washington Metropolitan area . . . for camping, hiking, fishing, sightseeing, and other recreational [and] aesthetic purposes,' and that these uses have been adversely affected by the increased freight rates."

They also claimed that the air they breathed in the Washington, DC, metropolitan area was more polluted as a result of the rate increase and that the increase had forced them to pay more for consumer products and more in taxes.[18]

A three-judge district court upheld the students' standing in less than a page. The court focused on allegations that the rate increase would disturb the students' enjoyment of streams and forests in the Washington area. The case was different from *Sierra Club*, it said, because the students alleged that they actually used the parks and forests they claimed were affected. The court did not explain the causal links that it supposed connected the rate increase to adverse impacts on the forests and parks, except to note that the theory of the students' case was that the rate increase would discourage the use of recyclable goods. It also brushed aside concerns that the students' allegations of injury did not distinguish them from many others with the same interests.[19]

Before the Supreme Court on review, the ICC and the railroads argued that the students' claims of injury fell far short of what *Sierra Club* required for standing. First, the claims were "vague and speculative"—sweeping, unproven, and, in the view of the ICC and the railroads, unprovable. There was no showing of how or to what extent the temporary rate increase would actually cause harm to the DC-area resources the students used. Second, the standing claims were, as U.S. Solicitor General Griswold said at oral argument, "entirely general. It is not said which forests, rivers, streams, or mountains. We don't even have a particular valley as we did in the *Mineral King* case last year. . . . It's obvious that these allegations could be made by any member of the public who wishes to make them." The students were merely seeking to vindicate their own policy preferences, which *Sierra Club* made clear was not a permissible basis for access to the federal courts. Nevertheless, the Court held that the students had alleged injury-in-fact sufficient to give them standing, although it reversed the lower court's issuance of a preliminary injunction against the rate increase.[20]

As in *Sierra Club*, the Court framed the standing issue as whether the students met the requirement of Section 10 of the Administrative Procedure Act that a person seeking judicial review be "adversely affected" or "aggrieved"—the statutory analogue of the constitutional standing requirement, which the Court has read to include the same elements of injury-in-fact and causation. Justice Stewart's opinion for the Court rejected the solicitor general's claim that the students' injuries were too general and too speculative to support standing. It granted that the scope of the impacts in this case was unlike the "specific and geographically limited" action in *Sierra Club*: "Rather than a limited group of persons who used a picturesque valley in California, all persons who utilize the scenic resources of the country, and indeed all who breathe its air, could claim harm similar to that alleged by the environmental groups here." But the universal scope of the injury did not mean that the students did not have standing. To hold otherwise, the Court concluded, would have the perverse effect "that the most injurious and widespread Government actions could be questioned by nobody." The Court showed no concern that by taking the case to protect broad majoritarian interests the courts would be intruding upon the policy prerogatives of the elected branches of government. That concern would await expression by critics of the decision, future-justice Scalia among them.[21]

The Court acknowledged the "attenuated line of causation" between the ICC's action and the "eventual injury" alleged but found the line strong enough to support standing. The influence of the ecological worldview was evident. The Court did not dwell on the contingencies in the "attenuated line of causation" leading from a 2.5 percent temporary nationwide surcharge in freight rates to increased deforestation, litter in the parks, and air pollution. Instead it accepted the plausibility of a highly interconnected system in which increased freight rates cause reduced recycling and adverse impacts of reduced recycling on natural resources ripple throughout the nation. Effects on the students individually might be small, but that did not make them less real or creditable ("an identifiable trifle is enough"). It would be hard to imagine a version of environmental injury and causation more encompassing.[22]

This was not, however, a worldview shared by Justice White in a dissenting opinion on the standing issue that was joined by Chief Justice Burger and Justice Rehnquist. The dissenters saw the majority as having abandoned common sense, "willing[ly] . . . suspend[ing] its judgment in the dim hope" that the alleged injuries and their nexus to the rate increase could be proved at trial. The allegations were "so remote, speculative, and insubstantial in fact" that they could not be a basis for standing. They were little different in effect from the allegations of general interest that the Court had found wanting in *Sierra Club*: a subterfuge for members of the public to litigate any official decision in which they might be interested but had no real personal stake.[23]

Nor was the Court's ecological worldview shared by future-justice Antonin Scalia. In his 1983 Suffolk law review article, he ridiculed *SCRAP*'s acceptance of the protracted causal chain linking the disputed rate surcharge with the claimed insults to the law students' environment—degradation of forests, caused by litter, caused by decreased recycling, caused by increased cost of recycled goods, caused by the general rate surcharge. The Court's acceptance of this thin account of injury and causation violated the separation of powers by allowing it to intrude into policy areas reserved for the other branches of government. Scalia took heart, however, from post-*SCRAP* opinions by the Court that explicitly acknowledged the relationship between standing and separation of powers. He predicted that the *SCRAP*-era approach to standing would "not endure."[24]

After his appointment to the Court in 1986, Justice Scalia worked with like-minded justices to curtail standing in public interest cases, with particular attention to the perceived excesses of citizen litigation in environmental cases. A warning shot came in 1990 with the Court's denial of standing in a nonenvironmental case, *Whitmore v. Arkansas*. Chief Justice Rehnquist's opinion for the Court in that case painted the student's claims in *SCRAP* as "probably the most attenuated injury conferring [Article] III standing." The decision in *SCRAP*, it said, "went to the very outer limit of the law." In the decade to follow, Rehnquist would join a series of opinions written by Scalia that, without purporting to overrule *SCRAP*, would shrink the world of standing for environmental plaintiffs to a fraction of its size.[25]

The first of these Scalia-authored environmental standing opinions, *Lujan v. Defenders of Wildlife* (*Lujan I*), came later the same year as *Whitmore* and brought a similar message. By a five to four vote in *Lujan I,* the Court rejected standing for environmentalists who claimed to use public lands that would be affected by the Bureau of Land Management's decisions to open up certain areas for mining development. Justice Scalia's opinion for the Court declared that the allegations of geographic nexus were too vague to withstand a summary judgment motion by defendants; the environmental plaintiffs claimed to use "unspecified portions of an immense tract of territory," on only some portions of which mining would likely occur. These allegations were insufficiently precise to give standing. The Court distinguished *SCRAP* (which had approved broad allegations of injury) on a technical point—that the standing issue in that case had been decided on a motion to dismiss, which "presumes that general allegations embrace those specific facts that are necessary to support the claim," rather than a motion for summary judgment, as in *Lujan I*, which required the environmental plaintiffs to "set forth specific facts showing that there is a genuine issue for trial." But it took a passing shot at *SCRAP*, describing it as a decision whose "expansive expression of what would suffice for [standing] has never since been emulated by the Court" and relegating it to the limbo of precedents that have lost their influence with a majority of the justices.[26]

Lujan II: Scalia, Agonist

A second *Lujan v. Defenders of Wildlife* (*Lujan II*), decided two years later, marked the high point of Justice Scalia's standing offensive and, not incidentally, a low point in the Court's openness to environmentalist perspectives.[27] In his opinion for the Court in *Lujan II*, concluding that environmental plaintiffs lacked standing, Scalia articulated a vigorous commitment to limited judicial access for beneficiaries of environmental legislation; voiced a corresponding skepticism of claims of universal injury of the sort credited in *SCRAP I*; and expressed special solicitude for the standing of the regulated community—all in a tone suggesting disdain for the environmentalist enterprise.

The plaintiffs in *Lujan II* sought to enjoin a rule issued by the secretary of the Interior limiting protections of the federal Endangered Species Act (ESA) to actions taken in the United States or on the high seas. The secretary's contested rule reversed a prior interpretation that ESA obligations extend to actions by federal officials supporting development projects in foreign countries. Plaintiffs sought reinstatement of the previous interpretation that required Section 7 consultation on U.S. actions that might affect threatened or endangered species abroad.[28]

Plaintiffs brought their action under the citizen suit provision of the ESA, which authorizes suits by "any person" against the "United States and any other governmental instrumentality or agency . . . who is alleged to be in violation" of the statute. They included Defenders of Wildlife and individual members of the group (collectively "Defenders") who claimed to be injured by Interior's new rule because they had visited habitats of endangered species in foreign countries threatened by U.S.-funded development projects and intended someday to visit these habitats again in hopes of seeing the species. Amy Skilbred, a wildlife biologist studying rare animals and their habitats, had traveled to Sri Lanka and observed the habitat of the endangered Asian elephant and leopard at what was now the site of a large U.S.-funded hydroelectric project. She intended to return and hoped "to be more fortunate in spotting . . . [the] elephant and leopard." Joyce Kelly had gone to Egypt and observed the habitat of the endangered Nile crocodile in the shadow of the Aswan dam, which was now being rehabilitated with U.S. assistance. She intended to go again and hoped "to observe the crocodile directly."[29]

The district court held that Defenders had standing and that the ESA applied to U.S.-sponsored projects abroad. The Court of Appeals for the Eighth Circuit affirmed on both issues. Defenders had standing because two of its members—Skilbred and Kelly—had made visits to the sites of contested projects, providing the geographical precision the Court had found lacking in *Lujan I*.[30]

In its arguments to the Court on review, the United States emphasized the contingencies in Defenders' standing claims. The members who had visited areas abroad had not shown that they had specific plans to return to those areas to actually witness the harm to species of interest to them. Nor had they shown that those species would indeed be jeopardized by U.S.-aided projects or that any adverse effects from those projects could be traced to the actions of U.S. officials, given the multiplicity of funding sources and decisionmakers, most of them foreign, involved in these projects. As Justice Scalia commented helpfully for the government during oral argument, "Well, this sounds very much like the house that Jack built. (Laughter.)" These contingencies, the government argued, cast doubt on whether Defenders had suffered any injuries at all, made the causal connection between any injuries and the secretary's rule "highly indirect," and made it unlikely that those injuries would be redressed by invalidation of the rule.[31]

Defenders focused on connections between their members' interests in endangered species abroad and the actions of U.S. officials that could meet the established injury-causation-redressability test. Chief among these connections were the past and intended future visits of members to sites of concern abroad ("geographic nexus"). But there were others, including ecological linkages transmitting harms to species from remote actions ("ecosystem nexus") and connections between those with special interests in studying or observing endangered species and the continuation of those species in the world ("animal" and "vocational nexus"). These overlapping "nexus" theories, Defenders argued, presented a network of relationships connecting Defenders' personal and professional interests to actions of U.S. officials. The injuries communicated through this network would be redressed, at least partially, by declaring Interior's rule invalid because that rule prevented Section 7 consultation that could reduce the risk to species abroad. Justice Scalia's opinion in the case would dismiss Defenders' "nexus" theories with a disdainful flourish, but other justices would find substance in them.

The voting among the justices was complicated. Justice Scalia wrote an opinion for the Court concluding that Defenders lacked standing and reversing the Eighth Circuit. His opinion dealt in separate sections with injury-in-fact, redressability, and "procedural injury." Chief Justice Rehnquist and Justices White and Thomas joined his entire opinion. Justices Souter and Kennedy joined all of it except the section on redressability, which they considered unnecessary given the Court's conclusion that Defenders had not shown injury-in-fact. Kennedy also filed a concurrence, joined by Souter, offering separate views on Defenders' nexus theories and on the role of Congress in defining injury and causation for standing. Justice Blackmun wrote a dissent, joined by Justice O'Connor. Justice Stevens wrote separately, also disagreeing with the Court's decision on standing but concurring in the result because he believed that Interior's rule was a correct interpretation of the law.

Justice Scalia's opinion for the Court rehearsed the separation-of-powers rationale for limited access to the federal courts and the three-part injury-causation-redressability test as the "constitutional minimum" for standing. This much was routine. Then the opinion introduced the distinction between "object" and "beneficiary" of regulation that anchored Scalia's 1983 standing article. In suits "challenging the legality of government action or inaction," the Court said, the difficulty of establishing standing "depends considerably upon whether the plaintiff is himself an object of the action (or foregone action) at issue." It justified this consideration with the argument that elements of injury, causation, and redressability would typically be clearly present for the object of regulation, but not so for the beneficiary of the regulation of "someone else." But this asymmetry brought with it the antiregulatory overtones of the 1983 article, in which it was clothed rhetorically in the desirability of executive branch nullification of excessive congressional regulatory policies. Cass Sunstein points out that the Court had implicitly recognized this asymmetry in *Allen v. Wright,* decided a year after the Scalia article, "but *Lujan* was the first case explicitly to mark out the categories."[32]

The Court's opinion ruthlessly dismembered the interdependence-based nexus theories. Injury, it emphasized, must be "concrete and particularized" and "actual or imminent," not "conjectural" or "hypothetical." Skilbred's and Kelly's allegations that they had visited habitats of endangered species in foreign countries affected by U.S.-supported development and intended someday to visit these habitats again did not meet the test. That they visited these areas before the development "prove[d] nothing"; the relevant injury would only occur if they returned to witness the harm caused to species by the unchecked development. Their "'some day' intentions—without any description of concrete plans, or indeed any specification of when the someday will be—do not support a finding of the 'actual or imminent' injury that our cases require."[33]

So much for Defenders' "geographic nexus." The opinion also roundly dismissed plaintiffs' efforts to establish injury-in-fact through the "ecosystem nexus," "animal nexus," and "vocational nexus." The "inelegantly styled 'ecosystem nexus' . . . proposes that any person who uses *any part* of a 'contiguous ecosystem' adversely affected by a funded activity has standing even if the activity is located a great distance away." Although not rejecting outright the notion that ecosystem effects could produce injury remote from the activity, the Court asserted that the "ecosystem nexus" cannot avail persons "who use portions of an ecosystem not perceptibly affected by the unlawful action in question."[34]

Lamenting similarly the inartful styling of the "animal nexus" and the "vocational nexus," the Court demolished these theories as well. It described them, respectively, as the notion that "anyone who has an interest in studying or seeing the endangered animals anywhere on the globe has standing" and that "anyone with a professional interest in such animals can sue." One might argue that actions threatening the continued existence of an endangered species, even actions that are geographically distant, have the potential to "injure" humans interested in the species. But Scalia's opinion for the Court did not allow room for such an argument, declaring that "this is beyond all reason." For those observing or working with animals, it imagined, injury may come from harm to particular animals in a particular locale. "It goes beyond the limit, however, and into pure speculation and fantasy, to say that anyone who observes or works with an endangered species, anywhere in the world, is appreciably harmed by a single project affecting some portion of that species with which he has no more specific connection."[35]

The insistence on direct, immediate linkages also figured in the plurality's conclusions that Defenders had not established causation and redressability. This portion of Justice Scalia's opinion dwelt on contingencies surrounding the behavior of third parties—federal funding agencies and foreign governments—not before the court. These contingencies left it "entirely conjectural" whether a ruling in favor of Defenders would save the species and habitats of concern to Defenders.[36]

The refusal of the Court in *Lujan II* to credit systemic mechanisms of injury and causation was in sharp contrast to *SCRAP*. One might try to reconcile these cases on the procedural distinction, offered by Justice Scalia in *Lujan I,* that *SCRAP* was decided at the pleading stage, on a motion to dismiss, whereas *Lujan II* was decided on a motion for summary judgment.[37] But, at bottom, these cases work from very different images of the world. In *SCRAP,* effects of human actions reverberate broadly with potentially serious consequences throughout the human-natural world. In the world of Justice Scalia in *Lujan II,* however, effects of actions are presumed to be discrete, limited to particular locales and, indeed, individual creatures. Contingencies characteristic of complex systems are disqualifying. The rhetorically heightened castigation of the various "nexus" theories seemed intended to marginalize, if not reject entirely, injury and causation arguments based on the genetic commons or on ecosystem effects and the interdependence model that those arguments assume.

As damaging as it was for environmentalists, Justice Scalia's opinion for the Court did not go as far as he originally planned in sealing off citizen access to the courts. In an early draft of his opinion circulated to the Court, he stressed that to qualify for standing citizen beneficiaries must demonstrate personal injury that was not only "concrete" but "particularized." Justices Souter and Kennedy, who were otherwise ready to join the opinion, read the draft to suggest that a qualifying injury would have to be not only personal and specific to the plaintiff but also not "universal" or widely shared by others. This implication was consistent with Scalia's observation in the Suffolk article that even a concrete injury might be so widely shared that it would not define as a "minority" group entitled to judicial protection, for example, "all who breathe" in *SCRAP*. For Justices Souter and Kennedy, however, this was a step too far. They requested changes to remove the suggestion that "the universality of an injury deprives anyone of standing," and Justice Scalia made the changes. This moderation of the Court's position bears significantly on standing based on systemic environmental injuries, particularly at the global level, as discussed in *MA v. EPA* later in this chapter.[38]

Despite the modest concession, Justice Scalia's opinion for the Court in *Lujan II* stands as a stark rejection of environmentalist ideas and values in law. The tone veered at times into the derisive, directed not at the object of legislative policy, as in the "snail darter case," but implicitly at the environmentalists themselves—the purveyors of the fuzzy-headed globalism that Scalia sensed in the nexus theories. The opinion's substance was one with its antagonistic tone. The Court refused to interpret its threshold requirement of injury to accommodate the environmentalists' ecological model and granted no deference to Congress's express intent that citizens have access to the federal courts to enforce environmental laws as written. *Lujan II* gives credence to Peter Manus's characterization of Justice Scalia's discussions of standing and separation of powers in environmental cases as "a consistent statement about the law's unwillingness to accept claims that require recognition of even the mildest tenets of environmentalism." Commentators have argued that the Court's opinion in *Lujan II* did not staunch the flow of environmentalist claims in the federal courts. "As usual," Michael Herz observed, "the Court's bark [was] worse than its bite." But the bark—the opinion's cultural message—was loud and clear.[39]

Other justices were more receptive to the plaintiffs' theories, including two who joined Justice Scalia's opinion (except for the part on redressability). Justice Kennedy's concurring opinion, joined by Justice Souter, offered conciliatory observations on injury and citizen suits that kept hope alive for the ecological model. This was an unwelcome development for Scalia. In a note to his boss, Justice Blackmun's law clerk, Jeff Meyer, reported that Scalia was said to be "irate at [Kennedy] for submitting his concurrence and felt that it 'scuttled' his majority opinion." Kennedy agreed that Defenders had not demonstrated concrete injury in this case, but he distanced himself from Scalia's trashing of the "nexus theor[ies]." Those theories could be viable "in different circumstances." That meant that at least two of the five justices in Scalia's standing majority were comfortable with the potential of nonlocal, systemic injuries to support standing.[40]

Justice Kennedy's concurrence also went some distance to retrieve a role for Congress in the standing debate. He agreed that Congress could not trump the requirement of concrete injury derived from Article III's "cases" and "controversies" limitation. But he also encouraged the Court to "be sensitive to the articulation of new rights of action that do not have clear analogs in our common-law tradition." This was an invitation for the Court to update its models of injury and causation, and Kennedy saw a role for Congress in that process. In his view, "Congress has the power to define injuries and articulate chains of causation that will give rise to a case or controversy where none existed before." He believed Congress had not done this in the citizen suit provision of the ESA, which does not by its own terms specify the injury that "any person" would suffer from a violation in giving that person the right to sue. As Justice Stevens pointed out in his opinion concurring in the judgment, Congress named a range of interests served by the ESA—from "aesthetic" to "ecological" and "scientific"—injuries to which could support standing for citizen plaintiffs. But this was not specific enough for Kennedy to relate the injury to the class of "persons" entitled to sue. His concurrence was nevertheless a signal, from within the majority, of a willingness to step beyond rigid adherence to the atomism associated with common law traditions and make room for the ecological model working through legislative enactment.[41]

In dissent, Justice Blackmun, joined by Justice O'Connor, continued the no-man-is-an island theme from Donne that he sounded in his *Sierra Club v. Morton* dissent. He urged the viability of plaintiffs' nexus theories. Drawing on the ecological model, he observed that "many environmental injuries . . . cause harm distant from the area immediately affected by the challenged action," such as disturbances affecting "animals traveling over vast geographical ranges." Also, eradication of an endangered species could cause harm to those with a "vocational or professional" interest in the species located far away. In failing to acknowledge these mechanisms of injury, Blackmun claimed, the Court applied "rigid principles of geographic formalism [that it would not apply] anywhere outside the context of environmental claims." This last shot provoked a counterthrust from Justice Scalia, who added in a footnote to his opinion that it was Blackmun, not he, who was crafting special standing rules for environmental cases by relaxing the traditional standards for establishing harm. But that did little to defuse

Blackmun's implication that Scalia's opinion for the Court was animated by antienvironmentalist sentiment.[42]

Justice Stevens concurred on the merits, agreeing with the Department of the Interior's rule that Section 7 of the ESA does not have extraterritorial application. However, like Justice Blackmun, he believed that Defenders had established injury-in-fact, even though they had no firm plans to return to their ecosystems abroad, because it was reasonable to conclude that they would. And even if they did not intend to return, they might be injured by changes in the aesthetics or ecology of the project areas by virtue of an interest in those areas that was analogous to a family relationship. "The interest that confers standing in a case of this kind is comparable, though by no means equivalent, to the interest in a relationship among family members that can be immediately harmed by the death of an absent member, regardless of when, if ever, a family reunion is planned to occur."[43]

Tucked at the end of a footnote, this analogy to family had at least two implications that were quite striking in the setting of a discussion about judicial access. First, it suggested that noninstrumental values may give rise to injury sufficient for standing. Kelly and Skilbred valued the threatened species and habitats for what they were, not just for the pleasure of seeing or being with them, as we value family members whom we may never see. Second, the family metaphor echoed the Leopoldian idea of a moral evolution of ethical attachments from being confined to a close group, the family, to encompassing a broader moral universe, including the land community. The death of a species or a functioning ecosystem takes on an emotional and moral significance "comparable" if not "equivalent" to the death of a family member to whom we are bound by ties of affection and obligation. Although Justice Stevens did not explore these implications, they suggested a space for further consideration of "injury" in an era of ecological interdependence. The family metaphor reserved this space for possible future development in much the same way as Justice Blackmun's invocation of Donne.

Justice Stevens's family analogy led to a humorous but revealing exchange with Justice Scalia, who added to the Court's opinion that it represented a "Linnaean leap" that the Court declined to join. Stevens wrote a memo to Scalia saying he liked the "reference to my 'Linnaean leap,' but . . . I had thought my natural development of standing jurisprudence had more of a Darwinian character." Scalia replied with his understanding that "Linne was responsible for the system of binomial nomenclature which is used for both plants and animals [i.e., species classification]. I had frankly thought of saying that you were reversing the process of Darwinian evolution but I thought it would be too cruel." Roughly translated, Stevens was claiming to assist the "natural" evolution of standing toward an extension of consideration to species and ecosystems. Scalia saw this as a violation of the natural order—the separate classification of animal species and humans—and a devolution of humans to status on a par with animals. This back-and-forth was lighthearted sparring between longtime colleagues, but it captured in brilliant miniature the debate over the moral status of the environmental other that was a subtext of the case.[44]

Justice Kennedy's concurrence had the effect of moderating the antagonistic, antienvironmentalist thrust of Justice Scalia's opinion for the Court in *Lujan II,* and the dissents provided further balance. The Court was not as aggressively hostile to environmentalist tenets in standing cases as Scalia would have had it, despite his command of a majority in the case. Some of these countercurrents would rise to prominence in the next cases discussed, *Laidlaw* and *MA v. EPA.*

After *Lujan II,* Justice Scalia authored two more opinions for the Court in environmental standing cases that concluded a string of setbacks for environmentalists. In one, *Bennett v. Spear,* the Court unanimously upheld the standing of ranch operators and irrigation districts adversely affected by endangered species protections. This case was a foil for *Defenders.* The plaintiffs managed land and water resources for economic gain. As Justice Scalia put it, they "[sought] to prevent application of environmental restrictions rather than to implement them" in their complaint that Interior's excessive enforcement of Section 7 reduced the amount of irrigation water available for their operations. These plaintiffs were exemplars of the regulation-burdened "minority" interests that, in the view of Scalia's 1983 article, were especially entitled to judicial protection. Scalia's opinion for the Court had little difficulty concluding that they met the three-pronged constitutional test for standing as well as the prudential "zone of interest" requirement. This time, there were no dissents.[45]

With *Lujan I* and *II* and *Bennett,* Justice Scalia had accomplished what he could only have dreamed in 1983 when he complained of the "judiciary's long love affair with environmental litigation." He had succeeded in "putting at the center of standing doctrine the private owner with an economic interest that motivates an antiregulatory legal claim" and in shutting out the claims of "the model subject of ecological interdependence, whose physical interdependence with, or moral and aesthetic evaluation of, a faraway part of nature runs beyond simple forms of causation." He had toughened the line on standing for public interest advocates generally, and he had put the environmentalists in their place.[46]

Justice Scalia concluded his standing sweep with *Steel Company v. Citizens for a Better Environment,* in which he wrote for the Court denying standing to environmentalists suing to enforce toxic release reporting requirements of the Emergency Planning and Community Right to Know Act (EPCRA). Steel Co. had not complied with EPCRA's reporting requirements for years. After receiving a notice of intent to file a citizen suit from Citizens for a Better Environment (CBE), however, it submitted all the required reports before suit was filed. The Court held that any injuries to CBE and its members were not redressable and that the plaintiffs therefore lacked standing. Nothing was to be accomplished by declaratory or injunctive relief by a court because Steel Co. had acknowledged its duty to report and carried out that duty prior to suit. The civil penalties that CBE sought for past violations were also not redress because the penalties, if assessed, would be paid to the U.S. Treasury, not to CBE. "In requesting them," Justice Scalia wrote for the Court, CBE "[sought] not remediation of its own injury . . . but vindication of the rule of law—the 'undifferentiated public interest' in faithful execution of EPCRA." All the justices agreed with the outcome in *Steel Co.*, although only a bare majority joined the Court's opinion in full and no fewer than four concurring opinions made clear that the justices were unsettled on the issues.[47]

Friends of the Earth v. Laidlaw: North Tyger River Nation

The run of Scalia-authored standing decisions ended in 1998 with *Federal Election Commission v. Akins,* which upheld standing for voters seeking to enforce lobbying disclosure requirements. Two years after *Akins* came another disappointment for the justice, *Friends of the Earth, Inc. v. Laidlaw Environmental Services (TOC), Inc.*, in which the Court gave standing to environmental plaintiffs in a citizen suit under the Clean Water Act (CWA). Justice Ginsburg wrote the opinion for the Court in *Laidlaw.* Appointed in 1993, Ginsburg replaced Justice White, who had joined the opinion for the Court in *Lujan II.* Her opinion in *Laidlaw* marked a modest swing toward greater receptivity to public interest plaintiffs in environmental cases and a restoration of the idea of interdependence in the Court's largely individualistic standing doctrine. The shift held out the possibility that *Lujan II*, rather than *SCRAP*, would end up the extreme outlier in standing jurisprudence.[48]

In 1986 Laidlaw Environmental Services (TOC), Inc. (Laidlaw) purchased a hazardous waste incinerator on the North Tyger River in Roebuck, South Carolina. The facility included a wastewater treatment plant, which treated water from the incinerator's air pollution control system prior to discharge into the river. South Carolina pollution control authorities issued Laidlaw a water discharge permit that incorporated state and federal pollution control requirements. The permit limited Laidlaw's discharge of a number of pollutants, including mercury, which is toxic to both aquatic life and humans in very small doses. Despite repeated efforts to improve the treatment plant's effectiveness, Laidlaw violated its discharge limit for mercury 489 times between 1987 and 1995, when it recorded the last violation.[49]

The original plaintiffs in the citizen suit were Friends of the Earth (FOE), a national organization, and Citizens Local Environmental Action Network (CLEAN), a South Carolina group. Sierra Club also joined as a plaintiff after the suit was filed in 1992. The lead counsel for these groups (collectively FOE) was Bruce Terris, who founded his "public interest law firm" in "the beginning of the environmental movement." The firm developed a specialty in finding and bringing citizen suit enforcement actions on behalf of FOE and others, funded by attorney fee awards available to the prevailing party in those actions. His firm was the "the biggest profit driven plaintiff-side environmental law firm in the country," Terris believed, but it was small and thinly resourced compared with firms working for the corporate defendants typically on the other side of these cases. The long and complex proceedings of *Laidlaw* would test its staying power.[50]

On April 10, 1992, FOE and CLEAN sent a sixty-day notice to Laidlaw stating their intent to bring suit for the company's CWA discharge violations. After an unsuccessful attempt by Laidlaw to prevent the suit through a sweetheart settlement with state environmental officials, FOE and CLEAN filed their complaint in federal district court on June 12, 1992. The mercury violations were ongoing then, but Laidlaw was in "substantial compliance" with its permit by August of that year, and its final violation was in 1995. The district judge found early in the case that FOE had standing, "albeit 'by the very slimmest of margins.'" In January 1997, after almost five years of proceedings, he issued his decision on the merits. He denied FOE declaratory or injunctive relief, because Laidlaw had no recent violations and because there was no "demonstrated harm" to the environment from its earlier violations. He did however impose a civil penalty on Laidlaw of $405,800.[51]

While appeals from the district judge's ruling in *Laidlaw* were pending before the Court of Appeals for the Fourth Circuit, the Supreme Court came down with its decision in *Steel Co.* On the basis of its understanding of that decision, the Fourth Circuit decided that FOE's case against Laidlaw was moot and ordered it dismissed.[52] It reasoned that with the district court's denial of declaratory and injunctive relief to FOE and FOE's failure to appeal that denial, the only relief available to FOE was civil penalties. Because *Steel Co.* held that civil penalties did not offer redress to environmental citizen suit plaintiffs, FOE had lost standing when the possibility of other remedies disappeared and with it the jurisdiction of the federal courts. This ruling, had it survived the Court's review, would have multiplied the damage done to environmental citizen suits by *Steel Co.*: "any sloppy polluter could potentially escape liability and payment of [attorneys'] fees merely by belatedly improving compliance efforts." The resources flowing to environmental groups and public interest lawyers such as Bruce Terris to prosecute these cases would have been cut drastically.[53]

The Supreme Court took review at FOE's request. The solicitor general of the United States was granted leave to file a brief and appear at oral argument on FOE's behalf, even though no federal agency was a party. In their briefs and oral arguments, the parties gave most of their attention to the Fourth Circuit's mootness holding and the related question of whether civil penalties could ever support standing. At the end of its brief, however, Laidlaw argued the issue that the Fourth Circuit did not reach—that FOE had not established the necessary injury for standing because Laidlaw's violations had no adverse effect on the environment. FOE's reply brief countered that proof of harm to the environment was not necessary where the plaintiff could show that the defendant's conduct had lessened its members' enjoyment of the river and reduced the economic value of their property near the river. This debate over injury-in-fact received little attention at oral argument, but it would emerge as a major issue in the opinions, reprising earlier exchanges over the same issue in *SCRAP, Sierra Club,* and *Lujan II.*[54]

Joined by six of her colleagues, Justice Ginsburg wrote for the Court reversing the Fourth Circuit; Justice Scalia wrote an agitated dissent, in which Justice Thomas joined. The Court's opinion addressed standing as well as mootness. Because the Court was overturning the Fourth Circuit's mootness ruling, it had to assure itself "that FOE had Article III standing at the outset of the litigation," and in concluding that FOE did, the Court addressed both injury-in-fact, examined more fully below, and redressability. The Court rejected the Fourth Circuit's interpretation of *Steel Co.* that civil penalties could never provide redress. *Steel Co.*'s holding was limited to cases in which violations ceased before suit was filed. In cases such as *Laidlaw,* where violations were ongoing at the time of suit and could continue, the deterrence effect of penalties could provide redress "by abating current violations and preventing future ones." In such cases, only if the litigation were later dismissed as moot would redressability be an issue. Morever, dismissal for mootness would only be justified if "it were absolutely clear that Laidlaw's permit violations could not reasonably be expected to recur," and that was disputed on the record in *Laidlaw.* These rulings by the Court, taken together, turned back the tide that had crested in *Steel Co.* and reopened the "judiciary's love affair with environmental litigation" or at least stemmed the hostility that Justice Scalia had helped sow.[55]

Of particular interest here is the Court's analysis of injury in *Laidlaw*. The plaintiffs had alleged—and the district court found—that discharges from Laidlaw's wastewater treatment plant into the Tyger River in South Carolina repeatedly violated the mercury limitations in Laidlaw's discharge permit. But the district court also found that the permit violations caused "no demonstrated proof of harm to the environment." Tissue studies found no fish in the North Tyger River with mercury levels approaching those that would threaten human health, and other tests showed no discernible effect of the discharges on the aquatic ecosystem. In dissent, Justice Scalia was quick to point out, as Laidlaw had in its arguments to the Court, "typically, an environmental plaintiff claiming injury due to discharges in violation of the Clean Water Act argues that the discharges harm the environment, and that the harm to the environment injures him." The district court's no-harm finding took that argument away.[56]

In finding injury-in-fact nonetheless, the Court began with the premise that "the relevant showing for purposes of Article III standing . . . is not injury to the environment but injury to the plaintiff." "We see nothing 'improbable' about the proposition that a company's continuous and pervasive illegal discharges of pollutants into a river would cause nearby residents to curtail their recreational use of that waterway and would subject them to other economic and aesthetic harms." The question was whether the plaintiffs' concerns about the river were reasonable. In finding that they were, the Court sketched the claims of five individual members of FOE and its sister organizations. Three of these individuals lived near the Laidlaw facility; two of them stated that, although they would like to, they no longer engaged in recreation (picnicking, hiking, bird watching) along the North Tyger River because of the effects of Laidlaw's illegal discharges, and the third stated that that Laidlaw's violations diminished the value of her property. Two others lived farther away but claimed that they too would like to camp, swim, picnic, or boat on the river near the facility but did not because of concerns about Laidlaw's violations. One of them who had canoed on the river forty miles downstream of the facility was afraid to canoe closer. The individualized injuries stood on their own, as they had to under the Court's standing doctrine, but in their number and overlapping concerns as laid out in the Court's opinion, they also created a sense of the effect of Laidlaw's discharges on the relationship of the entire community to the river.[57]

Limited to a discrete segment of the North Tyger River near Laidlaw's plant, *Laidlaw* was by no means a reprise of *SCRAP*, but it did revive in some limited measure the ecological model that animated that decision. In this, the Court's injury-in-fact inquiry showed some deference to the statutory context provided by the CWA. The purpose of the act is to protect and restore the "chemical, physical and biological integrity of the Nation's waters"; permit limitations are imposed to secure that purpose; and dischargers are strictly liable for violations of those limitations without a separate showing of environmental harm. This structure lends itself to a presumption that permit violations will impair "the integrity of the nation's waters." The Court in *Laidlaw* gave plaintiffs the benefit of this presumption: to require actual proof of injury to the environment, the Court said, would be "to raise the standing hurdle higher than the necessary showing for success on the merits in an action alleging noncompliance with [a discharge] permit."[58]

The Court's emphasis on the harm to humans rather than to the environment seemed to turn ecocentrism on its head. In Justice Douglas's dissent in *Sierra Club v. Morton,* the critical injury was to the natural system—"the river"—not to the individuals who might be appointed guardians to represent it. In *Laidlaw,* it was anthropocentrism all the way down. In another sense, however, as environmental law professor Daniel Farber has written, *Laidlaw* is consistent with "Justice Douglas's view that those who have an 'intimate relation with the inanimate object about to be injured, polluted, or otherwise despoiled are its legitimate spokesmen.' Just as private law protects the relationship between a property owner and land, so the Court [in *Laidlaw*] seems to recognize a protected relationship between natural resources and those whose lives are bound up with them." In *Laidlaw,* the Court may have gone as far as its doctrine of individualized injury would let it in framing standing in terms of the interdependencies between humans and their natural setting.[59]

The Court's model of the connections between dischargers, harm to the river, and injury to watershed dwellers' interests in the river was modest enough to draw the support of Chief Justice Rehnquist, who had joined with Justices Scalia, Thomas, and White (now no longer on the Court) in rejecting the nexus theories in *Lujan II*. It drew a vigorous objection from Scalia, however, joined by Thomas in dissent. Refusing to concede the linkages that would support a reasonable inference of adverse impacts from illegal wastewater discharges, Scalia concluded that the plaintiffs' claims were merely "subjective apprehensions" and that the Court's holding "makes the injury-in-fact requirement a sham." In Scalia's universe, human disturbances were not to be presumed to cause detrimental effects on natural systems, even at a local scale, in the absence of specific evidence of those effects. Nor was a relationship between humans and their environment that could produce harm to be presumed in the absence of those effects. The "subjective apprehensions" Scalia saw inherent in such presumptions would open the courthouse door wide to public interest environmental litigants.[60]

Massachusetts v. EPA: Global Interdependence

Chapter 3 explored *Massachusetts v. EPA*, the Court's 2007 decision that seemed to revive, if only by a slim margin, the Court's enthusiasm for the environmentalist enterprise apparent in decisions of four decades ago but lacking in more recent cases. The earlier discussion focused on the substantive issues in the case—the Clean Air Act's coverage of greenhouse gas emissions and the agency's duty to address those emissions under the precautionary endangerment standard set out in the act. But the decision also presented an issue of standing, which the Court resolved in the environmental petitioners' favor. In doing so, a majority of the Court raised the ecological model to a global level, crediting the complex causal linkages over space and time offered by climate change science—and drawing the scorn of the dissenters for creating "*SCRAP* for a new generation." But an unexpected turn of the decision limited both its practical and symbolic reach: the benefits of global interdependence for standing in climate change cases may be available only to states.

On review in the Court of Appeals for the District of Columbia Circuit, the environmentalist petitioners did not leave standing to chance. They submitted two volumes of declarations and exhibits that detailed the mechanisms, nature, and extent of global warming injuries from a variety of perspectives: declarants ranged from scientists and state officials to homeowners and recreationists. The defendants did not submit rebuttal materials.[61]

The three-judge panel split evenly on standing. Judge Randolph did not reach the issue. Taking a cue from Justice Scalia's opinion in *Lujan II,* Judge Sentelle concluded that the petitioners had not alleged harm that was "particularized" to them. Climate change was harmful, if it was harmful at all, "to humanity at large," and petitioners represented "segments of humanity at large," which did not meet the individualized requirements for standing. Judge Tatel, whose views would be vindicated by the Court's later decision, concluded that petitioners met all three elements of the standing test. Standing for only one of the petitioners was necessary for the case to go forward, and Judge Tatel focused on Massachusetts. He found injury that was "personal and individual" to the state (shoreline loss and increased flood damage), causation (sea level rise driven by global warming, driven by anthropogenic emissions, including those from automobiles in the United States), and redressability (moderation of Massachusetts losses resulting from reduced automobile emissions).[62]

The Court did not list standing as among the issues for review. As expected, however, the EPA raised standing in its brief, Massachusetts responded, and the issue was joined. Almost half the oral argument was spent on standing, with questions from all the justices except Justice Thomas, who very rarely speaks from the bench. The colloquy included the comments by Justice Scalia that questioned the imminence of climate change and its human origins. Most of the rest of the debate seemed to assume some level of human-induced climate change but swirled around the immediacy of the injury and the precision of the linkages necessary to establish causation and redressability. If nothing else, the debate highlighted the indeterminacy of standing doctrine as elaborated in the Court's decisions. James Milkey, the assistant attorney general who argued the case for Massachusetts and other petitioners, claimed that the state's injury was "much more direct and particularized" than what the Court found sufficient in *Laidlaw*, while Justice Scalia characterized the injury in *SCRAP* at the "far margin of our standing cases," as "a much more immediate kind of damage."[63]

Justice Stevens's opinion for the Court followed a line on standing similar to that laid out in Judge Tatel's dissenting opinion in the court of appeals. He credited the linkages connecting emissions from U.S. automobiles to a heightened greenhouse effect, to increased global temperatures, to sea level rise, and to the loss of Massachusetts's coastline. The EPA's failure to regulate greenhouse gas emissions from automobiles contributed to this loss and would continue to do so in the future. A correction of that failure would moderate the loss. Hence injury, causation, and redressability were all satisfied. It did not matter that U.S. automobile emissions represented only a small fraction (6 percent) of global emissions responsible for the damage to Massachusetts's coastline; nor did it matter that a reduction in those emissions would represent only a small decrease in that damage, one that might be overtaken by increased emissions in other parts of the world not under U.S. government or court control. Government rarely solved "massive problems in one fell regulatory swoop." "That a first step might be tentative does not by itself support the notion that federal courts lack the jurisdiction to determine whether that step conforms to law." To decide otherwise "would doom most challenges to regulatory action."[64]

The petitioners had submitted two volumes of material supporting the linkages on which Justice Stevens relied, but acceptance or rejection of them depended on the level of precision, specificity, and certainty that the Court required. In particular, standing in this case turned on the Court's readiness to credit global warming injuries that were remote in place and time from their diffuse causes (global and intergenerational in reach) and that defied precise quantification. It required recognition of the importance of incremental harms and corresponding remedial measures against the threat of "massive" (and potentially catastrophic) harms within the climate system as a whole. And it demanded an acceptance of causal relationships within that vast and complex system that could only be represented as trends or projections within a range of confidence rather than as precise one-to-one correspondences. In short, standing in *MA v. EPA* depended on a view of the evidence consistent with the ecological model, in this case raised to a global scale. John Donne's image of interdependence, introduced by Justice Blackmun in his *Sierra Club* dissent, took on literal force, as the Court credited Massachusetts's account of its coastline being "washed away by the Sea" and the state being "the lesse" for it.[65]

Justices Scalia, Thomas, and Alito joined Chief Justice Roberts's dissent on standing. Supreme Court commentator Linda Greenhouse described the opinion as "a declaration of [Roberts's] deepest jurisprudential beliefs and highest priorities . . . the most revealing portrait" in his eighteen months so far on the Court. Before this opinion, however, Roberts had not been reluctant to express his views on standing, both in his opinions as a judge on the District of Columbia Circuit and in his writings before he went on the bench. In an article written in 1993, while he was still in private practice, Roberts presented a stout defense of stringent standing requirements, based mainly, as Justice Scalia's Suffolk article had been, on the separation of powers. Although he avoided the provocative quips that made Scalia's piece notorious, he argued for "the key role that injury plays in restricting the courts to their proper function in a limited and separated government." He did offer an olive leaf to environmentalists, noting with approval that in *Sierra Club v. Morton* the Court had recognized aesthetic and recreational interests as a basis for standing and observed that "the fact that particular environmental interests are shared by the many rather than the few does not make them less deserving of legal protection through the judicial process." In his dissent in *MA v. EPA,* however, he appeared to renege on this concession in the face of the universal harm of climate change.[66]

Predictably, given Chief Justice Roberts's deep engagement with the standing issue, the tone of his dissent in *MA v. EPA* was intense and critical ("scathing") and the analysis, demanding. Massachusetts had not established injury that was "particularized" (global warming presented injury to "humanity at large"), "actual" (Massachusetts's unrebutted expert affidavit connecting global warming with sea level rise was "conclusory"), or "imminent" or "certainly impending" (the claimed injuries extended through 2100 and models used to predict them had high error ranges). His argument that Massachusetts's injury is not "particularized" because it is in some sense universally shared as an outgrowth of global warming seemed contrary to his placatory comment in the 1993 article that injuries were not disqualified simply because they were widespread. It also applied a meaning of "particularized" that the Court had backed away from at the urging of Justices Kennedy and Souter in *Lujan II*. The logical consequence of his point would be that that no one could take the government to court for unlawful failure to address climate change. But the federal courts would be open for individuals and industries burdened by climate change regulations.[67]

Chief Justice Roberts was equally fierce in deconstructing the Court's causation story. Domestic automobile emissions were a miniscule part of global greenhouse gas emissions. The linkage between those emissions and Massachusetts's coastal loss was fraught with complexity, "far too speculative to establish causation"—and far too speculative to make it likely that Massachusetts's specific loss would be redressed by any auto emission standards the EPA might impose. Roberts insisted that he was not debating the scientific case for global climate change or doubting its seriousness. He was simply taking Article III standing requirements seriously to keep courts out of policy and to maintain the tripartite allocation of power. But by separating the several elements of the causal chain and demanding particularized proof of each, his analysis necessarily rejected the environmentalists' presumptions of fragility, radiating harm, and serious consequence. Lest there be any doubt about the competing worldviews at work in these opinions, Roberts dubbed the Court's offensive standing opinion "*SCRAP* for a new generation."[68]

The triumph of environmentalist beliefs and values in the standing portion of *MA v. EPA* was qualified, if not seriously unsettled, by the special solicitude given to the status of Massachusetts as a state. It was "of considerable relevance," the Court wrote, "that the party seeking review here is a sovereign State and not, as it was in *Lujan [II]*, a private individual." This distinction was critical for Justice Kennedy, who had joined the Court's opinion in *Lujan II*. Evidence in the opinion confirms that the Court's special regard for the standing of states was designed to bring Kennedy into the majority. For example, the Court relied on *Georgia v. Tennessee*, a 1907 public nuisance action by Georgia to stop pollution from a Tennessee copper smelter, to support the special claim of states to federal jurisdiction. This was a case that the lawyers for Massachusetts had chosen deliberately not to cite, but Kennedy held it out to Assistant Attorney General Milkey during oral argument "as your best case," and it ended up as the centerpiece of the Court's argument for state exceptionalism.[69]

As a purely analytic matter, the Court's application of the injury-causation-redressability test supplies a separate and sufficient basis for standing in *MA v. EPA*. But the Court's emphasis of the special standing of states muddied the waters on both the practical application of the decision and its symbolic import. Practically, lower courts were left to struggle with whether only states had standing to bring climate change claims or whether others did too if they met the three-part test. In his dissent, Chief Justice Roberts put in his bid for the former interpretation, but lower courts have come out on both sides of the question.[70] Symbolically, by inserting the states as the arbiters of climate change injury, the Court diluted its opinion's environmentalist cast, stopping short of a full recommitment to the ecological model in its standing jurisprudence.

Subsequent decisions by the Court have not done much to make the decision or its meaning clearer. In *Summers v. Earth Island Institute,* decided in 2009, Justice Kennedy sided with a majority that rejected standing for environmentalists complaining about Forest Service regulations that cut off public participation for small-scale fire-rehabilitation activities and salvage-timber sales on federal lands. Justice Scalia's opinion for the Court was largely a reprise of *Lujan II.* It emphasized the special obstacles to standing for public interest plaintiffs, and it found that a declaration by one of the plaintiffs that he "want[s] to go" to forestlands affected by the regulations was too vague to establish imminent injury, like the "'some day' intentions" of the *Lujan II* plaintiffs. Two years later, in *AEP v. Connecticut,* an equally divided Court upheld the standing of "at least some of the plaintiffs" in a public nuisance action against large greenhouse gas emitters, holding the positions staked out in *MA v. EPA. MA v. EPA* remains the high-water mark in recent decades of the ecological model's influence on standing. But that mark has an asterisk. And the standing tides continue to ebb and flow.[71]

REJECTION OF THE INTERDEPENDENCE model in decisions such as *Lujan I* and *II* and in the energized dissents in *Laidlaw* and *MA v. EPA* would protect the rule of individualized standing and with it the autonomy, hierarchy, and mastery values that the rule favors against the competing values of much environmental legislation. Justice Scalia's visceral resistance to standing for environmental groups evinces a desire to not only end the federal judiciary's "love affair with environmental litigation" out of separation of powers concerns but also check the spread of the environmentalist paradigm. He said as much with his celebration of executive branch nullification of regulatory laws in his 1983 article; his derisive treatment of environmentalist theories in *Lujan II* and the *FOE* dissent confirmed it. Other colleagues, including Chief Justice Roberts, whose veneration of *Lujan II* was prominent in his *MA v. EPA* dissent, have tacitly joined this cultural enterprise.[72] As played out in environmental cases, the battle for a more or less individualistic notion of standing is a symbolic battle for the heart of the nation over environmentalist beliefs and values.

Acceptance of the interdependence model in decisions such as *SCRAP,* *Laidlaw,* and *MA v. EPA* has shown the capacity of the individualized version of standing in Court doctrine to adjust to the worldview embedded in environmental statutes and to accommodate the collectivist, egalitarian, and harmony values advanced by them. The defendants and associated interests in all of these cases—the railroads in *SCRAP,* the hazardous waste management company in *Laidlaw,* the fossil fuel interests behind the EPA in *MA v. EPA*—embodied contrary values that would have been shielded if the atomistic model had prevailed. Granting standing to environmental plaintiffs allowed the cultural conflict to be played out on the merits, as seen in the earlier analysis of the merits decision in *MA v. EPA,* but the conflict was also fully present in the very decision to grant judicial access.

Despite the Court's hedge in its grant of standing in *MA v. EPA,* the opinion suggests the power of the interdependence model when supported by extensive scientific evidence, as in the case of climate change. Voluminous evidence available to the Court, including not only the plaintiffs' declarations and exhibits but also scientific studies available in the public domain, validated the contentions of systemic injury and credited the urgency of predicted future harms. *MA v. EPA* was more than just *SCRAP* for a new generation. It was *SCRAP* with a formidable and growing body of science behind it and with much more than litter in the parks at stake. This urgency brought the Court, including Justice Kennedy, to revive its receptiveness to environmentalist suits on both jurisdiction and the merits. This at least raises the possibility that climate change has the capacity to not only activate the ecological model but also revive the transformative urgency that fueled the early days of the environmental movement across disparate cultural sets.

CHAPTER SEVEN

Federalism

FEDERALISM, the allocation of powers between the federal government and the states (and by extension local governments), is the vertical analogue to the separation of powers, as discussed in Chapter 6. Chief Justice Rehnquist supplied the rhetorical signature of the Supreme Court's federalism revolution: "the Constitution requires a distinction between what is truly national and what is truly local." Making that distinction, however, has proved contentious and has divided the Court along familiar cultural lines. Views among the justices on the reach of federal authority reflect differences not only on the merits of centralized power but also, as in the standing cases, on the desirability of public interest regulation and in ways of seeing the world. Where the Court draws the national/local line often reflects a belief about the level of interdependence that can or should be credited. The ecological model, with its expansive notions of causation and injury and its close connections within and between human and natural systems, has supported more generous interpretations of federal power. Resistance to that model characterizes less generous interpretations.[1]

Chapter 3 explored the beginning of the Court's federalism revolution with the 1992 decision in *New York v. United States*. Since then, the Court has been "rewriting federalism doctrine," giving new definition to the concept of a federal government of limited powers. This project has included reinvigoration of state sovereign immunity under the Eleventh Amendment, expansion of Tenth Amendment anticommandeering doctrine and related constraints on the spending power, and limitation of the commerce clause as the basis of federal regulatory controls. It has also reached collaterally into issues of federal preemption, the dormant commerce clause, and limitations on state authority under other provisions of the Constitution, such as the takings clause. Because federal environmental regulatory statutes are based primarily on the commerce power, this chapter will focus on the evolution of federalism doctrine under the commerce clause and the ripple effect of that doctrine in the Court's interpretation of the jurisdictional scope of environmental laws.[2]

Federalism under the Commerce Clause: Doctrine, Theories, and Values

The commerce clause gives Congress the power to "regulate Commerce . . . among the several States, and with the Indian Tribes." Court doctrine prescribes three permissible objects of federal regulation under the commerce power: Congress may regulate the "channels of interstate commerce," the "instrumentalities of interstate commerce," and "activities having a substantial relation to interstate commerce." Environmental laws rely predominantly on the third element—activities with a substantial relationship to interstate commerce. But the relationship between the activities that these laws regulate and "commerce" is often not self-evident. Whether the requisite connection exists depends not only on the definition of "commerce" but also on the types and magnitude of "activities" that will qualify as having a "substantial relation" to it. The Court's interpretations of its own "substantial relation" test reflect competing federalism theories and values that have been evolving since the framing of the Constitution.[3]

Spillovers, Race-to-the-Bottom, and Moral Minimums

Hardin's tragedy of the commons is at the heart of debates about federalism in regulation. As seen in the discussion of *New York v. United States*, Hardin's metaphor of herders' overuse of the grazing commons applies to interactions among states as well as individuals in the use and supply of common resources. In *New York,* the problem stemmed from externalized benefits: states that chose to supply waste disposal capacity bore all of the environmental burdens but enjoyed only some of the regional waste management benefits they provided. More typically, environmental commons problems among states grow from externalized costs. State A enjoys all of the benefit of commons-degrading economic activity (jobs, tax revenue) but incurs only some of the burdens (pollution, loss of ecosystem services), which are shared with state B. By allowing source states to avoid at least some of the costs of their use of the commons, interstate spillovers of this sort encourage states to overuse the resource. Regulatory intervention by a federal government that internalizes all the costs as well as the benefits offers a corrective.

By the same token, many regulatory theorists argue that in the absence of significant interstate externalities, state or local governments should make regulatory decisions because they are closer to the problem and more responsive to the preferences of the affected population and are therefore more likely to produce an optimal balance. This presumption is the basis for the oft-cited "matching principle," which holds that regulatory policy should be made by the smallest jurisdiction that encompasses all of the policy's significant costs and benefits. The concept is not new: constitutional law professor Michael McConnell has traced its pedigree back to debates on the ratification of the Constitution. Critics have used the matching principle to indict the reach of federal environmental laws to problems that do not have obvious interstate spillovers. In Professor Richard Stewart's colorful phrase, these laws are "nothing less than a massive [and unwarranted] effort at Soviet-style central planning of the economy."[4]

Environmentalists have also relied on a second theoretical justification for the federalization of environmental law, the race-to-the-bottom (RTB) theory. RTB hypothesizes that states compete with each other for job-creating businesses, offering reduced environmental requirements, among other inducements, to attract or keep businesses that might otherwise go elsewhere. The predicted result is undesirably lax environmental policies across the states, even in the absence of interstate spillovers. The federal environmental enactments of the 1970s and 1980s were written to address the problems that RTB predicted: Professor Richard Revesz has concluded that "race-to-the-bottom arguments explain far more of the Clean Air Act than do interstate externality arguments."[5]

Revesz and others have criticized RTB's foundational role in environmental federalism. Their main argument has been that competition among states could take the form of a functioning interstate market for industrial location rather than a strategic game. Rather than pushing states to under-regulate with the remorselessness of Hardin's tragedy, the market could be expected to yield welfare-maximizing outcomes—an efficient balancing of pollution and economic productivity for each state. Proponents of the RTB, the critics claim, have not produced empirical evidence to support their theory, although recent research suggests that at least some aspects of state environmental policy show progressive relaxation of environmental requirements in response to moves by other states. The debate continues over whether, under what circumstances, and to what effect RTB accurately characterizes environmental policy making by states.[6]

The matching principle, the RTB, and its opposing interstate market theory all assume that the goal of environmental regulation is efficiency:

an optimal balance between economic activity and environmental quality. As discussed, many environmentalists resist making efficiency the touchstone of regulatory efforts. They want policy to express nonwelfarist values. And to the extent they see these values as nationally defining, they are also determined that these values not be overridden by states or localities. This determination has led to a third, nonwelfarist rationale for centralized environmental policy—the need for a "moral minimum" protecting human health and the environment throughout the country.[7]

The Commerce Clause, Values, and Worldviews

The commerce clause says nothing about the matching principle, RTB, or moral minimums. The Court mediates these and other considerations bearing on the allocation of environmental decision-making authority through its "substantial relation to interstate commerce" test and other elements of its federalism doctrine. In this, the ecological model and its opposing atomistic model play an important translational role. In John Muir's universe, in which everything is "hitched to everything else," interdependence is all encompassing. It characterizes natural systems, human institutions such as markets and governments, and the relationships between them all. Environmental law scholar Jonathan Adler offers this description of the federalism implications of the ecological model at the extreme:

> It is, after all, a basic ecological postulate . . . that all activities have ecological impacts and that due to such effects and interconnections, everything is connected to everything else. The same can be said of economic interrelationships. Small changes in economic conditions, no matter how small, can ripple through the sea of interrelationships and exchanges that make up the modern economy.

With this understanding of the world, virtually any environmental disturbance could be argued to have a "substantial relation to interstate commerce." Even in the absence of observable interstate spillovers and regardless of whether states were operating in strategic games or markets, the close linkages in human-natural systems could be presumed to carry effects throughout those systems. In *National Association of Homebuilders v. Babbitt*, a case decided by the Court of Appeals for the District of Columbia Circuit, Judge Karen Henderson invoked this presumption to support commerce clause jurisdiction over the Delhi Sands flower-loving fly, a relict species of no known economic value found exclusively within an eight-mile radius in Southern California.[8]

Adler's treatment is not a sympathetic one, because he believes that the "Commerce Clause does not authorize such an all-encompassing regulatory power." Implicitly invoking the contrary presumptions of the atomistic model, he argues that the causal connections of the ecological model are too attenuated to activate the commerce power. Dissenting from the District of Columbia Circuit's finding of commerce clause jurisdiction in the Delhi Sands flower-loving fly case, Judge Sentelle applied a similar line of criticism to Judge Henderson's theory of ecological and economic interconnectedness. "There is no showing, only the rankest of speculation, that a reduction or even complete destruction of the viability of the Delhi Sands Flower-Loving Fly will in fact 'affect land and objects that are involved in interstate commerce.'" He went even further in deconstructing the interdependencies on which Judge Henderson's analysis rested. "The commerce clause empowers Congress 'to regulate commerce' not 'ecosystems.' . . . An ecosystem is an ecosystem, and commerce is commerce." Instead of one interconnected biotic community, as Leopold supposed, the law projects wholly separate domains.[9]

These competing worldviews attach to competing values in the federalism debate. Professor Adler and Judge Sentelle resist the implications of the ecological model for federalism because indulging those implications, they believe, would obliterate limits on federal regulatory power. And preserving those limits advances values that are important to them.

Federalism scholar Erin Ryan lists "the maintenance of checks and balances that safeguard individuals against tyranny" as a "primary value associated with American federalism." The Court's new federalism featured this value. It was at the heart of *New York v. United States,* which limited the reach of federal power to "secure to citizens the liberties that derive from the diffusion of sovereign power," and it figured centrally in later landmark federalism decisions, as explored in this chapter. In environmental federalism cases, mastery values were also prominent, resisting regulatory limits on economic development of land and other natural resources.[10]

Opposed to the autonomy values dominant in the federalism cases are collectivism values focused on public goods, such as environmental quality, which may be secured more certainly, efficiently, or comprehensively through federal regulation. Erin Ryan made herself an exemplar of these values when she wrote: "I proceed from the assumption that good government should address those market failures, negative externalities, and other collective action problems that individuals are ill-equipped to resolve on their own." In her analysis, "the nineteenth century dualism that haunts federalism theory"—emphasizing mutually exclusive domains of federal and state power—frustrates the legitimate ends of government. Collectivism values like hers, along with harmony values in environmental cases, animate the resistance to the Court's new federalism in concurring and dissenting opinions. They are closely associated in these opinions with an embrace of the interdependence model.[11]

Hodel v. Virginia Surface Mining & Reclamation Ass'n: Commerce Power to the "Nth Degree"

Hodel v. Virginia Surface Mining & Reclamation Ass'n was decided before the Rehnquist Court's federalism revolution. It remains the Court's only major decision that directly addresses the constitutionality of an environmental statute as within the commerce power. The decision upholding the statute provides a benchmark for assessing the later cases.[12]

In *Hodel,* the Commonwealth of Virginia, coal companies, and private landowners (mining interests) attacked the Surface Mining Control and Reclamation Act (SMCRA) on several constitutional grounds, including that it exceeded the commerce power and violated the Tenth Amendment. Mining interests challenged the act's provisions for interim federal standards governing surface mining operations, directing particular attention to requirements to restore "steep slopes" disturbed during mining to their original contours. They argued that the act's reclamation provisions regulated land use, and because land use was a local activity not affecting interstate commerce, it was not within the commerce power; contamination of air and navigable waters could lead to spillovers warranting federal regulation, but not local land disturbances. They also argued that SMCRA violated the Tenth Amendment by usurping traditional state prerogatives in land use regulation, again stressing the localized effects of land use decisions. The district court rejected the commerce clause attack but granted the Tenth Amendment claim because the act forced "relinquishment of state control of land use planning" and "loss of state control of its economy." Both sides sought review in the Supreme Court, which was granted.[13]

In conference after the oral argument, a number of the justices voiced unease with the scope of federal authority under SMCRA. Justice Blackmun recorded their comments. Chief Justice Burger: "The Commerce Clause has gone so far." Justice Stewart: "Is everything federal now?" Justice Rehnquist: "We have stood the Constitution on its head." He said that SMCRA's regulations were "OK" to the extent they bore on the mining itself but not to the extent that they prescribed "what must be done afterwards." In this he appeared to side with the district court's ruling on the reclamation provisions, although he disagreed with its reliance on the Tenth Amendment. Justice Powell: "I gag a lot." He took a pass on the reclamation provisions, observing that at some point the commerce clause "runs into the Tenth Amendment." Justice Powell wrestled with his concerns in a memorandum to Burger in which he complained that SMRCA's postmining regulations intruded pervasively into areas of "traditional state and local land use control" and considered voting to uphold the district court on this issue.[14]

These serious misgivings about the reach of federal power would eventually boil over into significant changes in Court doctrine, but in *Hodel* they remained largely confined. The justices ultimately were unanimous in upholding SMCRA against the mining interests' claims. In rejecting the miner's commerce clause attack, Justice Marshall's opinion for the Court observed that "the denomination of an activity as a 'local' or 'intrastate' activity does not resolve the question." A "local" activity that produces goods shipped in interstate commerce could be regulated under the commerce clause if the "'local' activity of producing these goods itself affects interstate commerce." Congress could also regulate local activity to prevent destructive interstate competition among states—that is, an RTB or interstate environmental spillovers. Congressional findings related to these commerce clause touchstones were reasonable, the Court found, and there was no "remaining foundation" for the mining interests' arguments keyed to characterization of SMCRA as land use regulation. The Court was also unpersuaded by the district court's Tenth Amendment ruling based on the act's intrusion on traditional state land use functions; SMCRA did not violate the Tenth Amendment because it regulated private concerns, not states.[15]

In dismissing the local as a determinative factor in commerce clause regulation, the Court in *Hodel* embraced "a web or ecosystem model" of commerce. It was quick to credit Congressional findings consistent with that model—adverse effects on interstate commerce, interstate environmental spillovers from local surface mining operations, and destructive interstate competition among coal mining states. And the Court rejected arguments that were inconsistent, particularly the miners' contention that land use was inherently local and within the states' traditional and primary power to regulate. The Court's indulgence of the interdependence model, its readiness to credit significant systemic effects flowing between and among states, has eroded in more recent federalism cases. In those cases, the Court has installed the states' "traditional and primary power over land and water use" as a presumption against federal jurisdiction.[16]

Chief Justice Burger and Justices Powell and Rehnquist wrote separate concurrences. Rehnquist concurred only in the Court's judgment (not its opinion) and registered concerns about the reach of federal power that he would later bring to dominance on the Court. He agreed reluctantly that SMCRA was supportable under the Court's commerce clause precedents, but the act, in his view, was congressional power stretched to the "nth degree." The job of the law, in protecting the values of federalism, was to draw lines and set limits within the endless web of interrelationships that could be imagined surrounding almost any activity. The Court's opinion, Rehnquist believed, had understated that role.[17]

To make his point, Justice Rehnquist quoted at length from two Justice Cardozo opinions from the 1930s that recognized a version of the interdependence model applied to socioeconomic systems: society as "an elastic medium which transmits all tremors throughout its territory." In Cardozo's view, as in Rehnquist's, however, to credit all these "centripetal forces" under the commerce clause would bring "an end to our federal system." It was imperative in commerce power cases to distinguish immediate from distant repercussions of local activities. The doctrinal device for this, Rehnquist argued, was a requirement sometimes (but not always) articulated by the Court that the regulated activity have a "substantial effect" on interstate commerce, not just "some nexus" with it, to fall within the commerce power. Drawing the line at "substantial effects" would enable the Court to distinguish, in Cardozo's words, "waves of causation [that] have radiated so far that their undulatory motion, if discernible at all, will be too faint or obscure, too broken, by cross-currents, to be heeded by the law." The Court's omission of "substantial" from its statement of the effects test in *Hodel*, Rehnquist worried, left federalism potentially at the mercy of an endless web of interrelationships. A decade later, now under Chief Justice Rehnquist's leadership, the Court would make "substantial" an unequivocal part of the effects test. It would be in the line-drawing business.[18]

United States v. Riverside Bayview Homes: Federalism in an Interconnected World

Also decided before the new federalism revolution on the Court, *United States v. Riverside Bayview Homes* did not address the commerce clause directly but upheld an expansive interpretation of federal regulatory jurisdiction under the Clean Water Act (CWA). Discharges of fill material and other pollutants into "navigable waters"—which the act defines as "waters of the United States, including the territorial seas"—are subject to federal permitting requirements under the CWA; discharges into anything other than navigable waters are not. At issue in *Riverside Bayview* was the Army Corps of Engineers' regulatory jurisdiction over wetlands "adjacent to" open waters. In a unanimous ruling, rendered in an opinion by Justice White, the Court agreed with the Corps that wetlands could qualify as "waters" and upheld the Corps' assertion of jurisdiction over adjacent wetlands as a reasonable interpretation of an ambiguous statute. The decision gave generous expression to the ecological model and values associated with it.[19]

The Court rested its decision on the stated purpose of the act: to protect and restore the "integrity" of the nation's waters. In its view, "this objective incorporated a broad, systemic view of the goal of maintaining and improving water quality." Although the wetlands at issue were physically adjacent to a stream that was "navigable" in the traditional sense of that term, they were not flooded or permeated by waters of that stream. The Court nevertheless observed that the wetlands were connected to the stream through the "hydrological cycle" and further that wetlands performed valuable ecosystem services such as water filtration, flood prevention, and "biological functions." Deferring to the "ecological judgment" of the Corps embedded in the regulatory definition, the Court concluded that "the evident breadth of congressional concern for protection of water quality and aquatic ecosystems suggests that it is reasonable for the Corps to interpret the term 'waters' to encompass wetlands adjacent to waters as more conventionally defined."[20]

Taking its cue from Congress, the Court in *Riverside Bayview* enthusiastically embraced a view of "waters" as highly interconnected aquatic systems, in which various components functioned together to provide natural services, including food and habitat. Congress's intent to protect these systems extended to their individual components, such as wetlands, even in the absence of an obvious connection, such as flooding, to traditional navigable waters. The Court concluded that "navigable" in the act's jurisdictional grant was of "limited import" given the broad statutory goals and the statutory definition of "navigable waters" as simply "waters of the United States." It reserved for a future day the "question of the authority of the Corps to regulate discharges of fill material into wetlands that are not adjacent to open bodies of water." Given the robust notion of interdependence that grounded the Court's unanimous decision in *Riverside Bayview*, it would not have been unreasonable to expect that these "isolated waters" would also be ruled as properly within the compass of the act. But by the time that issue came before the Court in *Solid Waste Agency of Northern Cook County v. U.S. Army Corps of Engineers* (*SWANCC*), the Court had acquired six new justices and in two ground-shifting decisions had declared a new commitment to limiting federal regulatory reach under the commerce clause.[21]

Lopez and *Morrison*: Resetting Commerce Clause Federalism

A decade after *Riverside Bayview*, the Court announced a new era in commerce clause jurisprudence with its decision in *United States v. Lopez*, striking down the Gun-Free School Zones Act of 1990. Five years later, it consolidated the new doctrine in *United States v. Morrison*, invalidating the Violence against Women Act. The statutes in these cases criminalized behavior that was intrastate and noncommercial in nature—possession of a firearm in the vicinity of a school in *Lopez* and violence against women in *Morrison*. Both cases were decided by five to four votes, with Justices Souter, Ginsburg, Stevens, and Breyer dissenting. Chief Justice Rehnquist wrote the opinion for the Court in both cases, joined by Justices O'Connor, Scalia, Kennedy, and Thomas. The Court invalidated the statutes as falling outside any of the three rationales for use of the commerce power, with particular attention to whether the activities regulated were substantially related to interstate commerce.[22]

As in Justice O'Connor's opinion for the Court in *New York v. United States,* limiting federal power under the Tenth Amendment, the Court in these cases left no doubt that the central value of federalism was liberty—in commerce clause cases, freedom from oppressive government regulation that might flow from unchecked federal power. The Court observed that the commerce clause supports federal regulation of intrastate activity as substantially affecting interstate commerce only if the activity is economic or commercial. *Lopez* made clear that the test was "substantially affect," not merely "affect," a vindication of Justice Rehnquist's concurring view in *Hodel.* If it was not clear from *Lopez, Morrison* made it clear that in determining substantial effects on commerce the Court would not, as a general matter, aggregate impacts of local activity that were noneconomic.[23]

Morrison, contrary to *Hodel*, suggested that "areas of traditional state regulation" provided a touchstone in affirmative commerce clause cases. Writing for the Court in *Morrison,* Chief Justice Rehnquist quoted from Justice Cardozo, as he had in *Hodel* and *Lopez,* on the daunting interrelatedness of our socioeconomic system and the need for judicial line-drawing to maintain the distinction between "what is national and what is local" against arguments based on attenuated causal relationships. In areas of traditional state concern such as family law, he acknowledged, "the aggregate effect of marriage, divorce, and childrearing on the national economy is undoubtedly significant," but it was the Court's job to protect areas of established state authority against wholesale federal intrusion and with them the values served by federalism. The Court's demanding "substantial effects" test was designed to do just that.[24]

In his dissent in *Morrison,* Justice Breyer saw the Court's effort to protect traditional enclaves of state and local authority as a vain attempt to resist "practical reality." The nation had modernized, moving past the conditions under which those traditional allocations of power developed: "We live in a Nation knit together by two centuries of scientific, technological, and environmental change." This advanced interconnectedness made "it close to impossible for the courts to develop meaningful subject-matter categories that would exclude some kinds of local activities from ordinary commerce clause 'aggregation' rules without . . . depriving Congress of the power to regulate activities that have a genuine and important effect on interstate commerce." Breyer would have left it to the political branches to strike an appropriate federal/state balance reflecting the conditions and preferences of the present.

The Court's resurrection of "areas of traditional state regulation" as a touchstone of federalism had particular significance for environmental cases because of the potential to privilege allocations of power based on pre-ecological understandings of environmental injury and causation. A "traditional" allocation tends to support a narrower scope of federal environmental regulation than would be warranted by modern ecological concepts. A narrower scope, in turn, broadens the discretion given solely to the states on whether and how far to regulate, and typically serves autonomy and mastery values over harmony and collectivist values that might be advanced by federal environmental regulation informed by the ecological model. This tendency played out in two CWA cases decided close on the heels of *Lopez* and *Morrison*.

Solid Waste Agency of Northern Cook County v. U.S. Army Corps of Engineers: A Line in the Waters

One year after *Morrison*, the Court revisited the scope of federal jurisdiction under the CWA in *Solid Waste Agency of Northern Cook County v. U.S. Army Corps of Engineers* (*SWANCC*). Although *SWANCC* was not a constitutional ruling, the Court's interpretation of the CWA was heavily influenced by its recent commerce clause holdings. The competing views on the balance of power between the central and the local that were evident in *Lopez* and *Morrison* surfaced again in *SWANCC* with distinct implications for environmentalist beliefs and values. In *SWANCC*, a majority of the Court suppressed the ecological model in limiting federal regulatory authority.[25]

Like its predecessor, *Riverside Bayview*, *SWANCC* addressed the scope of the Corps of Engineers' CWA permitting authority over "navigable waters." The "waters" in *SWANCC* were "a scattering of permanent and seasonal ponds of varying size and depth" (up to several feet). They evolved from old excavation trenches on an abandoned mining site, which over time had come to support "a successional stage forest." A consortium of twenty-three suburban Chicago municipalities, acting through the Solid Waste

Agency of Northern Cook County (SWANCC), purchased the site for the construction of a regional facility for disposal of their baled domestic solid waste, known as the "balefill."[26]

The Corps' regulatory definition of "waters of the United States" extended jurisdiction to isolated waters—waters not adjacent to other jurisdictional waters—if their "degradation or destruction . . . could affect interstate or foreign commerce." To clarify this part of its definition, the Corps added an interpretive gloss, the Migratory Bird Rule, which gave it jurisdiction over "intrastate" waters "which are or would be used as habitat by birds protected by Migratory Bird Treaties; or used as habitat by other migratory birds which cross state lines." The Corps initially declined jurisdiction over SWANCC's balefill site because it found no wetlands there, but later reconnaissance led it to conclude that the water areas were habitat for migratory birds. On the basis of the Migratory Bird Rule, the Corps claimed jurisdiction over the fill operations to construct the balefill, adding a federal Section 404 permit to the state and county permits already required.[27]

Opposition to the balefill came from citizens of the Village of Bartlett, located near the site. The grassroots center of the resistance, Citizens Against the Balefill (CAB), complained that the balefill would reduce local property values; unjustly make Bartlett a dumping ground for the waste of wealthier, more powerful localities; contaminate groundwater; and (after the Corps became involved) disturb the ecology of the site, including destruction of a colony of blue herons. The balefill received the necessary state and county permits. But through the intervention of Bartlett's U.S. Congressman, Dennis Hastert, CAB got the favorable attention of the Corps, and the Corps denied the federal permit. Its denial vindicated at least some of CAB's environmental objections: the balefill would cause "unmitigatable" harm to area species, "posed 'an unacceptable risk to the public's drinking water supply,'" and had not been shown to be the least environmentally damaging disposal alternative for the region's solid waste. SWANCC sued in federal court to overturn the denial.[28]

In *New York v. United States,* as discussed in Chapter 3, states supporting federal legislation to secure adequate and safe disposal capacity for low-level radioactive waste wore the environmentalist mantle. Much like them, SWANCC sought to secure adequate and safe capacity for disposal of the domestic waste of its member localities. But its litigation against the Corps put SWANCC in the position of discounting the impacts on wildlife and other environmental problems that the Bartlett activists claimed and that the Corps' denial validated. SWANCC came primarily to represent mastery values, albeit for a collective benefit, in its proposed disturbance of a landscape that was just regaining some semblance of ecological integrity after its earlier use for mining. The local activists fighting the balefill—NIMBYs to their adversaries—claimed the environmental high ground, wrapping themselves in the harmony values associated with allowing continued healing of the site and avoiding risks of groundwater contamination. In this, having been recruited by Congressman Hastert, the Corps became their champion.

SWANCC initially attacked both the Corps' jurisdiction over the balefill site and the merits of its permit denial. The district court upheld the jurisdiction under the Migratory Bird Rule, and SWANCC dropped its merits claim. On appeal, the Court of Appeals for the Seventh Circuit affirmed. The Migratory Bird Rule was within the commerce power because the destruction of migratory bird habitat and the resulting decrease in birds had a substantial aggregate effect on interstate commerce, measured in reduced opportunities to hunt and observe the birds across state lines. The circuit court also upheld the Migratory Bird Rule as a reasonable interpretation of the CWA, which in its view intended to extend the Corps' authority to the full extent of the commerce power.[29]

After the Court granted review in *SWANCC*, but before the briefing and argument on the merits, it decided *United States v. Morrison*. Lawyers for the Corps distanced themselves from the original rationale of the Migratory Bird Rule because it focused on an arguably noneconomic activity (the destruction of habitat) that might not be aggregable under *Morrison* to meet the substantial effects test. Instead, they characterized the activity regulated by the Corps as "the filling of ponds to construct a municipal landfill . . . plainly of a commercial nature." The Court would use this shift to bolster its assertion that the Corps had pushed the commerce clause to its outer limits, creating serious constitutional questions that should be avoided with a less expansive statutory interpretation.[30]

The Court's Opinion

The opinion for the Court by Chief Justice Rehnquist, joined by Justices Kennedy, Scalia, O'Connor, and Thomas, held that the Migratory Bird Rule exceeded the Corps' authority under the statute. While mentioning the act's ecosystem integrity goal, which had been at the heart of the decision in *Riverside Bayview*, it emphasized the statute's recognition of the "the primary responsibilities and rights of States" in achieving that goal. The Court acknowledged its statement in *Riverside Bayview* that "navigable" "was of 'limited import.'" But that did not mean that "navigable" was of "no effect whatever." In fact, "navigable" signified what Congress "had in mind as its authority for enacting the CWA: its traditional jurisdiction over waters that

were or had been navigable in fact or which could reasonably be so made."
The Court concluded:

> We thus decline respondents' invitation to take what they see as the next in-
> eluctable step after *Riverside Bayview Homes*: holding that isolated ponds,
> some only seasonal, wholly located within two Illinois counties, fall under
> § 404(a)'s definition of "navigable waters" because they serve as habitat for
> migratory birds.

Rather than a pointless atavism, as it seemed in *Riverside Bayview,* "navigable" in Chief Justice Rehnquist's hands became a tool to constrain the
act's expression of the ecological model and its associated values. The Migratory Bird Rule's effort to make nature into commerce was dead.[31]

The Court in *SWANCC* asserted that the limits of the Corps' permitting
authority were "clear." But even if they were not, the Court declined to give
deference to the Corps' regulatory interpretation, *Chevron* notwithstanding.
Chevron deference gave way to two constitutionally based clear statement
rules: the avoidance canon (the Corps' jurisdiction over the isolated waters would pose significant questions under the commerce clause, such as
"the precise object or activity that, in the aggregate, substantially affects
interstate commerce") and the federalism canon (the Corps' jurisdiction
would also "result in a significant impingement of the States' traditional
and primary power over land and water use"). Finding no clear indication
of congressional intent to force the issue on these questions, the Court interpreted the statute to avoid them.[32]

Clear statement rules protecting federalism existed before the Court's federalism revolution, but in 1991, on the eve of that revolution, the Court in
Gregory v. Ashcroft "adopted a powerful, generic" version of the canon,
and after that decision, the Court tended to apply it vigorously. In *SWANNC,*
the Court used the canon to turn its concern over protecting states' "traditional" regulatory domains into a restriction on the delegated policy-making
authority of the Corps under *Chevron.* The standard justification for the
federalism canon, like other constitutionally based canons, is that it reflects
values embodied in the Constitution. But as law professor John Manning,
an expert in statutory interpretation, has written, the Constitution advances
competing values in different settings—for example, the value of dual sovereignty in some settings and of strong national government in others. To
pick one value over another for purposes of a general interpretative rule,
as the federalism canon does, is a judicial value choice. In *SWANCC* that
value choice pervaded the Court's interpretation, both implicitly, in its
reading of ambiguous statutory terms to produce a "clear" meaning, and
explicitly, in its fallback invocation of the canon.[33]

The Court's interpretation of Section 404 was marked by a near-total absence of discussion of the possible ecosystemic consequences of filling the lakes and ponds north of Chicago. The Court briefly explained the contrary result in *Riverside Bayview* as based on "the significant nexus" in that case between the adjacent wetlands and "navigable waters." But it did not explore the possible nexus between the isolated waters in this case and other "waters of the United States" or the "aquatic ecosystem," as expansively portrayed in *Riverside Bayview*. It assumed that isolated waters were just that: "isolated" physically and biologically from "navigable waters" or "waters of the United States." It was as if by consigning these waters to the states' "traditional and primary power over land and water use," the Court disposed of the possibility that their disturbance would have significant extralocal effects warranting regulation under the CWA.[34]

Justice Stevens's Dissent

In his dissent, joined by Justices Souter, Ginsburg, and Breyer, Justice Stevens evoked the lost world of *Riverside Bayview* and placed isolated waters within it. In *Riverside Bayview*, he argued, there were two types of connections that justified regulation—hydrological (surface runoff from the wetland into the adjacent stream) and ecological. "Both types of connection are also present in many, and possibly most, 'isolated waters.'" Stevens's dissent emphasized the second, more comprehensive type of connection:

> As we recognized in *Riverside Bayview*, the interests served by the statute embrace the protection of "significant natural biological functions, including food chain production, general habitat, and nesting, spawning, rearing and resting sites" for various species of aquatic wildlife. For wetlands and "isolated" inland lakes, that interest is equally powerful regardless of the proximity of the swamp or the water to a navigable stream.

In Stevens's ecological worldview, the extensive connections between these waters and the larger system made them "anything but isolated," and they demanded recognition under a statute committed to the protection of aquatic systems.[35]

Because he concluded that the statute extends to isolated waters, Stevens completed the commerce clause analysis that the Court only began. The intrastate activity regulated in this case, development of a solid waste disposal site, was economic (a question on which the Court expressed doubt but left unresolved). Justice Stevens found that, in the aggregate, the filling of isolated waters serving as migratory bird habitat would harm the birds and substantially affect the interstate commerce generated by birdwatchers and hunters. As a response to interstate spillovers or "externalities" in the form of impacts on interstate bird populations, Stevens argued, the Migratory Bird Rule did not violate the distinction between "what is truly national and what is truly local" but rather honored it. This version of federalism—or perhaps better, nationalism—gave generous expression to the interdependence model and associated collectivist and harmony values operating at the national level.[36]

The meaning of *SWANCC* was complicated by the events that followed the decision. Individual and other private interests were not directly involved in *SWANCC*, although it is easy to see, as in *Rapanos v. United States,* how the Corps' jurisdictional claims could adversely affect those interests. The "tyranny" of immediate concern to the Court in *SWANCC* was the Corps' assertion of federal authority to override decisions of Illinois and Cook County officials that the balefill was in the public interest. But the specter of comparable tyranny was also present in Illinois's and Cook County's imposition of the balefill on an unwilling Village of Bartlett, tyranny about which the U.S. Constitution and the Court had nothing to say. The Court's decision seemed to leave the Village of Bartlett at Cook County's mercy, sweeping away the last regulatory barrier to the balefill. CAB and its allies continued to fight, however, targeting their efforts at the state legislature in an effort to override the County's decision to press forward with the project. With some additional help from Congressman Hastert, this effort was successful. Under threat of legislative disapproval, the adversaries reached a settlement in which SWANCC would abandon the balefill, sending its waste to private disposal facilities, which turned out to offer ample and reasonably priced capacity; the state would purchase the abandoned gravel pit for a forest preserve; and SWANCC would sell the remainder of the property that it had acquired for the project. SWANCC sold this property to residential developers and a mining company, which went on, with Bartlett's approval, to develop a mine, a sales lot for damaged autos, and an asphalt plant. One might ask, with Thomas Merrill, what the citizens of Bartlett were fighting for if they were content in the end with a mine and an asphalt plant in their community. But they now had the forest preserve too. Competing values were balanced. In this case, the balancing occurred within a complex political ecosystem, operating across many levels, in which the Court was an important, but not the controlling or even the most influential, player.[37]

Rapanos v. United States: Completing the Boundaries

The Court revisited the jurisdictional scope of the CWA for a third time in *Rapanos v. United States* and *Carabell v. United States Army Corps of*

Engineers (collectively *Rapanos*), decided together in June 2006. The array of opinions in *Rapanos* represented a modest shift in the cultural balance of *SWANCC,* offering a path of accommodation between the beliefs and values that seemed implacably at odds in the earlier case. This path of accommodation was the work of Justice Kennedy, whose lone concurrence arguably became the holding of the case.[38]

Rapanos addressed questions that *Riverside Bayview* and *SWANCC* had left open on the Corps' CWA jurisdiction over nonnavigable tributaries of navigable waters and wetlands adjacent to those tributaries. In the first case, the United States brought a civil enforcement action against John Rapanos, his wife, and a company controlled by him for unlawfully filling three tracts of wetlands that the Corps had determined were within its jurisdiction. Each of these tracts had a surface water connection with a ditch, drain, or stream that flowed ultimately into a traditionally navigable water. A federal district court upheld the Corps' jurisdiction over these wetlands, and the Sixth Circuit affirmed. In the second case, the Carabells sought and were refused a permit to fill a tract of wetlands adjoining a ditch that also drained ultimately into traditionally navigable waters but that was separated from the wetlands by a man-made berm that prevented, at least under normal conditions, surface water flow from the wetlands into the ditch. In the Carabells' appeal from the permit denial, a district court upheld the Corps' jurisdiction, and the Sixth Circuit, again, affirmed. The Court granted review in both cases.

The stormy figure of landowner-developer John Rapanos was at the symbolic heart of these cases. Rapanos envisioned a shopping center for one of his properties, the Salzburg site, but a state inspector told him that the site likely had wetlands that were "waters of the United States" and sent him an application for a permit under Section 404 of the CWA. A consultant hired by Rapanos confirmed that there were forty-eight to fifty-eight acres of jurisdictional wetlands on the site. An outraged Rapanos threatened "to destroy" the consultant if the report stood, and he vowed to bulldoze the site himself regardless of the findings. True to his threat, Rapanos began filling wetlands on all three properties without seeking state or federal permits and ignored state and federal administrative orders to stop. His defiance spurred the federal government to file the civil enforcement action that eventually led to the Supreme Court's review. The government also brought criminal charges against Rapanos for his actions at the Salzburg site, which resulted in a conviction. Like Rapanos, the Carabells were would-be-developers who objected to the Corps' interference with their plans to build on their wetlands. But they lacked Rapanos's provocative flair. In public discussions of the cases, John Rapanos was the polarizing figure—lionized by property rights advocates for his courageous stand against an overreaching federal government, disdained by environmentalists as a malicious law-breaker. The focus on the prerogatives of the individual property owner in *Rapanos* connects it symbolically to the takings cases discussed in Chapter 8.[39]

Before the Supreme Court, the issues were solely jurisdictional: Did the act authorize Corps jurisdiction over these wetlands and, if so, did that jurisdiction exceed the commerce power? The parties gave the great majority of their attention to the statute's scope, and oral argument made clear that the Court's attention was there also. Rapanos's lawyers argued that the act extended only to traditionally navigable waters and other waters that were "inseparably bound up" with them. A mere "hydrological connection" between wetlands and traditionally navigable waters supplied by nonnavigable tributaries of those waters was not enough. The Carabells' lawyers maintained that a hydrological connection with traditionally navigable waters was both necessary and sufficient for jurisdiction. Because that connection was lacking in the Carabells' case, their wetland was not within the reach of the act. The government argued that all wetlands that were "adjacent" to traditionally navigable waters or their tributaries were jurisdictional; a hydrological connection was not necessary. Even in one's absence, wetlands provided other important ecological functions, such as sediment capture and flood control, for adjacent waters that met the "significant nexus" test of *SWANCC*.[40]

The Court reversed and remanded both cases for further consideration by the lower courts. This result was complicated by the diversity of views expressed in separate opinions by five of the justices, three of whom are central to the analysis here. All justices agreed that the Corps' jurisdiction extended to traditionally navigable waters and wetlands adjacent to them, as the narrowest reading of *Riverside Bayview* would require. But beyond that, views of what the statute meant splintered. Joined by Chief Justice Roberts and Justices Thomas and Alito, Justice Scalia's plurality opinion extended jurisdiction only to "relatively permanent" standing or flowing bodies of water that drain to traditionally navigable waters and to wetlands with a "continuous surface connection" to such bodies of water. Justice Kennedy's lone concurrence extended the Corps' jurisdiction to nonnavigable waters and adjacent wetlands that the agency could show had a "significant nexus" to traditionally navigable waters, measured by impact on the aquatic system. Joined by Justices Souter, Ginsburg, and Breyer, Justice Stevens's dissent would have upheld the application of the Corps' regulations in these cases asserting jurisdiction over tributaries of traditionally navigable waters, whether permanent or intermittent, and wetlands adjacent to those tributaries.[41]

These diverse interpretations produced diverse cultural meanings. Justice Scalia's plurality opinion resisted the expansive pressure of the ecological model, as Chief Justice Rehnquist had in *SWANCC*, to make room for linked mastery and autonomy values emphasizing individual initiative in the manipulation of the environment for personal gain. Justice Stevens would have embodied a generous version of the ecological model in his interpretation of the statute, giving sway to the harmony and collectivist values associated with that model. Justice Kennedy's interpretation negotiated between these two poles, although he was relatively more responsive to the pull of the ecological worldview. These opinions produced three distinct jurisdictional maps, all of the same landscape but seen through different cultural lenses.

Justice Scalia's Plurality Opinion

John Rapanos was a made-to-order protagonist for Justice Scalia's autonomy-mastery narrative in the case—a feisty landowner thwarted by regulation from developing his property. Scalia used the first four pages of his plurality opinion to depict Rapanos's plight. He made no mention of Rapanos's abusive tactics to evade regulation, which both Justice Kennedy's and Stevens's opinions laid out, but instead stressed the heavy financial burdens and delays of seeking and obtaining a Section 404 permit and the oppressive penalties for violating the permit requirement. "In this litigation . . . for backfilling his own wet fields, Mr. Rapanos faced 63 months in prison and hundreds of thousands of dollars in criminal and civil fines." The sympathy for Rapanos was palpable, who only wanted to "backfill wet fields" (not build shopping centers on ecologically valuable wetlands), which were, after all, "his own."[42]

Against this model entrepreneur-landowner, Scalia posed the Corps, a bureaucracy with the "discretion of an enlightened despot" that had engineered an "immense expansion of federal regulation of land use" under the CWA. This expansion had converted up to 300 million acres of "swampy lands" (again, not ecologically valuable wetlands) into jurisdictional waters, "including half of Alaska and an area of the size of California in the lower 48 states." Indeed, he concluded, the Corps' claimed regulatory domain covered "any plot of land" to the extent connected, however tenuously, to the aquatic system. These characterizations drew an objection from Justice Kennedy, who wrote in his concurrence that they were "unduly dismissive of the interests asserted by the United States in these cases." They contributed to the plurality opinion's strong antiregulatory tone.[43]

Justice Scalia's opinion cut the aggressively colonizing aquatic ecosystem down to size and divided it into jurisdictional chunks small enough to protect traditional state and local land use prerogatives and, not incidentally, to make more room for the aspirations of property owners like the Rapanos and Carabells. He acknowledged the CWA's stated purpose to "restore and protect the chemical, physical and biological integrity of the nation's waters"—a purpose invoked by the Corps to justify its expansive jurisdictional claims as necessary to assure protection at the ecosystem level. But he argued that this purpose did not control the statute's meaning: in the CWA, Congress's goal of ecological protection was offset by its stated intent "to recognize, preserve, and protect the primary responsibilities and rights of the States . . . to plan the development and use . . . of land and water resources. . . ." Congress's commitment to its protection goal was also limited by the statute's key definitional terms. Using words in statutory text as devices of limitation, Scalia imposed strict boundaries on protean waters.[44]

The Court's focus in *Riverside Bayview* and *SWANCC* was on the role, if any, that "navigable" played in delimiting the CWA's jurisdictional scope. In Justice Scalia's plurality opinion in *Rapanos,* the attention shifted to "waters." Scalia mined that term to achieve two interpretational outcomes: First, to support Corps jurisdiction, "tributaries" to navigable waters had to be fixed bodies of water with continuous flows; intermittent or ephemeral streams do not qualify, even if they may impact downstream water quality. Second, to qualify as jurisdictional, wetlands had to have a continuous surface connection to a traditionally navigable water or a tributary; mere proximity was not enough, even if the wetlands performed ecological functions such as flood control.

"THE WATERS"

On the first issue, Justice Scalia's textual foothold was Congress's use of the definite article ("the") and the plural form ("waters") in the definitional term "the waters of the United States." From these features of the text he inferred that the reference was not to water in general, which could be present anywhere, but "more narrowly to water '[a]s found in streams and bodies forming geographical features such as oceans, rivers, [and] lakes.'" As Kennedy's concurrence and Stevens's dissent pointed out, there were less restrictive definitions of "waters," including "flood" or "inundation," that could have encompassed intermittent streams or even dry washes subject to periodic flooding. But Scalia dismissed these alternatives as more "poetic" than Congress could have intended in an "otherwise prosaic, indeed downright tedious, statute." Accommodating these additional meanings would have supported the very result that he wished to avoid, turning land (e.g., "wet meadows," "drain tiles," "dry arroyos in the middle of the desert") into regulated waters. This was just too silly or, as he put it, "beyond parody."[45]

Concluding that there was no ambiguity in the meaning of the CWA on this point, Justice Scalia granted no deference to the Corps' more expansive interpretation. But even if there had been ambiguity, he argued—just as Chief Justice Rehnquist did in *SWANCC*—that the avoidance canon and the federalist canon ruled out the Corps' interpretation. To leave no doubt about his dominant concern, Scalia reversed the order of citation of these canons, putting the recently reinvigorated federalism canon first—the anti-tyranny presumption that precluded extension of federal authority into areas of traditional state and local power, such as land use, without a "clear and manifest" statement of congressional intent to do so. This value-driven interpretive rule bolstered limiting the CWA's domain to a fraction of the aquatic ecosystem writ large.[46]

ADJACENCY

In his treatment of the adjacency issue, Justice Scalia similarly used verbal analysis to create limiting jurisdictional boundaries. But on this issue, Scalia was forced to address *Riverside Bayview,* in which the Court had upheld Corps jurisdiction over wetlands, albeit wetlands adjacent to "open waters" rather than to tributaries. He produced a minimalist reading of that decision that limited the relevance of ecological interconnectivity and the statutory purpose that supported it.

In *Riverside Bayview,* the Court had held that wetlands adjacent to open waters were jurisdictional but did not elaborate on what was required to establish adjacency. In *SWANCC,* the Court observed that the result in *Riverside Bayview* turned on the "significant nexus between the wetlands and the 'navigable waters' "—a nexus fatally absent for the isolated ponds in *SWANCC.*[47] Both Justice Kennedy's concurrence and Justice Stevens's dissent in *Rapanos* took this observation as justifying ecological interdependence as a basis for their more expansive jurisdictional interpretations. Scalia, however, sharply cabined it. *Riverside Bayview,* he argued, was a case in which the line between waters and land was ambiguous, as the wetlands merged into open waters with no clear line of demarcation. In those limited circumstances, the Court recognized that an ecological connection could justify treating abutting wetlands as waters. That alone was the point of *SWANCC'*s use of "significant nexus." Where there was no ambiguity where waters began and ended—as in *Carabell,* for example, where wetlands were dammed from neighboring waters by a berm—ecological considerations were irrelevant. In such cases, the line between land and waters was clear and no complicating notions of ecological connectivity could be allowed to blur it.

In sum, Justice Scalia's opinion established sharp boundaries between major features of the landscape—lands and waters—and used those boundaries to limit the Corps' regulatory encroachments. To accomplish this, he cut away features of *Riverside Bayview* that were resonant with the environmentalist paradigm and converted that holding into a narrow case of unclear boundaries. He mined "the waters," extracting hard-edged meanings for the term over more permeable possibilities compatible with notions of ecological interdependence underlying the Corps' jurisdictional claims. In his hands, the phrase became a tool to limit and close off wider connections within the regulatory landscape.

Justice Scalia is a textualist with a preference for rule-like interpretations of statutes that draw clear distinctions. One would expect his interpretation of the CWA or any statute to be based on a close parsing of the language and structure of the text and to yield relatively precise categories for application by lower courts and agencies. But this interpretive method leaves choices in its application. In *Rapanos*, Scalia insisted on select "natural" or "traditional" meanings of geographic or natural resource terms to limit federal regulation of systemic concerns. This interpretive strategy has become a staple of Scalia in environmental cases that have significant ecological dimensions. In his dissent on the merits in *MA v. EPA*, for example, he argued that the agency reasonably excluded greenhouse gas emissions from regulation as air pollutants because the "natural meaning" of "air pollution" was impurities "at ground level or near the surface of the earth," not gases disbursed in the "upper reaches of the atmosphere." He used the same approach in his 1995 dissent in *Babbitt v. Sweet Home Chapter of Communities for a Great Oregon*, discussed in Chapter 8.[48]

In *Rapanos*, Justice Scalia did not deny the ecological connections between or among waters or between waters and land. Indeed, the existence of those relationships seemed implicit in his effort to prevent their consideration in defining the CWA's scope. What he rejected were their implications for the federal regulatory scheme. He would control those implications by imposing a simplifying, limiting law grid on the living topography, dividing up the landscape in a manner consistent with preferred institutional arrangements and the values they reflect. In *Lujan II,* the Article III standing case, a dissenting Justice Blackmun accused Scalia of applying "rigid principles of geographic formalism" to defeat environmentalists' claims. In that case,

Scalia based this formalism on a reductive concept of injury; in *Rapanos* he based it on statutory text and canons of construction. But the effect on the legal landscape was similar.[49]

As in a number of other environmental opinions authored by Justice Scalia, the plurality opinion in *Rapanos* was revealing not only in its tactics but also in its tone. For the reasons already discussed, the ecological model threatens autonomy-mastery values, and the crucial, purpose-defining role of that model in the CWA helps explain the vigor with which Scalia deployed his textualist tools to cabin it. He truncated both the statutory term "waters" and the precedent of *Riverside Bayview* to create a rule-like construct that would control future courts and jurisdictionally aggressive agencies and provide some relief for the regulated community. He applied substantive canons of construction to bolster this outcome. His rhetoric was dismissive (Corps as "enlightened despot," "swampy lands," "beyond parody"), as in other cases in which he has rejected expansive regulation linked to the ecological worldview. In *Rapanos*, Scalia distinguished himself, in Justice Stevens's phrase, by an "antagonism to environmentalism" itself.[50]

Although federalism provided a framework for the legal analysis in *Rapanos*, the animus of Justice Scalia's plurality opinion seemed directed as much at the regulatory interference with Rapanos's development as at the federal source of that regulation. This antiregulatory cast was even starker in Scalia's vote in an earlier case with federalism overtones arising under the CWA, in which he joined Justice Thomas in arguing to protect federally licensed hydroelectric dams from the reach of state environmental regulations. The issue in *PUD No. 1 v. Washington Department of Ecology* was the permissible breadth of state water quality certifications required by the CWA as a condition of federally licensed projects discharging into navigable waters. Washington State's water quality certification for a proposed hydroelectric dam that required a federal license set minimum stream flows to protect salmon and steelhead runs. In an opinion written by one of the champions of the federalism revolution, Justice O'Connor, and concurred in by Chief Justice Rehnquist and five other justices, the Court cited the broad ecosystemic purposes of the CWA in holding that the state requirements were within the scope of the certification provision. Scalia joined Thomas's dissent complaining that the Court's reading would give the states virtually limitless veto authority over federally licensed energy projects, allowing "parochial environmental interests" to overpower the "*Nation's* power needs." The dissent would have switched federalist polarities, expanding federal authority at the expense of the states, but it served the same mastery values as the plurality opinion in *Rapanos*.[51]

Justice Stevens's Dissent

Justice Stevens's argument for affirmance was straightforward. In stating its purpose to protect "the chemical, physical, and biological integrity of the Nation's waters," Congress meant that the goal of maintaining and improving water quality was to be understood in broad, ecosystemic terms.[52] "Wetlands" "adjacent" to "tributaries" of traditionally navigable waters, as defined by the Corps, performed important functions for the aquatic ecosystem. The core jurisdictional term, "waters," was ambiguous, and therefore the Corps had discretion in defining its scope. Because they were a reasonable construction of ambiguous statutory language and fully consistent with Congress's purpose of protecting the aquatic ecosystem, the Corps' definitions were entitled to *Chevron* deference and should have been upheld. Stevens's opinion gave much greater weight to congressional purpose—and particularly the "integrity"-protecting purpose—than did Justice Scalia's. And consistent with this, it arrived at a much different understanding of the statutory text and relevant precedents.

Justice Stevens's reading of *Riverside Bayview* was the reverse image of Justice Scalia's, and he dismissed *SWANCC* as irrelevant, having "nothing to say about wetlands." In contrast to Scalia's minimalist rendering, Stevens read *Riverside Bayview* to sanction a principle of ecosystem protection broadly applicable to the universe of waters potentially subject to CWA jurisdiction. The Court in that case deferred to Corps' jurisdiction over "wetlands adjacent to navigable waters and their tributaries" as advancing "congressional concern for protection of water quality and aquatic ecosystems." It was stretching a point to say, as Stevens seemed to, that the specific issues in *Rapanos* were resolved by *Riverside Bayview*. What this earlier case legitimately offered him, however, was the embrace of a notion of "waters" as highly interconnected aquatic systems, in which various components function together to provide natural services, and the general understanding that Congress intended to extend protection to individual components of these systems.[53]

Justice Stevens also diverged from Scalia in his reading of the statutory text. Neither Webster's Second nor the practice of topographers, he claimed, supported Justice Scalia's definition of "waters" as requiring continuous flow; "common sense and common usage demonstrate that intermittent streams, like perennial streams, are still streams." Nor did the language of the statute require that wetlands be connected to other waters by continuous flow. Consistent with keeping the CWA open to the Corps' ecologically based regulatory approach, Stevens interpreted "waters" as largely open-ended, susceptible to interpretative possibilities consistent with Congress's ecological purpose. The jurisdictional words by themselves did not draw clear lines, in his view; they allowed lines to be drawn where necessary to protect ecosystem integrity. This was in sharp contrast to Scalia's use of the words as the source of boundaries to constrain the open-ended globalism of ecological protection.[54]

Finally, Justice Stevens disputed the plurality's reliance on the canons of avoidance of constitutional issues and intrusions into areas of traditional state authority. Congress had made the determination that water quality should be protected at the source, whether permanent or intermittent, and it plainly had the power under the commerce clause to regulate on a watershed or system-wide basis to protect navigable waters and their tributaries.[55]

In contrast to Justice Scalia, Justice Stevens was an intentionalist. He looked not only to statutory language and structure but also to legislative purposes and goals as a guide to interpretation. For intentionalists, as with the textualists, there are interpretive choices. How are statutory purposes to be defined, ranked, and integrated with text and structure? In his *Rapanos* dissent, Stevens gave sway to what he identified as the statute's underlying remedial purpose, aquatic ecosystem protection, and put to the side competing purposes, such as protecting the primary authority of states over their land and water resources. The convergence between this purpose and the Corps' broad jurisdictional claim enabled him to defer comfortably to the agency's interpretation, all in service of the ecological model and its associated values. In this he followed the interpretive strategy of his dissent in *SWANCC* and his opinion interpreting the Endangered Species Act (ESA) for the majority in *Babbitt v. Sweet Home Chapter of Communities for a Great Oregon.*[56]

One could argue that these different outcomes are simply due to different methods of statutory interpretation. But the indeterminacy of both methods creates room for expression of the justices' beliefs and values, and this expression is most likely in "political" cases such as *Rapanos,* in which the law is unsettled and cultural issues are salient. It was a surprise to no one that Justice Scalia used his textualist tools in *Rapanos* to divide up the jurisdictional landscape to protect autonomy and mastery values embodied by the Rapanos and Carabells or that Justice Stevens applied his intentionalist analysis to keep that same landscape open for expression of collectivist and harmony values under the Corps' regulations.

Justice Kennedy's Concurrence

In his concurrence, Justice Kennedy sought the middle ground. He agreed with Justice Stevens that Justice Scalia's plurality opinion misread the statutory text and precedents and gave insufficient deference to the protective purpose of the statute and to the Corps' authority to craft a program that achieves that purpose. Like Stevens, he criticized the plurality's reliance on the avoidance canons and argued the inapplicability of those canons to his own interpretation.[57] But he also criticized Stevens's dissent for ignoring the import of the word "navigable" in "navigable waters."

For Justice Kennedy, the jurisdictional touchstone was not ecological connectivity in general but whether nonnavigable waters, including wetlands, "are likely to play an important role in the integrity of an aquatic system comprising navigable waters as traditionally understood." The Corps might assert general jurisdiction over wetlands adjacent to traditionally navigable waters, as *Riverside Bayview* held, because it was reasonable to infer "ecologic connection" between those wetlands and the navigable-in-fact waters. The relationship between traditionally navigable waters and wetlands adjacent to tributaries, however, was more attenuated and uncertain. Under *SWANCC,* a significant ecological relationship between this more remote class of wetlands and navigable waters was crucial to the Corps' jurisdiction. This relationship could include a variety of functions—"pollutant filtering, flood control, and runoff storage" as well as hydrological connection—but it could not be presumed. The Corps' regulations, in Kennedy's estimation, did not ensure that this significant nexus test was met. Thus, at least until "more specific regulations" were adopted, Kennedy would have the Corps show a significant nexus on a case-by-case basis when it claimed jurisdiction over wetlands adjacent to nonnavigable tributaries.[58]

Justice Kennedy is a textualist, if not so committed a textualist as Justices Scalia or Thomas. Yet in *Rapanos* he moderated his textualism in search of a workable accommodation between competing worldviews and their associated values in these cases. His analysis included links to the text, but it extended beyond the text to reach a broad purpose-based jurisdictional test. Unlike Scalia, Kennedy framed the test as a standard rather than a rule, allowing the Corps considerable discretion in particularized applications of the test.

The phrase that anchored Justice Kennedy's analysis—"significant nexus"—did not appear in the statute but was drawn from *SWANCC*'s description of the Court's holding in *Riverside Bayview* as informed by "the significant nexus between the wetlands and the 'navigable waters.'" Kennedy did use the statutory text, "navigable waters," to limit the reach of his standard by requiring that, to qualify as jurisdictional, wetlands and nonnavigable tributaries must significantly affect systems incorporating navigable waters as conventionally understood. But the effect he gave "navigable" was modest. The "significant nexus" standard retained a decidedly purposive thrust, as a functional determination tied directly to the ecosystem protection objectives of the statute.[59]

Justice Kennedy's framing gave some rigor to the ecological model as a guide for statutory implementation and balanced the competing values advanced in the plurality opinion and the dissent. While the standard acknowledged the potential interconnectedness of aquatic systems, its application required a demonstration of the relevant connections in specific cases or classes of cases. Although, as both Kennedy and Stevens suggested, this requirement was not likely to make a big difference in outcomes, it provided a boundary of demonstrable "significance" to the ecological model and answered concerns that the Corps' regulations and the ecological model on which they relied were unconstrained. In this way, Kennedy attempted to balance the competing values associated with embracing or rejecting the ecological model in federalism cases. Although tilting toward an embrace, his approach at least gave the Rapanos and the Carabells arguments to make, as it sought to ensure that regulatory burdens were imposed only where they might make a real difference to affected systems.

The initial response to *Rapanos* was confusion. As Chief Justice Roberts pointed out in his separate concurrence, none of the opinions in *Rapanos* "commands a majority of the Court on precisely how to read Congress's limits on the reach of the Clean Water Act," and thus there were questions about how the Court's various pronouncements should guide the Corps and other implementing agencies on remand. Answers from the circuit courts have been diverse: some have applied only Justice Kennedy's "significant nexus" test; others have applied either that test or the plurality's test, or both; still others have reserved on the question of which test should govern and deferred to the agency's interpretation.[60] The Corps and Environmental Protection Agency have asserted jurisdiction over waters that meet either test.[61]

Riverside Bayview, SWANNC, and *Rapanos* reflected the rising tide of federalism values in the jurisdictional contours of a single statute. These cases coded the Court's acceptance or rejection of the ecological model in determining the jurisdictional scope of statutes seeking to protect natural systems. In *Riverside Bayview,* the Court minimized the importance of a potentially limiting statutory term ("navigable waters") to give effect to systemic considerations. By contrast, in *SWANCC* and *Rapanos,* Chief Justice Rehnquist and Justice Scalia used the words of the statute ("navigable waters," "*the* waters") to enforce limits on the reach of ecological concerns. They selected restrictive meanings of these words to mark boundaries on the legal landscape that largely ignored ecological contours. These boundaries gave expression to autonomy and mastery values against expansive federal regulation. In *Rapanos,* Scalia took on this line-drawing with Jesuitical flair suggesting a deep commitment to those values. Emphasizing the statute's protective purpose, Justice Stevens would have drawn jurisdictional lines—or allowed the Corps to draw them—that gave broad recognition to ecological relationships and made ample room for collectivist and harmony values. But that blank check for the ecological model had only minority support.

It was left to Justice Kennedy in *Rapanos* to keep the ecological model and the values tied to it in play in the CWA's further evolution. His "significant nexus" provides the controlling jurisdictional test or shares that honor with the plurality's test. While some commentators have doubted the practicality of the standard, and while the Corps and the EPA have struggled to define and implement it, it operates symbolically as a formula for reconciling competing worldviews and values. It suggests scientific demonstration of significant ecological connections as a way of disciplining claims based on the ecological model while not discounting them categorically.

Back to the Future: Waiting for the Other Shoe under the Commerce Clause

The Court's commitment to limiting federal power under the commerce clause shows no signs of weakening. In 2012, the Court upheld the individual mandate of the Patient Protection and Affordable Care Act, requiring those not participating in the health insurance market to purchase health insurance unless covered by an exclusion, as an exercise of the taxing power. But a majority of the justices made clear that the mandate would not survive scrutiny under the commerce clause. As Chief Justice Roberts put it: "The Framers gave Congress the power to *regulate* commerce, not to *compel* it."[62] More generally, the five justices in the majority on this issue expressed their resolve to extend the restrictive view of the commerce power announced in cases such as *United States v. Lopez* and *United States v. Morrison* and to cabin decisions suggesting a more generous view of that power. This resolve could affect future commerce clause rulings on the permissible scope of environmental statutes, such as the ESA.

Since *Hodel,* the Court has not ruled directly on the constitutionality of a federal environmental statute under the commerce clause, but it seems only a matter of time before it does. The lower courts have ruled on the constitutionality of other federal environmental provisions, including most prominently the ESA's prohibition on the taking of endangered animal species. In several cases, appeals courts have upheld the ESA's take provision as applied to intrastate species. But those rulings have rested on diverse and competing rationales and drawn pointed dissents. In one of these cases, *Rancho Viejo LLC v. Norton,* a three-judge panel of the District of Columbia Circuit upheld the ESA's antitake provision as applied to protect the arroyo toad, an endangered species of no economic value found only in California, but two judges dissented from the denial of an en banc rehearing in the case. One was Judge Sentelle, who had voiced vigorous dissent from the court's earlier decision upholding ESA's protection of the Delhi Sands flower-loving fly as within the commerce power. The other was then-judge John Roberts, who questioned whether the court had properly applied the substantial effects test from *Lopez* and *Morrison.* With his elevation to chief justice of a Court on which a majority of justices are identified with the new federalism, Roberts's reservations set the stage for a future confrontation with the ESA. That confrontation will feature technical debates about the application of the commerce clause doctrine, but informing those debates will be conflicting beliefs and values that have been implicated in other cases affecting legal protections for the environmental other.[63]

THE ECOLOGICAL MODEL and values associated with it are at the cultural center of the environmental federalism cases. The concern for Justice Rehnquist in *Hodel* was the elasticity of the social medium that "transmitted all tremors" and the threat that this elasticity would make everything fair game for federal regulation under the commerce clause. That threat only increases when, in the modern environmentalist's understanding, the socioeconomic system is linked to natural systems not directly involved in commerce. Justices resisting the extension of federal power based on those linkages must either reject the fact of interdependence or set limits on its legal relevance. In its affirmative commerce clause cases, the Court has set those limits by requiring that effects on commerce be "substantial" and that only local intrastate activities that are "economic" be aggregated to meet that test. These constructs work to sever the human system ("interstate commerce") from linked natural systems and the attenuated causalities within those systems. In *SWANCC* and *Rapanos,* the Court achieved the same objective through restrictive readings of statutory text.

   This distancing of the environmental other reflects a theme from Chapter 4. The Court's federalism cases sanction preferred political and economic systems. The natural systems that environmentalists see as intimately connected with those human systems are viewed at a remove. They are credited in the affirmative commerce clause cases only to the extent that they can be translated into economic transactions and credited in the CWA cases only to the extent that they can be linked to "navigable waters," a term historically identified with the value of waters as conduits of commerce in the nation's early expansion. This reluctance to recognize the claims of natural systems to protection in their own right may simply reflect the law: the language of the CWA demands a link to commercial navigability; the commerce clause, as Judge Sentelle reminded us, "empowers Congress 'to regulate commerce' not 'ecosystems.'" As my analysis suggests, however, legal interpretation at both the constitutional and statutory levels in these cases is values-infused. The interdependence model offers a frame for different constructions that expand rather than compress the space for the expression of collectivist and harmony values in federal environmental regulation.

CHAPTER EIGHT

Private Property

L AND OWNERSHIP RULES "set the physical platform for social and political institutions" and express prevailing cultural values.[1] The Supreme
Court's efforts to define those rules embody the tensions between private
rights and public claims that lie at the heart of our notions about freedom
and responsibility, individual autonomy, and collective interests. In modern
environmental disputes, this tension is heightened by the ecological model's recognition of complex systemic effects that challenge the boundaries
traditionally secured by property rules. I explore that tension here, particularly in two Fifth Amendment takings cases and a case interpreting the
Endangered Species Act (ESA).

In the last several decades, ecologically based regulation has burgeoned
in states and localities as well as at the federal level.[2] Modern state and local
land use controls seek to protect against cumulative systemic effects—such
as flooding, soil erosion, water pollution, habitat destruction, and even climate change—that are understood to flow from the myriad actions of individual landowners and developers. In advocating for these laws, environmentalists have not only stressed the complex interrelations of human-natural
systems but also argued that being part of the "land community" imposes
an obligation to protect it, invoking the collectivist and harmony values that
are associated with this way of seeing the world.[3] Their opponents have
questioned the degree of interconnectedness assumed by the environmentalists' model and have resisted the model's ethical extension to support constraints on the choices of private landowners. Their resistance to the inroads
of the ecological model on the prerogatives of property owners expresses
values of autonomy and mastery that are powerfully linked to private U.S.
land ownership.[4]

Property confers rights on the owners of things and assumes the existence of institutions to enforce these rights against nonowners, including government entities. The content of these rights is contested.[5] The Supreme Court has stated that owning property has three essential components: "the rights 'to possess, use and dispose of it.' "[6] This chapter focuses on the landowner's right to use, including the right to develop land and use it more intensively. This right is central in the debate about the perceived threat to private property posed by environmental regulation in the ecological age. It is not absolute. In common law, it is limited by the principle of *sic utere tuo, ut alienum non laedas* (use your own so as not to harm another).[7] This do-no-harm principle underlies the private nuisance doctrine, which prevents landowner A from using her land in a way that interferes with landowner B's use and enjoyment of her property. Nuisance accommodates the competing property interests of B by limiting the ownership rights of A; that is, A's bundle of rights does not include a right to uses that significantly impair B's use rights. The common law doctrine of public nuisance extends this limitation to uses that harm the public generally, enforceable by governmental entities. For many decades, however, the primary source of collective restraints on the uses of privately owned land has been not common law nuisance but regulatory legislation that pushes provocatively against received notions of landowners' prerogatives. This conflict between private ownership and land use regulation underlies many of the most culturally resonant conflicts in environmental law.[8]

Property Values (Culturally Speaking)

Private property in land, writes property scholar Robert Ellickson, "remains a particularly potent safeguard of individual liberty." The "individual liberty" that is secured by property is the same autonomy value that underlay the federalism cases of Chapter 7, but it plays an even more obvious role in direct conflicts between landowners asserting their use rights and governments seeking to limit those rights. Ellickson contrasts the autonomy values of private land ownership with the collectivist values of "communitarians," who doubt that "humans can flourish in atomized social environments" and who prefer group ownership as fostering "multi-stranded and enduring social relationships." Communitarians also tend to hold egalitarian values, he adds, which favor group ownership as a means of reducing distinctions in wealth, status, and power.[9]

Property's relationship to individual liberty is more complex than this suggests, however. Property secures autonomy but also serves the public interest by fostering economic development. It encourages owners to put their land to valuable uses, benefiting both themselves and the community. It offers a solution to collective action problems such as Hardin's tragedy of the commons by internalizing externalities and aligning individual incentives with socially desirable outcomes. "Land parcelization (private ownership)," Ellickson argues, "is generally more efficient than open commons or group ownership." Thus, property can serve both individual liberties and the collective good, but the two are not always compatible.

Environmentalists, a subgroup of Ellickson's "communitarians," question the utility—and morality—of strong property rights on other grounds. Parcelizing the environmental commons avoids the tragedy of overuse only if each owner's use does not impose significant, uncompensated burdens on others. Otherwise, the owner's liberty is likely to produce suboptimal outcomes, and that liberty also threatens the rights of others to be free of unconsented harms. The ecological model presumes serious and pervasive externalities among property owners and between owners and nonowners. For environmentalists, it demands a shift in emphasis from protecting the prerogatives of property owners to limiting them—a shift that activates the autonomy-collectivist opposition lurking in the multiple justifications for property. Law scholar and environmentalist Eric Freyfogle traces the historical emergence of private property in land as "a cultural ideal, . . . a mythical emblem of individual autonomy," but this ideal "shortchanges the [current] realities of economic power, social interdependence, and ecological interconnections."[10]

Property in land is also closely associated with mastery values. The relationship of the landowner to her property is conventionally one of dominion, the subjugation of land to human will. In Aldo Leopold's analogy, it mimics the relationship of the returning Odysseus to his slave-girls, whom he hanged at his whim. In the rapid settlement and conversion of vast U.S. land resources to intensive human use, an "expansionist, market-oriented, tame-the-land ethic" was prevalent among property owners, and this ethic continues to exert a strong cultural influence. It supported private ownership in land as vital to a laissez-faire economy and material prosperity. Leopold's hoped-for ethical revolution, in which humans would recast themselves from masters of their land to "mere citizen[s]" of it, engaged harmony values that were directly opposed to the mastery values conventionally tied to property in land. For Leopold, these harmony values flowed from his embrace of the ecological model—the "single premise . . . that the individual is a member of a community of interdependent parts." Contemporary environmentalists take a step beyond Leopold by advancing harmony values through governmental limits on the use rights of private owners.[11]

Lucas v. South Carolina Coastal Council: A Line in the Sand

Lucas v. South Carolina Coastal Council has been variously characterized as a breakthrough victory for the property rights movement and as "anticlimactic." In an opinion by Justice Scalia joined by Chief Justice Rehnquist and Justices White, O'Connor, and Thomas, with Justice Kennedy concurring in the judgment only, the Court declared a per se rule requiring compensation under the takings clause of the Fifth Amendment, "where regulation denies all economically beneficial or productive use of land," and restored the takings claim of landowner and developer David Lucas against the South Carolina Coastal Council. In his concurring opinion, Kennedy wrote that South Carolina should have more room to protect its fragile coastal system than the Court's per se rule would allow, but he agreed with the result. In separate dissents, Justices Blackmun and Stevens were sharply critical of the per se rule and would have denied Lucas's claim. Not far below the surface in each of these opinions were the ecological model's themes of the interconnectedness and fragility of human-natural systems and its implicit challenge to the strength of property boundaries, the use rights they secure, and the values they represent.[12]

The Divided Trail of Takings Cases Leading to *Lucas*

The Fifth Amendment's takings clause forbids the taking of "private property . . . for public use, without just compensation" and applies to actions of state and local governments as well as of federal authorities. The language is ambiguous on whether a "taking" can include government restrictions on property use as well as physical appropriations. Initially, the Supreme Court was inclined to limit Fifth Amendment takings to the latter. In *Mugler v. Kansas,* decided in 1887, the Court concluded that a regulation to prevent land uses "prejudicial to the public interest" was not a taking. *Mugler* upheld a Kansas statute's ban on the manufacture of spirits against the owner of an existing brewery despite the claim that the law would render the brewery of no value. Later rulings in the *Mugler* vein also declined to find a taking in the face of regulations prohibiting already established uses: for example, *Hadecheck v. Sebastian* (ordinance prohibiting an existing brickyard) and *Goldblatt v. Hempstead* (ban on continuation of a sand and gravel operation). These cases kept current a view that, as Justice Blackmun would later put it, the takings clause did not extend to "regulations imposed to arrest a significant threat to the common welfare, whatever their economic effect on the owner."[13]

In its 1922 decision in *Pennsylvania Coal v. Mahon,* however, the Court held for the first time that a public regulatory law—in this case a state statute that limited the exercise of subsurface mining rights to avoid undermining surface structures—was a Fifth Amendment taking. In the opinion for the Court in that case, Justice Oliver Wendell Holmes offered "the general rule . . . that while property may be regulated to a certain extent, if regulation goes too far it will be recognized as a taking." In dissent, Justice Louis Brandeis argued that, consistent with *Mugler,* a "restriction imposed to protect the public health, safety or morals from dangers threatened is not a taking." It was reasonable to regard sinking houses as a public harm if not a nuisance. The tension between *Mahon* and the *Mugler* line of takings cases would persist, unresolved, until the Court's 1992 decision in *Lucas v. South Carolina Coastal Council.*[14]

Deciding cases under Justice Holmes's "general rule" for regulatory takings proved difficult. What use rights were subject to regulatory takings? How far was "too far" in limiting those rights? In *Penn Central Transportation Co. v. City of New York,* the Court in 1978 added definition to the regulatory takings inquiry by naming three factors for consideration: the economic impact of the regulation on the owner, the interference with "distinct investment backed expectations," and the "character of the governmental action." But it declined to assign quantitative values or relative weight to these factors; the takings inquiry remained "essentially ad hoc" and "factual." The Court applied its three factors to reject a takings claim stemming from landmark preservation restrictions on development above New York City's Grand Central Terminal. It emphasized that the owner, Penn Central, retained the full use and benefit of the terminal itself, ensuring a "reasonable return" on its investment. Justice Rehnquist dissented, arguing that the elimination of Penn Central's use rights in the space above the existing station, as distinct from the rights they retained in the station itself, constituted a literal and obvious "taking" of substantial property rights.[15]

The Court's 1987 decision in *Keystone Bituminous Coal Ass'n v. Debenedictus* bolstered the *Mugler* line of cases against the challenge of *Mahon.* The Court rejected a takings claim against Pennsylvania's Subsidence Act, which required coal miners to leave a percentage of coal in place under threatened surface structures to prevent their collapse. The Subsidence Act bore a close resemblance to the Kohler Act, which occasioned the taking in *Mahon*: both laws regulated coal mining to limit the adverse effects of surface subsidence, to the detriment of the owners of subsurface mineral rights. But the Court distinguished *Mahon* in an opinion by Justice Stevens and reaffirmed the exercise of the "police power to abate activity akin to a public nuisance" without compensation. Chief Justice Rehnquist dissented, as he had in *Penn Central,* this time joined by Justices Powell, O'Connor, and Scalia, who had recently joined the Court. For him, the differences between the statutes in *Keystone* and *Mahon* were trivial. *Mugler* could not be read to ban compensation for restrictions under whatever a government might label a "nuisance regulation." Five years later in *Lucas,* a majority of the Court would redress *Mahon*'s eclipse in *Keystone.*[16]

Takings Values

Advocates for the compensation of private landowners for value lost due to government controls make several values-based arguments. Fairness is an important justification for compensation in cases where a landowner or small group of landowners bear a disproportionate regulatory burden. Advocates for generous compensation rules also make liberty and efficiency arguments, which echo the justifications for strong property rights. Legal scholar and libertarian Richard Epstein, for example, makes both types of arguments in his influential book, *Takings,* in which he urges a near-universal compensation for regulatory takings. His liberty-based argument rings familiar from earlier examination of the Court's federalism cases: "a nation in which private property is protected contains independent, decentralized sources of power than can be used against the state, reducing thereby the possibility that any group will be able to seize control over the sources of information or the levers of power." Epstein also argues that broad compensation is efficient because it forces the government to internalize the costs of its land use regulations. Although Epstein's views on compensation are at an extreme in the takings debate, the autonomy and efficiency concerns that he raises are common currency in that debate.[17]

In 1971, a year after the first Earth Day, environmental law pioneer Joseph Sax proposed a competing version of property rights and takings law that reflected environmentalists' communitarian values and the ecological model. Our new understanding of the world, he believed, revealed that spillovers from actions on private lands were pervasive, affecting not only neighbors' lands, as in private nuisance cases, but also commons shared by many—air, flowing water, viewsheds. The "public rights" of users of these environmental commons were entitled to equal consideration with the use rights of landowners. If the government prevents a use of private property that has no spillover effects, then compensation is due. But if (in the more likely case, Sax believed) the use restricted by the government has spillovers, no compensation is due. In the latter case, Sax concluded, the respective claims of the landowner and the public are "conflicting claims of right," appropriate for resolution by the political process, not "the constitutional law of property rights."[18]

These competing views of the takings clause and the values bearing on it were part of both the public discourse and the more specialized world of legal debate when the Supreme Court decided *Lucas* in 1992. The question was which paradigm would prevail—the atomized worldview of Epstein, in which land ownership is highly individualized and boundaries are unflinchingly enforced, or the interdependent worldview of Sax, in which ownership is communally inflected and boundaries are permeable. How would the Court conform its scattered precedents to its preferred model, and what cultural meanings would it attach to property rights in the modern environmental era?[19]

Beachfront Development and the Rise of David Lucas

In *Lucas,* the South Carolina Coastal Council applied the state's Beachfront Management Act (BMA) to prohibit the construction of houses on two beachfront lots owned by Lucas. The lots were in the Wild Dunes resort community on South Carolina's Isle of Palms, which had undergone rapid development in the 1970s and 1980s. Lucas had been a partner in the Wild Dunes development and bought the lots when he left the partnership in 1986. The lots were among the last four left in Wild Dunes, and for periods during the last forty years, they had been underwater or subject to daily inundation by the tides. Both lots were zoned single-family residential, and existing single-family homes stood on either side of them. Lucas commissioned plans for a house on each lot, one for his family's use and the other as a speculative investment. But the enactment of the BMA in 1988 put a stop to any construction before it began.[20]

The South Carolina legislature enacted the BMA to strengthen controls on coastal development using a comprehensive, systemic approach. Its purpose, according to the legislature, was to protect the integrity of the "beach/dune system," which the legislature found provided important ecosystem services such as protection of life and property against storms, support for the tourism industry, habitat for coastal flora and fauna, and "a natural healthy environment for the citizens of South Carolina." The legislature also found that development in the beach/dune system "jeopardized the stability of the . . . system, accelerated erosion, and endangered adjacent property." To restore and protect the beach/dune system's integrity, the BMA adopted a policy of gradual retreat from the shoreline, which included limiting placement of new structures in the system and rebuilding preexisting structures.

The council placed both of Lucas's lots within the act's protected coastal system subject to a ban on the construction of "occupiable improvements."[21]

David Lucas was not an everyday frustrated private landowner. He was a savvy developer and a committed conservative, and he turned the BMA's land use restriction into a cause célèbre for the property rights movement. Through his experience, he became—if he was not before—a culture warrior. In a book he authored after the Supreme Court's decision, *Lucas v. the Green Machine,* he celebrated himself as "an endangered species of American," hard-working, ambitious, freedom-loving, and successful. He was a "conservative Republican on most issues," was politically connected, and backed Ronald Reagan's presidential candidacy. His case against South Carolina, he wrote, championed individual liberty and initiative against "the Green Machine," a "malevolent axis between government and environmental groups [that] has become very wealthy and powerful during the last thirty years." Although Lucas, like Reagan, considered himself an "environmentalist," the fight against the Green Machine was not over the environment, he maintained, but "over the old issues of freedom, money, power and control."[22]

Lucas brought his dispute with the council to state court, where he claimed a taking under both the South Carolina and U.S. Constitutions. His lawyers conceded that the BMA was a valid exercise of the state's police power and did not dispute the validity of the council's line-drawing that put his lots in the no-construction zone. Instead they argued that the council's action had deprived Lucas's lots of all their economic value and that he was therefore entitled to compensation by the state. The trial court agreed.

The South Carolina Supreme Court reversed that ruling in an opinion by Justice Jean Toal, who before her appointment to the bench had been a champion of the BMA's passage in the state legislature. Drawing on the *Mugler* line of cases, Toal's opinion contended that where the land use restriction addressed "a serious public harm," as in the case of the BMA, no compensation was required. A dissent by Justice David Harwell argued that the *Mugler* cases did not apply because beachfront development was not a "noxious" land use and that under *Mahon* and later cases, total loss of value was sufficient, in the absence of nuisance-level concerns, to constitute a taking. Crediting the trial judge's finding that the lots were left with no economically viable use, Harwell concluded that the state had taken Lucas's land; his dissent provided the outlines of Justice Scalia's majority opinion in the Supreme Court.[23]

Arguments to the Court

The Supreme Court accepted review in November 1991, less than a month after Justice Thomas's ascension and consolidation of the Court's new "conservative majority." Lucas's lawyers argued aggressively that a land use restriction resulting in total loss of economic value was a per se taking. They conceded only an extremely narrow exception to their total takings rule—a "public necessity doctrine," limited to hazardous activities causing "imminent peril"—and that only as a "fall-back position."[24]

Among the numerous *amicus* briefs to the Court on both sides of the case, one that supported Lucas was from the Institute for Justice, represented by Richard Epstein, the law professor who had provided much of the intellectual power behind the movement to protect economic liberty and property rights. Lucas had met Epstein and lauded his book *Takings* as "very pro-private property rights and anti-big government." Epstein's brief supported Lucas's takings claim but criticized his lawyers' arguments as not going far enough to protect property owners who suffered less than a loss of all their property's value. Epstein insisted, as he had elsewhere, that a governmental restriction on use should be compensated under the takings clause if it resulted in any net diminution in value, unless the use would be prohibited anyway under the common law of nuisance.[25]

The council argued that the loss in the economic value of Lucas's lots, even if "virtually all," was not conclusive; under *Penn Central* this loss had to be balanced against the severity of the harm the BMA sought to prevent. The BMA fell within the *Mugler* cases finding no taking, the council claimed, because it addressed a "serious public harm," just as the state Supreme Court had held. In depicting the seriousness of that harm, the council's lawyers emphasized the risks of most direct human consequence—the threat of storms and erosion to the "life and property" of coastal dwellers—rather than the "incidental benefits" of "recreation and habitat for flora and fauna." The seriousness of the harm outweighed any loss in the economic value of the property. The council also disputed the critical factual premise of Lucas's argument: the trial court's finding, left intact by the South Carolina Supreme Court, that the BMA regulation had left Lucas's lots valueless. This attack on the "valueless" finding would win favor with four of the justices, but it did not stop the assumption of a "total taking" from becoming the lynchpin of the Court's opinion.[26]

The Court's disposition of a threshold procedural question—whether the takings issue was ripe for judicial consideration—signaled the intensity of the majority's desire to deal with the merits of Lucas's claim. After Lucas's case had been briefed and argued before the South Carolina Supreme Court but before that court's decision, South Carolina amended the BMA by authorizing the council to issue special permits for new home construction within the protected coastal zone. Lucas made no effort to obtain a special permit. On the basis of the Supreme Court's rigorous policing of ripeness requirements in prior land use takings cases, the council argued that because Lucas had not obtained a conclusive determination from the state on how he could use his land, he was not entitled to review on the merits of his taking claim. The Court proceeded to the merits nevertheless, stressing that ripeness was a prudential doctrine, subject to the Court's discretion, and concluding under the circumstances that it "did not think it prudent to apply that prudential requirement here." The reasoning was too clever by half for the dissenters. For environmental scholar and Supreme Court advocate Richard Lazarus, who was brought in at the last minute to shape the council's brief on the merits, the Court's uncharacteristically relaxed approach to ripeness, together with its uncritical acceptance of the no-economic-value finding, evidenced a majority that was "determined, and impatient, to issue a ruling favorable to the landowner."[27]

In the oral argument, Justice Scalia leveled his aim at the council's lawyer, C. C. Harness III, with strong support from Justice O'Connor. He questioned the seriousness of the harm that the BMA purported to address: Was this "an enormous amount of harm"? Did it rise "to the level of a threat to life and limb," "the highest . . . police power activity"? Why were there "houses all up and down the same street" on which Lucas had been denied the right to build? Scalia also attempted to force Harness into defending the position that the state could prohibit "any use of your property that harms others [regardless of its seriousness], even to the extent of depriving your land of all of its value, without compensation"—a position that the council had not taken before the Court and that would have been virtually impossible to defend in light of *Mahon*. From his spectator's seat at the argument, Lucas declared Scalia "our champion that day and the champion for property rights for all Americans."[28]

Among his colleagues on the Court, Justice Scalia had a less triumphal outing. In Richard Lazarus's account, the justices voted in conference seven to two in favor of Lucas, with Justices Blackmun and Stevens dissenting. When the dust settled, however, Scalia's opinion for the Court attracted only four other justices. "Justice Scalia's per se approach pushed Justice Kennedy away, as it did Justice Souter, both of whom would have likely joined an opinion that pursued something more akin to the *Penn Central* balancing approach." Moreover, Scalia likely added a portion of his opinion detailing a nuisance exception to the per se rule to assuage Justice O'Connor's concerns about the rule—an addition that threatened the opinion's internal coherence.[29]

Justice Scalia's Opinion for the Court

In advancing a per se rule for total takings, Justice Scalia's opinion for the Court took advantage of the latitude given by the Court's vague and poorly integrated takings precedents. It drew from dicta in prior cases that a taking should be found if regulation "denies [an owner] economically beneficial or productive use of [his or her] land" and narrowed the *Mugler* line of cases, on which the South Carolina Supreme Court relied. Acknowledging that those cases could be read to suggest "that 'harmful or noxious uses' of property may be proscribed without the requirement of compensation," the opinion argued that it made no sense to draw the takings line at the boundary between regulations that prevented a public harm and those that secured a public benefit because that boundary was illusory: a benefit secured could always be translated into a harm avoided. Instead, what the *Mugler* cases stood for was simply that regulating "harmful and noxious uses" was a legitimate exercise of the police power. Whether the effect of the regulation on the value of the property was "too much" was a separate question— answered in this case by the per se rule rather than *Penn Central*'s more open-ended inquiry. The South Carolina court's interpretation of *Mugler*, the Court claimed, would "essentially nullify" *Mahon*.[30]

LAND: "COMPACT" AND "CULTURE"

In justifying the per se rule, Justice Scalia's opinion for the Court highlighted the concern that land use regulations like those under the BMA would require "land to be left substantially in its natural state." Noting the "practical equivalence" of legislation pursuing conservation objectives through the exercise of eminent domain, the Court wrote that these regulations "carry with them a heightened risk that private property is being pressed into some form of public service under the guise of mitigating serious public harm."[31] The Court's broad concern (land required to be left in "its natural state") went beyond the BMA to take on a new generation of ecologically based legislation.[32]

The Court's opinion bore marks of the same antipathy to this new generation of environmental legislation found in the opinions authored by Justice Scalia in *Lujan II* and *Rapanos*. It expressed doubts about the political motives behind the BMA. South Carolina, the Court wrote, acted on an "expressed interest in intensively managing development activities in the so-called 'coastal zone.' " "So-called" implied that "coastal zone" might be a device for inflating the dangers of building on the beachfront and claiming false public importance for the regulation. "Expressed interest" suggested that another unspoken, less public-regarding interest lay behind the legislation's intensive management of development.[33] In a footnote, the opinion questioned the good faith of the legislature's finding that the building regulations were necessary to protect people and property, in light of the grandfathering of existing homes and a 1990 variance allowing new homes within the no-build zone.[34]

Despite this undercurrent of skepticism about the legislation, the Court's legal analysis assumed that South Carolina's findings of systemic harms offered a proper basis for regulation, as Lucas had conceded. The main work of the opinion, within the constraints of this assumption, was to limit the ecological model's threat to landowners' prerogatives. The Court drew a hard line at regulation that prohibits all economic development of land based on services that land provides in its natural state, such as erosion protection or wildlife habitat under the BMA. While tacitly entertaining the "emerging view of land as a part of an ecosystem," as Joseph Sax noted, it rejected that view as a basis for adjusting the legal entitlements of landowners.[35]

Perhaps inevitably, given the jumble of the Court's takings precedents, the Court resorted to history and societal expectations to bolster the per se rule. The Court would be guided "by the understandings of our citizens regarding the content of, and the State's power over, the 'bundle of rights' that they acquire when they obtain title to property." These "understandings" were particular to ownership of land. Owners of personal property were accustomed "to the State's traditionally high degree of control over commercial dealings" that might render the property worthless. But this was not so with property in land, which was different from personal property in ways that the Court did not pause to explain; perhaps it was less thoroughly subject to "commercial dealings" or traditionally more central to individual identity and material flourishing. That difference, whatever it was, was crucial to the expectations of landowners on the limits of uncompensated regulation.

> In the case of land . . . we think the notion pressed by the council that title is somehow held subject to the "implied limitation" that the State may subsequently eliminate all economically valuable use is inconsistent with the historical compact recorded in the Takings Clause that has become part of our constitutional culture.

Regulations that drained all economic value from land were "confiscatory," with implications of punitive and unjust use of governmental power.[36]

The Court's reliance on "historical compact" and "constitutional culture" as interpretative touchstones was both curious and revealing for the opinion's author, who has pressed hard for the "supremacy-of-text principle" in construing legal documents, including the Constitution.[37] In dissent, Justice Blackmun sampled takings practices from colonial times to the present to conclude that the Court's "historical compact" was a fabrication, constructed from a "grab bag of principles, to be adopted where they support the Court's theory and ignored where they do not."[38] "Historical compact" might have had less to do with legal history than with the Court's understanding of property in land as a prevailing cultural convention ("the understandings of our citizens")—a convention of which the law is, or should be, as much a reflection as a constitutive force.

A "constitutional culture" existing separately from the constitutional text likewise suggested a prevailing societal commitment to robust property rights, stout enough in this case to resist the erosive effects of the ecological model and its associated values. The Court's treatment did not address whether or how that "culture" might evolve in light of new understandings regarding the nature of land and the relationships among discrete parcels, as urged by the environmentalists. But that question came unavoidably to the fore in the Court's explanation of its nuisance exception to the per se rule.

THE CONSTRAINTS OF NUISANCE

The Court provided a narrow exception to its per se rule based on "background principles" of state property law and nuisance. It reasoned that because property uses in violation of these background principles were "*always* unlawful," they were never part of the owner's title. Thus, states and localities could adopt use prohibitions implementing the background principles without paying compensation; they would be "taking nothing." Courts applying the nuisance exception would have to consider what common law courts had always considered in finding a nuisance, including, as the Court wrote, "the degree of harm to public lands and resources, or adjacent private property." Critics of *Lucas* accused the Court of resurrecting the very notion of "harm" that it buried in neutralizing the *Mugler* cases, thereby making its opinion logically incoherent.[39]

Despite its risks to the opinion's consistency, the nuisance exception played a crucial role in conveying the rebuke to modern environmentalism that animated the opinion. By framing the exception in common law terms, the Court effectively drew a line between land use controls based on an ecological paradigm, as under the South Carolina statute, and environmental regulation of a more traditional kind. Common law nuisance had long addressed environmental insults involving direct harms, including various forms of pollution. Indeed, modern pollution control statutes are readily understood as elaborations of common law principles that evolved in response to industrial development. By the dawn of the modern environmental era, however, there had been a significant shift from common law to legislation. The emerging ecological model and the stewardship values associated with it found expression in statutes such as the South Carolina act rather than in further evolution of the common law, which courts had come increasingly to view as fixed.[40]

The Court in *Lucas* did acknowledge the common law's potential to evolve through "changed circumstances or new knowledge."[41] But it hedged this acknowledgment against the risk it posed to the use rights of landowners. The ecological paradigm, with its tendency to find injury at the human-natural interface, promised to greatly expand the universe of "harmful or noxious" uses that might gain status as nuisances.[42] To protect against this threat to the per se rule, the Court cautioned that common law principles would not typically prohibit uses that were already established in an area (e.g., beachfront homes on the Isle of Palms) or the construction of other "habitable or productive improvements." It also cautioned the state courts against lightly invoking the exception: they would have to determine that the state's existing nuisance law ("background principles") prohibited the intended use under the circumstances presented.[43] These admonitions hardened the exception to exclude the great majority of human uses traditionally assigned to land and to give ground only grudgingly to scientific and cultural change. Although there was some speculation after *Lucas* that state and local environmental controls adopted prior to a current owner's acquisition of property could provide a newly operative set of "background principles," the Court later rejected that possibility in *Palazzolo v. Rhode Island*, effectively freezing "background principles" against the ecological model's warming effect.[44]

The Court's message to regulators was if you choose to exercise your authorities in accord with the ecological paradigm and if the result is that property is to be kept in its natural state, the economic burden is yours, not the owner's. In this sense, the decision was not strictly libertarian. But the Court must have understood that it would dampen the appetite of legislatures for regulation to protect ecological services provided by land. This chilling effect on "manevolent" regulation was the ultimate goal of Lucas and his allies.[45]

Concurring and Dissenting Voices

In his opinion concurring in the result, Justice Kennedy maintained that the common law of nuisance was "too narrow a confine for the exercise of regulatory power in a complex and interdependent society." The key for Kennedy was the "reasonable expectations" of landowners. Those expectations were dynamic, responding, as state legislatures did, to "changing conditions." In applying the takings clause, courts were obligated to "consider all reasonable expectations whatever their source." Speaking ecologically, Kennedy observed that "coastal property may present such unique concerns for a fragile land system that the State can go further in regulating its development and use than the common law of nuisance might otherwise permit."[46]

Justice Stevens, in dissent, argued similarly against the nuisance exception as "too rigid and too narrow" and as "effectively freez[ing] the State's common law, denying the legislature much of its traditional power to revise the law governing the rights and uses of property." "The human condition is one of constant learning and evolution—both moral and practical. . . . New appreciation of the significance of endangered species; the importance of wetlands; and the vulnerability of coastal lands shapes our evolving understandings of property rights." Stevens's dissent was thus a more robust version of Kennedy's point: that changing ecological awareness and ethical sensitivities can and should, through the intermediary of the legislature, condition what property owners may reasonably expect to do with their land. This had the potential to translate into political and legal terms Aldo Leopold's "land ethic as a product of social evolution."[47]

Justice Blackmun's dissent began provocatively by accusing the Court of "launch[ing] a missile to kill a mouse." The "mouse" was the rare case in which regulation prohibited all economic use of land (a case the justice did not believe that *Lucas* actually presented); the "missile" was the Court's new per se rule and the wholesale recasting of the takings precedents to support it. The Court had never held that the ability of a state to regulate without compensation "turned on the availability of some residual valuable use," and the *Mugler* line of cases had privileged "legislative judgments" about public harms in rejecting takings claims.[48] Like Justice Stevens, Blackmun stressed that modern legislatures shared with courts the task of determining harmful uses that should be prohibited; the Court should respect those legislative judgments, as the South Carolina Supreme Court had in this case. The pointed tone of Blackmun's dissent made Justice Scalia so angry when he read it that he made numerous additions to his own opinion to take on the criticisms.[49]

The Meaning of *Lucas*

In an influential article on *Lucas* that builds on his earlier property rights accounts, Joseph Sax describes "two fundamentally different views of property rights . . . land in the 'transformative economy' and land in the 'economy of nature.'" Land in the "transformative economy" works off "an image of property as a discrete entity that can be made one's own by working it and transforming it into a human artifact"—an image expressive of both autonomy and mastery values. The demarcation between public and private land is clear, and private landowners "have no obligations." Land in the economy of nature, by contrast, is not "a passive entity waiting to be transformed by its landowner." Land is thought of not as "distinct tracts" with man-made boundaries but as consisting of systems defined by their function. It is property fit to the interdependence model. "The line between public and private is blurred," and landowners have a "custodial, affirmative protective role for ecological functions."[50]

The staunchly "transformative view" advanced in *Lucas,* Sax argues, "represents the Court's rejection of pleas to engraft the values of the economy of nature onto traditional notions of the rights of land ownership. Justice Scalia assumes that redefinition of property rights to accommodate ecosystem demands is not possible." One might quibble with this characterization of Scalia's assumption: not wise or not wanted perhaps, but not impossible. Both Justice Kennedy's concurrence and Justice Stevens's dissent offered suggestions for how the engrafting could be done. But their voices were peripheral. *Lucas* emboldened one of Sax's critics to consign him to a "Romantic period of takings scholarship," a phenomenon of the environmental movement's early years that federal takings doctrine had left behind. Extending Leopold's ecology-driven land ethic to limit the rights of landowners seemed out of the question.[51]

Sax's property rights foil, Epstein, also found the Court's ruling disappointing, but for different reasons. The per se rule for total takings pushed aside Epstein's more radical argument to the Court for takings in all cases of restricted use resulting in diminished value. Epstein was not forgiving: the welfare-maximizing justification for property required that partial as well as total takings be compensated. Adding insult to injury, the Court had failed to resolve the question of the property interest against which loss in value was to be measured: Was the basis for measuring a total taking the whole tract, or was it the portion of the tract burdened by the regulation? If the former, a complete loss of value would be much less likely (and the Court's rule would be much further from Epstein's ideal of universal compensation). The Court's failure to resolve the issue was "evasion in the name of cautious decisionmaking."[52]

In practice, it is not clear that *Lucas* led to compensation in a larger percentage of cases. But the cultural moment *Lucas* represented was profound. Carol Rose calls Epstein's complaints about *Lucas* "crocodile tears." Justice Scalia's opinion for the Court canonized a pro-property rights history of takings and framed new doctrine to honor that history. Its sweeping rhetoric supporting the per se rule ("historical compact," "constitutional culture") and denigrating "confiscatory regulation" mirrored the passions of the property rights movement. The opinion celebrated the movement's attachment to ownership in land as a last preserve of autonomy and a bulwark against the state. Property rights advocates, including Lucas, were jubilant; Scalia was indeed their champion, even if he could not be their savior.[53]

There are few, if any, more illuminating artifacts of the environmental culture wars than *Lucas*. It brought lastingly to the fore the deep tension between conceptions of land ownership emphasizing the owner's expression of individual will and material advancement and those emphasizing the owner's obligations as part of a larger "land community" that has both human and natural elements. It made apparent the challenge that the ecological model posed not just to our received understanding of how the world works but also to the prerogatives of ownership that rested comfortably in that understanding. Those competing concepts of ownership continue to play out daily, not just in judicial takings cases but in thousands of local land use debates that shape the nation's landscape. An ironic postscript to *Lucas* extended the fraught symbolism of the decision. After some legal skirmishing on remand to the trial court, the council agreed to buy Lucas's lots for $1.5 million (more than he paid for them) and issued special permits for the construction of homes on the lots, which Lucas conveyed to the council with his title. The council then sold the lots for development, and the new owners built houses on both. Property rights advocates shouted vindication. Just as Epstein would have predicted, when required to internalize the economic losses caused by its no-build rule, the council came to a much different view of the public interest. But property and land use scholar Vicki Been disputed this "cost internalization" account, attributing the council's about-face instead to the collapse of the BMA's protective regime under assault by beachfront property owners whose houses were damaged by Hurricane Hugo. The answer was no clearer in hindsight: requiring compensation might yield more efficient government policies (Epstein) or it might add to the already formidable power of property owners to thwart the collective good (Been). These competing interpretations of the postdecision history reflected the dueling interpretations of property in the decision itself. *Lucas* had done little to quiet the debate.[54]

The Court's Drift Away from *Lucas*

Later Supreme Court rulings limited *Lucas*'s doctrinal influence, putting Justice Scalia at odds with Justices O'Connor and Kennedy, who had agreed with him on the result in *Lucas,* and elevating the views of his frequent adversary, Justice Stevens. In *Palazzolo v. Rhode Island,* the Court held that a landowner was not prevented from asserting a takings claim just because the wetlands regulation he challenged was already in effect at the time he acquired his property. But the Court left open the question of whether and how the preexistence of the rule might be taken into account in a less decisive way.

Justices Scalia and O'Connor agreed with the holding but disagreed pointedly with each other on the question left open by the Court. In her concurrence, O'Connor favored a *Penn Central* balancing approach, believing that the existence of the regulation at the time of acquisition was entitled to some consideration. Otherwise, real estate speculators could reap a windfall by purchasing regulation-burdened properties at bargain rates and selling them for much more after successful takings claims. Scalia argued instead for a rule-like approach, as in *Lucas.* To give any weight at all to prior enactments was to give "the malefactor [i.e., the state] the benefit of its malefaction." The real "thief" was the government, the perpetrator of the offending regulation, not the opportunistic speculator. This government-as-thief image brought vividly to the surface the undercurrent of antiregulatory sentiment and suspicion of government in *Lucas.* Here, however, Scalia spoke for himself only.

In *Tahoe-Sierra Preservation Council, Inc. v. Tahoe Regional Planning Agency,* a majority of the Court distanced itself from Justice Scalia by refusing to extend *Lucas*'s per se rule to a temporary but total moratorium on land development surrounding Lake Tahoe and requiring use of the *Penn Central* balancing test instead. The opinion for the Court by Justice Stevens, a dissenter in *Lucas,* celebrated Lake Tahoe's "dazzlingly, brilliantly" clear waters and undisputed status as a "national treasure." The temporary moratorium was not a per se taking under *Lucas,* because the prohibition was only for a limited period (thirty-four months) and therefore did not extinguish all the development potential of the land. Justices Kennedy and O'Connor joined the Court's opinion, leaving Justice Scalia in a minority with Chief Justice Rehnquist and Justice Thomas, claiming that *Lucas* applied. Stevens's opinion for the Court not only limited the reach of *Lucas* but also made clear that a majority of the Court was not in the mood to adopt new per se takings rules favored by Scalia and replace *Penn Central*'s all-purpose test with more aggressive protections for property owners.[55]

After *Tahoe-Sierra,* it was clear that, at least for the time being, *Lucas* was a high-water mark for the property rights movement in regulatory takings cases. In the general run of these cases, the law remained without a "set formula," and in the great majority of them, the courts did not find takings. But in 2013, property rights advocates scored a significant victory in *Koontz v. St. Johns River Management District*, decided under the Court's unconstitutional conditions doctrine and explored later. That decision made plain that the cultural conflict underlying *Lucas* and other environmental takings cases continues unabated.[56]

Babbitt v. Sweet Home Chapter of Communities for a Great Oregon: Species Protection and the Simplest Farmer

The takings debates are values debates that have a natural home in the Fifth Amendment takings clause, but they are by no means confined there. *Babbitt v. Sweet Home Chapter of Communities for a Great Oregon* was not a takings case, although in Epstein's view it should have been. It emitted strong property rights vibrations in response to the assertion of the ecological paradigm under the federal ESA. Decided three years after *Lucas*, with Justices Ginsburg and Breyer having joined the Court in the interim, *Sweet Home* was in some ways a replay of *Lucas*, only this time in the guise of the interpretation of a statutory term (coincidentally "take"), rather than the Fifth Amendment's takings clause, and with the core of the majority in *Lucas*—Scalia, Thomas, and Rehnquist—now in the minority. It was an early indicator of the post-*Lucas* moderating trend on landowner rights that would mature in takings cases such as *Palazzolo* and *Tahoe-Sierra*.[57]

Section 9 of the ESA prohibits the "take" of an endangered species. "Take" is defined in the statute as "harass, harm, pursue, hunt, shoot, wound, kill, trap, capture, or collect, or to attempt to engage in any such conduct."[58] The Department of the Interior had defined "harm" to include "an act which actually kills or injures wildlife. Such act may include significant habitat modification or degradation where it actually kills or injures wildlife by significantly impairing essential behavioral patterns, including breeding, feeding or sheltering." Whereas Interior applied other components of the "take" definition to protect individuals of the species from being directly injured, the purpose of this regulation was to protect endangered species from indirect harm due to alteration of the ecosystems on which they depend.[59]

Opponents of the rule gathered a sympathetic group of plaintiffs: "small landowners, small logging companies, and families allegedly dependent on the forest products industry" for their livelihood. Their challenge in federal district court claimed that the rule exceeded the reach of Section 9's "take" prohibition by defining "harm" to include habitat modification. The district court upheld the rule, but a three-judge appeals court panel reversed after initially affirming the district court. Judge Stephen Williams, whose about-face produced the reversal, was concerned about the "extinction of private rights" that would result from Interior's "habitat modification concept of 'harm.'" In limiting the take prohibition to direct applications of force, his opinion for the court stressed the "gulf" between that concept, by which a "take" could occur indirectly, and the other terms of the definition of "take," which were of the form "A hit B."[60]

At oral argument before the Court, Justice Scalia delivered his own brief against Interior's rule in an exchange with the lawyer for Interior, Deputy Solicitor General Edwin Kneedler. "To take an animal refers to hunters," he said. He had "never heard [the word] used in any other way." Every word in the statute's definition of "take," including "harm," could be interpreted consistent with that "old-fashioned meaning," he insisted. Interior's expansive concept of "harm" fell far outside that definition. Kneedler did his best to answer the assault. The word "harm," he argued, rather than confirming the meaning of "take" in "ancient wildlife law," was added to accommodate the modern understanding of the importance of habitat to species survival and to advance the ESA's pervasive purpose of species protection. It was unlikely that Kneedler had any chance of swaying Scalia, given the vehemence of the justice's views, but he succeeded in attracting, or keeping, a majority of the Court. Scalia's ancient gloss became the core of his dissent.[61]

The opinion for the Court, authored by Justice Stevens and joined by Justices O'Connor, Kennedy, Souter, Ginsburg, and Breyer, upheld Interior's regulation. The Court found support in the dictionary definition of "harm," which encompassed indirect as well as direct injury, and in one of the act's central purposes: "to provide a means whereby the ecosystems on which endangered species and threatened species depend may be conserved." Rather than reading the other terms in the statutory definition of "take" to limit the meaning of "harm," as the District of Columbia Circuit did, the Court upheld the reasonableness of Interior's construction of "harm" as adding a meaning (indirect injury) not assigned to those terms. Embedded in this semantic dispute was the deeper struggle over the expression of the ESA's broad purpose of ecosystem protection, which the Court proclaimed was a central feature of "the most comprehensive legislation for the preservation of endangered species ever enacted by any nation." Interior's rule had the critical advantage of advancing that purpose over interpretations that left harmful habitat modifications out of the act's regulatory scope. The rule was entitled to *Chevron* deference.[62]

Justice Scalia's dissenting opinion, joined by Chief Justice Rehnquist and Justice Thomas, opened with a rhetorical flourish that might have been written for a Fifth Amendment takings case. Like Judge Williams, he was concerned about the rule's "extinction" of use rights, but that concern, in his hands, took on a populist tone:

The Court's holding that the hunting and killing prohibition incidentally preserves habitat on private lands imposes unfairness to the point of financial
ruin—not just upon the rich, but upon the simplest farmer who finds his land
conscripted to national zoological use.

This was, for Scalia, the specter of the BMA in *Lucas* revisited: the application of the ecological model to require preservation of land in its natural
state, complete with the image of the "simplest farmer" to dramatize the
burden. Here the issue before the Court was whether a federal statute supports such an imposition—a "conscript[ion] to national zoological use"—not
whether compensation was due. But the concern was the same: the restriction of individual landowners to provide a broad public benefit. The rhetoric
conveyed vividly Scalia's commitment to the "transformative economy," in
Sax's phrase. Privately owned endangered species habitat was not defined
by its ecological functions within a "land community"; it was property
subject to the will of its owner. The government's impressing land into "zoological use" offended that commitment.[63]

Justice Scalia's legal objections to the rule were that, contrary to the statute,
the rule did not require "an act" directed against endangered species (merely
an "*omission* will do"); did not require that habitat modifications that
cause death or injury to wildlife be foreseeable ("no more than cause-in-
fact" is sufficient); and encompassed injury to "populations of the protected
species" ("not only upon individual animals"). In his dissent he maintained,
as he had at oral argument, that "take" in Section 9 controlled the meaning
of its subordinate terms, including "harm." The meaning of "take" in wildlife law was primordial, "as old as the law itself." Scalia traced it back to
an eighteenth-century treatise and the *Digest of Justinian* to make the case
that the term was limited to affirmative actions done directly and intentionally to individual animals. This was also inescapably the meaning of
the other nine words the statute used to define "take," and like the District
of Columbia Circuit, he argued that the tenth word, "harm," should be limited accordingly. Using "harm" to leverage "take" beyond this meaning to
include the indirect and unintentional effects of habitat modification exceeded Interior's authority.[64]

The majority's reliance on the act's purpose of ecosystem protection, Justice Scalia argued, begged the question "by what *means* (and hence to what
length) Congress pursued that purpose." For him, the answer was in Section 5 of the ESA, which authorizes expenditure of federal funds for the
purchase of land for habitat protection. Congress did act to protect habitat for endangered species, but the means it chose was not regulation, im-

posing uncompensated burdens on landowners; rather, it was compensated land acquisition. The result for Scalia was very similar to *Lucas*: the legislature may pass laws based on the ecosystem paradigm, but the laws are not read to alter historical (i.e., pre-ecological era) expectations concerning what owners may do with their land. Where lands are appropriated for "zoological use," the expectation remains that compensation—either by statute or under the Fifth Amendment—will be provided.[65]

As in other cases in which he has confronted the ecological model, Justice Scalia bridled at the attribution of injury or harm through the intermediary of ecosystems. In his opinion for the Court in *Lujan II*, this concern was focused on expanded judicial access based on the nexus theories; in *Rapanos,* on the boundless scope of federal regulatory jurisdiction keyed to protection of aquatic ecosystems. In *Sweet Home,* he lamented the "large number of routine activities" on private land that could be brought within Section 9's prohibition under the rubric of habitat degradation, "no matter how remote the chain of causation and no matter how difficult to foresee (or to disprove) the 'injury' may be."[66]

Justice Scalia captured this concern in an image that expanded on the "simplest farmer" motif in the opening lines of his dissent. This was the specter that "a farmer who tills his field and causes erosion that makes silt run into a nearby river which depletes oxygen and thereby 'impairs [the] breeding' of protected fish has 'taken' or 'attempted to take' the fish." One could question the plausibility of this scenario, but its symbolic import was clear. Expansive application of the ecological model in interpreting Section 9 threatened the values of industry and independence embodied by the "simplest farmer" who virtuously "tills his field." In *Sweet Home,* as in *Rapanos,* Scalia would have used his textualist tools to block that threat.[67]

Justice O'Connor shared Scalia's concern over the regulatory implications of interconnectedness, but she reconciled this concern with upholding Interior's rule. She wrote separately to condition her concurrence on her understanding of the rule as limiting "harm" to habitat alteration causing "actual" (not hypothetical) death or injury to "identifiable protected animals" (not the species generally) and as applying principles of "proximate causation." Justice Stevens's opinion for the Court quietly accepted both conditions in a footnote.[68]

Proximate causation is a creature of the common law of tort that limits legal accountability to actions that are not only the actual, but-for cause of a harm but whose harmfulness is also reasonably foreseeable. Its purpose, O'Connor explained, was to protect against the unfairness of "imposing liability for remote consequences"—in this case, effects on endangered species through extended ecosystem causal chains. Proximate cause principles would avoid the unfortunate outcome predicted by Scalia for the farmer whose plowing sent soil into a stream. Only "the landowner" who killed an endangered fish while draining his pond would be culpable: he knew or should have known that fish deaths would result.[69]

Justice O'Connor's balancing between worldviews and values is reminiscent of Justice Kennedy's in *Rapanos*. She accepted the ecological model's expression in Section 9 but worked to constrain that expression in a way that was sensitive to the values defended in Justice Scalia's dissent. While tacitly agreeing with her colleague that "unfairness to the point of financial ruin" and wholesale conscription of property for "zoological use" were objectionable, she tailored the application of the ecological model in this regulatory setting to limit or avoid those outcomes.

Commentator J. B. Ruhl tagged *Sweet Home,* with its acceptance of Justice O'Connor's conditions, "a Pyrrhic victory" for environmentalists. While avoiding Justice Scalia's interpretation reducing Section 9 to little more than "an anti-hunting measure," he wrote, "the *Sweet Home* majority's hardnosed tort law approach to species protection can hardly be interpreted as a . . . shot of adrenalin for the ESA."[70] But the contrast with its constitutional analogue, *Lucas,* decided only three years earlier, marks *Sweet Home* as an important gesture in the environmentalists' direction. The purpose of ecosystem protection was privileged over the countervailing purpose that Scalia assigned to the ESA of protecting use rights through compensated acquisition of habitat. In *TVA v. Hill,* the Court had noted habitat destruction as the greatest threat to species survival and interpreted the act to categorically protect critical habitats threatened by federal actions. *Sweet Home* took a step of arguably even greater import, legally and culturally, by extending ESA authority to restrict habitat destruction on private lands in the face of prominent national norms of landowner rights and economic productivity. While in some ways less sweeping than *TVA v. Hill, Sweet Home* lacked the ambivalence of the earlier decision; the majority of the Court had found a way to settle comfortably with the environmentalists.

Koontz: Property Rights Redux

Property rights enjoyed a resurgence in the Court's 2013 decision in *Koontz v. St. Johns River Water Management District,* which arose under a special branch of Fifth Amendment takings law: "land-use exactions." Exactions cases differ from regulatory takings cases such as *Penn Central* and *Lucas* in that they do not address direct regulatory burdens on land use; instead, they deal with government demands that landowners give up property interests without compensation as a condition of obtaining development permits. The Court set the rules for judicial review of exactions in two cases decided during the freshet of pro-property rights decisions that ran from 1986 (when Justice Scalia joined the Court) to 1994 (when Justice Blackmun left it). To justify a demand that a landowner give up property in return for a development permit, the Court held, a permitting authority had to show that the property interest taken is directly related to a public purpose for which it might legitimately have denied the permit (*Nollan v. California Coastal Comm'n*) and that the demand was "roughly proportional" to the development's impact (*Dolan v. City of Tigard*). The Court argued that this heightened means-end review was necessary to protect against a government's using its monopoly power over land use regulation to "extort" concessions that were not warranted by the burdens a development would impose on the community.[71]

The initial reach of the exactions doctrine was limited by the facts of *Nollan* and *Dolan*—in both, the permitting authority had issued a permit conditioned on the landowner's turning over an interest in the property being developed (easements). The decisions left open several questions, including two of particular import for *Koontz*. The first was whether the doctrine extended only to cases in which a permit was issued with conditions or whether it also included cases in which a permit was denied for failure of the landowner to agree to the government's demands. The second was whether the doctrine applied to demands for payment of money as well as for interests in land. In answering yes to both questions, *Koontz* moved exactions to the mainstream of the property rights debate, injecting takings inquiry, in the view of dissenting Justice Kagan, into "the very heart of local land-use regulation and service delivery."[72]

To implement state laws "protect[ing] [Florida's] rapidly diminishing wetlands," the St. Johns River Water Management District required applicants for permits to develop in wetlands to offset the environmental damage "by creating, enhancing, or preserving wetlands elsewhere." Coy Koontz Sr. owned a 14.9-acre wetland parcel in the district—a northern section of 3.7 acres and a southern section of approximately 11 acres. In his application to the district for permits to build on the property, he proposed to limit development to the northern section and to foreclose development of the southern section by granting a conservation easement. The district determined that Koontz's mitigation proposal did not satisfy its mitigation policy and declined to issue the permit. The district did offer Koontz alternatives,

however, including paying a contractor to enhance wetlands on district property nearby or reducing his development to one acre and placing the rest of
the property in easement. By its account, the district was open to other pro-
posals for mitigation and offered to give Koontz time to negotiate. But
Koontz declined further discussions and brought suit.[73]

Justice Alito wrote the opinion for the Court, joined by Chief Justice
Roberts and Justices Scalia, Kennedy, and Thomas, reversing the Florida
Supreme Court's dismissal of Koontz's *Nollan* and *Dolan* claims. *Nollan*
and *Dolan* do not cease to apply, the Court held, simply because a government denies a permit rather than approves a permit with conditions. In either case, a government's actions could "run afoul of the Takings Clause . . .
because they impermissibly burden the right not to have property taken
without just compensation." More controversially, the Court ruled that
Nollan and *Dolan* applied to monetary exactions (e.g., payments to an
off-site contractor in *Koontz*) as well as exactions of real property. Because the government could easily convert a demand for an easement
into a money demand, excluding monetary exactions would allow it to
evade the protections of *Nollan* and *Dolan*. *Eastern Enterprises v. Apfel*
had held that the imposition of a monetary fee was not a taking, but the
Court found an exception for fees in cases such as Koontz's in which
"the monetary obligation burdened . . . ownership of a specific parcel of
land."[74]

The Court recognized the need to balance two "realities of the [land use]
permitting process"—protecting permit applicants from government coercion and forcing landowners to "internalize the negative externalities of their
conduct." The application of *Nollan* and *Dolan*, the Court argued, allowed
both "realities" to be accommodated. But its opinion emphasized the former
at the expense of the latter. It gave plausibility to Koontz's refusal to negotiate with the district ("Believing the District's demands to be excessive in
light of the environmental effects that his building proposal would have
caused, Koontz filed suit . . ."); indeed, it subtly celebrated Koontz's resistance ("He refused to yield"). It was saturated with the rhetoric of government abuse—"misuse of . . . power," "coercion," and "extortionate demands." The theme of exactions as susceptible to government "extortion,"
with its connotations of criminal behavior, appeared earlier in Justice Scalia's
opinion for the Court in *Nollan* and echoed his "government-as-thief" motif
in *Palazzolo*. On the other side, regarding the environmental externalities of
Koontz's development, the Court raised doubts about the presumed value of
his property as wetland, describing the section to be developed as already
degraded by a drainage ditch, high-voltage power lines, and a nearby major
toll road. In this case, as in *Lucas* and *Rapanos*, the story line—courageous

landowner battles oppressive governmental action based on dubious environmental benefit—followed the ruling's pro-property rights thrust.[75]

Justice Kagan dissented, joined by Justices Ginsburg, Breyer, and Sotomayor. Kagan agreed with the Court on the applicability of *Nollan* and *Dolan* to permit denials but did not agree that those decisions were applicable to permit monetary fees. The Court could not justify its claimed exception to the *Eastern Enterprises* ruling that fees are not takings: the monetary payment proposed by the district did not involve any specific property interest and could have been paid from any source. The analytical shortcomings of the Court's opinion left unclear how the fee in *Koontz* was to be distinguished from real property taxes or other common fees related to land ownership. The potential reach of its ruling, Kagan wrote, threatened "the heartland" of local government operations. There were other less intrusive legal doctrines to protect landowners from excessive monetary demands and there was no evidence of abuse that would require the heightened scrutiny of *Nollan* and *Dolan*.[76]

Like Justice Alito's opinion for the Court, the narrative of Justice Kagan's dissent mirrored her legal argument. She accorded respect to the state's determination of the need to "protect its rapidly diminishing wetlands" and the extension of that policy to Koontz's wetland property. She replaced the Court's government-as-abuser with a benign image of government. Arguing that the district did not "demand" anything of Koontz, she emphasized its openness to accommodation and negotiation while it sought to meet the requirements of state law. Koontz's curt refusal to negotiate—"saying (through his lawyer) that the proposal he submitted was 'as good as it can get' "—seemed unreasonable, not heroic, in her version of events. In the world of Kagan's dissent, government reliably serves good purposes, and refractory behavior like Koontz's can undermine mutually beneficial outcomes.

The practical effect of *Koontz* is much debated and will likely take years to unfold. Its symbolic import is clearer. Like other property rights decisions featured in this chapter, *Koontz* documented the clash of individualist and collectivist perspectives in a disputed social and physical landscape. Although the Court's rhetoric was relatively subdued compared with *Lucas*, its opinion marked the continuing power of the property rights narrative in opposition to the harmony and collectivist values of environmentalists. Once again, a majority of the Court subscribed to this narrative. The property rights movement may have faltered within the Court in the years after *Lucas,* but it found its voice again in *Koontz*.[77]

The Tides of Interdependence: A Coda

This chapter and Chapters 6 and 7 have tracked doctrinal shifts in standing, federalism, and property rights that resisted the interdependence model and accommodated values of autonomy, hierarchy, and mastery (e.g., *Lujan II, Lopez, Lucas, Koontz*). The Court perfected an individualized (and anti-collectivist) view of standing, advanced a new federalism that had individual liberty at its core, and strengthened the use rights of private landowners against government intrusion. The practical importance of these shifts for environmental regulation has been limited: In most cases, standing rules pose little more than technical pleading hurdles to be negotiated by environmental plaintiffs; the per se takings rule in *Lucas* has changed only a handful of case outcomes at the margins of land use regulation; the effect of *Koontz* is uncertain; and the Court has yet to invalidate an environmental statute because it exceeds the commerce power. But symbolically, these doctrinal innovations were significant for environmentalists because they all reflected values commonly understood as opposed to their movement. If nothing else, they testified to the continued vitality of those opposing values in the culture and their potential effect on the environmental movement's success.

The symbolic importance of these changes was qualified, however, by the vigorous dissents that accompanied them as well in some cases by the Court's opinions in subsequent cases (e.g., *Laidlaw, MA v. EPA, Tahoe-Sierra*). Within the Court, as in the larger society, the struggle over environmentalist worldviews and values continues. And even within the Court, as the opinions make plain, this is a struggle not just of ideas but also of emotions and wills.

Distinct patterns among recent and current justices with significant tenures on the Court help bring this struggle into focus. Justices Scalia and Thomas and, to a lesser extent, Chief Justice Rehnquist, have resisted the ecological model or sought to limit its implications for institutional arrangements between branches of government, state and federal governments, and governments and individual property owners. Two more recent arrivals, Chief Justice Roberts and Justice Alito, have followed this pattern, using legal constructs rooted largely in the pre-ecological era—such as nuisance, navigability, and the states' traditional power over land and water use—to counter expansive notions of causation and injury associated with the interdependence model as well as its normative overtones.

This alternative model is atomistic, emphasizing the boundaries, distances, and distinctions among components of human-natural systems. At the physical level, it is a world of discrete phenomena, with presumptively individual or local significance (*Lujan II, SWANCC,* dissent on standing in *MA v. EPA*). At the social level, it is a world of sharply demarcated and rigorously enforced property boundaries and jurisdictional lines (*Rapanos, Lucas,* dissent in *Sweet Home, Koontz*). It provides a setting consistent with the emphasis of these justices on individual liberty (positive freedom) and economic development of land and other natural resources, as well as the justices' acceptance of the unequal allocation of resources and burdens that the assertive use of resources may lead to.

Justice Scalia has been the voice for these justices in a number of the most prominent environmental cases, sometimes speaking for a majority, sometimes leading the dissenters. In constitutional rulings on standing, property rights, and the scope of federal regulatory power, and in his readings of ecologically based regulatory statutes, he has signed his allegiance to landowner autonomy and assertive resource use, combining it in environmental cases with hostility to the ecological model that has earned him a reputation as the Court's antienvironmentalist. His opinion for the Court in *Lujan II* denounced claims of universal injury flowing from the ecological model in limiting judicial access to beneficiaries of environmental legislation. Its rejection of expansive theories of standing based on ecological concepts, including the "ecosystem nexus" and the "animal nexus," was sweeping, its tone scathing. His opinion for the Court in *Lucas* called the state to account for "confiscatory regulations" enacted to protect a fragile coastal system. It conjured a "constitutional culture" of protection for private landowners' use rights, implicitly rejected stewardship obligations associated with the ecological model as limits on those rights, and invoked principles of nuisance law from the pre-ecological era to prevent states from imposing those obligations without compensation.[78]

Justice Scalia has shown a similarly intense resistance to the ecological model in statutory interpretation. In *SWANCC*, he joined Chief Justice Rehnquist for the Court in rejecting federal regulation of isolated waters based on their asserted ecological connections with distant waters. Writing for a plurality in *Rapanos*, Scalia vigorously rejected the ecological model's systemic imperatives. He led the dissenters in *Sweet Home*, taking particular offense at the contested rule's attribution of injury through extended ecosystem interactions and the "large number of routine activities" on private land that this would subject to regulatory prohibition. Dissenting again in *MA v. EPA*, he divided up the "air" into the local and the global to justify denial of federal jurisdiction over anthropogenic greenhouse gas emissions against a background of doubt that those emissions were causing global warming through the mechanism of the climate system.[79]

In these cases, Justice Scalia not only eschewed the "proenvironment" outcome but also expressed his antagonism to the basic precept of environmentalism—that humans are part of an interconnected human-natural system (Leopold's "biotic community") with attendant obligations to protect that community from adverse effects of their actions. His exemplars were not the wilderness enthusiasts of *Sierra Club* or the watershed dwellers of *Laidlaw*. Instead, he celebrated the landowners and entrepreneurs threatened by regulatory expansions inspired by the ecological model—the landowner-developers in *Rapanos* and *Lucas*, the "simplest farmer" in *Sweet Home*. The law map required hard boundaries, even if the natural world did not readily lend itself to them, to protect the values embodied by these figures.

Justices Stevens, Souter, Ginsburg, and Breyer (and recent additions Justices Kagan and Sotomayor) have more consistently embraced the ecological model. These justices have identified the model with new scientific knowledge and societal norms and have criticized the traditionalist constructs deployed by their colleagues to limit its expression, arguing that these constructs inhibit the evolutionary process of the law. Their model emphasizes connections among components of human-natural systems across space and time. It projects a world in which individual actions or local events are likely to have broader systemic effects (*Riverside, Laidlaw, Sweet Home, MA v. EPA*), and in which property boundaries and jurisdictional lines are permeable and conditional (dissents in *Lucas, SWANCC, Koontz*). It is closely associated with these justices' emphasis on subordination of individual interests to the collective good and living harmoniously with nature as well as on protecting against unequal burdens and status derived from nature-disturbing activities.

Justice Stevens became the ecological model's most vocal champion in the years before his retirement. He concurred in the judgment of the Court in *Lujan II* but, *contra* Justice Scalia, argued that standing could be based on an established interest in a distant species, which he likened to a family's communal interest in the life of an absent member. His opinion for the Court on standing in *MA v. EPA* credited causality within the earth's climate system in the linkage between U.S. automobile emissions and global harm. He dissented from Justice Scalia's opinion for the Court in *Lucas*. We must make room, he contended, for the evolution of property rights based on new knowledge of the vulnerability of species and ecosystems.

In interpreting ecologically based statutes, Justice Stevens stressed their protective purposes in pushing for broad regulatory coverage. He led the dissenters in *SWANCC*, arguing that even ostensibly "isolated" waters could support Clean Water Act (CWA) jurisdiction based on the statute's purpose to protect the integrity of the nation's waters and on likely hydrological and ecological connections with distant waters. Dissenting again, in *Rapanos,* he read the protection of an extended, interconnected aquatic ecosystem as Congress's controlling concern and the touchstone for an expansive regulatory jurisdiction under the CWA. He wrote for the majority in *Sweet Home,* upholding over Scalia's vehement objection an expansive regulatory scope for the ESA based on the importance of ecosystem protection to the statute's goal of saving endangered species.

For Justices Scalia and Stevens, interpretive method was honed to both outcomes and cultural meanings. Scalia's textualism consistently generated constraints on regulatory scope. He read words like "the waters," "take" and "air" as sharp-edged and limiting. The resulting statutory interpretations shrank and hardened legal boundaries, both vertical and horizontal, with the effect of containing regulatory domains driven by the ecological model. By contrast, Stevens used his intentionalism to read jurisdictional terms as open to the protective purposes of the statutes. This approach produced legal boundaries that were porous and responsive to the ecological model. The distinction between hard and soft interpretative modes, producing strict or permeable legal boundaries consistent with competing worldviews and values, also characterized these justices' views on related constitutional issues, such as the scope of individualized "injury" for standing, the strength of rights-protecting property boundaries for takings, and limits on federal powers.

Justice Ginsburg added an important voice to the environmentalist chorus often led by Justice Stevens. She concurred with Stevens in each of his opinions in these cases after she joined the Court and offered her own rendering of the land community in *Laidlaw*—one just as compelling in its way as Stevens's more florid accounts. Ginsburg has voted with environmentalists in a higher percentage of cases—and has arguably registered deeper sympathy with the environmentalist cause—than any other recent justice, despite a voice of restraint.

In character with their larger role on the Court, Justices O'Connor and Kennedy often occupied a middle ground in these cases. Kennedy in particular has with some consistency placed himself between the Court's ecologists and atomists, expressing a measured sympathy for the ecological model, albeit sometimes while concurring in a result seemingly in tension with the model. In his concurrence in *Lujan II,* for example, he undermined Justice Scalia's categorical dismissal of the "nexus" theories by arguing that "in different circumstances a nexus theory . . . might support a claim to standing." In *MA v. EPA,* he joined Justice Stevens's generous account of the systemic linkages between domestic auto exhaust and sea level rise along the Atlantic Coast. Concurring in *Lucas,* he maintained that the common law of nuisance was "too narrow a confine for the exercise of regulatory power in a complex and interdependent society."[80]

Justice Kennedy's bridging impulse has carried into his statutory interpretations. He joined the majority in *Sweet Home,* which shaped the ESA's regulatory scope to fit the purpose of ecosystem protection. With the majority in *SWANCC,* by contrast, he voted to reject ecological arguments for CWA jurisdiction over the isolated ponds, presumably because he agreed with the conclusion that there was no "significant nexus" between the ponds and traditionally navigable waters.[81] But in *Rapanos* he appropriated "significant nexus" to place ecological interdependence at the center of his singular interpretation of the CWA's reach. This synthesis both embraced the ecological model and disciplined it by requiring evidence of significant connections to support the Corps' jurisdiction. The effect was to balance among competing values.

In her concurrence in *Sweet Home,* Justice O'Connor offered a comparable gesture of reconciliation. She accepted the regulatory expression of interconnectedness in the Court's interpretation of the ESA but sought to constrain that expression using notions of foreseeability and individual harm. These gestures by Justices Kennedy and O'Connor suggest the possibility of a new synthesis for environmental thought and practice, an idea explored in Chapter 10.

CHAPTER NINE

The Eclipse of NEPA

SOON AFTER THE ENACTMENT of the National Environmental Policy Act (NEPA) in 1970, Congressman Henry Reuss called it "a Magna Carta for conservation." Later that year, Fred Fisher, cochair of the Sierra Club Legal Committee, extended the comparison in his remarks to an environmental law conference. He was "hopeful . . . that gradual common-law case-by-case type of development can make NEPA into something like an environmental Magna Charta." His statement made two important points. First, despite NEPA's sweeping language, the process of achieving Magna Carta status would be a gradual one, if it happened at all. Second, whether NEPA eventually achieved that status would depend on how the courts applied it.[1]

"Environmentalist Magna Carta" became a much-used moniker for NEPA, suggesting its potential to institutionalize an ecological imperative for all agencies of the federal government. Although the phrase has sometimes been used with an ironic edge, to suggest how far short of Magna Carta status NEPA has fallen, it continues to convey, wistfully perhaps, the high promise NEPA held for environmentalists at the time of its enactment. This chapter examines NEPA decisions by the Supreme Court over four decades that together frame a narrative of the Court's engagement with this distinctive environmental law.[2]

Two features of NEPA make it uniquely suited for attention in this book. The first is NEPA's high symbolic content. Other environmental statutes focused on particular environmental concerns—air or water pollution, hazardous waste, or species loss. NEPA dealt with the environment as a whole. It was also, as the name made clear, a policy statute, unlike other statutes that had a remedial or regulatory focus. According to one of its chief architects, political scientist Lynton Caldwell, its function was to articulate broad "national environmental goals and values which the Federal government is directed to honor in cooperation with State and local governments and other concerned public and private organizations." It did this in elevated rhetoric that embraced the new environmental paradigm (NEP). The breadth and boldness of this articulation had a quasi-constitutional cast that invited the Magna Carta epithet. NEPA's policy could be read—and was by many—as an embodiment of the cultural transformation that the environmental movement sought to bring about. It could also be read—as it ultimately was by the Court—as hand waving.[3]

The second important feature of NEPA is related to the first. Because it is a policy statute, NEPA lacks the detailed prescriptive machinery at the heart of regulatory statutes such as the Clean Water Act (CWA) and Clean Air Act. Its "action-forcing" provisions addressed to federal officials are few and succinct. Most of NEPA's language is general, giving latitude to the executive branch and the courts in determining how it should be understood and applied. Extending Fred Fisher's early insight, Justice Marshall wrote: "this vaguely worded statute seems designed to serve as no more than a catalyst for development of a 'common law' of NEPA." Council on Environmental Quality (CEQ) regulations interpreting NEPA are accorded "substantial deference" by reviewing courts, but these regulations themselves are largely a codification of prior case law and leave substantial room for judgment in specific applications. This common law aspect of NEPA interpretation leaves more space for judicial importation of beliefs and values from the ambient culture than do more constrained statutory environments.[4]

These related qualities of NEPA create a potentially fruitful field for studying the cultural dimensions of the Court's deliberations.

NEPA and the Court: An Overview

Judged only by their outcomes, the Supreme Court's NEPA decisions signify a profound rejection of NEPA and environmentalism. In his masterful inside account of the decisions, Richard Lazarus documents the extreme one-sidedness apparent on the face of the Court's record. Although review may be sought in a NEPA case by any party from an adverse appellate court ruling, the Court has much more often accepted review when the federal agency is the petitioner, having lost below on the basis of a finding of a NEPA violation, than when an environmental party is the petitioner, having failed to persuade the lower court of a violation. Indeed, in more than four decades of NEPA litigation, the Court has granted review in only one NEPA case at the behest of an environmental petitioner. In virtually all other cases, the Court has granted review at the request of the solicitor general on behalf of an agency complaining of an overly strict reading of NEPA by the court below. The record on the merits is even more lopsided. Of the seventeen NEPA cases that the Court has decided on the merits, the government has won them all. And in all but a handful, the decision has been unanimous. As Lazarus observes, "I doubt there is any other area of law in which the Court has been so repeatedly and so unanimously opposed to the arguments advanced by one set of parties."[5]

This one-sidedness has led to general condemnation, at least within the scholarly community, of the Court's disparagement of NEPA. But Lazarus argues that the record is not as one-sided as it seems. Regarding the Court's extreme tendency to favor petitions for review by the government over those by environmentalists, he offers explanations that do not rest on hostility to NEPA; these include the effects of injunctive relief issued against the government by the lower court on the Court's sense of a case's importance and the "dynamic nature of NEPA litigation," which may influence the Court's perception of the efficacy of review where environmentalists have lost below. On the merits decisions, Lazarus demonstrates how at least one of the seventeen losses for environmentalists was in fact a victory—a small consolation for environmentalists perhaps, but palpable nonetheless. More generally, he shows how the solicitor general, as gatekeeper for federal agencies seeking access to the Court, has adroitly maximized the government's success under NEPA by appealing only winnable cases and by conceding points that might otherwise have prompted judicial rebuke. He also shows that the Court has sometimes narrowed the reach of its opinions to avoid unnecessarily undermining the importance of NEPA's action-forcing provisions and that this careful tailoring helps explain the unanimity of the justices in these cases.[6]

Professor Lazarus's account shifts the narrative away from one of unmitigated hostility on the Court's part to NEPA and its environmentalist roots. But he does not say that the result is parity. "It cannot be doubted that [environmentalists] have still lost more than they have won before the Court, in terms of NEPA's potential."[7] The residual disparity is a result, Lazarus argues, of particularly effective advocacy by the solicitor general and by justices—including Chief Justice Rehnquist—who worked to limit NEPA's force and effect. His analysis of the decisions bears out the importance of advocacy effectiveness in both these respects. But comparison with environmental decisions in other legal contexts suggests there is more to the story. In non-NEPA cases, the government does not have a perfect record in the Court when pitted against environmentalists. In *TVA v. Hill,* for example, the attorney general himself argued on behalf of a governmental petitioner against environmental respondents and lost. By the same token, although Rehnquist was an extremely effective chief justice, in other areas of particular interest to him, such as environmental federalism, he was less successful in producing a unanimous Court.[8] In other legal domains explored in this book, dissenting opinions have been the rule in culturally salient environmental decisions, whether for or against environmental interests. In NEPA cases, the Court has stood as one, with few exceptions, against more environmentally generous interpretations. In this chapter, I explore what this says about NEPA, the Court, or both.

If NEPA is the litmus test of adherence to the NEP, one is left to wonder whether there are any environmentalists on the Court, with the exception perhaps of Justice Ginsburg, who in *Winter v. Natural Resources Defense Council, Inc.* wrote the first full dissent from a NEPA decision upholding the government's view in almost thirty years.[9] Perhaps the egalitarian-collectivists who joined in dissenting from decisions such as *Lujan II, Lucas,* and *Rapanos* did not share the full range or intensity of environmentalist commitments that NEPA may be read to embody.[10]

NEPA: Origins and Aspirations

NEPA combines a comprehensive statement of national environmental policy with action-forcing measures to realize that policy. Section 101(a) "recognize[s] the profound impact of man's activity on the interrelations of all components of the natural environment . . . and recognize[s] further the critical importance of restoring and maintaining environmental quality to the overall welfare and development of man." It declares "the continuing policy of the Federal government . . . to foster and promote the general welfare, to create and maintain conditions under which man and nature can exist in productive harmony, and fulfill the social, economic, and other requirements of present and future generations of Americans." Elaborating on this general statement, Section 101(b) lists six policy goals that it is the "continuing responsibility" of the federal government to secure: "fulfill the responsibilities of each generation as trustee of the environment for succeeding generations"; "assure for all Americans safe, healthful, productive, and esthetically and culturally pleasing surroundings"; "attain the widest range of beneficial uses of the environment without degradation"; "preserve important historic, cultural, and natural aspects of our national heritage, and maintain, wherever possible, an environment which supports diversity and variety of individual choice"; "achieve a balance between population and resource use which will permit high standards of living and a wide sharing of life's amenities"; and "enhance the quality of renewable resources and approach the maximum attainable recycling of depletable resources."[11]

In elevated rhetoric unusual for legislation on any subject, NEPA's Section 101 expresses the environmentalist beliefs and values identified in Chapter 1. It picks up the strains of egalitarianism ("wide sharing of life's amenities") and collectivism ("promote the general welfare") that Dan Kahan and others have associated with environmental concern. It twice extends its concerns to future generations. It expresses autonomy values in the "variety of individual choice" that flows from an unspoiled environment rather than in the individualism of property ownership and entrepreneurship. It embraces the ecological model and related elements of fragility and urgency ("profound impact of man's activity on the interrelations of all components"). And it captures environmentalism's distinctive harmony values ("conditions under which man and nature can exist in productive harmony"). The language suggests an ecocentric cast, stressing harmony and interrelatedness, but it also connects a holistic concern for nature to human well-being ("the overall welfare and development of man"), closing the potential gap between ecocentric and anthropocentric strains of environmentalism. The result is a succinct, compelling articulation of the NEP.

Section 101's character as an environmentalist manifesto took shape in the early stages of the legislative process. NEPA's main intellectual instigator was Lynton Caldwell, a political scientist who served as an advisor to Senator Scoop Jackson, chair of the Senate Committee on Interior and Insular Affairs and the chief political architect of the law. In 1968, with the assistance of committee counsel William Van Ness, Caldwell drafted a report for the committee that argued for a national environmental policy and a comprehensive system for information gathering and reporting to carry it out.[12]

Caldwell's report traced familiar environmentalist themes. The situation was urgent and unprecedented—"a circumstance that is totally new in human history." The crisis had its roots in undue emphasis on autonomy and mastery values: "exaggerated doctrines of private ownership and an uncritical popular tolerance of the side effects of economic production." An effective response demanded recognition of the environment as an interconnected whole, earth's "life-support systems." The primary justification for the new policy was anthropocentric, with an apocalyptic turn. At stake was nothing less than "the survival of man, in a world in which decency and dignity are possible." But the report also incorporated ecocentric strains—a "philosophy of reverence for life."[13]

The report provided the basis for S. 1075, which was introduced by Senator Jackson and, combined with Congressman John Dingell's House bill in conference, became the primary source of NEPA's text. Its visionary cast reflected an intent on the part of key legislative drafters that the "notion of a new ecological conscience be a fundamental part of NEPA's language and its interpretation." The enacted language of Section 101, as discussed above, reflected that intent, but interpretation would remain a matter for the agencies and the courts.[14]

The challenge was to ensure that Section 101 was not a hollow pronouncement. In hearings before Jackson's committee on S. 1075, Caldwell proposed that "an action-forcing, operational aspect" be added to the bill. This proposal resulted in NEPA's Section 102. Section 102(1) generally requires that federal laws and regulations "be interpreted and administered in accordance with the policies set forth" in Section 101 "to the fullest extent possible." Section 102(2) establishes specific procedural mandates, including requirements that federal agencies prepare an environmental impact statement (EIS) for "major federal actions significantly affecting the quality of the human environment" and consider alternatives to their actions.[15]

In Caldwell's view, the goal of NEPA, like that of the movement he drafted the act to serve, was transformative: to link "principle and process to transform . . . national ethos from the pioneer ethic to one of environmental custody and care." The express directives of the statute were to federal officials, but it implied a broader purpose of "'public' education and persuasive teaching." The "action-forcing" provisions of Section 102—and the EIS requirement in particular—were subservient to NEPA's transformative goal. Section 101(2)(C), Caldwell later wrote, was not the "essential purpose" of the act, as the courts—and particularly the Supreme Court—had come to interpret it. Instead, the EIS provision was intended "to force agency compliance with the substantive provisions of the Act." This was NEPA's "precautionary strategy for the future."[16]

The Supreme Court has been less than hospitable to the broad purposes of Section 102 as Caldwell conceived it. It has rendered Section 102(1) unenforceable and, while magnifying the enforceability of Section 102(2), has isolated its requirements from the policy of Section 101.

Calvert Cliffs v. AEC: Brave Beginnings

The seminal decision that commenced an era of judicial review under NEPA was handed down not by the Supreme Court but by a panel of the Court of Appeals for the District of Columbia Circuit in the 1971 case of *Calvert Cliffs' Coordinating Committee v. U.S. Atomic Energy Commission*. Prior to this, the Supreme Court had had only one encounter with NEPA, and it was inconclusive: In *Named Members of San Antonio Conservation Society v. Texas Highway Department,* local environmentalists sought review of a Fifth Circuit decision allowing state and federal authorities to proceed with plans for an expressway through a city park in San Antonio without having prepared an EIS under Section 102(2)(C). The setting was similar to *Citizens to Preserve Overton Park, Inc. v. Volpe,* which the Court would decide a year later in favor of the highway opponents. In *San Antonio,* however, the Court denied certiorari, allowing the highway project to go forward.[17]

The Court in *San Antonio* gave no reason for its action, as is typical for denials of certiorari. The move attracted two blazing dissents, however: one by Justice Black, joined by Justices Douglas and Brennan, and the other by Douglas, joined by Black and Brennan. Both dissents extolled the virtues of urban parkland and decried its destruction in images even more vivid than the Court would later use in *Overton Park.* Black described the San Antonio park as "a lovely place for people to retreat from the frantic pace of bustling urban life to enjoy the simple pleasures of open space, quiet solitude, and clean air." That quiet retreat would be broken by the "ugly, smelly stream of traffic pouring down a super six-lane 'North Expressway.'" Douglas offered his own dire condemnation of the "ruination of a sanctuary created for urban people" and its "awful . . . consequences." He would have granted review and used the Court's opinion to "let the bureaucracy know that [Section] 102(2)(C) is the law of the land to be observed meticulously." Despite the vehemence of the dissents, however, the silence of the majority made the import of the case obscure. The task of elucidating the significance of NEPA—particularly its Section 101(2)(C)—was left, as it happened, to the District of Columbia Circuit.[18]

Calvert Cliffs was not the first appeals court decision to address NEPA, but it was the first to come to terms with the act's broad significance and the role of the courts in its implementation. Judge Skelly Wright, who authored the court's opinion in the case, had a history of decisive judicial action in socially charged settings. As a federal district judge in his home state of Louisiana, he had bravely enforced Supreme Court antidiscrimination rulings against hostile state and local institutions.[19] Now, as an appellate judge on the District of Columbia Circuit, he took on the role of crusader for the environmental values that Congress, "at long last," sought to protect in NEPA.

The first paragraph of Judge Wright's opinion was portentous:

These cases are only the beginning of what promises to become a flood of new litigation—litigation seeking judicial assistance in protecting our natural environment. Several recently enacted statutes attest to the commitment of the

Government to control, at long last, the destructive engine of material "prog-ress." But it remains to be seen whether the promise of this legislation will be-come a reality. Therein lies the judicial role. In these cases, we must for the first time interpret the broadest and perhaps most important of the recent stat-utes: the National Environmental Policy Act of 1969. . . . Our duty . . . is to see that important legislative purposes, heralded in the halls of Congress, are not lost or misdirected in the vast hallways of the federal bureaucracy.[20]

In this remarkable passage, Wright internalized the environmentalist view of the destructiveness of "material 'progress' " and the urgent need to con-tain it. The quotes around "progress" set off his ironic use of the term, and the image of progress as an "engine" conveyed its dehumanized relentless-ness. "Material 'progress' " was mastery values run amok. NEPA's purpose was finally to bring the "destructive engine" to heel; the courts' role, to secure this purpose against the entrenched indifference of government functionaries—the faceless denizens of the bureaucracy's "vast hallways." Wright gladly welcomed the "flood of new litigation" that would allow the courts to enact that role. Commentator Dan Tarlock distills the import of this paragraph: to the question of whether NEPA created judicially enforce-able duties, Wright answered "with a resounding 'yes' in the ringing tones of an Old Testament prophet and thus launched environmental law."[21]

The court applied these duties to the Atomic Energy Commission's (AEC) licensing of nuclear power plants—an early target of environmentalists be-cause of perceived risks of radioactive exposure. Rules newly adopted by the AEC to implement NEPA required that the EIS for a proposed facility "accompany the [license] application through the Commission's review pro-cesses" but provided that the statement would not be considered in licensing hearings unless a party to the proceedings raised an environmental issue. Al-though arguably the rule was in literal compliance with Section 102(2)(C)'s requirement that an EIS "accompany the proposal through the existing agency review process," the court pilloried the AEC's "crabbed interpretation" as "mak[ing] a mockery of the Act." Section 102 required the agency's active consideration of environmental factors at every stage of the process, regard-less of whether there was an environmental "intervenor with the information, energy and money" to mount a challenge.[22]

Judge Wright's opinion was welcomed by environmentalists both for its oracular announcement of a new era of environmental governance and for advancing legal principles that seemed to secure a central role for the courts in promoting the cultural shift that NEPA's originators envisioned. Two of these principles were definitive; a third was tentative but rich with possi-bility: First, NEPA created a cause of action for judicial review of agency compliance with the act. Second, Section 102(2)(C), requiring EISs for environmentally significant federal actions, created judicially enforceable duties. Third, the opinion suggested that a procedurally sound agency decision might nevertheless be reviewed to determine whether "the actual balance of costs and benefits that was struck was arbitrary or clearly gave insufficient weight to environmental values." This last principle held out the prospect that federal courts would police agency fidelity to NEPA's policy goals. It remained undeveloped, because *Calvert Cliffs* did not present a question of substantive review. Other federal courts, taking their cue from that case, also entertained possible substantive review under NEPA.[23]

Although celebrated among environmentalists, *Calvert Cliffs* set the stage for a judicial backlash. In the coming decades, a series of Supreme Court decisions worked to undo Judge Wright's enthusiastic embrace of NEPA. The Court left intact *Calvert Cliff*'s first principle—that NEPA provides a cause of action for review. But it significantly qualified the second—the judicial enforceability of NEPA's procedural requirements—by limiting the extent of judicial review. Those limitations weakened the link between substance and procedure that was central to *Calvert Cliffs'* model of NEPA—and Caldwell's initial concept. Finally, the Court mounted a decisive assault on substantive review under NEPA, as entertained by *Calvert Cliffs* and other lower federal courts. By enlarging agency discretion and expunging substantive review, the Court's goal seemed not only to stem the flood of NEPA litigation that Judge Wright had welcomed but also to put itself at arm's length from NEPA's environmentalist commitments.

Substantive Review under NEPA

The argument for substantive review has a basis in the language of NEPA. The first part of the statute's "action-forcing" provision, Section 102(1), is general: "the Congress authorizes and directs that, to the fullest extent possible[,] the policies, regulations, and public laws of the United States shall be interpreted and administered in accordance with the policies set forth in this [Act]." More specific directives, including the EIS requirement, are set forth in Section 102(2). There is no suggestion in the language or structure of the statute that the general directive is of less force or effect than the specific directives. The qualifying language—"to the fullest extent possible"—applies equally to both parts of Section 102. And according to the report accompanying S. 1075 as it emerged from House-Senate conference, the language was "not to be used by any Federal agency as a means of avoiding compliance with the directives set out in Section 102." According to Caldwell, Section 102(1) places an "explicit obligation on the agencies to reconcile their decisions with the principles (or values) declared in Section 101."[24]

Section 102(1)'s mandate supports at least two theories of substantive judicial review of agency actions subject to NEPA. The first and more assertive theory is that courts may review agency decisions under NEPA to ensure that they give proper weight to the values articulated in Section 101. Such review would determine whether the balance struck by an agency was "in accordance with law" as provided by NEPA. In 1977, the CEQ stated on the basis of the decisions of five federal circuit courts that "NEPA's Section 101 present[ed] sufficiently definite standards to permit meaningful judicial review." A second, more modest theory is that courts may review agency decisions to determine whether they are "arbitrary and capricious." Under this second theory, courts would require not that agencies give any particular weight to environmental considerations but that the balance struck be reasonable.[25]

Section 102(1) notwithstanding, in a series of four NEPA decisions between 1976 and 1989, the Supreme Court made it increasingly clear that federal judges were not to review the substance of agency decisions under NEPA. Two of these decisions were unanimous. Justice Marshall dissented in the other two—joined by Justice Brennan in one, alone in the other. At a practical level, this quartet stifled judicial oversight of the reconciliation of agency missions with NEPA's values. At a cultural level, it discounted those values against competing values embodied in existing agency missions and practices.[26]

Kleppe v. Sierra Club: Planting the Seed

The Court's suppression of NEPA's values in judicial review began obscurely in *Kleppe v. Sierra Club*, decided in 1976. The issue in *Kleppe* was procedural, whether Section 102(2)(C) required the Department of the Interior to prepare a regional EIS for coal leasing on federal lands. But the Court used the case to lay the foundations for judicial noninterference on the substance of agency decisions.[27]

The passage of NEPA in 1969 had major implications for Interior's program to lease coal reserves on federal lands for private development. The department took steps to comply with Section 102(2)(C), including commencing work on a national-scale "coal programmatic" EIS and preparing EISs on individual leases with significant environmental effects. Environmental groups, however, demanded that Interior also prepare a regional impact statement on leasing activities across the "northern Great Plains region," which they defined as covering portions of six states, including northeastern Wyoming, eastern Montana, and western North and South Dakota. The department had commenced a regional study, the Northern Great Plains Resources Program (NGPRP), to gather information on economic and environmental issues for planning purposes. But it declined to do the regional EIS that the environmentalists demanded.[28]

The district court dismissed the environmentalist claim that a regional EIS was required because it found no proposal for federal action at the scale of the "Northern Great Plains region." In an opinion by the author of *Calvert Cliffs,* Judge Wright, the District of Columbia Circuit reversed and remanded the case for further consideration. The circuit court was concerned about the cumulative effects of individual leasing decisions that might escape full consideration in both lease-specific impact statements and in the national programmatic EIS. Unsure about whether Interior's northern Great Plains study had ripened into a "proposal," however, the court remanded to allow the department to decide initially whether and when a regional EIS would be prepared.[29]

The Supreme Court reversed in an opinion by Justice Powell. The government had reduced its legal vulnerability by conceding its obligation to prepare a national programmatic EIS and regional impact statements where necessary to deal with related actions, as well as statements on individual leases with significant impacts. The only issue left was whether the appropriate scope of a regional impact statement was the Northern Great Plains region, as environmentalists had defined it, or some other specific geographical configuration. On this issue, Justice Powell's opinion for the Court adopted a literalist interpretation of Section 102(2)(C). No Northern Great Plains regional EIS was required because there was no regional "proposal" for federal action. The department's NGPRP was a "regional study" not a "proposal." The mere possibility of a future proposal for federal action at that regional scale was not enough to trigger the courts' involvement. The time at which the EIS requirement becomes ripe and a court may intervene "is the time at which [an agency] makes a recommendation or report on a *proposal* for federal action" and not before. This spare reading of Section 102(2)(C) left the District of Columbia Circuit's anticipatory intervention with no legal footing.[30]

The Court did agree with the Sierra Club on a theory not developed by the circuit court that cumulative environmental impacts of several proposed federal actions might demand a "comprehensive" EIS, even in the absence of a regional proposal. But the presence of such impacts and the scale at which they might be best considered were matters within the expert discretion of the action agency. The Court declined to disturb Interior's view that cumulative impacts were better addressed at subregional scales, on the basis of "basins, drainage areas, and other factors."[31]

The Court's decision brought a partial dissent by Justice Marshall, joined by Justice Brennan, the only justice remaining on the Court from the trio of proenvironmentalist dissenters in *San Antonio*. Marshall's interpretation of NEPA's procedural requirements was keyed less to the statute's literal terms and more to its policy-shifting aspirations. The problem with postponing judicial involvement until the moment of "a recommendation or report on a proposal," the justice argued, is that by then agency officials may have made up their minds without the benefit of an adequate environmental analysis. Where this is the case, a judicial order to undertake an EIS is not likely to produce the receptivity to environmental values that NEPA intended, producing only "*post hoc* rationalizations." To ensure real consideration of environmental consequences, courts should be able to step in pre-proposal when the agency obligation to do an EIS is clear and its "violation blatant." Marshall's emphasis on the actual internalization of NEPA's values by agency officials was absent from the Court's more formal concept of "consideration" of environmental issues based on an EIS.[32]

Missing from the ranks of the dissenters were those, such as Justices Blackmun and Stevens, who often took a proenvironmentalist stance in split decisions under other environmental statutes. According to Blackmun's notes of the conference, Stevens, like others in the majority, believed that the court of appeals's position lacked statutory support. Blackmun himself was torn. He had revealed his environmentalist sympathies in *Sierra Club v. Morton* and would go on to write ringing dissents in *Lujan II* and *Lucas*. But here he leaned toward reversal. In a memorandum he wrote for himself before oral argument, he expressed concern about "regional impact and irrevocable commitment once the first plan is approved." But he also wrote that "we should be realistic about all this." Increasing demand for energy meant that the nation would do everything it could to develop new energy sources. "All this . . . means that a lot of what we regard as natural environment is going to be destroyed. I think that is just as inevitable as it can be."[33] This candid comment suggested the futility of changing the course of environmental degradation, despite what NEPA and the courts might require. It left the possibility that his vote was an act of acquiescence in the "inevitable" rather than one of strong legal conviction.

Justice Powell's opinion for the Court gave the District of Columbia Circuit no quarter. The opinion's bright spot for the Sierra Club—the recognition of cumulative environmental impacts as the basis for comprehensive impact statements—was based on arguments advanced by the Sierra Club, not the circuit court. The deconstruction of the lower court's rationale, carried out with relentless precision, conveyed that there was more at issue than simply an innocent misapprehension of statutory requirements by the lower court. This sense matured in a footnote near the end of the opinion in which the Court cautioned that NEPA does not

> contemplate that a court should substitute its judgment for that of the agency as to the environmental consequences of its actions. . . . The only role for a court is to insure that the agency has taken a "hard look" at environmental consequences; it cannot "interject itself within the area of discretion of the executive as to the choice of the action to be taken."[34]

There was no obvious occasion for this admonition. The Sierra Club had not argued for substantive review before the Court, nor had the District of Columbia Circuit purported to exercise substantive review in its holding. That the Court thought the note was necessary suggested a concern that environmentalist values had seeped into the circuit court's assessment of Interior's procedural compliance. "Hard look" review saved a space for federal courts' enforcement of agency NEPA obligations, but the depth and scope of that role remained unclear. The Court's emphasis was on the limitations of the judicial role—a first step in its progressive marginalization of NEPA's policy thrust.[35]

Vermont Yankee Nuclear Power Co. v. Natural Resources Defense Council, Inc.: The Escalation

In *Vermont Yankee,* the Court's suspicion that the District of Columbia Circuit's review of procedural compliance with NEPA was inflected by environmental values came out of the shadows. What was a footnote in *Kleppe* became a textual admonition in *Vermont Yankee,* bringing into full view the Court's emerging doctrine barring substantive review under NEPA. And in *Vermont Yankee,* unlike *Kleppe,* there was no dissent. As Richard Lazarus puts it, the case "marked the true beginning of the demise of NEPA in the Supreme Court."[36]

Vermont Yankee consolidated review of two decisions by the District of Columbia Circuit. Both were petitions for review by environmental groups opposing Atomic Energy Commission licenses for nuclear power facilities. (During the pendency of the proceedings, Congress transferred the licensing functions of the Atomic Energy Commission to the Nuclear Regulatory Commission; both are referred to here as the commission.[37]) In the first case, the Natural Resources Defense Council (NRDC) and others attacked the commission's issuance of an operating license for the Vermont Yankee

Nuclear plant near Brattleboro, Vermont, for failure to consider the impacts of the nuclear fuel cycle (including reprocessing of spent fuel and the disposal of nuclear waste) in the licensing decision. They also objected to a rulemaking that the commission undertook in connection with the Vermont Yankee licensing. The rulemaking determined that the environmental effects of the fuel cycle were "relatively insignificant" for individual plants and limited consideration of those effects in licensing cases to a set of numerical values provided in the rule. In the second case, Saginaw Nuclear Power Study Group (Saginaw) and others objected to the commission's issuance of construction permits for twin nuclear reactors in Midland, Michigan. Their issues included the refusal of the commission to consider energy conservation as an alternative to the nuclear plants or to allow inquiry into the conclusions of the Advisory Committee on Reactor Safeguards (ACRS), which acted in an advisory role to the commission on nuclear safety issues.

Chief Judge Bazelon's opinions for the District of Columbia Circuit in these cases built on the principle of *Calvert Cliffs* that NEPA requires "a careful and informed decisionmaking process." In *Vermont Yankee*, the court set aside the commission's fuel cycle rule. The "statutory context created by NEPA" required that the agency consider "'responsible scientific opinion concerning possible adverse environmental effects' which is contrary to the official agency position." The commission's informal rulemaking proceedings, it concluded, did not meet this standard. Without requiring a different substantive outcome or specifying the additional procedures that might be necessary, the court sent the rule back to the agency for further ventilation. In the *Midland* case, the court ruled that the EIS was inadequate under Section 102(2) because of a failure to consider the alternative of energy conservation and sent the issue back for consideration by the commission. The court also ordered the return of the ACRS safety report for elucidation of "other problems" alluded to but not specified in the report.[38]

Justice Rehnquist's opinion for the Court reversing the court of appeals in both cases was unanimous, but immediately after oral argument it was not clear that the opinion would be unanimous or even that the Court would decide the case on the merits. The Court's deliberations were complicated by events following the District of Columbia Circuit's decisions. The commission had replaced the 1974 fuel cycle rule overturned by the court of appeals with a new interim rule that included new values for consideration of fuel cycle impacts, and it had applied those values to the Vermont Yankee plant. It had also stated publicly that consideration of fuel cycle impacts in individual licensing proceedings would be "consistent with the legal requirements and spirit of NEPA."[39]

Given these developments, Justice Brennan argued that the writ of certiorari should be dismissed as improvidently granted: the fuel cycle issues were moot "as a practical matter" and the rest of the issues in the case did not warrant review. A majority of justices voted against dismissal, however, and Justice Rehnquist circulated a memorandum in the form of draft opinion reversing the District of Columbia Circuit on the merits. In a footnote to the draft, Rehnquist insisted that the Court address the circuit court's handling of the fuel cycle rule because it was a harmful precedent for the judicial imposition of administrative procedures not required by law and continued to have direct adverse effects on the commission's proceedings. He rejected the contrary views of Justices Brennan and Marshall on this question, but he did accept other suggestions by these justices, including increasing the prominence given to the commission's concession that NEPA required environmental assessments for individual reactors to address fuel cycle issues. Congratulating Rehnquist on being a "damned good fisherman," Brennan "acquiesce[d] in [his] catch in these cases," as did Marshall.[40]

Justice Rehnquist's opinion for the Court found that the court of appeals "improperly intruded into the agency's decisionmaking process." In overturning the commission's fuel cycle rule, "the ineluctable mandate of the [lower] court's decision [was] that the commission's rulemaking procedures were inadequate." However, it was "absolutely clear" from the Court's precedents that agencies are "free to fashion their own rules of procedure" absent exceptional circumstances not present in these cases. The commission's rulemaking more than met the minimal process requirements of the Administrative Procedure Act (APA). And the Court rejected the District of Columbia Circuit's reliance on NEPA as a source of requirements for new agency procedures. The only procedural requirements NEPA imposes are "stated in the plain language of the Act." The notion that NEPA might alter the larger procedural environment within which federal agencies operated was dead in its infancy.[41]

The Court also reversed the District of Columbia Circuit's rulings on the Midland EIS (failure to consider energy conservation alternative) and the ACRS report (remand for "further elaboration"). This latter issue provoked the opinion's remarkable closing paragraph:

> All this leads us to make one further observation of some relevance to this case. To say that the Court of Appeals' final reason for remanding is insubstantial at best is a gross understatement. Consumers Power first applied in 1969 for a construction permit. . . . To then nullify that effort seven years later because one report refers to other problems, which problems admittedly have been discussed at length in other reports available to the public, borders on

the Kafkaesque. Nuclear energy may some day be a cheap, safe source of power or it may not. But Congress has made a choice to at least try nuclear energy. . . . The fundamental policy questions appropriately resolved in Congress and in the state legislatures are *not* subject to reexamination in the federal courts under the guise of judicial review of agency action. . . . NEPA does set forth significant substantive goals for the Nation, but its mandate to the agencies is essentially procedural. . . . It is to insure a fully informed and well-considered decision, not necessarily a decision the judges of the Court of Appeals or of this Court would have reached had they been members of the decisionmaking unit of the agency. Administrative decisions should be set aside in this context, as in every other, only for substantial procedural or substantive reasons as mandated by statute, . . . not simply because the court is unhappy with the result reached.[42]

Although addressed specifically to the ACRS issue, this passage worked as a coda for the whole opinion ("of some relevance to this case"). There was an unvarnished, off-the-record quality to it. The tone was forceful and at times scathing: "insubstantial at best," a "gross understatement," and "Kafkaesque," which carried disturbing, nightmarish connotations. "Borders on" moderated this effect, but the condemnatory note was still powerful. In the judicial setting, the reference evoked Kafka's surreal novel *The Trial*, in which the protagonist, Joseph K., is tried and executed by a remote and unaccountable judicial authority. Although "Kafkaesque" was increasing in general usage in the 1970s, this was its first use by the Supreme Court. And it remains the Court's only use of the word in a majority opinion except to quote a lower court or a party's brief.[43]

One might have expected that other justices prone to protect the honor of the District of Columbia Circuit and the importance of NEPA, such as Justices Brennan and Marshall, might object. But none did. Brennan teased Rehnquist about "border[ing] on the Kafkaesque" in a memorandum on other aspects of the case. But he did not urge its deletion. I do not find evidence that any other justice commented on the last paragraph, and given its tone and breadth, this absence may say as much about *Vermont Yankee* as the unanimity in the result. The Court not only reversed but reversed with a harsh rebuke of the lower court that swept up NEPA.[44]

The message on NEPA was an amplification of Justice Powell's footnote in *Kleppe*. NEPA does not change the basic mandates of mission agencies such as the commission (i.e., to "try" nuclear energy); its requirements are "essentially procedural," not substantive; and federal judges may not surreptitiously inject NEPA's values under the guise of procedural review. As in *Kleppe*, the message came as dictum. The issue of substantive review was not presented by the case; none of the parties briefed the issue.

Vermont Yankee can be read as a gratuitous slap at NEPA, devaluing the statute's substantive goals even while acknowledging them as "significant," all in the absence of an issue of substantive review. There is another reading less inimical to NEPA. Both the text of the opinion and the record of the Court's deliberations might support the view that Justice Rehnquist's pique was aimed at what he saw as the overreaching of the court below rather than at NEPA itself. NEPA was merely the shoehorn by which the District of Columbia Circuit had tried to squeeze itself into the commission's shoes. On this understanding, the Court's emphasis on NEPA's limitations was a collateral effect of its efforts to bring the lower court into line.

This left open the possibility that the Court had backed itself into a corner on substantive review, without necessarily intending the implications for future cases, and might be led to reconsider. But later cases brought no reconsideration. When the Court reached cases that did present issues of the substantive application of NEPA, it treated these dicta as law to apply. And it applied them to virtually foreclose review of federal agencies' integration of NEPA's policy goals. In *Kleppe* and *Vermont Yankee,* the Court had put itself, deliberately as it turned out, on a path to deny NEPA substantive effect. The author of *Vermont Yankee,* Justice Rehnquist, played a crucial role in guiding the Court down that path to "a legal position he seemed to have long maintained."[45] The slap was not gratuitous at all.

Strycker's Bay Neighborhood Council, Inc. v. Karlen: Making It Plain

Strycker's Bay was the first case in which the issue of substantive review was presented to the Court, providing the occasion to turn the dicta of *Kleppe* and *Vermont Yankee* into hard law. The "federal action" under review was approval of a federally funded low-income housing project at "Site 30" on the Upper West Side of Manhattan. The federal funding agency—the Department of Housing and Urban Development (HUD)—decided that the project did not require an EIS, and this decision was not disturbed on review. In an initial round of litigation on the project, however, the Court of Appeals for the Second Circuit did order that HUD "consider reasonable alternatives to the development of Site 30 as a . . . low-income housing project" under what is now NEPA 102(2)(E).[46]

HUD complied by preparing a Special Environmental Clearance Report, which assessed nine alternatives to Site 30. The report found that one of the alternatives, Site 9, "could be superior to Site 30" for low-income housing "from the standpoint of social environmental impact" because it would produce a greater dispersal of low-income people. Against the environmental benefits of Site 9, however, HUD considered the "environmental costs" of the minimum two-year delay associated with a change in sites; these were the costs of failing to reduce the low-income housing deficit for the length of the delay. Balancing the benefits of an alternative site against these delay costs, HUD concluded that "the benefits seem insufficient to justify a . . . substitution." Accordingly, it continued to support Site 30.[47]

The federal district court upheld HUD's decision, but the Second Circuit reversed. Although the legal rationale was not entirely clear, the Second Circuit's inquiry went well beyond agency documentation of impacts and alternatives. NEPA supplied the "substantive standards necessary" for review of the merits of an agency decision under the APA. The concentration effects of building a 100 percent low-income high-rise in an area already "lined with low-income housing" (Site 30) were contrary to the social and economic "integration contemplated by NEPA." HUD had given "consideration" to alternatives, as ordered, but the department also had to make a "reasoned choice" among the alternatives. Delay, HUD's main reason for continuing with Site 30, "is not to be regarded as an overriding factor . . ." and "environmental factors, such as crowding low-income housing into a concentrated area, should be given determinative weight" as Congress intended in authorizing the federal housing program.[48]

The Second Circuit's opinion was ambiguous on its theory of substantive review. HUD's elevation of delay over other environmental concerns may have prevented a "reasonable choice between alternatives," and the decision therefore was "arbitrary and capricious" or an "abuse of discretion." Or HUD's decision may have violated a legal hierarchy of values established by NEPA or by HUD's authorizing legislation and was therefore "not in accordance with law." Although the opinion tilts more to the latter than the former, it contains elements of both. The Supreme Court would limit itself to the second rationale, with the effect of obscuring the possibilities of the first.[49]

The parties did not brief or argue the case on the merits before the Supreme Court, because the Court decided the case only on the basis of the briefs for and against the petitions for a writ of certiorari by the United States and others. In a footnote in its certiorari brief, the government made a significant concession that agency action under NEPA might be overturned as arbitrary and capricious "when an agency gives little or no weight at all to environmental values or when it rejects an environmentally preferable alternative for no apparent reason." But that, it contended, was not what the Second Circuit had done. Instead, it had erroneously assumed that NEPA's values carried determinative weight and reversed HUD's decision as otherwise not in accordance with law. NEPA does not assign "appropriate weights": an agency may choose an environmentally more damaging alternative where "required by other considerations of national policy."[50]

The parties seeking to uphold the Second Circuit were careful in response. No doubt mindful of the Court's dicta in *Kleppe* and *Vermont Yankee,* they did not advance the more assertive theory of substantive review that the court below had used at least in part to justify its ruling—that is, that NEPA's values carried determinative weight. Instead, they built on the government's concession that courts might reverse NEPA decisions that were arbitrary and capricious and argued that that's what the Second Circuit had done. What separated them from the government in the end was not their view of the law but their characterization of the Second Circuit's decision.[51]

A majority of justices voted initially to grant review, with only two opposed. But the justices also authorized Justice Rehnquist to draft an opinion summarily reversing the Second Circuit. Rehnquist's per curiam opinion drew the support of all the other justices except Justice Marshall, who filed a dissent. It read the Second Circuit's opinion as mandating an order of values based on NEPA rather than holding that HUD had acted arbitrarily and capriciously. The rest of the analysis followed from *Kleppe* and *Vermont Yankee*: NEPA's requirements are "essentially procedural," and "the only role for a court is to insure that the agency has considered the environmental consequences." "There is no doubt that HUD considered the environmental consequences of its decision," as the Second Circuit itself concluded. "NEPA requires no more."[52]

Justice Marshall stood alone in dissent; it would be the last dissent on the merits of a NEPA case for almost three decades, during which environmentalists would lose eight of these cases by unanimous votes.[53] Marshall framed the case as falling within "the normal scope of review of agency action to determine it if is arbitrary, capricious, or an abuse of discretion." *Vermont Yankee* acknowledged that agency decisions under NEPA, as in other statutory settings, might be set aside for substantial "*substantive*" as well as procedural shortcomings. And *Kleppe* authorized arbitrary and capricious review to ensure that "the agency 'has taken a "hard look" at environmental consequences.'" The Court's opinion risked limiting "the reviewing court to the essentially mindless task of determining whether an agency 'considered' environmental factors . . . in reaching its conclusion." These limits on NEPA review were unusual in administrative law, stricter than would be expected "in a different factual setting." NEPA and the environmental concerns it addressed, Marshall suggested, were being especially discounted.[54]

In response to Justice Marshall's draft dissent, Justice Rehnquist added a footnote to the per curiam: "If we could agree with the dissent that the Court of Appeals held that HUD had acted 'arbitrarily,' . . . we might also agree that plenary review is warranted." This opened the possibility of arbitrary and capricious review of agencies' substantive decisions under NEPA—as the government had granted in its brief—but the body of the opinion worked against it. The Court cut off exploration by refusing to consider the Second Circuit's decision within the framework of arbitrary and capricious review; it emphasized the "essentially procedural" limitation from *Vermont Yankee,* suggesting that NEPA imposed no significant nonprocedural requirements; and it reinforced this suggestion by stating that the "*only* role for a court is to insure that the agency has considered the environmental consequences."[55] There was nothing requiring that an agency's "consideration" be meaningful or, as Justice Marshall put it, preventing an agency, having "considered" environmental factors, from effectively ignoring them in its decision. The debate begun in *San Antonio* continued. Increasingly in the Court's construct of NEPA, however, "consider" took on a distinctly formal cast.

The lower courts got the point, conveyed as much by the tone as by the content of these decisions. On the basis of their review of NEPA decisions in lower courts after *Strycker's Bay,* Richard Goldsmith and William Banks found that "the courts are enforcing NEPA with diminished rigor. This judicial retreat has primarily taken the form of a contraction in the scope of judicial review. . . . Indeed, under the influence of *Strycker's Bay,* some of the lower courts now seem to be reviewing agency action under NEPA far less closely than they review other types of agency action."[56] In Justice Marshall's reading, this is exactly what the Court's opinion portended.

Robertson v. Methow Valley Citizens Council, Inc.: Exclamation Point

In case any of the lower courts or other members of its audience had missed the point of *Strycker's Bay,* the Court made it emphatic in *Robertson v. Methow Valley Citizens Council, Inc.* The facts were similar to those of *Sierra Club v. Morton*: the Forest Service issued a special use permit for the development of a ski resort on federal land overlooking the Upper Methow Valley in Washington's Cascade Mountains. The main environmental impacts were on air quality and the health of a large mule deer herd that used the valley as a migration corridor and overwintering habitat. Most of the impacts would be indirect, stemming from secondary development generated by the resort on private lands under state and local jurisdiction.[57]

The Forest Service's EIS discussed these impacts, noting the difficulty of predicting the off-site effects and the possible mitigation measures. These were primarily steps that could be taken by state and local governments to reduce the impacts of secondary development. The EIS did not specify measures to be carried out, but the issuance of the special use permit was conditioned on execution of an agreement on mitigation that was to be worked out among the Forest Service, the state, and the county in which the resort would be located. This condition would be enforceable in later stages of federal review and approval.[58]

A federal district court in Oregon upheld the Forest Service on review; the Court of Appeals for the Ninth Circuit reversed. The Ninth Circuit held that the EIS was inadequate in several respects and that the Forest Service had not met its substantive obligation to adopt mitigation measures before approving the permit. Impacts on air quality or the mule deer herd could not be adequately evaluated without knowing what the measures, if any, would be. If the Forest Service could not produce the information to "make a reasoned decision" on the impacts, including the effectiveness of mitigation measures, it was required to conduct a "worst-case analysis," assessing impacts based on the worst consequences that could reasonably be projected. Separately, the appeals court held—or seemed to hold—as a substantive matter that NEPA required specification in the EIS of the mitigation measures that would be undertaken.[59]

In granting certiorari, the Court identified three issues for review: the adequacy of the EIS's discussion of impacts and failure to include a worst-case analysis and the substantive issue of whether NEPA required a "fully developed mitigation plan" for the issuance of the special use permit. Counsel for opponents of the project, David Bricklin, conceded two of these issues. Struggling for footing on the terrain established by *Strycker's Bay* and its precursors, he agreed in oral argument that the Ninth Circuit's suggestion that NEPA imposed substantive duties was "not consistent with this . . . Court's statements or the Act." But this suggestion was only dicta, he argued. The basis of court of appeals' decision was the inadequacy of the impact statement given the conclusory nature of its discussion of mitigation—a procedural, not substantive, ruling. Bricklin also conceded the "worst-case" analysis issue, in light of changes in the CEQ's regulations on the issue.[60]

With three other justices, Justice Stevens voted in conference to affirm. In the end, however, he authored a unanimous opinion for the Court reversing the Ninth Circuit; Justice Brennan wrote a one-sentence concurrence stressing the importance of EIS discussion of mitigation measures. Stevens's opinion for the Court dealt with the one live issue remaining—the adequacy of the EIS's discussion of mitigation measures. Although NEPA required an

EIS to include "a detailed discussion of possible mitigation measures," it did not require, as the Ninth Circuit had concluded, an EIS to have "a fully developed [mitigation] plan." The opinion avoided the question of whether the EIS's mitigation discussion, which the Court described as "merely conceptual," was adequate under an appropriate test. This restraint was essential, in Lazarus's view, to the decision's unanimity, given a diversity of views among the justices on the appropriate measure of adequacy.[61]

But the opinion was not at all restrained on the issue of substantive review. In the Court's description of Section 101 of NEPA as containing "strong precatory" language, "precatory" drained the strength out of "strong." The Court elaborated:

> Although [NEPA's] procedures are almost certain to affect the agency's substantive decision, it is now well settled that NEPA itself does not mandate particular results. . . . In this case, for example, it would not have violated NEPA if the Forest Service, after complying with the Act's procedural prerequisites, had decided that the benefits to be derived from downhill skiing at Sandy Butte justified the issuance of a special use permit, notwithstanding the loss of 15 percent, 50 percent, or even 100 percent of the mule deer herd.[62]

The Court had said this before: the issue was now "well settled." But it was compelled to say it again in terms no one could mistake. As it noted, the Forest Service and the Washington Department of Game had argued over the likely impact of the resort on the deer herd: the Forest Service had estimated a possible 15 percent reduction in the herd; the state had argued that the impact might exceed 50 percent. But nothing in the facts rehearsed by the Court suggested that the herd might be eliminated. The "100 percent" was a rhetorical gesture to drive the Court's point home: under a statute making it national policy "to create and maintain conditions under which man and nature can exist in productive harmony," there was no bar to wiping out the largest deer herd in Washington, because the language of Section 101, though "strong," was "precatory." Review of the Forest Service's weighing of costs and benefits under the APA's arbitrary and capricious standard remained a theoretical possibility but not one that the Court addressed. The Court's rhetoric drove that possibility further into the shadows. Former CEQ General Counsel Nicholas Yost commented that in *Methow,* "essentially procedural" became "exclusively procedural."[63]

This left the question of how, if at all, agencies would be held accountable for integrating the values of Section 101. The Court identified two alternative modes for accountability. First, "the strong precatory language of [Section] 101 of the Act," together with the EIS requirement, would "inevitably bring pressure to bear on agencies 'to respond to the needs of environmental quality.' " The source of this pressure was not clear—was it the agency's leadership or an environmentally sensitized White House? Second, NEPA played a "larger informational role" by assuring the public that the agency considered environmental concerns and by giving a basis for political objection if it did not. This "larger" role extended to citizen groups and to other governmental bodies, such as the state and local agencies with jurisdiction over impacts flowing from the ski resort. In short, accountability for the substantive implementation of NEPA was left to the political process.[64]

Interpreting the Substantive Review Story

Lazarus's account suggests that the Court's march on the substance of NEPA was less inevitable than it might seem on the surface. Concessions by the government and ameliorating adjustments by the justices kept the march going when it might otherwise have foundered. In the end, however, the Court's determination seemed stronger than any contingency. Its decisions left NEPA on an uncertain doctrinal island, where even the normal rules of judicial review seemed not to reach or to reach with less force than elsewhere. This legal isolation was metaphor for putting NEPA's values in their place.

The symbolic import of these cases grows not just from their outcomes but from the tone and texture of the judicial texts agreed to by all or lopsided majorities of the justices. The opinions did include language favorable to environmentalists, voicing the importance of NEPA's values and the expectation that agencies would heed them. But the Court's refusal to give legal substance to these values created a kind of doubletalk. "Significant values" for the nation meant values of no particular weight. "Consideration" of these values included the ability to sacrifice them to competing values. The "strong" language of Section 101 was in the form of an entreaty, not a command, relying for its realization on the same political system that Congress, in passing NEPA, had found gave scant weight to environmental concerns. The erosive tone in these opinions reached its height in *Methow*, with the hypothetical (and legally permissible) elimination of the entire Methow Valley mule deer herd.

A full consideration by the Court of the legal merits of substantive review might have cut against an interpretation of these decisions as implying resistance to NEPA's values, but that consideration did not occur. Arguments against the strong form of substantive review applied by the Sixth and Ninth Circuits certainly exist. A number of commentators, including some sympathetic to NEPA's transformative goal, have made them. Environmental policy scholar R. N. L. Andrews wrote that the six values principles in Section 101(2) are by themselves "merely non-operational advice. They . . . contain no specific objectives, criteria, or benchmarks by which their achievement might be measured." Environmental law scholar and environmentalist Oliver Houck was more to the point: the principles "are inspiring, but they are not law." The substance of an agency action could not fail to be "in accord with law" under NEPA because NEPA supplied no relevant legal content. The United States made precisely this argument against the Second Circuit's application of the strong form of substantive review in *Strycker's Bay*.[65]

But the issue was never joined before the Court. The strongest argument in favor of substantive review lies in Section 102(1)'s command that agencies interpret and apply their authorities consistent with the policies of Section 101. That argument was not raised by the parties in these cases, and the Court did not discuss Section 102(1) in its opinions in *Strycker's Bay* and *Methow*. The environmental parties conceded the position that Section 102(1) supported; the Second and Ninth Circuits' assertions of NEPA's substantive thrust went undefended. Instead, they advanced the less assertive "arbitrary and capricious" theory, which the Court sidelined. The Court's pronouncements on substantive review in these opinions had an ex cathedra quality, with minimal legal analysis, again suggesting an unspoken resistance to NEPA's aspirations.[66]

It is possible that the Court was simply reacting to the generality of the statute's values, or to what it sensed as lack of real commitment to NEPA's values in the broader society. This latter possibility recalls Justice Blackmun's sense of the futility of NEPA's quest for harmonious relations between humans and nature, captured by his reflection in *Kleppe* that the destruction of the natural environment under development pressure "is just as inevitable as it can be." Or as Gerald Rosenberg put it, the Court "failed to force substantive environmental change because the political and economic system was not ready for such change." The inertia of that system and the durability of the beliefs and values that supported it were formidable, particularly within development-oriented agencies. The CEQ, the champion of NEPA's policies within the executive branch, was institutionally weak. Presidents of both parties did not move aggressively to put NEPA's values into action. And Congress did not act to strengthen NEPA against weak executive and judicial enforcement. NEPA was a bold stroke by environmentalist legislators and intellectuals seeking to jumpstart a cultural shift, but it was unable to produce that shift by itself. In this account, the Court was merely being "realistic," in Justice Blackmun's phrase, complicit in the deflation of NEPA but not an instigator.[67]

Enforcing the Procedural Requirements

In contrast to its treatment of substantive review, the Court endorsed judicial enforcement of the procedural requirements of Section 102(2). This included judicial review of an agency's decision not to prepare an EIS (threshold determination) and of the adequacy of information on impacts and alternatives in a completed EIS. *Kleppe* stated that the courts' role in these cases was "to insure that the agency has taken a 'hard look' at environmental consequences." "Hard look" was a gloss on the "arbitrary and capricious" standard of review under the APA that promised to hold agencies to a high level of compliance with NEPA's analytical and disclosure requirements. It offered to extend to NEPA the kind of "searching and careful" review of agency decisions that the Court had prescribed in *Overton Park*. This promise of tough policing of NEPA procedures would be undercut, however, by the Court's deference to agency expertise, concerns about the feasibility of agency compliance, and limits on the reach of NEPA's obligations. Both in tone and content, the Court's opinions persistently undermined *Calvert Cliffs'* enthusiastic projection of a robust role for the courts in NEPA procedural compliance, putting it at an even further remove from the values that the procedures were to serve.[68]

Kleppe: "Hard Look"

The hard look doctrine reflected in *Overton Park* originated in the District of Columbia Circuit. Judge Harold Leventhal, the doctrine's main author, laid it out in *Greater Boston Television Corp. v. Federal Communication Commission,* a nonenvironmental case decided shortly before *Overton Park.* The doctrine required not only that agencies take a "hard look at the problem areas" but also that they "set forth with clarity grounds of reasoned decision which we think permissible." Reviewing courts were to give deference to the scientific, technical, and programmatic expertise of agencies, but their duty remained to ensure "reasoned consideration to all the material facts and issues."[69]

In a 1974 law review article, Judge Leventhal argued that hard look review should be even more demanding in NEPA procedural cases than in cases in which agencies have acted within the scope of their recognized expertise. "When an essentially nonenvironmental agency has made a determination downplaying the environmental consequences of its action, the court may cock a skeptical eye and insist on the kind of justification that *Overton Park* seems to contemplate." But the Supreme Court did not heed Leventhal's call for searching review in procedural cases under NEPA.

Instead, it granted generous deference to the environmental determinations of mission agencies, both on threshold applicability and adequacy issues.[70]

An early example was *Kleppe,* the case that announced hard look review for NEPA cases. The Court acknowledged that a regional Northern Great Plains EIS would be necessary if individual leasing actions threatened cumulative or synergistic impacts that could be adequately dealt with only in an impact statement of that scope. But it ruled against the Sierra Club because the Department of the Interior "appear[ed] to have determined that the appropriate scope of comprehensive statements should be based on basins, drainage areas, and other factors." The Court's uncritical reliance on the presumed environmental expertise of the action agency to uphold a decision the agency "appear[ed]" to have made gave its hard look review a distinctly soft touch. Although it applied more searching scrutiny of NEPA procedural determinations in later cases, the Court continued to stress the deference due to agency expertise. It has never upheld a lower court's finding that an agency was arbitrary and capricious in carrying out its procedural obligations under NEPA.[71]

Kleppe further enlarged the discretion of action agencies by making administrative feasibility relevant to NEPA procedural compliance. Even if it could be shown that impacts were regional in scope, the Court observed, "practical considerations of feasibility might well necessitate restricting the scope of comprehensive statements." This additional insulation for agencies against judicial oversight of their NEPA compliance came in the face of statutory language that required compliance "to the fullest extent possible." In *Calvert Cliffs,* the District of Columbia Circuit "stress[ed] as forcefully as possible that this language does not provide an escape hatch for footdragging agencies; it does not make NEPA's procedural requirements somehow 'discretionary.' " In *Flint Ridge Development Co. v. Scenic Rivers Ass'n,* another NEPA case decided only days before *Kleppe,* Justice Marshall's opinion for the Court declined to rely on an argument made by the solicitor general that administrative burdens limited NEPA obligations. *Kleppe* credited the argument, however, and gave agencies the opening that *Calvert Cliffs* had so "forcefully" tried to close.[72]

Vermont Yankee: Tightening the Reins on *Calvert Cliffs*

Reflecting a focused effort by Justice Rehnquist, in his opinions and behind the scenes, to limit the influence of *Calvert Cliffs,* the Court in *Vermont Yankee* again pushed back on the strict application of NEPA's procedural obligations.[73] The District of Columbia Circuit found the commission's failure to address energy conservation alternatives in the EIS arbitrary and capricious. Although reductions in energy demand through conservation might reduce the need for new nuclear plants, the commission had applied a "threshold test" in deciding that Saginaw's showing on the issue was not enough to require reasonable minds to inquire further.[74] Tracking *Calvert Cliffs* closely, the lower court held that the threshold test, as applied, flouted the agency's duty to independently investigate environmental issues.

In reversing, the Court qualified the requirement that an EIS consider alternatives. "The concept of alternatives must be bounded by some notion of feasibility" and was also "an evolving one," contingent on knowledge at the time of the EIS. "Energy conservation" was not well defined and represented "unchartered territory" for the agency, gaining serious public attention only after the EIS was completed. The environmental intervenor, Saginaw, raised this alternative in comments on the draft EIS but declined to clarify or offer evidence to support it. Under these circumstances, the NRC's threshold test was reasonably applied to rule out further inquiry.[75]

Justice Rehnquist's opinion for the Court implicitly cut back on *Calvert Cliffs'* expansive interpretation of the duty of environmental inquiry under NEPA. *Calvert Cliffs* stood for the obligation of agencies to take a hard look at environmental issues, even if not raised by environmental intervenors. *Vermont Yankee* qualified that obligation, at least to the extent of requiring environmentalists to participate "meaningfully" in the process. The Court saved some of its strongest language for the environmentalists, whom it warned against "engag[ing] in unjustified obstructionism by making cryptic and obscure reference to matters that 'ought to be' considered and then, after failing to do more to bring the matter to the agency's attention, seeking to have that agency determination vacated on the ground that the agency failed to consider matters 'forcefully presented.'" *Vermont Yankee* recast the "bad guys" in the NEPA narrative from the recalcitrant bureaucrats in *Calvert Cliffs* to the obstructionist environmentalists.[76]

Department of Transportation v. Public Citizen: Limiting the Reach of NEPA's Disclosure Requirements

Finally, in *Department of Transportation v. Public Citizen* (*DOT*), the Court put limits on the principle in *Calvert Cliffs* that NEPA "makes environmental protection a part of the mandate of every federal agency" and compels every agency to take "environmental values into account." The question in the case was whether NEPA supplements statutory authorizations limiting agency consideration to factors that do not include environmental concerns. As Richard Lazarus points out, thirty years before *DOT,* the Court faced the same question in *Flint Ridge Development Co. v. Scenic Rivers Ass'n.* Although his fellow justices were prepared to answer "no" to this question, Justice Marshall wrote an opinion for the Court that decided the case on narrower grounds less detrimental to NEPA's standing. This move turned what would have been a broad defeat for environmentalists into a decision with "virtually no precedential effect." But it turned out to be only a holding action. In *DOT,* nearly thirteen years after the departure of Marshall from the Court, the Court got what it had been expecting in *Flint Ridge*—and a diminished NEPA in the bargain.[77]

In *DOT,* the Federal Motor Carrier Safety Administration (FMCSA) declined to prepare an EIS on safety regulations governing Mexican trucks operating in the United States. FMCSA is an agency of the Department of Transportation that registers motor carriers in the United States and sets requirements for their safety and financial responsibility. For almost twenty years, Congress and the president had maintained a general moratorium on Mexican trucks operating in the United States, although limited operations were allowed in border areas. In 2001, after the president said he would lift the moratorium, Congress prohibited the processing of applications for Mexican trucks to travel in the United States until FMCSA adopted special registration and safety-monitoring regulations for Mexican carriers. FMCSA issued the rules, and the president lifted the moratorium.[78]

Before issuing the rules, FMCSA prepared an environmental assessment that did not consider the air quality impacts of allowing more Mexican trucks on the nation's highways, reasoning that those impacts would be the result of the president's lifting the moratorium, not of its regulations. Because the other effects of its rules did not "significantly" affect the quality of the human environment, it decided that an EIS was unnecessary. The Ninth Circuit held that this decision was arbitrary and capricious. Even though the lifting of the moratorium was the president's decision, the court argued, Mexican trucks would not be admitted into the United States without FMSCA's special rules. Given the president's stated intention to lift the moratorium, the increase in emissions from the influx of Mexican trucks was a "reasonably foreseeable" effect of the rules that required consideration under NEPA.[79]

The Court reversed. A unanimous opinion by Justice Thomas stressed the limits of FMCSA's regulatory reach. The agency had no authority to regulate air emissions from trucks or to prevent Mexican trucks from entering the United States because they would add to domestic emissions. It had no choice but to register ("shall register") a motor carrier that complied with its safety and financial responsibility requirements. The Court agreed that FMCSA's rules were a but-for cause of increased pollution from Mexican trucks: under Congress's edict, the trucks could not come in without them. But this was not enough to make FMCSA responsible for the air quality effects of these trucks under NEPA.[80]

To defend this result, the Court consulted the dual purposes of NEPA's procedural requirements as outlined in *Methow*: to inform the agency's deliberations and to inform the public (the "larger informational role"). These purposes were essential to the political accountability that *Methow* offered in lieu of substantive judicial involvement to advance NEPA's values. The Court, however, concluded that an EIS in this case would serve neither because "FMCSA simply lacks the power to act on whatever information might be contained in the EIS." In the absence of that power, an EIS could not make a difference in FMCSA's action, and, for that reason, could not give useful leverage to "the larger audience" outside the agency. The Court generalized this result: "Where an agency has no ability to prevent a certain effect due to its limited statutory authority over the relevant actions, the agency cannot be considered a legally relevant 'cause' of the effect," and "the agency need not consider these effects" in complying with NEPA.[81]

The Court's opinion gave short shrift to arguments by the EIS proponents that would have enlarged the scope of the agency's considerations and the relevant audience of an EIS. In dismissing the possibility that FMCSA had any meaningful discretion to act on environmental concerns (e.g., by setting safety requirements to get older, high-polluting trucks off the road), the Court did not squarely confront the respondents' argument that NEPA added environmental concerns to the other considerations that FMCSA was bound to consider.[82] Its opinion made this key legal point almost invisible.

Also, in rejecting the relevance of the EIS's "larger informational role," the Court dismissed in a footnote the possibility that the purpose of the EIS requirement extended beyond action by the agency itself, as environmental respondents had argued. In *Methow*, the purpose of this "larger informational role" reached to "other governmental bodies," including state and local agencies not subject to NEPA, that could address the environmental consequences lying outside the action agency's authority to control (e.g., impacts of secondary development on private lands). In limiting this "larger" role to public participation in the FMCSA rulemaking itself, the Court in *DOT* did not address the potential importance of a full analysis of air quality effects for other political actors able to respond to the environmental consequences of Mexican truck traffic, such as state and local air quality management officials, state legislative bodies, or Congress itself. It did not acknowledge *Methow*'s more generous construction of the "larger information role" or explain why it should not apply in this case; it simply stated in a footnote that "NEPA's core focus" was "on improving agency decisionmaking."[83]

DOT confined the agency's responsibility to consider environmental factors to the four corners of its "statutory [i.e., non-NEPA] mandates." Having made the political system the engine of NEPA's substantive implementation in *Methow*, the Court now limited the flow of information to fuel that engine based on a conventionally narrow construction of agency statutory authority. The effect was to confine NEPA to a narrower bureaucratic niche than *Calvert Cliffs'* "mandate" language had promised and to further marginalize the values the act was meant to promote.[84]

Interpreting the Procedural Review Story

In *Calvert Cliffs,* Judge Wright put federal courts at the center of a dawning environmental consciousness and assigned them the job of forcing change on recalcitrant agencies through strict enforcement of NEPA's procedural requirements. The Court's decisions rejected that assignment. Compared with *Calvert Cliffs'* expansive reading of NEPA and assertive role for the courts, the Court's treatment was limiting and deferential. Language in its opinions extolled the importance of NEPA's procedural requirements, but the decisions invariably sanctioned a lower level of compliance than the courts below had required.[85] Rather than impose a stricter version of the hard look doctrine in NEPA cases, as Judge Leventhal urged, the Court gave generous deference to the scientific and programmatic expertise of agencies whose decisionmaking NEPA sought to reform. It deflated the bold pronouncements of *Calvert Cliffs*: allowing agencies to consider administrative feasibility as well as legal permissibility in interpreting their obligations, putting the burden of due diligence on environmentalists as well as agencies, and limiting the reach of NEPA's mandate in the face of narrow statutory authorizations. In the Court's narrative, federal officials were not law-shirkers skulking in the vast hallways of the federal bureaucracy but public servants whose decisions deserved respect. And environmentalists could sometimes be obstructionists.

Some retrenchment from *Calvert Cliffs* may have been inevitable as NEPA matured within the complex realities of existing agency missions and practices. But the Court's systematic assault on Judge Wright's opinion, led by Justice Rehnquist but supported by or at least acquiesced to by his colleagues, went beyond retrenchment to disavowal. This decanonization of *Calvert Cliffs* conveyed not only a reduced role for the courts but also a diminution in NEPA's status. It supported the view—increasingly prevalent in the years after NEPA's passage—that the statute was a "paper tiger" largely within the manipulation and control of the mission agencies rather than an empowering environmentalist Magna Carta. Because NEPA was identified so closely with the new environmentalism, it was a symbolic blow to the movement as well.

Injunctive Relief: Balancing the Equities

When a court finds a NEPA violation, it must decide an appropriate remedy. In NEPA cases, the remedy is typically a permanent injunction prohibiting an agency from acting until it has corrected the violation. A court may also issue a preliminary injunction pending the final outcome of litigation over a claimed violation where it concludes that the plaintiffs are likely to prevail. Whether the injunction is preliminary or permanent, the plaintiffs must show that they have suffered or are likely to suffer irreparable injury, the balance of harms is in their favor, and the injunction would serve the public interest.[86] Unlike the initial decision on NEPA compliance, made by the agency subject to judicial review, the appropriateness of injunctive relief is decided by the court, on the basis of its own determination of what lies in the public interest. In remedy selection in NEPA cases, therefore, the values of the judges are likely to be even closer to the surface than in the review of agency decisions.

The Court's 1978 decision in *TVA v. Hill* raised a question about the scope of the Court's equitable discretion under the new generation of environmental laws. One could read *TVA v. Hill*—holding that the Endangered Species Act left the Court no choice but to enjoin the Tellico Dam—to suggest that injunctive relief was mandatory upon a finding of a violation under other environmental statutes as well. Four years later, in *Weinberger v. Romero-Barcelo,* however, the Court made clear that this was not what it meant. There the Court upheld a district court's refusal to enjoin the U.S. Navy's firing of ordnance into the waters of Puerto Rico in violation of the CWA based on a finding of no significant environmental harm from the violation. With this ruling, the Court reasserted its capacity—and will—to avoid outcomes giving undue (in its judgment) priority to environmental concerns, recapturing territory that it seemed to have ceded to Congress in *TVA v. Hill*. The Court extended this assertiveness to two NEPA cases in which it limited or denied injunctive relief granted by the lower courts.[87]

Winter v. United States: Of Whales and Submarines

Decided in 2008, *Winter v. United States* elevated military readiness over the protection of marine mammals in the face of the Navy's likely violation of NEPA. A federal district court issued a preliminary injunction restricting antisubmarine sonar training operations by the U.S. Navy to avoid harm to marine mammals. The district court found that the Navy had likely violated NEPA by failing to prepare a full EIS on the training exercises, the exercises carried a "near certainty" of irreparable harm to marine mammals affected by the sonar, and the balance of harms and the public interest favored the restrictions. The Navy contended that its exercises in Southern California waters would have no significant environmental effect, but the district found evidence to the contrary, including mass strandings of whale species following similar sonar training operations in other parts of the Pacific. The Court of Appeals for the Ninth Circuit upheld the district court's injunction.[88]

The Navy sought review by the Court of two of the six restrictions imposed by the lower courts. In an opinion by Chief Justice Roberts, joined by Justices Scalia, Kennedy, Thomas, and Alito, the Supreme Court reversed the circuit court and vacated the parts of the district court's injunction that the Navy challenged. Justice Breyer, joined by Justice Stevens, wrote an opinion concurring in part and dissenting in part. Justice Ginsburg dissented, joined by Justice Souter.

The Court ruled that the balance struck by the lower courts was an abuse of discretion, because the interests in national security outweighed any injury to marine mammals, even if irreparable. Roberts's opinion for the Court magnified the importance of national defense interests and minimized the competing ecological interests. It began with a quote from George Washington's first annual address to Congress stressing the importance of military readiness as "one of the most effectual means of preserving peace" and ended with a quote from Teddy Roosevelt urging the necessity of "practice at sea" to make "a navy . . . efficient." Between these unimpeachable sources for the preeminence of war preparations, the Court elaborated the need for field training in sonar detection as essential to defense against submarine attacks, citing the testimony of "some of the Navy's most senior officers." The lower courts had not properly deferred to the expertise of these officers in limiting the Navy's exercises.[89]

Correspondingly, the Court minimized the environmental threats of the sonar training. It acknowledged the potential injuries to marine mammals, but it emphasized the voluntary measures the Navy had taken to minimize those injuries and the absence of clear evidence of harm. The Court stressed—in five separate mentions—that the antisubmarine training off Southern California had gone on for forty years without documented proof of injury to a marine mammal, a "fact" that the government had harped on in its briefs and at oral argument.[90]

In the crucial portion of its opinion on balancing the equities, the Court's account of the potential environmental harm was removed and abstract, compared with its vivid and detailed treatment of the security risk. The focus was on harm to humans' "ecological, scientific, and recreational interests in marine mammals," not the life interests of the mammals themselves. The Court summed the environmental risk in the following sentence: "For the plaintiffs, the most serious possible injury would be harm to an unknown number of the marine mammals that they study and observe." This anthropocentric framing shifted the measure of harm from the maiming and death of beaked whales and other species projected by the environmentalists to a much less disconcerting disturbance of human study and observation. Rhetorically as well as substantively, by the end of the Court's opinion, there was simply no contest.[91]

There was urgency in the Court's opinion, but it was attached to national defense, not the protection of whales. The court of appeals had invited the Navy "to request relief [from the district court] on an emergency basis" if it turned out that the preliminary injunction actually impaired defense readiness. But by the time the Navy would be able to meet the Ninth Circuit's condition, the Court observed, it would already have suffered increased vulnerability to enemy submarines. "By then it may be too late." Compared with the grim emotion of this statement, the Court's account of the environmental harms was bloodless. While it claimed not to "discount the importance of plaintiffs' . . . interests in marine mammals," it distanced itself emotionally from those interests—and the nonhuman species that lay behind them. The Court's heart as well as its mind was fully with the defense of the nation.[92]

Justice Ginsburg would have affirmed the Ninth Circuit. The Navy's training exercises "serve[d] critical interests," but the mitigation measures imposed by the lower courts were not an abuse of discretion. She based this conclusion on "the likely, substantial harm to the environment," the Navy's persistent refusal to accept what was almost certainly its legal obligation to prepare an EIS, and "the public interest." She mined the Navy's own environmental assessment to enlarge the scope and seriousness of the "likely harm" beyond the depiction in the Court's opinion. Her rendering of that harm was vivid and direct. She detailed the effects of sonar with anatomical precision to include "mass strandings of marine mammals, hemorrhaging around the brain and ears, acute spongiotic changes in the central nervous system, and lesions in vital organs." And these injuries were to the animals themselves—"the environment"—not merely to the interests of their human observers. These rhetorical choices signaled identification with the marine life at risk that was missing entirely from the Court's opinion and supported her conclusion that the public interest was on the environment's side.[93]

War—which includes manipulation of the environment to harm one's enemies—is inevitably in conflict with environmentalist values. As Justice Breyer commented at oral argument, "the whole point of the armed forces is to hurt the environment." How could environmental protection, he implied, have any role in the conduct of military action? He asked counsel for NRDC, Richard Kendall, "You go on a bombing mission, do they have to prepare an environmental impact statement first?" Kendall answered that NEPA requirements do not apply to combat. No one argued that the training activities in *Winter* were exempt from NEPA, but the activities were directly linked to readiness for combat in time of war. In this clash between the mastery values expressed in self-defense and the harmony values of environmentalists, the issue was, in the majority's view, not even close.[94]

Monsanto v. Geertson Seed Farms: Industrial Agriculture in the Balance

Six years later, the Court again stressed the limits of the lower courts' equitable discretion in providing remedies for NEPA violations. In *Monsanto*, a district court had enjoined virtually all use of genetically modified alfalfa, pending completion of an EIS by the Animal and Plant Health Inspection Service, and the Ninth Circuit affirmed. The Court overturned a portion of the district court's order that kept the Animal and Plant Health Inspection Service from amending its decision to allow partial use of the modified crop while the EIS was being prepared. The Court held that this condition was excessive because it was possible that a decision allowing partial use of the genetically modified crop would not involve significant environmental risk and therefore require no EIS. The district court, in the view of all the justices but one, had been unduly risk-averse in the constraints it had imposed.

In a lone dissent, Justice Stevens protested that the Court had unduly subordinated the risks of genetically modified crops to the interests of the manufacturers and farmers using those crops. The district court had evidence that genetic contamination was likely and would be difficult to control. "In enjoining partial deregulation until it had the benefit of an EIS to help parse the evidence, the court acted with exactly the sort of caution that Congress endorsed in NEPA." The Court's ruling subverted NEPA's precautionary principle.[95]

Winter and *Monsanto* completed the deflation of NEPA begun in the substantive review cases. In the latter cases, the Court sought to prevent lower courts from importing NEPA's values into their review of agency action—by either insinuating those values into their procedural review (*Kleppe, Vermont Yankee*) or overtly tipping the scales in favor of those values through substantive application of NEPA (*Strycker's Bay, Methow*). In the injunction cases (*Winter* and *Monsanto*), the Court's concern was similar, although in a different legal context: the lower courts had given NEPA's values more sway than they should have. The Court discounted these values relative to competing concerns (defense readiness, economic reliance on bioengineered crops) in overturning the equitable balance struck by the courts below. Having accorded generous discretion to agencies in narrowing their NEPA obligations, the Court limited the discretion of the lower courts to enforce those obligations.

THE VISION OF NEPA as culture-changing has not been realized. The act has increased information on environmental effects and alternatives and has forced mission agencies to bring on new staff with environmental expertise. It has compelled changes in some projects to minimize public criticism and avoid more demanding procedural requirements. And it has resulted in the cancellation of a few of the worst, or politically most vulnerable, projects. But few would argue that it has changed the internal compass of the mission agencies, which remain tightly linked to the economic and political interests that are their natural constituencies.[96] The failure to internalize the values of NEPA may be primarily the fault of the president, for not insisting that agencies give NEPA substantive force, or of Congress, for failing to legislate further when that failure became apparent. But the Court was a contributor in this—practically in holdings that validated government decisions limiting the scope and effect of NEPA, and symbolically in the tone and tenor of opinions that pushed NEPA toward the periphery of the concerns of mission agencies.

Although some of the opinions proclaimed the statute's importance, the burden of the Court's NEPA narrative was to the contrary. The course of these cases seems, at least in retrospect, to have been deliberate. The Court reached out to foreclose substantive review under NEPA before that issue was presented and through its dicta in *Kleppe* and *Vermont Yankee* discouraged a full airing of the issue in later cases. It pushed back persistently on *Calvert Cliffs* over decades, undercutting that decision's bold gesture of judicial oversight, protecting agency discretion, and limiting the reach of NEPA's requirements. It used the injunctive relief cases to make normative points about the relative importance of the environmental values embodied in NEPA.

The Court's rhetoric matched the trend of its holdings: the characterization of the District of Columbia Circuit's procedural enhancements for environmental inquiry as verging on the "Kafkaesque," the blessing of an imagined elimination of the entire Methow Valley mule deer herd to nail shut the prospect of substantive review, and the rating of the competition between defense training and the welfare of marine mammals in *Winter* as not a close question. The connotations of the marginalization of NEPA accumulated through these cases and gave credence to Joseph Sax's early characterization of the statute as a "legal sentimentality" not designed to be taken seriously. Although Sax later recanted that view, the Court has not.[97]

These cases raise the question of whether there have been any true environmentalists on the Court since Justice Douglas left in 1975. Douglas's dissent in *San Antonio*, the Court's first NEPA case, adopted an apocalyptic tone in depicting the environmental ills NEPA was enacted to avoid—the despoliation of parkland "sanctuaries," their conversion to "a biological desert," the use of federal funds in a "predatory manner" to bring about these "awful" consequences. Joined by Justices Black and Brennan, his opinion represented a significant minority of justices aligned behind robust interpretation of NEPA. But that dissenting trio disbanded with the departures of Black and Douglas in 1971 and 1975.[98]

Justice Marshall wrote more dissents in NEPA cases than any other justice, and he also authored the opinion for the Court in *Flint Ridge* that protected environmentalist interests while handing a narrow victory to the government. He may have been drawn to environmentalist viewpoints through his experience in the civil rights movement, as was Judge Wright.[99] His role in the cases is largely in the nature of damage control, however, perhaps inevitably given the posture of the issues and the disposition of his colleagues. His partial dissent in *Kleppe*, joined by Justice Brennan, was reserved compared with Justice Douglas's passionate embrace of NEPA in *San Antonio*. In *Strycker's Bay*, Marshall stood alone in dissent but limited his argument to a modest version of substantive review that even the majority seemed willing, at least obliquely, to acknowledge.

Almost thirty years after *Strycker's Bay*, Justice Ginsburg wrote her dissent in *Winter*. Although it also lacked the surface passion of Justice Douglas's *San Antonio* dissent, its weighing of the potential harms to marine mammals was a classic application of environmentalist values advanced by NEPA. In her matter-of-fact style, Justice Ginsburg conveyed an empathy for nature that eluded both the majority opinion and Justice Breyer's partial concurrence and dissent. But *Winter* remains Justice Ginsburg's only dissent in a NEPA case, although she has often reflected environmentalist perspectives in other legal settings. Justice Stevens, frequently a voice for environmentalists in other settings, likewise dissented in only one NEPA case, while authoring the opinion for the Court in *Methow* that sealed shut the possibility of substantive review. Other justices, such as Blackmun and Breyer, who often joined proenvironment justices on a divided Court, never dissented in a NEPA case.

The thin support for NEPA among justices otherwise favorably disposed to environmentalist positions has several possible explanations. Among them are the solicitor general's pivotal role in selecting NEPA cases and positioning the issues for the Court and the effectiveness of advocates on the Court, particularly Justice Rehnquist, all as Richard Lazarus has described. Another explanation (not exclusive of the others) lies in NEPA itself. The act may be at once too ambitious and too weak to attract strong defenders among justices otherwise well-disposed to environmentalist concerns: too ambitious because it harbors a transformative goal aimed not just at federal officials but ultimately at the nation, and too weak because it lacks the machinery to credibly execute that transformation. Egalitarian-communitarians such as Justices Blackmun, Breyer, and Stevens have supported legal-policy resolutions that give an edge to environmentalist values in determining the public interest in particular settings. An unchanneled commitment to "productive harmony" across all types of human endeavor, however, may have represented a stretch for these justices, particularly in the absence of a well-elaborated mechanism for determining how that harmony is to be interpreted and applied. Only Justice Ginsburg, among sitting justices, has been willing to consider the implications of such a commitment in the face of the most serious of competing concerns.

CHAPTER TEN

Environmentalist Futures

D URING THE ORAL argument in *Department of Transportation v. Public Citizen* in 2004, Justice Breyer, brushing back a correction by the counsel for the environmental respondents, quipped, "You're against bad environment. All right. We're all against that."[1] But, if "we're all against [bad environment]," why has the Supreme Court rejected environmentalist positions in many of its decisions, limiting protections and distancing itself from the values and beliefs that have animated the movement? In the first half of this chapter, I attempt to answer that question by distilling the Court's response to environmentalism from the earlier case analyses and exploring what that response may say about the Court or environmentalism or both. In the second half, I use the findings to frame possible futures for environmentalism in the United States.

The environmental movement has been remarkably successful and durable, but it is stymied now by a deepening U.S. cultural divide, even as it faces problems of unprecedented difficulty, including climate change. Others have offered broad prescriptions for addressing the movement's predicament. My account is largely descriptive, focusing on emerging expressions of the movement that challenge conventional cultural oppositions and draw energy and innovative power from a diversity of methods, means, and values. Under the pressure of still-unresolved environmental problems and the early promise of new approaches, the movement is working out a new future for itself, although that future is still much contested. The Court is positioned as an arbiter of that future, both legally and culturally.

What the Court's Decisions Show

The last four decades of Court decisions do not offer environmentalists a reassuring story. In a study of environmental cases decided by the Court from 1960 to 1988, Richard Levy and Robert Glicksman concluded that the decisions after 1976 "reflect a trend seemingly at odds with congressional policy, reaching prodevelopment results far more often than proenvironmental results." Richard Lazarus reached a similar conclusion based on his review of one hundred environmental cases decided by the Court through 1998. He found that "the Court as a whole [was] steadily becoming less responsive to environmental protection." This trend may have leveled out. But in the Court's environmental decisions since Lazarus's study, proenvironment outcomes have continued to be in the minority.[2]

From my cultural analysis of the cases, the story may be even more discouraging for environmentalists. In a number of them, the Court rejected or questioned the urgent priority for environmental concerns that was the movement's motivating force. Although it reached a proenvironment result in *TVA v. Hill*, the Court insinuated its view that saving an obscure species of "little fish" at the expense of a virtually completed dam was not sensible; in *NAHB*, it limited the sweep of the Endangered Species Act's (ESA) precautionary Section 7, undercutting its super statute status. *Entergy* also had a subtext of irrational excess—the absurdity of spending a billion dollars to save a fish. In *Winter*, the Court found no contest between projected harm to marine mammals and the requisites of national defense readiness. *Lyng* resonated at the level of rights rather than welfare, but it concluded similarly by subordinating values associated with Native American spiritual traditions to mastery and hierarchy values associated with the sovereign's property rights. In *New York v. United States*, the Court subordinated the environmental "crisis of the moment" to the autonomy values it saw enshrined in the federalist structure.

In diverse legal settings, the Court also restricted operation of the ecological model, the core of the environmentalist cosmology. In *SWANCC* and *Rapanos*, it truncated aquatic ecosystems under the Clean Water Act (CWA) to facilitate public and private development. *Lucas* and *Koontz* discounted claims of ecological harm in privileging the rights of private owner-developers. *Lujan II* denounced theories of ecosystemic injury as a basis for judicial access. In these cases, the Court emphasized boundaries among tracts, jurisdictions, and institutions to accommodate mastery, hierarchy, and autonomy values that seemed to fit more comfortably in an atomistic model. Ecological interdependence was disputed in fact or made legally irrelevant.

A number of these decisions (*New York v. United States, Lucas, Koontz, Lujan II*) advanced major doctrinal shifts in standing, federalism, and property rights. These changes were inimical generally to those seeking governmental protection of the public interest, not just to environmentalists. Environmental disputes were frequently the vehicle for these changes, however, as justices showed particular concern about the implications of environmentalism for preferred institutional arrangements. Before ascending to the Court, then-judge Scalia complained about the "judiciary's long love affair with environmental litigation," and once on the Court, he pressed his colleagues to end the affair. The environmental laws of the 1970s helped institutionalize the environmental movement. The Court's later revisions to standing, federalism, and takings doctrine helped institutionalize the countermovement, although in each of these areas it might have gone further than it did.

The Court marginalized the nation's environmental stewardship act, the National Environmental Policy Act (NEPA). Rather than applying NEPA to constrain agency actions with significant adverse impacts on the environment, the Court minimized the act's effect. It foreclosed substantive review of agency actions, emphasized agency discretion in implementing the law's procedural requirements, and limited the reach of those requirements. In decisions on injunctive relief for NEPA violations, it subordinated the values NEPA advanced. Although, as Richard Lazarus has shown, there is more for environmentalists in these cases than meets the eye, it is difficult to read them as other than a repudiation of the act's transformative aspirations.

The story has another side: this book's selected cases also yielded important legal and symbolic victories for environmentalists. Several cases vindicated environmentalist priorities against competing concerns. In the first years of the movement, *Citizens to Preserve Overton Park, Inc. v. Volpe* reinterpreted standards of judicial review to give meaningful protection against threats to the vanishing "green havens." A unanimous decision in *ATA* upheld the primacy of human health concerns over economic interests, despite Justice Breyer's reservations about a return to the Stone Age. And in a landmark victory for environmentalists, *MA v. EPA* (the merits) underwrote the urgency and priority of action on climate change; the Court reaffirmed *MA v. EPA*'s core ruling in *AEP* and *UARG*, although these cases tempered the earlier decision's bold tone as well as its substance.

The ecological model and related values also fared well in a number of these cases. *Sweet Home* ratified the extension of the ecological model in the Department of the Interior's ESA regulation against harmful modifications of species habitats—this, in the face of Justice Scalia's impassioned defense of property rights and economic activity, figured in the "simplest farmer." *Friends of the Earth, Inc. v. Laidlaw Environmental Services (TOC), Inc.* countered the extravagant rejection of the environmentalist worldview in *Lujan II*. Legitimizing the connection between watersheds and their human communities, it granted local citizens standing to police local clean water violations. The standing decision in *MA v. EPA* endorsed a model of global interdependence in crediting harm to the state from climate change. Even *Rapanos* sanctioned a version of the ecological model in Justice Kennedy's "significant nexus" test for CWA jurisdiction.

These decisions were important affirmations of an environmentalist worldview. More generally, the Court has preserved a working core of environmental regulatory authority against concerted attacks by industry, developers, and other resource users. And it has limited the reach of doctrinal innovations on citizens' standing, property rights, and the scope of federal authority in ways that offer a measure of accommodation to environmentalists.

In the final analysis, however, the resistance to environmentalist beliefs and values in the selected cases overshadows the gains for environmentalists. Much in these cases presents as a cultural rearguard action, the importation of pre-ecological values and practices into judicial doctrine and the statutes of a new ecological era. This rearguard action has stirred the emotions and deep allegiances of the justices, pro and con, and has succeeded enough of the time to check the transformative promise of the environmental law revolution. At the symbolic level, just as in outcomes, environmentalists have lost more before the Court than they have won.

What the Decisions May Tell Us about the Court, Environmentalism, or Both

There are at least two reasons for believing that the Court may be distinct enough from the ambient culture that its resistance to environmentalism has little to say about the movement's progress or future success. First, for reasons of its institutional makeup and function, the Court may be more inclined than other (and more broadly influential) institutions, such as Congress and the president, to resist the inroads of environmentalism. Second, the ideological makeup of the Court over the last several decades may have pushed its decisions in environmental cases in directions that do not meaningfully reflect the movement's progress in the larger society.

Of the major institutions of national government, the Court might seem most likely to reflect the dominant social paradigm (DSP) and least likely to be receptive to a social movement such as environmentalism. The justices who serve on the Court enjoy lifetime tenure, are not directly accountable to the electorate, and are to that extent insulated from shifts in public sentiments. Moreover, although it also interprets legislation, the Court's most visible role is as interpreter of the Constitution, which lacks an environmental clause and embodies values opposed to those that have animated the environmental movement. Finally, the Court's traditional adherence to precedent and an incrementalist case-by-case approach may make it less receptive to large-scale change than the political branches. These features suggest both a commitment to the pre-ecological dominant worldview and an institutional conservatism that would make the Court, on the face of it, an unlikely champion for the environmental movement and more likely than its sister institutions to resist a fundamental reordering of the kind environmentalists have sought.

But this account may prove too much. Whether one subscribes to the embeddedness model or agency model of its interactions with the larger culture, the Court has shown its capacity to respond affirmatively to social movements in decisions such as *Brown v. Board of Education* (civil rights) and *Lawrence v. Texas* (gay rights). Even while resisting environmentalist claims in many of its recent cases, the Court's decision in *MA v. EPA* represented a comparable breakthrough for the greens, albeit at the level of statutory rather than constitutional interpretation. This and other environmentalist successes remind us that the Court's response to environmentalism has hardly been monolithic, as would be more likely if that response were institutionally compelled. Although the Court's unique institutional perspective is important to understanding the outcomes and meanings of these cases, there is more to the story.

The Court's resistance might also stem from an ideological imbalance among current and recent justices that works against environmentalists. Even if the Court has the institutional capacity to be receptive to environmentalist views, its particular lineup of justices may cut off that capacity, at least in those cases where antienvironmentalists on the Court are able to assemble a majority. A brief review of the Court's ideological alignment over the period of the environmental movement offers a mixed verdict on this question; claims and counterclaims regarding political imbalance have been the rule and continue to swirl around the present Court.

The conservative movement that began in the 1950s was gathering strength as the environmental movement matured and found broad expression in federal law. In the modern environmental era, there have been three chief justices of the Court—Burger (1969–1986), Rehnquist (1986–2005), and Roberts (2005–present)—all appointed by Republican presidents. Although the views of conservative justices on the Burger Court often did not prevail, they did set the stage for future rebukes to liberals in areas such as federalism and property rights. When conservatives consolidated their majority in 1991 under Chief Justice Rehnquist, there was a decided rightward shift in the Court's rulings in some areas (e.g., federalism, standing, property rights) but not in others (e.g., affirmative action, civil rights). Although accused by its critics in the 1990s of judicial activism to advance conservative values, the Rehnquist Court trended left in its last years.[3]

Critics accuse the Roberts Court of turning again to the right, and early studies do suggest a rightward shift, for example, in cases involving economic activity. Even if that rightward pull continues, however, the Roberts Court may still be within the mainstream of public values. In a 2013 Gallup poll, 30 percent of respondents thought the Court was too liberal in its recent decisions, 23 percent thought it was too conservative, and 41 percent thought it was about right. In a majority of the fourteen Gallup polls that have asked that question since 1991, higher percentages have rated the Court as too liberal rather than too conservative. If the Court has become more conservative over the last several decades, perhaps so has the American public.[4]

This analysis suggests that despite the Court's increased conservatism (or perhaps because of it), the Court has operated generally within the cultural mainstream during the period of this study, giving some confidence that its environmental decisions offer useful insights on the status of environmentalism in the larger society. This is not to say that a majority of the American public would have approved of any of the decisions analyzed here or that the balance of these decisions reflects a public consensus. But it is to say that the structure of many of these decisions—resistance by of a block of the justices (sometimes a majority) to environmentalist perspectives, balanced by a block of sympathetic justices (sometimes a majority)—is instructive beyond the domain of law. This structure reflects the limits of the movement's success and the continuing resistance from still vigorous elements of the DSP. This sense of environmentalism's limits is consistent with concerns about the future of the movement voiced by environmentalists themselves and with evidence of growing divisions within the public on environmental questions.

Environmentalism has shown remarkable and enduring strength in bringing about the changes in both laws and values in the United States, weathering the assaults on these laws by Ronald Reagan in the 1980s and by congressional Republicans in the mid-1990s, and preserving the gains of the movement to the present. But environmentalists themselves lament the movement's failure to complete the transformation, and some of them believe that the movement has stalled, having lost the vision and vigor that brought its early successes. Most famously among the latter are Ted Nord-haus and Michael Shellenberger, who published *The Death of Environmen-talism* in 2004, followed by a more in-depth treatment, *Break Through*, in 2007. Environmentalism was not dead, they argued, but it needed to die, because it had "become just another special interest" and had lost the vi-sionary force of its early expression. Even while criticizing Shellenberger and Nordhaus's indictment of the movement, other environmentalists ac-knowledged the movement's loss of energy and failure to remedy pressing problems.[5]

Although interpreting the cultural implications of public opinion polls is tricky, recent trends in polling data suggest a weakening in environmen-talism's status. In 2010, sociologist and longtime student of the movement Riley Dunlap wrote that "while it still enjoys majority support, the envi-ronmental movement is less consensual than it was a decade ago." He pointed to polling data that showed "a 10-point drop (from 71% to 61%) in the overall percentage of Americans holding a positive orientation toward the environmental movement over the [preceding] decade [2000–2010]." A full 36 percent of the public now believes that the movement has done more harm than good. Suggesting the influence of a strong and growing ideo-logical divide, the biggest shifts on this and related questions were among Republicans, who registered increasingly negative views of the movement.[6]

Similar erosion appears in the public's prioritization of environmental pro-tection and economic growth, which can serve as a proxy for the relative strength of environmentalist values. Since 1984, Gallup has periodically polled the public on whether "protection of the environment should be given priority, even at the risk of curbing economic growth (or) economic growth should be given priority, even if the environment suffers to some extent." For over two decades when Gallup asked this question respondents favored environmental protection over economic growth, often by margins of 30 percentage points or more. In 2008, however, as the economic crisis mounted, the priorities flipped for the first time (51 percent to 42 percent for eco-nomic growth). This new relative ranking has persisted despite the economic recovery, although the gap has narrowed. This shift is consistent with a 2012 Gallup poll showing a decline in the percentage of Americans who worry about environmental problems. In open-ended surveys in which respondents are asked what they believe is the most important problem facing America today, the environment is rarely cited.[7]

Even if one does not interpret these data as evidence of environmentalism in decline, they suggest a movement that has exhausted its transformative surge. Rather than being poised to make substantial new inroads on public thought, it appears to be fighting merely to hold its place. The data are consistent with a public embrace of environmentalism that is broad but contingent and not very deep. They also show that identification with the movement increasingly follows cultural fault lines associated with conservative and liberal ideologies.[8]

The story told by the polls is replicated in the politics. The movement has been largely successful at maintaining its early institutional gains, but at considerable cost. Much of its energy goes to fighting off attempts by opposing forces to weaken laws and policies previously achieved. There has been no significant new federal environmental legislation for more than two decades. The push for comprehensive climate change legislation in the 111th Congress was successful in the House but failed decisively in the Senate in 2010. There is no realistic chance for such legislation in the current political dispensation. In 2012, the GOP's platform called on Congress to prohibit the Environmental Protection Agency's (EPA) regulation of greenhouse gas emissions because of impacts on economic growth and risks to "liberty, the central organizing principle of the American Republic and its people."[9]

Reasons for the Flattening of the Environmental Movement

I focus here on three leading explanations for the flattening of the movement, out of many possibilities: environmentalism has dissipated its power in interest group politics, it is a victim of its own success in improving the environment, and it has encountered a resurgence of opposing values. These hypotheses are not mutually exclusive, and it is likely that each has had at least some role in determining the current state of the movement. The cases examined here offer some corroboration for each hypothesis, although the strength of that support varies among the theories. The cases offer the most support for the third hypothesis in their depiction of recurring conflict between beliefs and values identified with environmentalism and those running counter to the movement.

Environmentalism as Interest Group Politics

The legal transformation of the 1960s and 1970s was a signal achievement for the U.S. environmental movement, but institutionalization also brought changes that some commentators believe have undermined the movement's visionary power and left it unable to deal with current threats. As movement scholar Cary Coglianese has described, the new federal environmental legislation forced environmental groups to "strengthen their presence in

Washington, DC," centralizing to effectively engage with federal governmental actors. The movement also became professionalized. Implementing the new laws posed complex issues of science, engineering, economics, and law, and environmental groups hired full-time scientists, economists, lawyers, fund-raisers, and media consultants to raise money, analyze issues, and advocate for their positions.[10]

With the institutionalization of the movement, major environmental groups began to work within the system using techniques, such as legislative and administrative lobbying and litigation, typical of special interests. Environmentalists' "use of litigation became relatively more routine and incremental. . . . Instead of seeking a broad transformation of American law, environmentalists turned to the courts to enforce and maintain the legislative victories they had previously secured." Coglianese summarizes this progress in an image of an environmental movement domesticated by its own success:

> Instead of existing as a minority voice in the political process, the environmental movement had become a part of the American political and social fabric. Environmentalism has matured from a social movement to an extensive network of interest group organizations with a presence in Washington, DC, like that of any other political lobby.[11]

Environmentalists critical of their own movement have blamed its present doldrums on reduction to interest group status. According to Nordhaus and Shellenberger, by acting as "just another special interest," environmentalists have limited themselves to narrow tactical thinking. They have put the "technical policy cart before the vision-and-values horse." This approach, they argue, ignores the reality that environmentalism must engage "core American values" to succeed on issues such as climate change. Although he disagrees with Nordhaus and Shellenberger on much of their critique, Gus Speth also has placed blame for environmentalism's shortcomings on the choice to work within the "system." In his view, the transformative change needed to address continuing environmental decline instead requires deep changes in national values and politics.[12]

Some of the downsides of this "pragmatic and incrementalist" environmentalism are apparent in federal environmental litigation. Most federal environmental cases, including those that the Court has taken for review, lie at the interstices of complex statutory frameworks or deal with the fine points of constitutional law doctrines in areas such as standing, federalism, and property rights. These cases often seem narrow and technical compared with those, for example, on free speech, affirmative action, or gay rights—not well suited to galvanize a constituency or make visible a new or emerging norm. (Ironically, this results in part from the success of the movement in institutionalizing its objectives in detailed prescriptive statutes.) And in the aggregate, environmental litigation—at least in those cases decided by the Court—has not broadly advanced environmentalists' values or even their "interests."

The decisions examined here, however, qualify the claim that emphasis on lobbying and litigation narrows the movement's focus. Within the constraints of existing federal law and doctrine, environmentalists have pursued cases that can fairly be called transformative in their reach and importance, including *TVA v. Hill,* which secured strong protections for species against government resistance, and *MA v. EPA,* which made way for federal regulation of greenhouse gas emissions, also despite government opposition. Environmentalists have also helped procure and defend landmark agency decisions favoring protection, such as the Department of the Interior's regulation against the destruction of species' habitats in *Sweet Home* and the cost-blind application of national air quality standards in *ATA.* These decisions have driven strong national protections that would not necessarily have matured in the absence of "special interest" lobbying and litigation.

In addition, the Court's decisions belie the suggestion that environmental litigation, which falls in Shellenberger and Nordhaus's class of "narrow tactical thinking," is necessarily disconnected from the values animating the movement. As my analysis shows, even in cases involving legal actions with limited practical or policy significance, environmentalist beliefs and values are not far below the surface. The regulation in *Entergy,* for example, dealt narrowly with cooling water intake structures at electric power plants, but it brought the Court to struggle with the basic tension between biological protection and human welfare. *Friends of the Earth, Inc. v. Laidlaw Environmental Services (TOC), Inc.* was a suit against a local waste treatment facility that closed during the litigation and whose CWA violations environmentalists could not show were harmful to the river. But the Court used it to sanction a "protected relationship" between humans and their natural setting. Although framed in the specialized language of the law ("the system"), these and other cases examined here were cultural as well as tactical encounters. They were not separate from the larger cultural war that Shellenberger and Nordhaus claim is missing from the world of "special interest" environmentalism; they were in the middle of it.

Environmentalism as a Victim of Its Own Success

Coglianese observes that "the existence the environmental laws and regulatory institutions secured by the environmental movement makes it less likely future crises will materialize to mobilize the public outrage necessary for future reform." These laws and institutions have seen marked improvements in air, water, waste management, and species protections. To the extent that they convinced the public that problems were being dealt with and future crises would be avoided, they muted the urgency that led to them—and that would be necessary to maintain them and respond to new threats.[13]

The trajectory of the decisions in this study is consistent with this theory. Decisions in the early 1970s shared a sense of urgency in addressing environmental concerns. The threat to the last "few green havens that are the public parks" animated the Court's decision in *Overton Park*. In *SCRAP*, the Court crafted an expansive standing doctrine to ensure a judicial remedy against environmentally "injurious and widespread government actions." Even in *Sierra Club v. Morton*, which environmentalists lost, the Court showed sympathy for them by crediting aesthetic and conservation interests as bases for standing.

As the movement matured and protective measures took hold, however, the Court's embrace of environmentalist urgency gave way to a more neutral stance and, in some cases, to skepticism and even animosity, as in Justice Scalia's castigation of environmentalist theories in *Lujan II*. In other cases, the Court implied or concluded outright that Congress or the implementing agencies had overcorrected (e.g., *TVA v. Hill*, *SWANNC*, *Rapanos*) or that environmentalist claims, if granted, would lead to regulatory excess (e.g., *Entergy*). This drop in the Court's identification with the movement is plausibly related to a reduced salience of environmental issues owing to the movement's success. But there are other possible explanations, including political changes on the Court, discussed earlier, or the emergence of a strong cultural countermovement, a possibility explored in the next section.

The victim-of-its-own-success theory does help explain the apparent anomaly of *MA v. EPA*, which came within the same three-year span as the Court's rejection of environmentalist views in *Entergy, Rapanos*, and *Winter. MA v. EPA* recaptured the urgency of earlier environmental decisions and ranks high in the Court's environmental canon in both symbolic and policy importance. One explanation for the Court's resurgent identification with environmentalists in this case was the majority's view that climate change was a critical problem that political institutions had failed to address. The refusal of the Bush administration to take on "the most pressing environmental issue of our time" stoked a renewed sense of urgency among a majority of the justices absent in other settings in which a regulatory response was already in place. This suggests the possibility that climate change, which some consider the environmental movement's Waterloo, also holds the key to the movement's renewal.

Environmentalism as Awakening Its Cultural Opposition

A third possibility is closely related to the second: that once it became institutionalized, environmentalism spawned its own cultural opposition. The environmental laws of the 1960s, 1970s, and 1980s were of high symbolic, as well as policy, moment. Passed by broad majorities from both political parties, they seemed to represent a reordering of societal values and priorities. By the 1990s, however, it was clear that if there was or had ever been a national consensus around environmentalism, it was not as complete or as enduring as it had seemed.[14]

Legal scholars Don Elliott, Bruce Ackerman, and John Millian have cast the emergence of concerted opposition to these laws as a political economy story: the laws' rapid passage in the absence of a strong national interest group presence either on the part of environmentalists or economic interests was followed by resistance and revisionist pressures as economic interests organized effectively to counter them. The story lies not only at the level of "rational self-interest," however, but also at the level of cultural values that were reenergized in reaction to environmentalism. In his study of the culture of environmentalism, Jedediah Purdy wrote that opposition to "the ephemeral consensus [of the 1960s and 1970s] came from cultural attitudes that turned out not to have changed as quickly or as completely as many imagined." These cultural attitudes organized around themes of economic freedom, property rights, and resource use. They found voice in the wise use and property rights movements. We have encountered their champions in the cases—developer David Lucas fighting South Carolina's Beachfront Management Act in *Lucas,* the Klamath ranchers fighting ESA protections in *Bennett v. Spear*.[15]

Associated with the emergence of antienvironmentalist movements has been a larger cultural sorting. As the bipartisan consensus of the 1970s crumbled, environmentalism became closely identified with the Democratic Party, which aligned more consistently with egalitarian-collectivist values and the new environmental paradigm. The Republican Party became more consistently the redoubt of individualist-hierarchs and the defender of the DSP. The 2012 Democratic Party platform featured environmental protection as a top priority, celebrated the benefits of environmental regulatory initiatives, and promised further protection through government action. The 2012 Republican Party platform on the environment stressed economic growth and "wise development," attacked the "job-killing punitive mentality" of federal environmental officials, and argued for private stewardship based on strong property rights as an alternative to regulation. Polls show an increasingly less positive view of the environmental movement among rank-and-file Republicans than among their Democrat counterparts. More and more, receptivity to the environmental movement appears to follow cultural fault lines reflected by the dominant political parties.[16]

My interpretation of the Court's environmental decisions offers strong support for the cultural-opposition theory of environmentalism's current struggles. It shows that environmentalism, while registering broad public appeal, challenged beliefs and values that were deeply embedded in U.S. institutions and proved to be enduring elements of the culture. The movement did not create these opposing values, but its success stimulated their expression in the environmental realm. Although the movement's early surge generated favorable public response, including the cascade of federal environmental legislation, the Court and other institutions worked to level out that response over time in recognition of competing values that were subordinated in the surge but that remained strongly engrained in the culture.

An example of this leveling was *New York v. United States,* in which the Court subordinated an environmental concern (siting adequate disposal capacity for radioactive wastes) to autonomy values ("liberty"). Although it agreed that the environmental concern was real and important, the Court insisted that it be addressed consistent with the liberty-enhancing constitutional principles of federalism. The environmental "crisis of the day" took second priority. The values conflict was not direct or unavoidable: there was no suggestion that it would be unwise to increase radioactive waste disposal capacity, and Justice O'Connor's opinion for the Court outlined how that could be done without offending the Constitution. But it determined the legality of the siting legislation's take-title provision. The case both marked the beginning of the Rehnquist Court's federalism revolution and illustrated the persistence of values opposing environmentalism's new urgency.

Other environmentalist defeats followed this pattern. None of the justices in the majority in these cases argued that it was good to harm the environment. One may take Justice Breyer's comment at face value and assume a consensus among the justices that, considered by itself, harming the environment is not a good thing. But in each loss for the environmentalists, some other value—sometimes only implicit in the Court's interpretive rationale—emerged to trump the protective impulse.

The cases examined represent neither the defeat nor the triumph of environmentalism but depict instead an ongoing struggle among the justices. Only a small minority of the selected cases, whether decided for or against the environmentalist cause, were without a dissent or a significant concurrence. The values debate pervaded them. Although cast in the specialized language and reasoning of the law, it reflected the conflict over environmentalism within the larger culture. Both on the Court and in society more generally, the sides seem stalemated. But for environmentalists seeking to complete the transformation they began in the 1960s and 1970s, stalemate can seem like defeat.

The full depth and persistence of the cultural opposition in these cases is masked by the variability among the decisions. Sometimes the environmentalist perspective prevails, sometimes it fails; a majority of the Court seems open to either perspective depending on the circumstances. But the abiding poles of the debate are clear in the commitments of individual justices.

Although just one of five "conservative" justices currently on the Court, Justice Scalia has distinguished himself as the Court's archetypal antienvironmentalist. Although he wrote the opinions for the Court in *ATA* and *City of Chicago* upholding environmentalist positions, the environmental harms in those cases were within the frame of traditional nuisance concerns.[17] Scalia has ardently resisted modern environmentalism's ecological perspective. He has shown particular aversion to the notion of humans as part of a larger community of life with obligations to avoid harm to that community, as in his opinion for the Court in *Lujan II*. He has used his interpretive skills repeatedly to limit regulation to prevent ecological injury not connected to direct human health impacts (e.g., protections for species in *Sweet Home,* coastal and aquatic ecosystems in *Lucas* and *Rapanos,* the global climate system in *MA v. EPA*). And he has often matched his intellectual opposition to environmentalism with a tone of disparagement. His opposition is felt as well as thought—and meant to be felt by the readers of his opinions.

There are several justices that one might place opposite Justice Scalia. Justice Douglas internalized environmentalism as thoroughly as Scalia has its antithesis, but he served only a short time in the modern environmental era and never when Scalia was on the Court. Justice Blackmun revealed his environmental sympathies in his *Sierra Club v. Morton* dissent, earning a pat on the back from Douglas that might be taken as a passing of the mantle. Blackmun's dissents in *Sierra Club* and *Lujan II* advanced the environmentalist theme that legal relationships should accommodate the systemic nature of environmental risks. In *Lucas,* he sharply dissented from the Court's pro-property rights ruling and was also with the dissenters in *Lyng* for protecting Native American earth religions. But he joined Justice Powell's dissent in *TVA v. Hill,* arguing the absurdity of stopping the dam to save the fish, and in the NEPA cases Blackmun seemed overwhelmed by the futility of efforts to prevent environmental loss, as he wrote to himself in *Kleppe.* He also left the Court in 1994 before many of the selected cases were decided.

Justice Stevens, who was appointed to fill Justice Douglas's seat on the Court, at first offered environmentalists a lukewarm embrace. He joined the majority in *Lyng,* for example, and he wrote the Court's opinion in

Methow, which extinguished the last faint hope of substantive review under NEPA. He went on, however, to be a foil for Justice Scalia in many of the most prominent cases—*Lujan II, Rapanos, Lucas, Sweet Home, Entergy, MA v. EPA*—trading majority opinions and dissents (and in *Lujan II* a concurrence in the result). In these, Stevens championed the environmentalist worldview that Scalia decried, going so far in *Lujan II* as to invite comparison of our connection to the environmental other to relationships within a human family.

Among justices still on the Court, Justice Ginsburg is Justice Scalia's strongest counterpart. She joined Justice Stevens's opinions in all the above-mentioned cases that were decided after she joined the Court, and she contributed her own voice for the environmentalist perspective in decisions such as *Laidlaw.* In her dissent in *Winter,* she made clear that her egalitarian-collectivist values extended to the environmental other, in this instance exceeding even Stevens in her empathy. Her precise, neutral style—so different from Scalia's colorful rhetoric—might seem dispassionate, but it can have the opposite effect. In *Winter,* it conveyed an intensity that dignified her act of solidarity with the marine mammals affected by the Navy's training.

Defining the poles of the environmentalism debate on the Court also helps bring into focus the dynamics of the center. Justices in the middle in this debate have been more likely to show ambivalence or oscillate between views on environmental issues and have been more likely to seek accommodation of views. Whereas positions at the poles typically have held out little hope of reconciliation, the middle has intimated synthesis and new direction. Among sitting justices, two—Justices Kennedy and Breyer—are key to understanding the middle and what it may have to suggest about environmentalism's future.

Justice Kennedy, who with Justice O'Connor's departure from the Court now owns sole title to swing justice, has shown sympathy for ecological perspectives. He joined the majorities in *Sweet Home* and in *MA v. EPA,* an environmentalist triumph that would not have happened if he had held ranks with other conservatives on the Court. Even in cases where he has supported an antienvironment outcome, he has written concurrences receptive to the ecological model's implications for standing, property rights, and regulatory scope. He resisted Justice Scalia's wholesale rejection of the "nexus" theories in *Lujan II,* argued in *Lucas* for appropriate room for land regulation in an interdependent world, and in *Rapanos* appropriated the concept of ecological nexus to mediate between protecting the integrity of aquatic systems and limiting federal jurisdiction. (O'Connor's concurrence in *Sweet Home* offered a similar gesture toward synthesis—accepting ecological interdependence as a rationale for regulation but constraining it with common law notions.)

Justice Breyer's middle-ness has been to a different effect than Justice Kennedy's. In environmental cases, he has voted mostly with the liberal block (the egalitarian-collectivists). He has differentiated himself from his liberal colleagues, however, in two concurrences questioning the urgency that environmentalists assign to their concerns. In agreeing hesitantly to join the unanimous decision in *ATA*, he worried that failure to balance environmental benefits against the costs of regulation threatened a return to the "Stone Age." In *Entergy*, he agreed with the conservative majority that the CWA authorized a rough cost-benefit balancing to weed out irrationally demanding regulation to protect aquatic life. This concern about regulatory extremes allied him with Justice Scalia in that case and echoed a particular concern with environmentalist excesses from his previous writings and judicial encounters.

Justice Kennedy exemplifies a conservative who is sympathetic with core environmentalist concepts; Justice Breyer, a liberal who resists environmentalist exceptionalism. Their opinions do not define an environmental future in which the current conflicts can be transcended. But they do highlight areas for further exploration in overcoming the current impasse. Kennedy points to the potential of the ecological model to be applied in ways that limit conflict with elements of the DSP such as limited government, property rights, and economic development. Breyer's concurrences suggest the capacity of liberal welfarism to temper environmental regulatory enthusiasm in a way that moderates conflict with the DSP. These seeds of synthesis are explored in the analysis that follows.

Environmentalist Futures

Building on the analysis of how beliefs and values from the larger culture have colored the Court's environmental decisions, this last section switches the primary focus from the Court to society. It explores possible futures for the environmental movement, including new approaches that hold out some promise of crossing the cultural barriers that have limited the movement's success or at least rearranging those barriers to positive effect for the environment. My account is illustrative, not exhaustive. It does not anoint a single future but instead considers a diversity of practices and the possibilities they suggest.

The environmental movement has become "more fragmented," Cary Coglianese noted, even as it has become institutionalized.[18] The movement has always had plural strains, but this diversity has grown and become institutionalized among groups that appeal to different interests, values, and practices. At the national level, major groups vary in their understanding of the proper relationship to nature, their preferred tools, and their willingness to engage with resource users and corporations. The lodestar of Defenders of Wildlife, for example, is "the inherent value of wildlife and the natural world, regardless of whether individual species are recognized as having utilitarian and aesthetic value to human kind." The Nature Conservancy (TNC), while also devoted to nature conservation, embraces both ecocentric ("lov[ing] nature for its own sake") and anthropocentric ("practical reasons for protecting nature") strains. TNC also emphasizes land acquisition and voluntary programs rather than confrontation, government regulation, and litigation—strategies more likely to appeal to political conservatives. Greenpeace uses "peaceful protest and creative communication" to draw public attention to practices it opposes, and the Center for Biological Diversity channels its activism in regulatory litigation and "creative media." The Natural Resources Defense Council relies on political organizing, lobbying, and litigating to address a range of environmental issues, but it also touts its partnerships with businesses "who create prosperity and protect the environment at the same time." The Environmental Defense Fund has staked its claim as the leader among environmental groups in the use of market mechanisms (making "environmental protection pay") and collaborations with businesses and resource users and in the embrace of "economic sustainability" as a necessary condition of environmental sustainability.[19]

The variety of perspectives extends through a multitude of international groups, with which many U.S. groups are affiliated, and through groups at the state and local levels, which offer opportunities for pragmatic effort on culturally divisive issues such as climate change that may be impossible at the national or international levels.[20] Adding to the mix are private-sector ventures, discussed below, that are outside the movement as conventionally understood but are no less engaged in realizing a vision of the proper human-natural relationship.

This diversity creates a rich cultural marketplace for U.S. environmentalism. Although fragmentation could dissipate the movement's energy and render it ineffective, at this moment, when the movement is searching for new footing, diversity may be salutary. Having a suite of expressions of environmentalism, effective across a range of audiences and settings, might be more effective in a polarized society than a more univocal movement. Diversity can make room for innovation. Competition can help sort out which approaches maximize the cultural viability of protective actions, enabling the movement to adapt to meet the environmental challenges that remain.

Prescriptions for Change

In response to environmentalism's struggles, some have urged radical change. These critics view the existing system as either inherently indifferent to environmental harm or beyond the reach of environmentalism to meaningfully effect.[21] They argue for the system's destruction or transformation and prescribe their preferred future for society, the environmental movement, or both. I consider two of the most prominent of these deep critiques, before offering a more tentative (and less prescriptive) exploration of environmentalism's future.

Once described as the "ultimate insider" for his prior service as environmental advisor to two presidents and administrator of the U.N. Development Program, environmentalist Gus Speth now offers a radical assessment of the present system. He argues that the political economy is failing pervasively and that this failure calls for a broad political movement for transformative change in virtually every aspect of our public life—from the electoral process to wealth distribution, consumption, money and finance, and corporate governance. In this, Speth commits environmentalism's future to the triumph of a sweeping movement of the left, a green progressivism. "Environmentalists need for liberals to succeed," he writes, and succeed big.[22]

Nordhaus and Shellenberger offer a different critique—theirs focused as much on the shortcomings of environmentalism itself as on the system at large—but with comparably radical implications for the movement's future. Whereas Speth ties the future of environmentalism firmly to the progress of liberalism, they work to wrest environmentalism from liberals, whom they classify as "an aggregation of the aggrieved." As a "liberal interest group," they argue, environmentalists have defined themselves by resentment of human power, an emphasis on limits, and a quasi-religious commitment to protection of an essentialized nature. The authors reject this reproachful, restrictive, and biophilic construct—a "politics of limits"—in favor of a "generous, adaptive, contingent and *anthropophilic* politics"—a "politics of overcoming."[23]

Both critiques demand sweeping and fundamental change—Speth in society at large as essential to environmentalism's success, Nordhaus and Shellenberger in the environmental movement in order to succeed in a "post-material" society. These accounts offer important insights on cultural contradictions and barriers impeding environmentalism's success, but they also have important limitations. Speth ties environmentalism so securely to the advance of "liberalism" that he cuts off any alternative expression or evolution of the movement. If environmentalism is to succeed, it must overwhelm the opposition, and Speth cannot offer any immediate prospect of the deep systemic changes that he argues are necessary. Similarly, Nordhaus and Shellenberger's bracing tonic is not backed by a theory of political or cultural change that would support the promise of better environmental outcomes. As Doug Kysar has written, "the authors . . . offer us nothing but the politics of perceptual and cultural manipulation."[24]

Against these sweeping, prescriptive critiques, I offer a more modest, largely descriptive account—one that emphasizes overcoming, or dispelling, cultural resistance to the movement's progress through a process of cultural experimentation and testing while staying connected to the movement's historical roots. Although less revolutionary than either Speth or Nordhaus and Shellenberger, this account does not confine itself to the narrow version of environmentalism that the movement's critics describe variously as working "within the system" or "interest group politics." That version—plodding, visionless, in-the-box—not only is normatively unattractive, as the critics intend, but also is not accurately descriptive of the current movement, which although, and perhaps because, it is stressed, is becoming increasingly innovative and diverse.[25]

My account looks for indications of a further evolution in cultural values and practices regarding the environment. It features new modes of engagement with existing institutional and values frameworks that challenge the conventional perception and application of those frameworks. These innovations might be the first steps toward broad transformations of the sort that Speth or Nordhaus and Shellenberger envision, or they might not. But they have promise in their own right and might help establish, if nothing else, more robust support within what we might generously call our "existing system" for addressing environmental concerns, including the daunting challenge of climate change. Such a shift could reshape the movement's interactions with the Court, among other major institutions.

Bridging Divides

My analysis has emphasized the divide between environmentalism and its cultural opponents. But these lines of opposition do not necessarily control societal outcomes. Cultural values "orient mass opinion through complex social and cognitive mechanisms," but most people remain "relatively tolerant." Their initial values-based orientation on an issue can evolve through new information and deliberation on the merits. Policies and practices that appeal to multiple cultural perspectives or dampen conflict between them can make space for that deliberation to occur. For example, consideration of a revenue-neutral carbon tax or reliance on nuclear power as policies to address climate change might increase agreement on climate change science. Within the ceaseless interaction of competing cultural viewpoints and changing material circumstances, new positions and practices can emerge that appeal to diverse perspectives and create new opportunities for consensus on environmental science and policy—or at least reduce the extreme polarization that we now experience.[26]

CLIMATE CHANGE AS CATALYST

Pressures for cultural rapprochement come from rising threats to planetary systems—climate change, ocean degradation, biodiversity loss, and disturbance of the nitrogen cycle—that are not being effectively dealt with. Among these threats, climate change is most daunting. Commentators have variously dubbed it a "super wicked problem" and "a perfect moral storm." It is wicked because of the extremely broad dispersion of causes and effects, both spatially across the entire planet and temporally across generations, and the inadequacy of international institutions to deal with the problem at a global scale. Added to these recalcitrant features are cultural barriers that have discouraged meaningful deliberation on the science of climate change and policies to address it. Individualist-hierarchs rate the risks of climate change significantly lower than do egalitarian-communitarians because high ratings would lead to "restrictions on commerce and industry," the types of activity that individualist-hierarchs value. Their discounting of climate change risks is only exacerbated by the linkage of the science, through the Intergovernmental Panel on Climate Change, to an international framework for reductions in fossil fuel emissions by industrial nations and payments to developing countries suffering the effects of climate change.[27]

For all of these reasons, climate change is environmentalism's biggest challenge, and so far, its biggest failure. But the very enormity of the problem, the force of its wickedness, may help prepare the movement for another transformative surge. In response to the climate change challenge as well as other pressing issues, we see the emergence of new strains of environmentalism that are more accepting of—indeed, reliant on—markets, technology, and economic development. These recastings carry the dual promise of enhancing practical effectiveness and increasing the cultural pluralism of environmental deliberations.[28]

STEWARDSHIP, CHOICE, AND MARKETS

TVA v. Hill told the story of environmentalists' fight to save an endangered species from landscape-transforming technological development (the Tellico Dam)—a clash, as interpreted earlier, between mastery and harmony values. But there is another narrative embedded in the facts of the case that has a much different cultural resonance. Among the dam's opponents were farmers, some from families who had owned and worked land in the Tennessee Valley for generations. Their land was taken by the government to accommodate the reservoir, and holdouts were forcibly evicted. In November 1979, United States marshals forced a seventy-five-year-old widow, Nellie McCall, to leave the ninety-acre farm that she had owned with her deceased husband. These were the "simplest farmers" that Justice Scalia offered as exemplars of autonomy values against the heavy hand of government regulation in *Sweet Home*. But in this case, government was crushing their autonomy in the name not of species protection but of claimed economic development. This story hidden in *TVA v. Hill* opens the possibility that autonomy values and the market systems with which they are associated might support norms of environmental stewardship rather than oppose them.[29]

Before there was environmental law and policy as we now know it, Aldo Leopold was working out the implications of ecological interdependence for personal ethics. The "land ethic" that grew from his understanding of the world as a "biotic community" was framed to inform the choices of individual landowners, who were encouraged by their own choice to become "citizens" of the land community. In this pure form, Leopold's land ethic is not just consistent with autonomy values; it emphasized the choices that they protect. Concerns about externalities and free rider problems led to the prevailing view among environmentalists that effective implementation of the land ethic requires collectivist measures, but its original conceptualization as an ethical evolution (not a governmental program) holds out another possible path of realization—one fully in line with the 2012 Republican national platform, which declared its belief "in the moral obligation of the people to be good stewards of the God-given natural beauty and resources of our country."[30]

Environmentalists sniggered when President George W. Bush, speaking to the Cattlemen's Association in 2002, told the cattlemen that they were the embodiment of our national land ethic. But Wolf Creek Farm in Wolftown, Virginia, meets a demanding sustainability checklist that ranges from all-grass-fed natural beef and home-raised calves to no antibiotics, hormones, pesticides, or chemical fertilizers and that includes "animal welfare approved" and "all natural land stewardship." Wolf Creek "selected cattle to be the mainstay of our farm due to our affinity with this truly gentle creature that has historically connected mankind with the natural world." One might guess that the farm's owner, John Whiteside, is a strong egalitarian-collectivist seeking harmony with the land and community. By his own description, Whiteside is a "radical environmentalist," but he is also a libertarian who sees autonomy values as not only consistent with a virtuous relationship to the land but essential to it. Practicing stewardship through private exchange allows Whiteside and his local clientele to simultaneously express a deep commitment to the land and a preference for limited government. Voluntary associations such as the American Grassfed Association connect Whiteside to like-minded farmers.[31]

In his path-breaking piece, "Private Environmental Governance," Michael Vandenbergh depicts a host of private orderings around sustainable practice, some in concert with environmental groups, others not. Voluntary certification and labeling systems for forest products, fish, bananas, and coffee govern the terms under which these resources are grown and harvested. Approximately 40 percent of private U.S. forestland is managed under one of two voluntary forest stewardship certification associations. One of these associations, keyed to small forest owners, "certifies 244 million hectares of forest owned by over 750,000 forest owners."[32]

Private standards established by the U.S. Green Building Council (USGBC) anchor the green building movement. USGBC's Leadership in Energy and Environmental Design (LEED) program is a voluntary certification system for sustainable commercial and residential construction and neighborhood development projects. "As of 2012," Vandenbergh writes, "LEED-certified buildings accounted for two billion square feet of occupied space in the U.S." Supply chain contracts required by large retailers such as Wal-Mart and Hewlett-Packard impose environmental requirements on their suppliers in the United States and abroad. Vandenbergh estimates that the potential benefits of these bilateral requirements of performance beyond "public legal requirements may be larger than many current international or national regulatory measures."[33]

Voluntary approaches of this kind have the potential to address global issues such as climate change in the face of governmental inaction at the national and international levels. Energy efficiency requirements in corporate supply chain contracts can bring down greenhouse gas emissions in supplier countries; LEED certification offers some promise of reducing the carbon footprint of buildings, which currently account for 30 percent of greenhouse gas emissions in the United States.[34] The UK-based Carbon Disclosure Project (CDP) represents global investors in obtaining voluntary reports from corporations on the amounts of their greenhouse gas emissions and efforts to reduce them, among other sustainability measures. In 2013, 722 investors representing $87 trillion in assets asked for reports from the world's 500 largest corporations. Over 80 percent of those companies responded with information, which CDP publically assessed as to its completeness and effectiveness.

These diverse private orderings for environmental benefit are consistent with values favoring market transactions and voluntary group associations, and they invite a more culturally inclusive construction of the stewardship ethic. They do not necessarily represent a deep commitment to that ethic by their participants. They may be motivated by the personal values of resource owners or corporate officials, as appears in John Whiteside's case, but they may also be responding to prods from environmental groups, veiled threats of governmental regulation, or investor or consumer demands. This leaves concern among environmentalists about "greenwash," programs "designed to give the appearance of environmental benefits without delivering actual benefits." More information is needed for a full assessment, but on the basis of the existing literature, Vandenbergh generally concludes that these programs can drive positive results.[35]

The model of private environmental governance assumes minimal government involvement beyond the operation of contract and property law that provides the understory of our laissez-faire economic system. A major shift to this model away from regulation would move environmental litigation from public to private law issues and doubtless produce many fewer environmental cases in the Supreme Court. Such a shift is unlikely, however. Although private orderings offer useful alternatives to government programs and may enlarge environmentalism's cultural appeal, their potential is limited by collective action problems, such as free riding, which are likely only to increase with the costs of effective response.

EFFICIENCY, PRICE SIGNALS, AND THE SOCIAL COST OF CARBON

Even if more robust government involvement is necessary, however, the use of flexibility devices, such as pollution taxes and emissions trading, can expand the appeal of environmental protection by offering more room for choice and greater efficiency than do other forms of regulation. In the early decades of the modern movement, environmentalists resisted these devices in favor of more prescriptive regulation because they believed the devices offered less certain protections and condoned environmental harm. In *Chevron*, as discussed, the Natural Resources Defense Council (NRDC) opposed a plantwide bubble under the Clean Air Act (CAA) that the Court's 1984 decision upheld as a reasonable accommodation between economic growth and environmental protection. Since then, however, environmentalists have increasingly embraced flexibility mechanisms. The acid rain trading provisions of the CAA Amendments of 1990 were "heavily influenced by an emissions-trading proposal" developed by the Environmental Defense Fund (EDF) and supported by President George H. W. Bush as a market-friendly approach to environmental protection. Broad support among environmental groups for the EPA's regional bubble and trading approach in *EME Homer* is further evidence of this shift. The shift has important cultural as well as policy implications: it reflects acceptance of flexibility and efficiency by environmentalist egalitarian-communitarians as consistent with their protective goals and offers to neutralize the skepticism of individualist-hierarchs about those goals by "embracing markets and empowering commercial firms to combat a social problem."[36]

Support for market-based approaches to climate change regulation is nearly universal among mainstream environmental groups, although some environmental justice advocates oppose them, fearing they could lead to increased concentrations of conventional pollutants in poor and minority neighborhoods. The NRDC, which led the charge against the plantwide bubble in *Chevron,* was among the many environmental groups that rallied behind the Waxman-Markey climate change cap-and-trade bill that passed the House of Representatives in 2009. The receptivity of these groups to "an economy-wide market-driven approach that includes cap-and-trade as a core element" enabled a coalition with business groups to support the legislation. Environmental groups similarly rallied around a carbon tax bill introduced into the House of Representatives in 2013.[37] Although these efforts have not borne legislative fruit and are not likely to soon, they reduce the cultural dissonance on climate change and create space for meaningful engagement. Conservative environmental law scholar Jonathan Adler has endorsed action on climate change in the form of a revenue-neutral carbon tax while urging fellow conservatives to move past their reflexive dismissal of environmental concerns through renewed consideration of institutional responses consistent with limited government and free enterprise.[38]

In *Entergy,* environmentalists fought against the use of cost-benefit analysis (CBA) and the efficiency paradigm in setting policy for aquatic organisms; the National Wildlife Federation and Sierra Club argued in their amicus brief that "the value of the ecological integrity of the nation's waters cannot be quantified." In other settings, however, environmentalists have begun to use monetization of environmental benefits to tactical advantage. The social cost of carbon is a construct that estimates the marginal benefits of climate change protections, expressed as the value of impacts avoided by the reduction of a ton of CO_2 or its equivalent. This number is used in CBAs of the EPA's greenhouse gas emission rules, as required by Executive

Order 12866; it could also be used in setting the cap for an emission trading program or the amount of a carbon tax. Environmental groups, including NRDC and EDF, successfully urged the administration to increase its so- cial cost of carbon estimates to reflect the current climate science and then helped defend the higher estimates.[39] Working within a framework that was put in place by a conservative Republican president to make regulation ef- ficient enables environmentalists to take the climate change debate to op- ponents on their own terms. Widespread acceptance of CBA and the effi- ciency paradigm, as urged by Revesz and Livermore, would represent a cultural sea change for environmentalists with implications for a host of policy and legal questions, including the cost-blind premise of *American Trucking*.

Mastery, Technology, and Nature

Environmentalists have resisted mastery values expressed through techno- logical manipulation of the environment and economic growth. In his dis- sent in *Sierra Club v. Morton,* Justice Douglas represented these values as the "bulldozers of 'progress,'" poised to "plow under all the aesthetic won- ders of this beautiful land" and reduce "priceless bits of Americana . . . to the eventual rubble of our urban environment."[40] Virtually all of the con- tested actions and policies in this book's selected cases were variants of the "bulldozers of 'progress'"—from dams, highways, and nuclear plants to land development, mining, and industrial emissions. In opposing them, environ- mentalists sought more harmonious relations with nature, reducing the human footprint and limiting technological intrusions. Mastery for envi- ronmentalists, however, is less straightforward than this account suggests.

RECONSIDERING THE ANTIMASTERY NARRATIVE

The founding text of the movement, Rachel Carson's *Silent Spring,* begins with her "A Fable for Tomorrow," depicting a rich and harmonious world threatened by death-dealing synthetic chemicals. Critics have attacked this narrative as a harmful romanticization. Nordhaus and Shellenberger, for example, argue that it falsely depicts nature as Edenic and the natural im- pulse of humans to control it as sinful, aping the myth of the fall in the book of Genesis. "It is this reality—human agency—that most bothers en- vironmentalists like Carson," they write. "For her, human attempts to con- trol nature inevitably end in tragedy."[41] But Carson's actual response to the crisis she depicted was more complex—and much less antimastery—than this criticism presumes. She did not urge retreat to a prechemical past but instead encouraged the development of a "science of biotic controls" that could offer comparable protections for agriculture with fewer ecological risks than chemical poisons: for example, chemical sterilization to wipe out the screwworm fly in the southeastern United States. This was hardly a return to Eden.[42]

The valence of mastery has only become more complex with increasing awareness of the pervasiveness of human impacts on the environment and the recognition that technological and economic development will be essential to manage at least some of those impacts, most notably climate change. In *The End of Nature*, environmental activist Bill McKibben ruefully argued that anthropogenic climate change pervaded nature in a way that made human dominance complete. Although we had intruded on nature before, "we never thought we had wrecked [it] . . . we never really thought we could." Climate change, however, changed the meaning of nature from something reassuring and secure to something contingent, subdued. On the basis of a comprehensive tracing of the human imprint across ecosystems and landscapes, the Nature Conservancy's (TNC) chief scientist, Peter Kareiva, and his colleagues confirm that "virtually all of nature is now domesticated." By "domesticated," they mean nature "exploited and controlled."[43]

If nature is thoroughly domesticated, the question for environmentalists may shift from how we put it back or set it free to how we manage it to best effect. This shift in perspective revealed itself dramatically in the split among environmentalists over the Cape Wind project off Nantucket. Environmentalist Robert F. Kennedy Jr. proclaimed his support for wind power but drew the line at a project that would compromise the beauty of his beloved Cape Cod. He framed the case against Cape Wind as an antimastery narrative, emphasizing the industrial scale of the project and its violation of the Massachusetts coastal environment. "130 giant turbines whose windmill arms will reach 417 feet above the water [will] be visible for up to 26 miles," "hundreds of flashing lights . . . will steal the stars and nighttime views," and "a transformer station rising 100 feet above the sound would house giant helicopter pads and 40,000 gallons of potentially hazardous oil." Kennedy compared siting the project on Nantucket Sound to building a wind farm in Yosemite Park. The Massachusetts coast, while "far from pristine," was itself a kind of wilderness, necessary for the "spiritual renewal" of people in nearby cities, like Boston, and vulnerable to the wind farm's disruptions.[44]

Nordhaus and Shellenberger criticized mainline environmental groups, such as NRDC, for not taking Kennedy, one of their own, to task; Kennedy's opposition, they argued, was selfish NIMBYism. But a number of environmentalists did object to Kennedy's stance, including Bill McKibben, probably the nation's most prominent environmentalist and climate change advocate. In an open letter to Kennedy, McKibben and others wrote that the adverse impacts of Cape Wind were trivial when measured against the need to address the climate change crisis, which "will require the dramatic transformation of America's energy economy." They offered a future not of technological and economic restraint but of "cutting-edge technologies, and rewarding high-paying jobs." In his 2010 approval of Cape Wind, Secretary of the Interior Ken Salazar celebrated its grand scale, job creation, and carbon-reducing benefits while taking steps to reduce local disruptions, including "visual impacts from the Kennedy Compound National Historic Landmark."[45]

Kennedy and the environmentalists who opposed him differed not only on the outcome—a vote yes or no for Cape Wind—but on the values they invoked to explain their respective positions. This latter difference has significance for environmentalists' efforts to expand support for action on climate change and other contentious issues. Kennedy's appeal was narrowly to egalitarian-collectivist values, stressing the technological appropriation of the commons for economic gain and the adverse effects on local fishermen and marine life. The pro–Cape Wind environmentalists embraced technological mastery and economic opportunity in a way more likely to resonate with individualist-hierarchs favoring private entrepreneurship and material abundance, while their commitment to solving the global commons problem retained appeal for egalitarian-collectivists.

Renewable energy technologies, such as the wind turbines off Cape Cod, have a different cultural valence than conventional pollution-control technology. The latter operates as a constraint on primary economic productivity; the former offer themselves as the engines of a new economy. Deployment of renewable technologies at a scale to deal meaningfully with climate change would represent a massive industrial retooling, with opportunities for entrepreneurial success and economic growth in portions of the energy and other sectors, albeit with economic decline in others.

Environmentalists almost universally embrace renewable energy development, although troublesome issues about siting remain, as in Cape Wind. Many remain skeptical, however, of another technology to reduce greenhouse gas emissions: nuclear power, which from the early days of the movement has embodied dangerous technological hubris (e.g., *Calvert Cliffs, Vermont Yankee*). But climate change scientist and activist James Hansen and other prominent environmentalists have argued that the movement will have to accept it, albeit in a more advanced, safer form. That's because, by Hansen's calculation, renewable sources cannot scale up fast enough to prevent "dangerous climate change." Were it to be widely embraced by the environmental community, this position would have an important expressive as well as policy dimension. Dan Kahan and his coinvestigators found that individualist-hierarchs were more receptive to scientific representations of human-caused climate change when those representations were linked to nuclear power as a solution rather than to "anti-pollution regulation."[46]

Environmentalists' receptivity to industrial-scale renewable energy technologies goes with recognition of the economic transformation needed to develop and deploy those technologies at the scale necessary to address climate change. This has helped them connect with groups outside the movement, partnering with industries and labor unions to champion economic investment and job growth in the "clean economy." These partnerships may be simply marriages of convenience, common in interest group politics. But there have been moments suggesting a deeper convergence. The BlueGreen Alliance joins major environmental groups (e.g., NRDC, EDF, National Wildlife Federation) with major labor unions (e.g., United Steel Workers, United Auto Workers, Amalgamated Transit Workers) to increase the number and quality of jobs in the new energy economy. Speaking on behalf of the alliance in April 2013, AFL-CIO President Richard Trumka proclaimed that climate change had brought environmentalists and labor together in "values" as well as "interests," and it was now possible to imagine "a movement that combines environmentalists and labor and business." Saying doesn't make so, but being able to say what before there seemed no cultural room to say is itself something new.[47]

"OLD GREENS VERSUS NEW"

Reconsideration of the antimastery narrative extends beyond climate change and embraces a collection of revisionist views on technology, nature, and the goals of environmental stewardship. Mark Lynas, a self-described environmentalist and former advisor to the president of the Maldives on climate change, argues in his book *The God Species* that Earth is stressed across a number of its major system processes, and humans have transgressed the boundaries of three of them: biodiversity loss and excessive nitrogen (eutrophication) in addition to climate change. To reestablish sustainable practices in these areas and avoid exceeding other planetary boundaries, Lynas writes, we must reject

> the standard Green creed . . . that playing God is dangerous. Hence the reflexive opposition to new technologies. . . . My thesis is the reverse: playing God (in the sense of being intelligent designers) at a planetary level is essential if creation is not to be irreparably damaged or even destroyed by humans unwittingly deploying our newfound powers in disastrous ways.

Lynas seems intentionally to challenge Leopold's foundational trope: god-like Ulysses is called not to humble himself as a "mere citizen" of the biotic community but to assert his prowess, albeit with a knowledge of the natural limits of the systems within which he must live. This recast stewardship urges the development and use of technologies and economic strategies across a range of planetary problems. These tools are to be used wisely within the real constraints that nature imposes, but their purpose is not to establish a prelapsarian state. It is to secure the conditions for sustained human flourishing in a nature unalterably different from that which would have been if the "god species" had never appeared.[48]

Like Lynas, new environmentalist Peter Kareiva challenges the antimastery narrative by undercutting the movement's received wisdom. In a 2011 lecture, he provocatively marked the cultural break with traditional environmentalists by disparaging the views of prophets of the movement such as Thoreau and Abbey. Thoreau and Abbey were hypocrites in their sanctification of pristine nature: Thoreau's mother did his laundry while he lived at Walden Pond; Abbey privately expressed his loneliness while publically celebrating the "loveliness" of his wilderness experience. Although he has been kinder to Rachel Carson, lauding her role in bringing about needed environmental protections, Kareiva dismisses her "fragility trope" (with its corollary of apocalypse) as inconsistent with data showing nature's resilience.[49]

The Aspen Institute cast the struggle as generational, "old greens versus new," suggesting that if only as a matter of life expectancy, the "new" will eventually prevail. A panel at the institute's 2012 Environment Forum pitted "traditional conservationists [whose] goal has been to preserve as much wild nature as possible from encroaching human civilization" against "a new breed of pragmatists . . . advocating that we accept the growing needs of humanity as a starting point for conservation—along with the reality that there is no untouched wilderness left to preserve." The climax of the panel was a face-off between Emma Marris, the youthful author of *The Rambunctious Garden,* in which she argued for "throwing out the 'pristine wilderness' ideal" and coming to terms with altered nature, and E. O. Wilson, eminent octogenarian biologist and ecocentrist. Marris opined that the Burmese Python, an invasive species in the Florida Everglades, was "likely here to stay" despite efforts to eliminate it and should be accepted and managed as part of the ecosystem. Wilson's response: Marris was showing "a white flag of surrender."[50]

The promise of these change initiatives is not only a more pragmatic approach to looming environmental challenges but also a cultural inclusivity that could lead to broader acceptance of the scientific basis for urgent action as well as agreement on forms that action should take. The risk is that they will dissolve the environmentalist perspective into an undifferentiated sea of competing interests and value preferences. In a world of trade-offs, one may question what remains of environmentalism's transformative aspirations. It is unclear, in the end, what Shellenberger, Nordhaus, and their followers offer other than the cultural status quo and the indifferent environmental outcomes that we might expect from it.

My own view is that although the movement needs to come to terms with the Anthropocene (and is already doing that), it would be a mistake to abandon its traditional wellsprings, as Kareiva and others have urged. There is power in the idea of nature, although we understand that nature is, and perhaps has been since humans appeared in numbers on the planet, beyond recall in a "pristine" state. "People feel that nature matters and act on that conviction."[51] That primary connection to nature has set environmentalism apart from the other great social movements of our time. It has rallied the movement's adherents. To give up that idea entirely is to abandon the allegiances that have powered the movement—to show the white flag, as Wilson quipped—and abdicate its enterprise of deep change.

A cultural synthesis is plausible. Seminal figures such as Aldo Leopold and Rachel Carson offer bridges between the old and the new. Leopold was an advocate of wilderness protection, but he also valued working landscapes, including the Wisconsin farm that he brought back into productive use from past abuse and neglect. His land ethic is the fount of ecocentric theories that would limit human intervention. But it also lends itself to anthropocentric interpretations. Carson defended an idyllic harmony from the harms of pesticides but envisioned a chemically managed future for modern high-yield agriculture. Contemporary environmentalist writer and activist Bill McKibben wrote *The End of Nature* but remains an advocate for wildness in multiple forms. "For me," he writes, "the idea that there's no such thing as pure wilderness has made the relative wild all the more precious."[52]

The synthesis may take the form of benign mastery: the world is what we make it, but we make it out of concern not only for ourselves.[53] Benign mastery need not imply allegiance to intrinsic value theories, but it does imply an attitude of respect for nature in all its forms—our own bodies included. Justice Douglas's *Sierra Club* dissent imagined an assemblage of species of the Mineral King Valley "standing before the Court" in their own right. But because we cannot speak with the environmental other, there may be little practical difference between this view of an egalitarian council of life and the more anthropocentric but empathetic views of Justice Blackmun's dissent or even the Court's opinion. These views all support a more generous consideration than a narrow utilitarian or instrumentalist perspective would grant. The challenge going forward would be to deepen and broaden that consideration to encompass diverse environments, technologies, knowledge systems, and cultural idioms. In this version of the movement's future, as Jedediah Purdy wrote, the triad of Leopold's land ethic—"integrity, stability, and beauty"—stand not as "qualities of unchanged 'wild' nature, but goals for active management, both of wilderness and of densely inhabited places."[54]

One might argue that continuing the emphasis on our connectedness to nature is not based on reason, but flatters instead the movement's mystical or quasi-religious side, risking romantic excess or policy irrelevance. Even reason has its limits, however. It cannot by itself force change beyond prevailing conventions of reasonableness. Movements may appeal to reason; they may use the implements of reason, such as CBA, to advance their aims. But they are not powered by reason, and reason may arbitrarily limit their horizons. This was the point of David Brower, who knew something about what made a movement, when he claimed provocatively that "objectivity is the greatest threat . . . today."[55] The continued tenacity and power of the movement may depend on keeping its roots deep in the cultural soil from which it grew, even as its expressions take on new, adaptive forms.

IN THE SELECTED CASES, contending worldviews inflect the justices' assessment of environmental risks and societal responses to those risks. The divisions among the justices reflect the competition between these worldviews in the larger culture. The cases are consistent with other evidence that the modern environmental era, despite its rush of bold legislation, did not bring about the deep cultural change that might have been imagined. Opposing beliefs and values proved to be enduring and deeply embedded in our institutions and practices. Indeed, during the span of the modern environmental movement, and sometimes with the Court's help, those beliefs and values seem more entrenched than in the 1970s.

The movement struggles with its maturity. Commentators from within and outside it are skeptical of its ability, in its present form, to deal with a new generation of environmental problems of daunting scale and complexity. If, as the Court's cases suggest, the movement's difficulties stem from cultural stalemate, its future success may depend on neutralizing the cultural opposition. I highlighted emerging beliefs and practices that might contribute to that end: an increased reliance on private associations, markets, and market mechanisms; an embrace of transformative technologies to reduce environmental impacts while underwriting economic growth; and a move away from "nature" or the "natural" as an orienting idea. But these strategies, even as they promise greater compatibility with dominant cultural strains, are of uncertain outcome and may threaten the sources of environmentalism's distinctive power—in particular, its "deep sense of engagement with the landscape, with profound connections to surroundings and to natural processes central to all life."[56]

Whatever the movement's future directions, the Court will continue in its role as legal and cultural arbiter. It has already engaged with the central question facing the movement (What is our proper relationship to the natural world?) in cases such as *Sierra Club, TVA v. Hill, Lyng,* and *Laidlaw.*[57] It will likely have occasion to do so again as the movement and the institutions through which it engages evolve. The Court is likely to use environmental cases for further development of constitutional doctrine on property rights, standing, and federalism—to deal with unanswered questions on the reach of *Koontz,* standing for nongovernmental climate change plaintiffs under *MA v. EPA,* or the scope of the Commerce Power for ecological statutes such as the ESA. It will also be inclined to make additional investments in its portfolio of cases on instrument choice (*Chevron, EME Homer*) and CBA (*ATA, Entergy*), including—if Revesz and Livermore have their way—revisiting *ATA*'s legal and policy premises. Finally, the Court's significant investments in culturally salient statutory issues—such as the EPA's authority to regulate greenhouse gas emissions under the CAA—will call for future installments.

In the absence of legislative change, the Court's task in environmental cases may be even more challenging than in the past, as efforts to accommodate a changing physical and cultural environment further stretch the limits of existing environmental laws, as glimpsed in *UARG* and *EME Homer.* That difficulty, however, may only increase the importance of the Court's role as reason-giver, conveying law's meanings as well as determining its outcomes.[58]

Appendix: Selected Cases

Acknowledgments

This book has many authors. It builds on a body of literature in the diverse fields of cultural analysis, social science, and law. In addition to the many sources on which it draws explicitly, its unspecified debt to scholars in these and related fields is immense. It also has a distinguished company of direct contributors. Richard Lazarus and an anonymous reviewer read and commented on the text for Harvard University Press. Jedediah Purdy, Stephen Cushman, and John Hanson also generously reviewed the entire manuscript. Zygmunt Plater and his class at Boston College Law School made critiquing a draft of the book a collective undertaking. John Monahan, Michael Vandenbergh, Doug Laycock, Michael Livermore, Risa Goluboff, and Nancy Sherman brought their expertise to individual chapters, and participants in the Boulder Environmental Law Workshop commented on a draft of Chapter 10. The diverse perspectives from leading scholars and practitioners added greatly to the book's coherence, balance, and accuracy.

My work was aided throughout by the wonderful research librarians at the University of Virginia Law School. Leslie Ashbrook led the final source checking and production of the manuscript, aided by research assistants Paul Ritchey, Will Grossenbacher, and David Soltes. A long line of student researchers assisted in the book's evolution over many years, including Isak Howell, Daniel Foster, Emily Davis, Keiko Seno, Liam Paskvan, Brandon Bullard, James Dean, and Matthew Skanchy.

I am deeply grateful to all who contributed their energies and skills to bringing this project to fruition. Its merits owe much to their generous contributions; the flaws that remain are my own.

My earlier article, "Environmentalism and the Supreme Court: A Cultural Analysis" (*Ecology Law Quarterly* 33, no. 2 [2006]), informs the themes and discussions of this book. My other previous articles inform the discussions in particular portions of the book: "The Significance of *Massachusetts v. EPA*" (*Virginia Law Review in Brief* 93 [2007]) in Chapters 3 and 6; "Sounds of Silence: Cost-Benefit Canons in *Entergy Corp. v. Riverkeeper, Inc.*" (*Harvard Environmental Law Review* 34, no. 2 [2010]) in Chapter 5; and "Words and Worlds: The Supreme Court in *Rapanos* and *Carabell* (*Virginia Environmental Law Journal* 25, no. 3 [2007]) in Chapter 7.

Notes

Epigraphs

Epigraphs on p. ix: Ralph Waldo Emerson, *English Traits, Representative Men, and Other Essays* (London: J. M. Dent & Co., 1908), 24. Letter to Florens Christian Ring, December 9, 1923, trans. by Manfred R. Jacobson and Evelyn M. Jacobson, in *The Correspondence of Walter Benjamin 1910–1940*, ed. Gershom Scholem and Theodor W. Adorno (Chicago: University of Chicago Press, 1994), 225.

Chapter 1: Environmentalism

1. Philip Shabecoff, *A Fierce Green Fire: The American Environmental Movement*, rev. ed. (Washington, DC: Island Press, 2003), 104–105.
2. See P. Wesley Schultz and Lynnette Zelensky, "Values as Predictors of Environmental Attitudes: Evidence for Consistency across 14 Countries," *Journal of Environmental Psychology* 19, no. 3 (1999): 258, citing Victor Barnouw, *Culture and Personality* (Homewood, IL: Dorsey Press, 1985). See also Amir N. Licht, Chanan Goldschmidt, and Shalom H. Schwartz, "Culture, Law and Corporate Governance," *International Review of Law and Economics* 25 (2005): 233 ("Culture refers to the complex of meanings, symbols, and assumptions about what is good or bad, legitimate or illegitimate that underlie the prevailing practices and norms in a society"); Geerd Hofstede, *Culture's Consequences: International Differences in Work-Related Values* (Beverly Hills, CA: Sage Publications, 1980), 25 (Culture is "'the collective programming of the mind which distinguishes the members of one human group from another.' . . . Culture, in this sense, includes systems of values; and values are among the building blocks of culture.").
3. See Naomi Mezey, "Law as Culture," in *Cultural Analysis, Cultural Studies, and the Law: Moving beyond Legal Realism,* ed. Austin Sarat and Jonathan Simon (Durham, NC: Duke University Press, 2003), 42.

4. See Robert Post, "Law and Cultural Conflict," *Chicago-Kent Law Review* 78, no. 2 (2003): 487–494.

5. Michael McCloskey, foreword to *Ecotactics: The Sierra Club Handbook for Environment Activists*, ed. John G. Mitchell and Constance L. Stallings (New York: Pocket Books, 1970), 11.

6. Shabecoff, *Fierce Green Fire*, 287.

7. David P. Daniels et al., "Public Opinion on Environmental Policy in the United States," in *The Oxford Handbook of U.S. Environmental Policy*, ed. Sheldon Kamieniecki and Michael E. Kraft (Oxford: Oxford University Press, 2013), 461–467.

8. Riley E. Dunlap and Kent D. Van Liere, "The 'New Environmental Paradigm': A Proposed Measuring Instrument and Preliminary Results," *Journal of Environmental Education* 9, no. 4 (1978): 10–19. The authors conducted surveys from two samples of Washington state residents in the summer of 1976. One group was based on names drawn from telephone directories across the state, and the other was based on names drawn from the mailing list of a statewide environmental organization. For further elaboration of the NEP, see Lester W. Milbrath, "The World Is Relearning Its Story about How the World Works," in *Environmental Politics in the International Arena: Movements, Parties, Organizations, and Policy*, ed. Sheldon Kamieniecki (Albany: State University of New York Press, 1993), 24–29.

9. Riley E. Dunlap et al., "Measuring Endorsement of the New Ecological Paradigm: A Revised NEP Scale," *Journal of Social Issues* 56, no. 3 (2000): 432.

10. Willett Kempton, James S. Boster, and Jennifer A. Hartley, *Environmental Values in American Culture* (Cambridge, MA: MIT Press, 1995), 39–62, 87–95, 215–216. The authors used "semistructured" interviews and form surveys of randomly selected "laypeople," such as workers at sawmills and dry cleaners, and "specialists" whose work or interests relate to the environment, such as Sierra Club members. Kempton, Boster, and Hartley, *Environmental Values*, 2, 22.

11. Riley E. Dunlap and Aaron M. McCright, "Social Movement Identity: Validating a Measure of Identification with the Environmental Movement," *Social Science Quarterly* 89, no. 5 (2008): 1051. Critics of Kempton, Boster, and Hartley's earlier methodology and conclusion that environmentalism is a "consensus view" include Thomas Greider, "Claims-Making as Social Science: A Review of *Environmental Values in American Culture*," *Journal of Political Ecology* 2, no. 2 (1995), http://jpe.library.arizona.edu/volume_2/griedervol2.htm; Herve Varenne, review of *Environmental Values in American Culture*, by Willett Kempton, James S. Boster, and Jennifer A. Hartley, *American Ethnologist* 23, no. 4 (1995): 1062–1063; Jonathan Baron, "Book Review," review of *Environmental Values in American Culture*, by Willett Kempton, James S. Boster, and Jennifer A. Hartley, *Journal of Policy Analysis and Management* 15, no. 2 (1996): 292–295. For Kempton, Boster, and Hartley's response to Greider, their harshest critic, see Willett Kempton, "Response to 'Review of *Environmental Values in American Culture*,'" *Journal of Political Ecology* 2, no. 2 (1995), http://jpe.library.arizona.edu/volume_2/kemptonvol2.htm.

12. Riley E. Dunlap and Kent D. Van Liere, "Commitment to the Dominant Social Paradigm and Concern for Environmental Quality," *Social Science Quarterly*

65, no. 4 (1984): 1013, quoting Dennis Clark Pirages, "Introduction: A Social Design for Sustainable Growth," in *The Sustainable Society: Implications for Limited Growth,* ed. Dennis Clark Pirages (New York: Praeger, 1977), 6.

13. See William E. Kilbourne, Suzanne C. Beckmann, and Eva Thelen, "The Role of the Dominant Social Paradigm in Environmental Attitudes: A Multinational Examination," *Journal of Business Research* 55, no. 3 (2002): 194; Dunlap and Van Liere, "Commitment to the Dominant Social Paradigm," 1018; Milbrath, "World Is Relearning," 24.

14. Dunlap and Van Liere, "Commitment to the Dominant Social Paradigm," 1018–1021. For recent work on the DSP and the environment, see Kilbourne, Beckmann, and Thelen, "Role of the Dominant Social Paradigm," 193–204.

15. See Mary Douglas, *Natural Symbols: Explorations in Cosmology* (London: Routledge, 1996), 54–68; Mary Douglas and Aaron Wildavsky, *Risk and Culture: An Essay on the Selection of Technical and Environmental Dangers* (Berkeley: University of California Press, 1982).

16. Dan M. Kahan, "Cultural Cognition as a Conception of the Cultural Theory of Risk," in *Handbook of Risk Theory,* ed. Sabine Roeser (London: Springer Science+Business Media, 2012), 2: 725–760.

17. Kahan, "Cultural Cognition as a Conception," 727–728. See also Dan M. Kahan and Donald Braman, "Cultural Cognition and Public Policy," *Yale Law and Policy Review* 24, no. 1 (2006): 149–163.

18. Dan M. Kahan et al., "The Polarizing Impact of Science Literacy and Numeracy on Perceived Climate Change Risks," *Nature Climate Change* 2 (2012): 732.

19. Kahan et al., "Polarizing Impact," 732, 733.

20. Aaron M. McCright and Riley E. Dunlap, "The Politicization of Climate and Polarization in the American Public's Views of Global Warming," *Sociological Quarterly* 52, no. 2 (2011): 155–194.

21. Kahan and Braman, "Cultural Cognition and Public Policy," 158.

22. Jonathan Haidt, *The Righteous Mind: Why Good People Are Divided by Politics and Religion* (New York: Pantheon Books, 2012), 130–154. Matthew Feinberg and Robb Willer, "The Moral Roots of Environmental Attitudes," *Psychological Science* 24, no. 1 (2013): 56–62.

23. Feinberg and Willer, "Moral Roots," 56–62.

24. Shalom H. Schwartz and Galit Sagie, "Value Consensus and Importance: A Cross-National Study," *Journal of Cross-Cultural Psychology* 31, no. 4 (2000): 492; Shalom H. Schwartz and Maria Ros, "Values in the West: A Theoretical and Empirical Challenge to the Individualism-Collectivism Cultural Dimension," *World Psychology* 1, no. 2 (1995): 91; Schultz and Zelensky, "Values as Predictors," 262; Milbrath, "World Is Relearning," 36. Bill McKibben, *Deep Economy: The Wealth of Communities and the Durable Future* (New York: St. Martin's Griffin, 2007), 102.

25. René Dubos, *So Human an Animal* (New York: Charles Scribner's Sons, 1968), 27.

26. Paul B. Sears, "Ecology—a Subversive Subject," *Bioscience* 14, no. 7 (1964): 11.

27. David Lowenthal, introduction to *Man and Nature; or, Physical Geography as Modified by Human Action,* by George Perkins Marsh (Seattle: University of Washington Press, 2003), xxxii (originally published 1864); Robert D. Richardson

Jr., *Emerson: The Mind on Fire* (Berkeley: University of California Press, 1995), 141–142; John Muir, *My First Summer in the Sierra* (Boston: Houghton Mifflin Company, 1911), 157; Aldo Leopold, *A Sand County Almanac, with Essays on Conservation from Round River* (New York: Ballantine Books, 1966), 190, 246; Rachel Carson, *Silent Spring* (Boston: Houghton Mifflin, 1962), 189; John McPhee, *Encounters with the Archdruid* (New York: Farrar, Straus and Giroux, 1971), 79, 84.

28. George Perkins Marsh, *Man and Nature* (Seattle: University of Washington Press, 2003), 36 (originally published 1864).

29. Carson, *Silent Spring,* 1–2.

30. Cary Coglianese, "Social Movements, Law, and Society: The Institutionalization of the Environmental Movement," *University of Pennsylvania Law Review* 150, no. 1 (2001): 90, citing Richard N. L. Andrews, *Managing the Environment, Managing Ourselves: A History of American Environmental Policy* (New Haven, CT: Yale University Press, 1999), 137–148; Berton Rouché, "Fog," *The New Yorker,* September 30, 1950, 33.

31. Carson, *Silent Spring,* 16.

32. For example, Paul R. Ehrlich, *The Population Bomb* (New York: Ballantine Books, 1971) (originally published 1968) (population crisis); James Lovelock, *The Revenge of Gaia: Earth's Climate Crisis and the Fate of Humanity* (New York: Basic Books, 2006) (global climate crisis); Theo Colborn, Dianne Dumanoski, and John Peterson Myers, *Our Stolen Future* (New York: Dutton, 1996) (endocrine disruptors); Bill McKibben, *The End of Nature* (New York: Random House, 2006), 87 (climate change and other developments affecting the "basic integrity and equanimity of earth"); James Gustave Speth, *Red Sky at Morning: America and the Crisis of the Global Environment,* ed. Nota Bene (New Haven, CT: Yale University Press, 2005) (climate change); Edward O. Wilson, *The Future of Life* (New York: Vintage Books, 2002) (loss of biodiversity). See sources cited in Jonathan H. Adler and Andrew P. Morriss, "Introduction: The Virtues and Vices of Skeptical Environmentalism," in "Symposium on Bjorn Lomborg's *The Skeptical Environmentalist,*" symposium issue, *Case Western Reserve Law Review* 53 (2002): 249–262.

33. Gregg Easterbrook, *A Moment on the Earth: The Coming Age of Environmental Optimism* (New York: Penguin Books, 1995), 25, 83–85.

34. Bjorn Lomborg, *The Skeptical Environmentalist: Measuring the Real State of the World* (Cambridge: Cambridge University Press, 2001), xix (originally published in Danish in 1998). But see Michael Grubb, "Relying on Manna from Heaven?" review of *The Skeptical Environmentalist: Measuring the Real State of the World,* by Bjorn Lomborg, *Science,* November 9, 2001, 1285–1287; Stuart Pimm and Jeff Harvey, "No Need to Worry about the Future," review of *The Skeptical Environmentalist: Measuring the Real State of the World,* by Bjorn Lomborg, *Nature,* November 8, 2001, 149–150; John Rennie et al., "Misleading Math about the Earth," *Scientific American,* January 2002, 61–71; Douglas A. Kysar, "Some Realism about Environmental Skepticism: The Implications of Bjorn Lomborg's *The Skeptical Environmentalist* for Environmental Law and Policy," *Ecology Law Quarterly* 30, no. 2 (2003): 223; Peter H. Gleick,

"Is the Skeptic All Wet? *The Skeptical Environmentalist,*" *Environment: Science and Policy for Sustainable Development* 44, no. 6 (2002): 36–41; Speth, *Red Sky at Morning,* 113–115.

35. Jedediah Purdy, "The Politics of Nature: Climate Change, Environmental Law, and Democracy," *Yale Law Journal* 119, no. 6 (2010): 1177. Christina R. Foust and William O'Shannon Murphy, "Revealing and Reframing Apocalyptic Tragedy in Global Warming Discourse," *Environmental Communication* 3, no. 2 (2009): 152; Anthony Leiserowitz, "Communicating the Risks of Global Warming: American Risk Perception, Affective Images and Interpretive Communities," in *Creating a Climate for Change: Communicating Climate Change and Facilitating Social Change,* ed. Susanne C. Moser and Lisa Dilling (New York: Cambridge University Press, 2007), 44–63.

36. Daniel B. Botkin, *Discordant Harmonies: A New Ecology for the Twenty-First Century* (New York: Oxford University Press, 1990), 62, 190; Daniel B. Botkin, *The Moon in the Nautilus Shell: Discordant Harmonies Reconsidered* (Oxford: Oxford University Press, 2012), xvi–xvii.

37. Leopold, *Sand County Almanac,* 239–241; Shabecoff, *Fierce Green Fire,* xv.

38. See Andrew Brennan and Yeuk-Sze Lo, "Environmental Ethics," in *The Stanford Encyclopedia of Philosophy,* ed. Edward N. Zalta, Fall 2011 ed., accessed February 14, 2014, http://plato.stanford.edu/archives/fall2011/entries/ethics-environmental, quoting Arne Naess, "The Shallow and the Deep: The Long-Range Ecology Movement," *Inquiry* 16 (1973): 95–100.

39. Henry David Thoreau, *"Walden, or Life in the Woods" and "On the Duty of Civil Disobedience,"* Signet Classic ed. (New York: New American Library, 1962), 92, 97; Henry David Thoreau, "Walking," *Atlantic,* June 1862, 657, 660.

40. Leopold, *Sand County Almanac,* 240, 243.

41. Carson, *Silent Spring,* 1, 297; Dubos, *So Human an Animal,* 7; Ted Nordhaus and Michael Shellenberger, *Break Through: From the Death of Environmentalism to the Politics of Possibility* (Boston: Houghton Mifflin, 2007), 134.

42. McPhee, *Encounters with the Archdruid,* 166.

43. Citizens to Preserve Overton Park, Inc. v. Volpe, 401 U.S. 402 (1971); Robertson v. Methow Valley Citizens Council, Inc., 490 U.S. 332 (1989).

44. See Hofstede, *Culture's Consequences,* 209–278.

45. Garrett Hardin, "The Tragedy of the Commons," *Science,* December 13, 1968, 1243–1248.

46. Stewart L. Udall, *The Quiet Crisis* (New York: Holt, Rinehart and Winston, 1963), 66–68.

47. McKibben, *Deep Economy,* 2, 95–105.

48. Eric T. Freyfogle, "Property and Liberty," *Harvard Environmental Law Review* 34, no. 1 (2010): 78–84, 102. See Mark Sagoff, "On Markets for Risk," *Maryland Law Review* 41, no. 4 (1982): 761–762, 764.

49. Shabecoff, *Fierce Green Fire,* 227–230; Solid Waste Agency of Northern Cook County v. U.S. Army Corps of Engineers (SWANCC), 531 U.S. 159 (2001); Friends of the Earth, Inc. v. Laidlaw Environmental Services (TOC), Inc. (Laidlaw), 528 U.S. 167 (2000); Rapanos v. United States, 547 U.S. 715 (2006); Lucas v. South Carolina Coastal Council, 505 U.S. 1003 (1992).

50. Murray Bookchin, *Toward an Ecological Society* (Montreal: Black Rose Books, 1980), 75–83 (emphasis in original).

51. Robert D. Bullard, *Dumping in Dixie: Race, Class, and Environmental Quality,* 2nd ed. (Boulder, CO: Westview Press, 1994), 1–11, 14 (originally published 1990).

52. Sheldon Kamieniecki and Michael E. Kraft, "The Evolution of Research on U.S. Environmental Policy," in *The Oxford Handbook of U.S. Environmental Policy,* ed. Sheldon Kamieniecki and Michael E. Kraft (Oxford: Oxford University Press, 2013), 11–12; Robert C. Ellickson et al., *Land Use Controls: Cases and Materials,* 4th ed. (New York: Wolters Kluwer Law & Business, 2013), 843–845; Lyng v. Northwest Indian Cemetery Protective Association, 485 U.S. 439 (1988).

53. Leopold, *Sand County Almanac,* 261, 262. See Wilson, *Future of Life* (knowing, loving, and taking responsibility for the nonhuman world as the basis of a "conservation ethic").

54. See J. Baird Callicott, "Non-Anthropocentric Value Theory and Environmental Ethics," *American Philosophical Quarterly* 21, no. 4 (1984): 299–309; J. Baird Callicott, ed., *Companion to A Sand County Almanac: Interpretive & Critical Essays* (Madison: University of Wisconsin Press, 1987); Jedediah Purdy, "Our Place in the World: A New Relationship for Environmental Ethics and Law," *Duke Law Journal* 62, no. 4 (2013): 857 (offering a new interpretation of the land ethic to bridge the gap between theory and practice in environmental law and practice). William Boyd, Douglas A. Kysar, and Jeffrey J. Rachlinski, "Law, Environment, and the 'Nondismal' Social Sciences," *Annual Review of Law and Social Science* 8 (2012): 191–192.

55. Roderick Frazier Nash, *The Rights of Nature: A History of Environmental Ethics* (Madison: University of Wisconsin Press, 1989), 70–71; Leopold, *Sand County Almanac,* 239–240.

56. Christopher D. Stone, "Should Trees Have Standing? Toward Legal Rights for Natural Objects," *Southern California Law Review* 45, no. 2 (1972): 450–501, quoting Charles Darwin, *The Descent of Man, and Selection in Relation to Sex,* 2nd ed. (New York: A. L. Burt, 1874), 139–141; Sierra Club v. Morton, 450 U.S. 727, 741–742 (1972) (Douglas, J., dissenting); Christopher D. Stone, *Should Trees Have Standing? Law, Morality, and the Environment,* 3rd. ed. (Oxford: Oxford University Press, 2010).

57. Nash, *Rights of Nature,* 73; McKibben, *End of Nature,* 147.

58. Kempton, Boster, and Hartley, *Environmental Values,* 113.

59. Bryan G. Norton, "Environmental Ethics and Weak Anthropocentrism," in *Environmental Ethics,* ed. Andrew Light and Holmes Rolston III (Malden, MA: Blackwell, 2003), 163–174. See also Jill Ker Conway, Kenneth Keniston, and Leo Marx, ed., *Earth, Air, Fire, Water: Humanistic Studies of the Environment* (Amherst: University of Massachusetts Press, 1999), 10–11. Wilson, *Future of Life;* Christopher D. Stone, *Earth and Other Ethics: The Case for Moral Pluralism* (New York: Harper & Row, 1987).

60. Lynn White Jr., "The Historical Roots of Our Ecologic Crisis," *Science,* March 10, 1967, 1205, 1206.

61. Willis Jenkins, "After Lynn White: Religious Ethics and Environmental Problems," *Journal of Religious Ethics* 37, no. 2 (2009): 283–309; Pope John Paul

II, Apostolic Letter Inter Sanctus, 29 November 1979, in *Acta Apostolicae Sedis* (Vatican: Typis Polyglottis Vaticanis, 1979), 71: 1509; Pope John Paul II, "Peace with God the Creator, Peace with All Creation: World Peace Day Message," Vatican, January 1, 1990, http://www.vatican.va/holy_father/john_paul_ii/mes sages/peace/documents/hf_jp-ii_mes_19891208_xxiii-world-day-for-peace _en.html; Al Gore, *Earth in the Balance: Ecology and the Human Spirit* (Boston: Houghton Mifflin, 1992), 242–248, 262–263.

62. Thomas Berry, *The Dream of the Earth* (San Francisco: Sierra Club Books, 1988), 81, 184. For example, Annie L. Booth and Harvey M. Jacobs, "Ties That Bind: Native American Beliefs as a Foundation for Environmental Consciousness," *Environmental Ethics* 12, no. 1 (1990): 30n10 and sources cited therein.

63. Robert H. Nelson, "Environmental Religion: A Theological Critique," *Case Western Reserve Law Review* 55, no. 1 (2004): 51, quoting John Muir, Joseph Sax, and Theodore Roszak, among others; Roderick Frazier Nash, *American Environmentalism: Readings in Conservation History,* 3rd ed. (New York: McGraw-Hill, 1990), 97, excerpting from John Muir, *The Yosemite* (New York: Century, 1912), 262; Joseph L. Sax, *Mountains without Handrails: Reflections on the National Parks* (Ann Arbor: University of Michigan Press, 1980), 103–104; William Cronon, "The Trouble with Wilderness: A Response," *Environmental History* 1, no. 1 (1996): 47–55. See also foreword to Thomas R. Dunlap, *Faith in Nature: Environmentalism as Religious Quest* (Seattle: University of Washington Press, 2004), xiii–xiv; McPhee, *Encounters with the Archdruid*. But see Robert H. Nelson, "Rethinking Church and State: The Case of Environmental Religion," *Pace Environmental Law Review* 29, no. 1 (2011): 149–166; Nelson, "Environmental Religion," 62–66 (tracing the evolution of environmentalism as a secular religion not to the Druids, but to the Calvinists).

64. Nelson, "Environmental Religion," 55.

65. Kamieniecki and Kraft, "Evolution of Research," 29; J. H. Dales, *Pollution, Property and Prices: An Essay in Policy-Making and Economics* (Toronto: University of Toronto Press, 1968). William F. Baxter, *People or Penguins: The Case for Optimal Pollution* (New York: Columbia University Press, 1974), 5. See also Allen V. Kneese and Charles L. Schultze, *Pollution, Prices, and Public Policy* (Washington, DC: Brookings Institution, 1975); Robert Dorfman and Nancy Dorfman, ed., *Economics of the Environment: Selected Readings* (New York: Norton, 1972).

66. Baxter, *People or Penguins*, 7–8.

67. See, for example, Amy Sinden, Douglas A. Kysar, and David M. Driesen, "Cost-Benefit Analysis: New Foundations on Shifting Sand," review of *New Foundations of Cost-Benefit Analysis* by Matthew D. Adler and Eric A. Posner, *Regulation & Governance* 3, no. 1 (2003): 63–66; Frank Ackerman and Lisa Heinzerling, *Priceless: On Knowing the Price of Everything and the Value of Nothing* (New York: New Press, 2004); Douglas A. Kysar, *Regulating from Nowhere: Environmental Law and the Search for Objectivity* (New Haven, CT: Yale University Press, 2010), 101; Mark Sagoff, *The Economy of the Earth: Philosophy, Law, and the Environment* (Cambridge: Cambridge University Press, 1988), 92–95.

68. See, for example, Randall Lutter, John F. Morrall, and W. Kip Viscusi, "The Cost-Per-Life-Saved Cutoff for Safety-Enhancing Regulations," *Economic Inquiry* 37,

no. 4 (1999): 599; Cass R. Sunstein, *Risk and Reason: Safety, Law, and the
Environment* (New York: Cambridge University Press, 2002), 35; Matthew D.
Adler and Eric A. Posner, *New Foundations of Cost-Benefit Analysis* (Cam-
bridge, MA.: Harvard University Press, 2006), 1–23.

69. Cass R. Sunstein, *The Cost-Benefit State: The Future of Regulatory Protection*
(Chicago: American Bar Association, 2002); Robert H. Nelson, *The New Holy
Wars: Economic Religion vs. Environmental Religion in Contemporary
America* (University Park: Pennsylvania State University Press, 2010).

70. Kysar, *Regulating from Nowhere,* 64, quoting Sonja Boehnmer-Christiansen,
"The Precautionary Principle in Germany—Enabling Government," in *Interpreting the Precautionary Principle,* ed. Timothy O'Riorday and James Cameron
(London: Earthscan, 1994), 34, 38; Cass R. Sunstein, *Laws of Fear: Beyond
the Precautionary Principle* (New York: Cambridge University Press, 2005),
18–20; Cass R. Sunstein, "Beyond the Precautionary Principle," *University of
Pennsylvania Law Review* 151, no. 3 (2003): 1011–1020; U.N. General As-
sembly, Report of the United Nations Conference on Environment and Development (Rio Declaration on Environment and Development), A/CONF.151/26
Annex I, 1992, http://www.un.org/documents/ga/conf151/aconf15126–1annex1
.htm. See Science and Environmental Health Network, "Wingspread Conference on the Precautionary Principle," accessed August 5, 2013, http://www.sehn
.org/wing.html.

71. Sunstein, *Laws of Fear,* 26–27; Sunstein, "Beyond the Precautionary Principle,"
1020, 1039. See also John D. Graham, "Risk and Precaution" (remarks delivered at the Brookings–AEI Conference on "Risk, Science, and Public Policy:
Setting Social and Environmental Priorities," St. Regis Hotel, Washington, DC,
October 12, 2004), http://georgewbush-whitehouse.archives.gov/omb/inforeg
/speeches/101204_risk.html; Richard B. Stewart, "Environmental Regulatory
Decision Making under Uncertainty," in *An Introduction to the Law and Economics of Environmental Policy: Issues in Institutional Design,* vol. 20, *Re-
search in Law and Economics,* ed. Timothy Swanson (Amsterdam: Elsevier
JAI Press, 2002), 71–126; Kysar, *Regulating from Nowhere,* 64, quoting
Sonja Boehnmer-Christiansen, "The Precautionary Principle," 34, 38.

72. Mark Dowie, *Losing Ground: American Environmentalism at the Close of the
Twentieth Century* (Cambridge, MA: MIT Press, 1995), 205; Bullard, *Dumping
in Dixie;* Douglas Bevington, *The Rebirth of Environmentalism: Grassroots
Activism from the Spotted Owl to the Polar Bear* (Washington, DC: Island
Press, 2009), 23. See Nordhaus and Shellenberger, *Break Through.*

73. Philip Shabecoff, *Earth Rising: American Environmentalism in the 21st Century* (Washington, DC: Island Press, 2000), 186.

Chapter 2: Environmental Law, the Court, and Interpretation

1. Gerald N. Rosenberg, *The Hollow Hope: Can Courts Bring About Social
Change?* 2nd ed. (Chicago: University of Chicago Press, 2008), 271–273.

2. Edmund S. Muskie, "Foreword," *Cornell Law Review* 55, no. 5 (1970): 663.
See E. F. Roberts, "The Right to a Decent Environment; E=MC2: Environment

Equals Man Times Courts Redoubling Their Efforts," *Cornell Law Review* 55, no. 5 (1970): 690–701; Joseph L. Sax, *Defending the Environment: A Strategy for Citizen Action* (New York: Knopf, 1970), 158–163.

3. Douglas A. Kysar, *Regulating from Nowhere: Environmental Law and the Search for Objectivity* (New Haven, CT: Yale University Press, 2010), 229n1.

4. Barton H. Thomson Jr., "Constitutionalizing the Environment: The History and Future of Montana's Environmental Provisions," *Montana Law Review* 64, no. 1 (2003): 157, 158.

5. Kysar, *Regulating from Nowhere,* 229n3; Thomson, "Constitutionalizing the Environment," 158. But see Robinson Township, Washington County v. Commonwealth, 83 A.3d 901 (Penn. 2013) (overturning fracking law as violative of state's Environmental Rights Amendment).

6. U.S. Const. art. III; Lujan v. Defenders of Wildlife (Lujan II), 504 U.S. 555 (1992).

7. U.S. Const. amend. X; U.S. Const. art. I, § 8; U.S. Const. art. IV, § 3, cl. 2.

8. New York v. United States, 505 U.S. 144 (1992); Rapanos v. United States, 547 U.S. 715 (2006).

9. U.S. Const. amend. V; Pennsylvania Coal Company v. Mahon, 260 U.S. 393 (1922); Lucas v. South Carolina Coastal Council, 505 U.S. 1003 (1992).

10. Jedediah Purdy, "The Politics of Nature: Climate Change, Environmental Law, and Democracy," *Yale Law Journal* 119, no. 6 (2010): 1180–1189.

11. Richard J. Lazarus, *The Making of Environmental Law* (Chicago: University of Chicago Press, 2004), 67, 69–70.

12. Cary Coglianese, "Social Movements, Law, and Society: The Institutionalization of the Environmental Movement," *University of Pennsylvania Law Review* 150, no. 1 (2001): 98 (describing the environmental legislation of this period as "quasi-constitutional in scope").

13. Lazarus, *Making of Environmental Law,* 69–70.

14. Compare Jay D. Wexler, "The (Non)Uniqueness of Environmental Law," *George Washington Law Review* 74, no. 2 (2006): 315–316, with Jedediah Purdy, "American Natures: The Shape of Conflict in Environmental Law," *Harvard Environmental Law Review* 36, no. 1 (2012): 172.

15. 42 U.S.C. § 4344 (2012).

16. U.S. Environmental Protection Agency, "Planning, Budget, and Results," accessed January 20, 2014, http://www.epa.gov/planandbudget/budget; Office of Management and Budget, "2013 Report to Congress on the Benefits and Costs of Federal Regulations and Agency Compliance with the Unfunded Mandate Reform Act," (Washington, DC: Office of Management and Budget, 2014), 11, table 1–1.

17. Toxic Substances Control Act § 6(c)(1), 15 U.S.C. § 2605(c)(1) (2012); Federal Insecticide, Fungicide and Rodenticide Act § 2(bb), 7 U.S.C. § 136(bb) (2012).

18. See Exec. Order No. 12,291, 3 C.F.R. 127 (1981) (repealed 1993); Exec. Order No. 12,866, 3 C.F.R. 683 (1993), reprinted as amended in 5 U.S.C. 5 § 601 note (2012); Unfunded Mandates Reform Act, 2 U.S.C. § 658 et seq. (2012). Provisions of this act relating to CBA are codified at 2 U.S.C. 1531–1538.

19. Kasie Hunt, "Newt Gingrich Proposes Abolishing EPA," Politico, January 25, 2011, accessed August 14, 2013, http://www.politico.com/news/stories

/0111/48143.html; Stephen Lacey, "Bachmann Pledges to Have the EPA's 'Doors Locked and Lights Turned Off,'" Grist, August 9, 2011, accessed August 14, 2013, http://www.grist.org/politics/2011-08-08-michele-bachmann -pledges-epas-doors-locked-and-lights-turned-off; "Fox News–Google GOP Debate Transcript," FoxNews.com, September 22, 2011, accessed August 14, 2013, www.foxnews.com/politics/2011/09/22/fox-news-google-gop-2012-presi dential-debate/ (Herman Cain picking EPA as federal agency he would eliminate).

20. See Chapter 9. George S. Sessions, "Anthropocentrism and the Environmental Crisis," *Humboldt Journal of Social Relations* 2, no. 1 (1974): 80; Kysar, *Regulating from Nowhere,* 248.

21. 16 U.S.C. §§ 1531–1544, § 1531(b)-(c) (2012); Tennessee Valley Authority v. Hill, 437 U.S. 153, 184–185 (1978).

22. 33 U.S.C. § 1251(a) (2012); Purdy, "Politics of Nature," 1184–1185nn211–213 and sources cited therein.

23. Solid Waste Agency of Northern Cook County v. United States Army Corps of Engineers, 531 U.S. 159 (2001); Rapanos v. United States, 547 U.S. 715 (2006).

24. 42 U.S.C. § 7401(b) (2012); Whitman v. American Trucking Ass'ns, 531 U.S. 457 (2001).

25. U.S. Environmental Protection Agency, "Planning, Budget, and Results," 14; President Barack Obama, "Statement by the President on the Ozone National Ambient Air Quality Standards," September 2, 2011, accessed August 14, 2013, http://www.whitehouse.gov/the-press-office/2011/09/02/statement-president -ozone-national-ambient-air-quality-standards.

26. Clean Air Act, 42 U.S.C. § 7604 (2012) (CAA); Clean Water Act, 33 U.S.C. § 1365 (2012) (CWA); Endangered Species Act, 16 U.S.C. § 1540(g) (2012) (ESA).

27. Richard J. Lazarus, "Restoring What's Environmental about Environmental Law in the Supreme Court," *UCLA Law Review* 47, no. 3 (2000): 735–736; Daniel A. Farber, "Is the Supreme Court Irrelevant? Reflections on the Judicial Role in Environmental Law," *Minnesota Law Review* 81, no. 3 (1997): 568n101; Richard E. Levy and Robert L. Glicksman, "Judicial Activism and Restraint in the Supreme Court's Environmental Law Decisions," *Vanderbilt Law Review* 42, no. 2 (1989): 346, 405–408. See also Stephen M. Johnson, "The Roberts Court and the Environment," *Boston College Environmental Affairs Law Review* 37, no. 2 (2010): 317–364; Albert C. Lin, "Erosive Interpretation of Environmental Law in the Supreme Court's 2003–04 Term," *Houston Law Review* 42, no. 3 (2005): 565–635.

28. Naomi Mezey, "Law as Culture," in *Cultural Analysis, Cultural Studies and the Law: Moving Beyond Legal Realism,* ed. Austin Sarat and Jonathan Simon (Durham, NC: Duke University Press, 2003), 39, 51–59.

29. See Frederick Schauer, *Thinking Like a Lawyer* (Cambridge, MA: Harvard University Press, 2009), exploring whether and how lawyers think differently from others.

30. Pierre Bourdieu, "The Force of Law: Toward a Sociology of the Juridical Field," trans. Richard Terdiman, *Hastings Law Journal* 38, no. 5 (1987): 839.

31. Robert Post, "Introduction: The Relatively Autonomous Discourse of Law," in *Law and the Order of Culture,* ed. Robert Post (Berkeley: University of California Press, 1991), xiii, citing Bourdieu, "Force of Law," 839, 805–854.

32. Paul W. Kahn, *The Cultural Study of Law: Reconstructing Legal Scholarship* (Chicago: University of Chicago Press, 1999), 105.

33. James B. Beam Distilling Co. v. Georgia, 501 U.S. 529 (1991) (Scalia, J., concurring) (emphasis in original). Oliver Wendell Holmes, "The Path of the Law," *Harvard Law Review* 10, no. 8 (1897): 466. For example, Post, "Introduction: The Relatively Autonomous Discourse of Law," xiii. Robert Post, "Law and Cultural Conflict," *Chicago-Kent Law Review* 78, no. 2 (2003): 499. Lucas v. South Carolina Coastal Council, 505 U.S. 1003, 1028 (1992).

34. For example, James L. Gibson and Gregory A. Caldeira, "Has Legal Realism Damaged the Legitimacy of the U.S. Supreme Court?" *Law and Society Review* 45, no. 1 (2011): 195–196; Michael Gilbert, "Does Law Matter? Theory and Evidence from Single-Subject Adjudication," *Journal of Legal Studies* 40, no. 2 (2011): 333–365; William M. Landes and Richard A. Posner, "Rational Judicial Behavior: A Statistical Study," *Journal of Legal Analysis* 1, no. 2 (2009): 775–831; Jeffrey A. Segal and Harold J. Spaeth, *The Supreme Court and the Attitudinal Model Revisited* (New York: Cambridge University Press, 2002).

35. See Keith J. Bybee, *All Judges Are Political Except When They Are Not: Acceptable Hypocrisies and the Rule of Law* (Stanford, CA: Stanford Law Books, 2010), 122, citing public opinion poll by Syracuse University's Maxwell School.

36. See Gilbert, "Does Law Matter," 350–356.

37. Segal and Spaeth, *Supreme Court and the Attitudinal Model Revisited,* 86.

38. Post, "Introduction: The Relatively Autonomous Discourse of Law."

39. Gregory Mitchell and Philip E. Tetlock, "Cognitive Style and Judging," in *The Psychology of Judicial Decision-Making,* ed. David Klein and Gregory Mitchell (New York: Oxford University Press, 2010), 279–284; Shai Danziger, Jonathan Levav, and Liora Avnaim-Pesso, "Extraneous Factors in Judicial Decisions," *Proceedings of the National Academy of Sciences of the United States of America* 108, no. 17 (2011): 6889–6892.

40. Justin Driver, "The Consensus Constitution," *Texas Law Review* 89, no. 4 (2011): 797–798, citing Texas v. Johnson, 491 U.S. 397 (1989), and Lee v. Weisman, 505 U.S. 577 (1992).

41. Lani Guinier, "Beyond Legislatures: Social Movements, Social Change, and the Possibilities of Demosprudence," *Boston University Law Review* 89, no. 2 (2009): 553–554.

42. Robert A. Dahl, "Decision-Making in a Democracy: The Supreme Court as a National Policy-Maker," *Journal of Public Law* 6, no. 2 (1957): 281–285. See also Barry Friedman, *The Will of the People* (New York: Farrar, Straus and Giroux, 2009), 369–372; David S. Law, "A Theory of Judicial Power and Judicial Review," *Georgetown Law Journal* 97, no. 3 (2009): 729–730; Robert G. McCloskey, *The American Supreme Court,* 3rd ed. (Chicago: University of Chicago Press, 2000), 231 (Court has "learned to be a political institution"). But see Daryl J. Levinson, "Parchment and Politics: The Positive Puzzle of Constitutional Commitment," *Harvard Law Review* 124, no. 3 (2011): 734–737 (agreeing generally with Dahl that the Court "typically operates not against

but as 'part of the dominant national alliance' " but noting instances in which the Court enjoyed continued public support even when it produced unpopular decisions). Sandra Day O'Connor, "Public Trust as a Dimension of Equal Justice: Some Suggestions to Increase Public Trust," *Court Review* 36, no. 3 (Fall 1999): 13. Mark Tushnet, *The New Constitutional Order* (Princeton, NJ: Princeton University Press, 2003), 106.

43. Dahl, "Decision-Making in a Democracy," 284, 293; Rosenberg, *Hollow Hope*, 422. Compare Patrick J. Egan and Jack Citrin, "Opinion Leadership, Backlash, and Delegitimation: Supreme Court Rulings and Public Opinion," (working paper, 2009), 1–42, http://papers.ssrn.com/sol3/papers.cfm?abstract _id=1443631, with James W. Stoutenborough, Donald P. Haider-Markel, and Mahalley D. Allen, "Reassessing the Impact of Supreme Court Decisions on Public Opinion: Gay Civil Rights Cases," *Political Research Quarterly* 59, no. 3 (2006): 419–433. Michael J. Klarman, "Brown and Lawrence (and Goodridge)," *Michigan Law Review* 104, no. 3 (2005): 445n102.

44. Michael J. Klarman, *From Jim Crow to Civil Rights: The Supreme Court and the Struggle for Racial Equality* (New York: Oxford University Press, 2004), 443. Michael J. Klarman, *From the Closet to the Altar: Courts, Backlash, and the Struggle for Same-Sex Marriage* (New York: Oxford University Press, 2013), 165–172.

45. Rosenberg, *Hollow Hope*, 271–292. J. B. Ruhl, "The Endangered Species Act's Fall from Grace in the Supreme Court," *Harvard Environmental Law Review* 36, no. 2 (2012): 491–492, citing Richard J. Lazarus, "Thirty Years of Environmental Protection Law in the Supreme Court," *Pace Environmental Law Review* 17, no. 1 (1999): 1–17; Kenneth A. Manaster, "Justice Stevens, Judicial Power, and the Varieties of Environmental Litigation," *Fordham Law Review* 74, no. 4 (2006): 1965.

46. Driver, "Consensus Constitution," 775n124, citing David J. Garrow, "Hopelessly Hollow History: Revisionist Devaluating of *Brown v. Board of Education*," *Virginia Law Review* 80, no. 1 (1994): 151–160, 776–777, 786n184.

47. See Clifford Geertz, *The Interpretation of Cultures* (New York: Basic Books, 1973), 311.

48. David E. Pozen, "Judicial Elections as Popular Constitutionalism," *Columbia Law Review* 110, no. 8 (2010): 2070.

49. William D. Popkin, *Evolution of the Judicial Opinion: Institutional and Individual Styles* (New York: New York University Press, 2007), 114–122.

50. Guinier, "Beyond Legislatures," 549–550.

51. Robert Post, "Law Professors and Political Scientists: Observations on the Law/ Politics Distinction in the Guinier/Rosenberg Debate," *Boston University Law Review* 89, no. 2 (2009): 584.

52. Kahn, *Cultural Study of Law,* 136.

53. Geertz, *Interpretation of Cultures,* 30.

54. Robert C. Post, "Foreword: Fashioning the Legal Constitution: Culture, Courts, and Law," *Harvard Law Review* 117, no. 1 (2003): 111.

55. See Jane Baron, "The Rhetoric of Law and Literature: A Skeptical View," *Cardozo Law Review* 26, no. 6 (2005): 2274.

56. Although law clerks hired by the justices from among the elite of recent law school graduates do much of the drafting of opinions—more for some justices than for others—the justice who signs the opinions adopts the words as his or her own and therefore has functional authorship.

57. Peter Brooks, "Law and Humanities: Two Attempts" (draft paper on file with author).

58. See Baron, "Rhetoric of Law and Literature," 2276: "Nor is the appreciation that our rhetorical choices have moral dimensions entirely new" (citing literary critic William Wimsatt).

59. The group of 150 includes the 103 environmental cases identified by Lazarus, "Restoring What's Environmental," 773, app. A, current through 1999, as well as an additional forty-seven environmental cases decided through June 2014 (list on file with author). James Salzman and J. B. Ruhl, "Who's Number One," *Environmental Forum* 26, no. 6 (2009): 36–40 (results of survey to establish "the most significant environmental cases").

60. Michael Allen Wolf has made a significant contribution with *The Supreme Court and the Environment: The Reluctant Protector* (Los Angeles: Sage, 2012), in which he weaves an account of American environmental law that integrates the Court's environmental decisions with actions by other public and private entities.

Chapter 3: Environmental Urgency and Law

1. United States v. Standard Oil Company, 384 U.S. 224, 225–226 (1966); Citizens to Preserve Overton Park, Inc. v. Volpe, 401 U.S. 402, 412–413, 404 (1971); United States v. Students Challenging Regulatory Agency Procedures (S.C.R.A.P.), 412 U.S. 669 (1973).

2. Federal Highway Administration, "History of the Interstate Highway System," accessed September 13, 2013, http://www.fhwa.dot.gov/interstate/history .htm. Judy Davis, "Consequences of the Development of the Interstate Highway System," *Transit Cooperative Research Program, Research Results Digest* 21 (August 1997): 7.

3. Department of Transportation Act of 1966, § 4(f), Public Law 89–670, 80 Stat. 931, 934 (1966). Federal-Aid Highway Act of 1968, Public Law 90–495, 82 Stat. 815, 823–824 (1968).

4. "Overton Park," The Cultural Landscape Foundation, October 16, 2009, http://tclf.org/landslides/overton-park. *Citizens to Preserve Overton Park, Inc.*, 401 U.S. at 406 (1971). See J. P. Young, ed., *Standard History of Memphis, Tennessee* (Knoxville, TN: H. W. Crew, 1912), 19, 331.

5. Peter L. Strauss, "*Citizens to Preserve Overton Park v. Volpe*—of Politics and Law, Young Lawyers and the Highway Goliath," in *Administrative Law Stories*, ed. Peter L. Strauss (New York: Foundation Press, 2006), 262–263, 284–285, 291–298. For a helpful chronology of the events of the Overton Park story, see Strauss, "*Citizens to Preserve Overton Park*," 264–268.

6. *Citizens to Preserve Overton Park, Inc.*, 401 U.S. at 408.

7. Strauss, "*Citizens to Preserve Overton Park*," 284–285. "Citizens to Preserve Overton Park," accessed September 6, 2013, www.overtonparkforever.org.

8. Jerry L. Mashaw, Richard A. Merrill, and Peter M. Shane, *Administrative Law: The American Public Law System Cases and Materials,* 6th ed. (St. Paul, MN: Thomson/West, 2009), 803.

9. Citizens to Preserve Overton Park, Inc. v. Volpe, 309 F.Supp. 1189, 1195 (W.D. Tenn. 1970); Citizens to Preserve Overton Park, Inc. v. Volpe, 432 F.2d 1307, 1314–1315 (6th Cir. 1970).

10. Transcript of Oral Argument at 4, 24–28, Citizens to Preserve Overton Park, Inc. v. Volpe, 401 U.S. 402 (1971) (No. 1066) (Mr. Vardaman for CPOP and other petitioners, Solicitor General Griswold for respondents). *Citizens to Preserve Overton Park, Inc,* 401 U.S. at 409.

11. Justice Blackmun, Memorandum (1971), Box 130, Folder 70–1066, Harry A. Blackmun Papers, 1913–2001, Library of Congress, Washington, DC.

12. *Citizens to Preserve Overton Park, Inc.,* 401 U.S. at 404.

13. Ibid. at 413.

14. Webster's Third New International Dictionary, s.v. "haven." Henry David Thoreau, "From 'Huckleberries,'" in *American Earth: Environmental Writing since Thoreau,* ed. Bill McKibben (New York: Library Classics of America, 2008), 35.

15. *Citizens to Preserve Overton Park, Inc.,* 401 U.S. at 415–416.

16. Ibid. at 421, 422 (Black, J., separate opinion) (agreeing with the judgment of the Court).

17. Strauss, "*Citizens to Preserve Overton Park,*" 260–261; Peter L. Strauss, "Revisiting *Overton Park*: Political and Judicial Controls over Administrative Actions Affecting the Community," *UCLA Law Review* 39, no. 5 (1992): 1251–1329; Peter L. Strauss, "On Capturing the Possible Significance of Institutional Design and Ethos," special issue, *Administrative Law Review* 61 (2009): 271–274.

18. Massachusetts v. EPA, 549 U.S. 497 (2007). Robert V. Percival, "Massachusetts v. EPA: Escaping the Common Law's Growing Shadow," *Supreme Court Review,* no. 1 (2007): 160; Richard J. Lazarus, "A Breathtaking Result for Greens," *Environmental Forum* 24, no. 3 (2007): 12; Jody Freeman and Adrian Vermeule, "Massachusetts v. EPA: From Politics to Expertise," *Supreme Court Review,* no. 1 (2007): 108. Ronald A. Cass, "Massachusetts v. EPA: The Inconvenient Truth about Precedent," *Virginia Law Review in Brief* 93 (May 21, 2007): 75, http://www.virginialawreview.org/volumes/content /massachusetts-v-epa-inconvenient-truth-about-precedent.

19. Intergovernmental Panel on Climate Change home page, accessed September 6, 2013, http://www.ipcc.ch/organization/organization.shtml#.Uitokn_lfms. Intergovernmental Panel on Climate Change, "Summary for Policymakers," in *Climate Change 2007: The Physical Science Basis* (New York: Cambridge University Press, 2007), 5, 10. Freeman and Vermeule, "Massachusetts v. EPA," 61n32.

20. Freeman and Vermeule, "Massachusetts v. EPA," 60. "An Inconvenient Truth (2006)," *New York Times,* accessed August 5, 2014, http://www.nytimes.com /movies/movie/342290/An-Inconvenient-Truth/awards; "A Global Warning," An Inconvenient Truth: The Official Website of the Award-Winning Film, ac-

cessed August 5, 2014, http://www.takepart.com/an-inconvenient-truth/film. "Gallup Poll, Environmental Worries, March 11–14, 2007," in *The Gallup Poll: Public Opinion 2007* (Lanham, MD: Rowman & Littlefield, 2007), 120 (61 percent responding that increases in Earth's temperature over the last century are more attributable to the effects of pollution from human activities than to natural changes); New York Times/CBS News Poll, April 20–24, 2007, accessed October 28, 2014, http://www.cbsnews.com/news/poll-global -warming-worries-grow/ (52 percent responding that global warming is a very serious problem that should be one of the highest priorities for government officials).

21. I was EPA General Counsel at the time.

22. Clean Air Act § 302(g), Public Law 88–206, 77 Stat. 392 (1963), codified at 42 U.S.C. § 7602(g).

23. Jamie Gibbs Pleune, "Is Scalian Standing the Latest Sighting of the Lochner-ess Monster?: Using Global Warming to Explore the Myth of the Corporate Person," *Environmental Law* 38, no. 1 (2008): 295–296.

24. 42 U.S.C. § 7521(a)(1) (2012).

25. Control of Emissions from New Highway Vehicles and Engines, 68 Federal Register 52,929–52,931 (September 8, 2003).

26. Brief of Amici Curiae Climate Scientists David Battisti et al., in support of petitioners at 9–10, Massachusetts v. EPA, 549 U.S. 497 (2007) (No. 05–1120). Transcript of Oral Argument at 30, Massachusetts v. EPA.

27. Massachusetts v. EPA, 415 F.3d 50 (D.C. Cir. 2005).

28. Lisa Heinzerling, "Climate Change in the Supreme Court," *Environmental Law* 38, no. 1 (2008): 6–8. Massachusetts v. EPA, 549 U.S. at 506.

29. Transcript of Oral Argument at 3–5, Massachusetts v. EPA.

30. Dan M. Kahan et al., "The Tragedy of the Risk-Perception Commons: Culture Conflict, Rationality Conflict, and Climate Change" (Working Paper No. 89, Cultural Cognition Project, Yale University Law School, 2011), 15.

31. Dan M. Kahan and Donald Braman, "Cultural Cognition and Public Policy," *Yale Law and Policy Review* 24, no. 1 (2006): 168.

32. Massachusetts v. EPA, 549 U.S. at 504–505.

33. National Research Council, *Climate Change Science: An Analysis of Some Key Questions* (Washington, DC: National Academy Press, 2001), quoted at Massachusetts v. EPA, 549 U.S. at 511.

34. Transcript of Oral Argument at 26, Massachusetts v. EPA; Brief for the Federal Respondent at 37, Massachusetts v. EPA.

35. Massachusetts v. EPA, 549 U.S. at 529, 532.

36. Ibid. at 533–534.

37. Mashaw, Merrill, and Shane, *Administrative Law,* 964.

38. Cass, "Massachusetts v. EPA," 81. Freeman and Vermeule, "Massachusetts v. EPA," 78–87. See also Jonathan Adler, "Massachusetts v. EPA Heats Up Climate Policy No Less than Administrative Law: A Comment on Professors Watts and Wildermuth," *Northwestern University Law Review Colloquy* 102 (2007): 37, http://www.law.northwestern.edu/lawreview/Colloquy/2007/20 /LRColl2007n20Adler.pdf (arguing that the Court's opinion clarified the test

for review of denial of petitions for rulemaking "but it did not depart from established precedent").

39. For example, EPA used an argument based on Department of Transportation mileage standards "to shirk its environmental responsibilities," Massachusetts v. EPA, 549 U.S. at 532; engaged in "reasoning divorced from the statutory text," 549 U.S. at 532; read "judgment" in Section 202(a)(1) as a "roving license to ignore the statutory text," 549 U.S. at 532; offered "no reasoned explanation for its refusal to decide," 549 U.S. at 534.

40. Freeman and Vermeule, "Massachusetts v. EPA," 108.

41. Kathryn A. Watts, "From Chevron to Massachusetts; Justice Stevens's Approach to Securing the Public Interest," *UC Davis Law Review* 43, no. 3 (2010): 1026, 1059.

42. See, for example, Antonin Scalia, "Assorted Canards of Contemporary Legal Analysis," *Case Western Reserve Law Review* 40, no. 3 (1990): 586.

43. Massachusetts v. EPA, 549 U.S. at 549–560.

44. Jonathan Haidt, *The Righteous Mind: Why Good People Are Divided by Politics and Religion* (New York: Pantheon Books, 2012), 131–134, 146–153.

45. Massachusetts v. EPA, 549 U.S. at 550–551.

46. Ibid. at 560.

47. American Electric Power Company, Inc. v. Connecticut, 131 S.Ct. 2527, 2530 (2011).

48. Ibid. at 2533n2.

49. Utility Air Regulatory Group v. EPA, 134 S.Ct. 2427 (June 23, 2014).

50. Ibid. at 2445.

51. Ibid. at 2444.

52. Ibid. at 2452–2454 (Breyer, J., concurring in part and dissenting in part).

53. Endangerment and Cause or Contribute Findings for Greenhouse Gases under Section 202(a) of the Clean Air Act, 74 Federal Register 66,496 (December 15, 2009). 75 Federal Register 25,524 (May 7, 2010). Prevention of Significant Deterioration and Title V Greenhouse Gas Tailoring Rule, 75 Federal Register 31,514 (June 3, 2010). Barack Obama, "Remarks by the President on Climate Change" (remarks, Georgetown University, Washington, DC, June 25, 2013), http://www.whitehouse.gov/the-press-office/2013/06/25/remarks-president -climate-change.

54. New York v. United States, 505 U.S. 144 (1992).

55. Compare Mark Tushnet, *The New Constitutional Order* (Princeton, NJ: Princeton University Press, 2003), with James F. Simon, *The Center Holds: The Power Struggle inside the Rehnquist Court* (New York: Simon and Schuster, 1995). See, for example, Erwin Chermerinsky, "Speech," *Williamette Law Review* 41, no. 5 (2005): 827–828 (speech on Rehnquist Court and federalism); Kathleen Sullivan and John Yoo, "Holding Court: The Legacy of the Rehnquist Court," interview by Peter Robinson, *Uncommon Knowledge with Peter Robinson,* Hoover Institution, May 26, 2005, http://www.hoover.org/research/ holding-court-legacy-rehnquist-court.

56. See Fry v. United States, 421 U.S. 542, 549 (1975) (Rehnquist, J., dissenting). Erin Ryan, "Federalism at the Cathedral: Property Rules, Liability Rules, and

Inalienability Rules in Tenth Amendment Infrastructure," *University of Colorado Law Review* 81, no. 1 (2010): 39. New York v. United States, 505 U.S. at 159.

57. *New York,* 505 U.S. at 149–150, 182. United States Nuclear Regulatory Commission, "Low-Level Waste," March 25, 2013, http://www.nrc.gov/waste/low-level-waste.html.

58. *New York,* 505 U.S. at 150. See Richard C. Kearney, "Low-Level Radioactive Waste Management: Environmental Policy, Federalism, and New York," *Publius* 57, no. 3 (1993): 60–61.

59. Low-Level Radioactive Waste Policy Act Amendments of 1985, Public Law 99–240, 99 Stat. 1842 (1985) (codified in various sections of 42 U.S.C.). New York v. United States, 505 U.S. at 150–154, quoting 42 U.S.C. § 2021e(d)(2) (C).

60. New York v. United States, 505 U.S. 154, 181. U.S. General Accounting Office, *Nuclear Waste: Slow Progress Developing Low-Level Radioactive Waste Disposal Facilities,* GAO/RCED-92-61 (Washington, DC: Government Accounting Office, 1992), available at http://www.gao.gov/products/RCED-92-61. State of New York v. United States, 757 F. Supp. 10 (N.D.N.Y. 1990); 942 F.2d 114 (2nd Cir. 1991); Transcript of Oral Argument at 7, New York v. United States, 505 U.S. 144 (1992) (Nos. 91–543, 91–558, and 90–563).

61. New York v. United States, 505 U.S. at 156–157. The tautology language was suggested by Justice Souter in comments on a draft of Justice O'Connor's opinion. Robert V. Percival, "Environmental Law in the Supreme Court: Highlights from the Blackmun Papers," *Environmental Law Reporter* 35 (2005): 10,637, 10,650. National League of Cities v. Usery, 426 U.S. 833, 852 (1976); Garcia v. San Antonio Metropolitan Transit Authority, 469 U.S. 528 (1985). See Mark Tushnet, "Why the Supreme Court Overruled National League of Cities," *Vanderbilt Law Review* 47, no. 5 (1994): 1623–1655. Garcia, 469 U.S. at 579 (Rehnquist, J., dissenting), 580 (O'Connor, J., dissenting).

62. Robert V. Percival, "Highlights from the Blackmun Papers," 10,637, 10,650.

63. New York v. United States, 505 U.S. at 161–176.

64. Ibid. at 169.

65. Herman Schwartz, "The Supreme Court's Federalism: Fig Leaf for Conservatives," in "The Supreme Court's Federalism: Real or Imagined," ed. Frank Goodman, *Annals of the American Academy of Political and Social Science* 574 (March 2001): 124. See also Erwin Chermerinsky, "The Values of Federalism," *Florida Law Review* 47, no. 4 (1995): 516–517 (accountability rationale in NY v. United States is "troubling aspect"; "factual assumptions behind Justice O'Connor's position are highly questionable").

66. New York v. United States, 505 U.S. at 181–182, quoting Coleman v. Thompson, 501 U.S. 722, 759 (1991) (Blackmun, J., dissenting). For a foreshadowing of this theme by Justice O'Connor in a statutory case, see Gregory v. Ashcroft, 501 U.S. 452, 458–459 (1991) (extolling the "federalist system [as] a check on abuses of government power" and locating "the promise of liberty" in the constitutional balance between federal and state power).

67. Schwartz, "Supreme Court's Federalism," 124.

68. New York v. United States, 505 U.S. at 149, 187.
69. Ibid. at 189–190, 199, 206 (White, J., dissenting).
70. Ibid. at 190, 193, 210 (White, J., dissenting).
71. Tushnet, *New Constitutional Order,* 44–45.
72. National Federation of Independent Business v. Sebelius, 123 S.Ct. 2566, 2578 (2012), opinion of Roberts, C. J., part IV, 2602, citing New York v. United States in arguing that individual liberty would suffer if state power gave way to central government, opinion of Scalia, Kennedy, Thomas, and Alito, JJ., dissenting, part IV.
73. For example, Babbitt v. Sweet Home Chapter of Communities for a Great Oregon, 515 U.S. 687 (1995), 708–714 (O'Connor, J., concurring).

Chapter 4: Law for the Environmental Other

1. See Christopher D. Stone, *Should Trees Have Standing? Law, Morality, and the Environment,* 3rd ed. (Oxford: Oxford University Press, 2010), 8–17 (includes original article as chapter 1).
2. Sierra Club v. Morton, 405 U.S. 727 (1972); Tom Turner, *Wild by Law: The Sierra Club Legal Defense Fund and the Places It Has Saved* (San Francisco: Sierra Club Books, 1990), 3.
3. Turner, *Wild by Law,* 5. Transcript of Oral Argument at 23, Sierra Club v. Morton, 405 U.S. 727 (1972) (No. 70–34). 405 U.S. at 728.
4. Tom Turner, *Wild by Law,* 5, 9, 13, 16; 405 U.S. at 729.
5. Susan R. Schrepfer, "Perspectives on Conservation: Sierra Club Strategies in Mineral King," *Journal of Forest History* 20, no. 4 (1976): 177. Philip Shabecoff, *A Fierce Green Fire: The American Environmental Movement,* rev. ed. (Washington, DC: Island Press, 2003), 65–66. John L. Harper, *Mineral King: Public Concern with Government Policy* (Areata, CA: Pacifica, 1982), 161. "Earth Justice," accessed October 15, 2013, http://earthjustice.org/about.
6. "Walt Disney Receives Audubon Medal," *Audubon Magazine* 58 (1956): 25. William O. Douglas, *Go East, Young Man: The Early Years; The Autobiography of William O. Douglas* (New York: Random House, 1974), 206–207, 207, quoting Michael Frome.
7. 5 U.S.C. § 702 (2012); Sierra Club v. Morton, 405 U.S. at 732–733. Sierra Club v. Morton, 405 U.S. at 735n8 (quoting paragraph 3 of Sierra Club's complaint in the district court); Sierra Club v. Hickel, No. 51464, 1 Environmental Law Reporter 20 (N.D. Cal. 1969); Sierra Club v. Hickel, 433 F.2d 24 (9th Cir. 1970).
8. Association of Data Processing Service Organizations, Inc. v. Camp, 397 U.S. 150 at 154 (quoting lower court opinions) (1970); Barlow v. Collins, 397 U.S. 159 (1970). Sierra Club v. Morton, 405 U.S. at 734.
9. Reply Brief for the Petitioner at 1–2, Sierra Club v. Morton; Sierra Club v. Morton, 405 U.S. at 735–736 n. 8; Transcript of Oral Argument at 12–15, Sierra Club v. Morton, 405 U.S. at 727 (1972) (No. 70-34).
10. Michael McCloskey, "Sierra Club Executive Director: The Evolving Club and the Environmental Movement, 1961–1981," interview by Susan R. Schrepfer, 1981, *Sierra Club History Series* (Berkeley, CA: Bancroft Library University of California, 1983), 171–172.

11. Stone, *Should Trees Have Standing?*, xiv. Sierra Club v. Morton, 450 U.S. 727, 741–742 (1972) (Douglas, J., dissenting).

12. Del Dickson, ed., *The Supreme Court in Conference, 1940–1985: The Private Discussions Behind Nearly 300 Supreme Court Decisions* (New York: Oxford University Press, 2001), 133–134. Robert V. Percival, "Environmental Law in the Supreme Court: Highlights from the Blackmun Papers," *Environmental Law Reporter* 35, no. 10 (2005): 10,637.

13. *Sierra Club,* 405 U.S. at 734–735, 740–741.

14. See ibid. at 742–743.

15. Melvin L. Urofsky, introduction to *The Douglas Letters: Selections from the Private Papers of William O. Douglas,* ed. Melvin L. Urofsky (Bethesda, MD: Adler & Adler, 1987), xviii.

16. William O. Douglas, *A Wilderness Bill of Rights* (Boston: Little Brown, 1965), 26–27, 37, 150–151; Douglas, *Go East, Young Man,* 206.

17. Sierra Club v. Morton, 405 U.S. 727, 741–742, 752, quoting from Leopold, *A Sand County Almanac,* 204: "The land ethic simply enlarges the boundaries of the community to include soils, waters, plants, and animals, or collectively: the land" (1972).

18. Ibid. at 741, 750, 751, 752; Douglas, *Wilderness Bill of Rights,* 37.

19. Peter Manus, "Wild Bill Douglas's Last Stand: A Retrospective on the First Supreme Court Environmentalist," *Temple Law Review* 72, no. 1 (1999): 142 (emphasis in original).

20. *Sierra Club,* 405 U.S. at 743.

21. Ibid. at 743–745, 752; Manus, "Wild Bill," 150; George T. Frampton, Memorandum on Sierra Club (Mar. 30, 1972), Box 137, Folder 7, Harry A. Blackmun Papers, 1913–2001, Library of Congress.

22. Manus, "Wild Bill," 183, 187.

23. Stone, *Should Trees Have Standing?*, 159–164. See also Manus, "Wild Bill," 186–194. Palila v. Hawaii Department of Land and Natural Resources, 852 F.2d 1106, 1106–1107 (9th Cir. 1988), cert. denied, 429 U.S. 839 (1976).

24. Sierra Club v. Morton, 405 U.S. 727, 758 (1972) (Blackmun, J., dissenting). Bob Woodward and Scott Armstrong, *The Brethren: Inside the Supreme Court* (New York: Simon & Schuster, 1979), 164.

25. *Sierra Club,* 405 U.S. at 755–756; Justice Blackmun, Letter Scot Powe (April 28, 1972), Box 137, Folder 7, Blackmun Papers; Woodward and Armstrong, *The Brethren,* 164; Peter Manus, "The Blackbird Whistling—The Silence Just After: Evaluating the Environmental Legacy of Justice Blackmun," *Iowa Law Review* 85, no. 2 (2000): 429–515.

26. Stone, *Should Trees Have Standing?*, 165–168.

27. 16 U.S.C. § 1536(a)(2) (2012); 16 U.S.C. § 1531(a)(3), (a)(5) (2012).

28. Daniel A. Farber, "A Tale of Two Cases," *Virginia Environmental Law Journal* 20, no. 1 (2001): 34. 437 U.S. 153, 156–158 (1978).

29. Tennessee Valley Authority Act, Public Law No. 73–17, §§ 22–23, 48 Stat. 58, 69 (1933). Zygmunt J. B. Plater, *The Snail Darter and the Dam: How Pork-Barrel Politics Endangered a Little Fish and Killed a River* (New Haven, CT: Yale University Press, 2013), 15–17; Holly Doremus, "The Story of TVA v. Hill: A Narrow Escape for a Broad New Law," in *Environmental Law Stories,* ed.

Richard J. Lazarus and Oliver A. Houck (New York: Foundation Press, 2005), 111. 437 U.S. at 156.

30. Plater, *Snail Darter and the Dam*, 6–7, 22–23, 46; TVA v. Hill, 437 U.S. at 157.

31. Endangered Species Act of 1973, Public Law 93–205, 87 Statutes at Large 884 (1973) (codified at 16 U.S.C. §§ 1531–1544). See 437 U.S. at 158–159. See also Environmental Defense Fund v. TVA, 371 F. Supp. 1004 (E. D. Tenn. 1973) (dissolving preliminary injunction), *aff'd* 492 F. 2d 466 (6th Cir. 1974).

32. Doremus, "Story of TVA v. Hill," 120–123; Zygmunt J. B. Plater, "In the Wake of the Snail Darter: An Environmental Law Paradigm and Its Consequences," *University of Michigan Journal of Law Reform* 19, no. 4 (1986): 811; Plater, *Snail Darter and the Dam*, 33–36, 56–61; 40 Federal Register 47,505–47,506 (Oct. 8, 1975) (listing); 41 Federal Register 13,926 (Apr. 1, 1976) (critical habitat). The snail darter is still listed at 50 C.F.R. § 17.11(h) (2013).

33. Hill v. TVA, 419 F. Supp. 753, 757, 759–760 (E. D. Tenn. 1976); Hill v. TVA, 549 F.2d 1064, 1074–1075 (6th Cir. 1977).

34. Percival, "Highlights from the Blackmun Papers," 10,637, 10,642; Justice Stevens, Dissenting opinion (2nd draft), TVA v. Hill (Oct. 27, 1977), Box 268, Folder 9, Blackmun Papers; Doremus, "Story of TVA v. Hill," 126–128.

35. Chief Justice Burger, Note to Justice Powell (Oct. 25, 1977), Box 268, Folder 8, Blackmun Papers.

36. The government's brief to the Court, while presenting the arguments for TVA in the body of the brief, had included contrary arguments on behalf of the Department of the Interior in an appendix. Brief for Petitioner, TVA v. Hill, 437 U.S. 153 (1978) (No. 76–1701). Bell's argument to the Court, however, only presented TVA's side. Transcript of Oral Argument at 5–6 (questions from Justice Stevens), 20–21 (comments of Justice Marshall), TVA v. Hill (attribution of justices' questions from copy of transcript available at Boston College Law School, Snail Darter Documents, http://lawdigitalcommons.bc.edu/darter_materials/44).

37. Transcript of Oral Argument at 13, 20–23, TVA v. Hill.

38. Plater, *Snail Darter and the Dam*, 220, 247–249; Transcript of Oral Argument at 44, TVA v. Hill. See Daniel S. Cohen, "Judicial Predictability in the United States Supreme Court Advocacy: An Analysis of the Oral Arguments in Tennessee Valley Authority v. Hill," *University of Puget Sound Law Review* 2, no. 1 (1978): 104.

39. Transcript of Oral Argument at 47–50, TVA v. Hill.

40. Justice Blackmun, Notes of Conference, TVA v. Hill (Apr. 2, 1978), Box 268, Folder 8, Blackmun Papers; Doremus, "Story of TVA v. Hill," 130.

41. TVA v. Hill, 437 U.S. at 178, 184–185, 193–195.

42. Ibid. at 187–188.

43. See David E. Cole, "Judicial Discretion and the 'Sunk Costs' Strategy of Government Agencies," *Boston College Environmental Affairs Law Review* 30, no. 3 (2003): 710–714. See also Douglas Laycock, "The Neglected Defense of Undue Hardship (and the Doctrinal Train Wreck in Boomer v. Atlantic Cement)," *Journal of Tort Law* 4, no. 3 (2012), doi: 10.1515/1932-9148.1123.

44. TVA v. Hill, 437 U.S. at 194.

45. Zygmunt J. B. Plater, "Endangered Species Act Lessons over 30 Years, and the Legacy of the Snail Darter, A Small Fish in a Pork Barrel," *Environmental Law* 34, no. 2 (2004): 305. See Doremus, "Story of TVA v. Hill," 130–131; Percival, "Highlights from the Blackmun Papers," 10,643.

46. TVA v. Hill, 437 U.S. 153, 172 (1978); Abraham Lincoln, "Second Inaugural (Washington, DC, March 4, 1865)," in *Noted Speeches of Abraham Lincoln,* ed. Lilian Marie Briggs (New York: Moffat, Yard & Company, 1911), 53–56. I am indebted to my colleague, Stephen Cushman, for pointing out this parallel.

47. TVA v. Hill, 437 U.S. at 159nn7, 8. John C. Jeffries Jr., *Justice Lewis F. Powell, Jr.* (New York: Fordham University Press, 2001), 248–249 (originally published New York: Scribners' Sons, 1994).

48. TVA v. Hill, 437 U.S. 195.

49. Ibid. at 196, 204–205, 210 (Powell, J., dissenting), 213 (Rehnquist, J., dissenting).

50. Doremus, "Story of TVA v. Hill," 131 (internal quotations omitted); Endangered Species Act Amendments of 1978, Public Law No. 95–632, 92 Stat. 3751 (1978) (codified as amended at 16 U.S.C. §1536(e) (2012)). Endangered Species Committee, "Proceedings, January 23, 1979," 26, available at Boston College Law School Snail Darter Documents, http://lawdigitalcommons.bc .edu/darter_materials/ 2?utm_source=lawdigitalcommons.bc.edu%2Fdarter _materials%2F2&utm_medium=PDF&utm_campaign=PDFCoverPages; William Bruce Wheeler and Michael J. McDonald, *TVA and the Tellico Dam, 1936–1979: A Bureaucratic Crisis in Post-Industrial America* (Knoxville: University of Tennessee Press, 1986), 211, quoting from transcript of a committee meeting; Plater, *Snail Darter and the Dam,* 5.

51. Energy and Water Development Appropriation Act, 1980, Public Law No. 96–69, 93 Stat. 437 (1979).

52. National Association of Home Builders v. Defenders of Wildlife, 551 U.S. 644, 661 (2007).

53. Ibid. at 664.

54. Ibid. at 675, 678. J. B. Ruhl, "The Endangered Species Act's Fall from Grace in the Supreme Court," *Harvard Environmental Law Review* 36, no. 2 (2012): 507.

55. Douglas A. Kysar, *Regulating from Nowhere: Environmental Law and the Search for Objectivity* (New Haven, CT: Yale University Press, 2010), 181.

56. Ruhl, "Endangered Species Act's Fall," 490–491; J. B. Ruhl, "Climate Change and the Endangered Species Act," *Environmental Law Reporter* 39, no. 8 (2009): 10,735, 10,735n4.

57. Plater, "Endangered Species Act Lessons," 302. Transcript of Oral Argument at 56, Entergy Corporation v. Riverkeeper, Inc., 556 U.S. 208 (2009) (Nos. 07–588, 07–589, and 07–597).

58. Plater, *Snail Darter and the Dam.*

59. William O. Douglas, *The Three Hundred Year War: A Chronicle of Ecological Disaster* (New York: Random House, 1972), 18. Kristen A. Carpenter, "A Property Rights Approach to Sacred Sites Cases: Asserting a Place for Indians as Nonowners," *UCLA Law Review* 52, no. 4 (2005): 1068, quoting Laurie

Anne Whitt et al., "Belonging to Land: Indigenous Knowledge Systems and the Natural World," *Oklahoma City University Law Review* 26, no. 2 (2001): 705.

60. Lyng v. Northwest Indian Cemetery Protective Assocation, 485 U.S. 439, 473 (Brennan, J., dissenting) (1988).

61. Brian Edward Brown, *Religion, Law, and the Land: Native Americans and the Judicial Interpretations of Sacred Land* (Westport, CT: Greenwood Press, 1992), 122.

62. Amy Bowers and Kristen A. Carpenter, "Challenging the Narrative of Conquest: The Story of Lyng v. Northwest Indian Cemetery Protection Association," in *Indian Law Stories,* ed. Carole Goldberg et al. (New York: Foundation Press/ Thomson Reuters, 2011), 495–497.

63. Dorothy J. Theodoratus, Joseph L. Chartkoff, and Kerry Kona Chartkoff, *Cultural Resources of the Chimney Rock Section, Gasquet-Orleans Road, Six Rivers National Forest* (Fair Oaks, CA: Theodoratus Cultural Research, 1979), 105, 419–420, 422..

64. U.S. Const. amend. 1; Sherbert v. Verner, 374 U.S. 398 (1963); Wisconsin v. Yoder, 406 U.S. 205 (1972).

65. Bowen v. Roy, 476 U.S. 693, 696, 699–700 (1986).

66. Ibid. at 707.

67. Northwest Indian Cemetery Protective Association v. Peterson, 565 F. Supp. 586, 594–595 (N.D. Cal. 1983). See Bowers and Carpenter, "Challenging the Narrative of Conquest," 510–512. Northwest Indian Cemetery Protective Association v. Peterson, 795 F.2d 688, 704 (Beezer, J., dissenting).

68. See Bowers and Carpenter, "Challenging the Narrative of Conquest," 516–522.

69. Brief for Petitioner at 16–17, 29, Lyng v. Northwest Indian Cemetery Protective Association, 485 U.S. 439 (1988) (No. 86–1013).

70. Reply Brief for Petitioner at 18, Lyng v. Northwest Indian Cemetery Protective Association; Transcript of Oral Argument at 20, Lyng v. Northwest Indian Cemetery Protective Association.

71. Brief for the Indian Respondents at 32–34, Lyng v. Northwest Indian Cemetery Protective Association; Transcript of Oral Argument at 28–41, Lyng v. Northwest Indian Cemetery Protective Association.

72. Justice Blackmun, Conference Notes, No. 86–1013, Lyng v. Northwest Indian Cemetery (Dec. 2, 1989), Box 496, Folder 8, Blackmun Papers.

73. Lyng v. Northwest Indian Cemetery Protective Association, 485 U.S. at 447–449, citing Bowen v. Roy, 476 U.S. 693, 699 (1986), 451–452, 456–458.

74. Ibid. at 452–453 (emphasis in original). See generally Christopher E. Smith, "The Supreme Court's Emerging Majority: Restraining the High Court or Transforming Its Role?" *Akron Law Review* 24, no. 2 (1990): 393–422 (discussing "majoritarianism" on the Court and citing *Lyng* in the context of "slighted" religious minorities).

75. See *Lyng,* 485 U.S. 439, 461 (citations omitted); 485 U.S. at 464, quoting from the Ninth Circuit's opinion below (modification in original); 485 U.S. at 472–476 (Brennan, J., dissenting); see also Marcia Yablon, "Property Rights and Sacred Sites: Federal Regulatory Responses to American Indian Religious Claims on Public Land," *Yale Law Journal* 113, no. 7 (2004): 1632–1634.

76. *Lyng,* 485 U.S. at 457–458. Employment Division, Department of Human Resources of Oregon v. Smith, 494 U.S. 872 (1990).

77. Bowers and Carpenter, "Challenging the Narrative of Conquest," 525.

78. Ibid. at 532 (quoting *Lyng,* 485 U.S. 439 at 453). See Carpenter, "A Property Rights Approach," 1065.

79. Allison M. Dussias, "Ghost Dance and Holy Ghost: The Echoes of Nineteenth-Century Christianization Policy in Twentieth-Century Native American Free Exercise Cases," *Stanford Law Review* 49, no. 4 (1997): 850.

80. Lynn White Jr., "The Historical Roots of Our Ecologic Crisis," *Science,* March 10, 1967, 1205–1206.

81. Brown, *Religion, Law, and the Land,* 158, 173; Thomas Berry, *The Dream of the Earth* (San Francisco, CA: Sierra Club Books, 1988), 81. Gary Snyder, *Turtle Island* (New York: New Directions, 1974), 99.

82. Smith River National Recreation Area Act, Public Law No. 101–612, 104 Stat. 3209, 3212 (1990) (codified at 16 U.S.C. § 460bbb-3(b)(2)(H) (2012)). Jonathan Cannon and Jonathan Riehl, "Presidential Greenspeak: How Presidents Talk about Environment and What It Means," *Stanford Environmental Law Journal* 23, no. 2 (2004): 244–245, 248.

83. Kysar, *Regulating from Nowhere,* 181.

Chapter 5: Efficiency

1. Chevron v. Natural Resources Defense Council, Inc., 467 U.S. 837 (1984); Jody Freeman, "The Story of Chevron: Environmental Law and Administrative Discretion," in *Environmental Law Stories,* ed. Richard J. Lazarus and Oliver A. Houck (New York: Foundation Press, 2005), 173; and Thomas W. Merrill, "The Story of Chevron: The Making of an Accidental Landmark," in *Administrative Law Stories,* ed. Peter L. Strauss (New York: Foundation Press, 2006), 399.

2. Steven Kelman, *What Price Incentives? Economists and the Environment* (Boston: Auburn House, 1981), 2–3, 101, 108, 114–115.

3. Chevron, 467 U.S. at 865; 42 U.S.C. §§ 7411(b), 7475, 7503 (2012).

4. 40 Federal Register 58,416, 58,419 (Dec. 16, 1975); ASARCO, Inc. v. EPA, 578 F.2d 319, 327 (D.C. Cir. 1978); 42 U.S.C. § 7411(a)(3) (2012).

5. 43 Federal Register 26,380, 26,39 (June 19, 1978); Alabama Power Co. v. Costle, 636 F.2d at 401–402 (D.C. Cir. 1979).

6. Merrill, "Story of Chevron," 405, 408.

7. 46 Federal Register 50,766 (Oct. 14, 1981); Natural Resources Defense Council, Inc. v. Gorsuch, 685 F.2d 718, 726 (D.C. Cir. 1982); Brief for the Administrator of the Environmental Protection Agency at 37, Chevron v. Natural Resources Defense Council, Inc., 467 U.S. 837 (1984) (Nos. 82–1005, 82–1247, & 82–1591).

8. Brief for the Administrator of the Environmental Protection Agency at 56, 59, Chevron v. Natural Resources Defense Council, Inc; Transcript of Oral Argument at 39–40, Chevron v. Natural Resources Defense Council, Inc.

9. Brief for Respondents Natural Resources Defense Council, Inc. at 66–69, Chevron v. Natural Resources Defense Council; Transcript of Oral Argument at 21–23, Chevron v. Natural Resources Defense Council.

10. Freeman, "Story of Chevron," 192–194 (confusion at oral argument); Merrill, "Story of Chevron," 415–418 (confusion and uncertainty at conference).

11. Chevron, 467 U.S. at 842–843, n.9, 844.

12. Ibid. at 860–862.

13. Ibid. at 863nn36, 37.

14. Environmental Defense Fund, "Economic Incentives," accessed October 22, 2013, http://www.edf.org/approach/markets; World Resources Institute, "What We Do," accessed July 25, 2014, http://www.wri.org/our-work; James Gustave Speth, *The Bridge at the Edge of the World: Capitalism, the Environment, and Crossing from Crisis to Sustainability* (New Haven, CT: Yale University Press, 2008), 93–94.

15. EPA v. EME Homer City Generation, L.P., 134 S.Ct. 1584 (2014).

16. 42 U.S.C. § 7410(a)(2)(D)(i) (2012); EME Homer City Generation, L.P. v. EPA, 696 F.3d 7, 21 (D.C. Cir. 2012).

17. EME Homer, 134 S. Ct. at 1607.

18. Matthew D. Adler, "Cost-Benefit Analysis," in *Encyclopedia of Law and Society: American and Global Perspectives*, ed. David S. Clark (Los Angeles: Sage, 2007), 1: 304; Cass R. Sunstein, *The Cost-Benefit State: The Future of Regulatory Protection* (Chicago: American Bar Association, 2002), ix; Richard Revesz and Michael A. Livermore, *Retaking Rationality: How Cost-Benefit Analysis Can Better Protect the Environment and Our Health* (Oxford: Oxford University Press, 2008), 15; Matthew D. Adler and Eric A. Posner, *New Foundations of Cost-Benefit Analysis* (Cambridge, MA: Harvard University Press, 2006), 52–53.

19. Eyal Zamir and Barak Medina, "Law, Morality, and Economics: Integrating Moral Constraints with Economic Analysis of Law," *California Law Review* 96, no. 2 (2008): 326–327; Frank Ackerman and Lisa Heinzerling, *Priceless: On Knowing the Price of Everything and the Value of Nothing* (New York: New Press, 2004), 8, 37–40; Amy Sinden, Douglas A. Kysar, and David M. Driesen, "Cost-Benefit Analysis: New Foundations on Shifting Sand," review of *New Foundations of Cost-Benefit Analysis,* by Matthew D. Adler and Eric A. Posner, *Regulation & Governance* 3, no. 1 (2003): 55, 58–59; Steven Kelman, "Cost-Benefit Analysis: An Ethical Critique," *Regulation* 5, no. 1 (1981): 36; Mark Sagoff, *The Economy of the Earth: Philosophy, Law, and the Environment* (Cambridge: Cambridge University Press, 1988), 92–97. But see Carol M. Rose, "Environmental Faust Succumbs to Temptations of Economic Mephistopheles; or, Value by Any Other Name Is Preference," review of *The Economy of the Earth: Philosophy, Law, and the Environment,* by Mark Sagoff, *Michigan Law Review* 87, no. 6 (1989): 1631–1639. For a more recent assertion of the fundamental distinction between political and economic domains, see Mark Sagoff, *Price, Principle, and the Environment* (Cambridge: Cambridge University Press, 2004), 13.

20. Douglas A. Kysar, *Regulating from Nowhere: Environmental Law and the Search for Objectivity* (New Haven, CT: Yale University Press, 2010), 101, 117; Sinden, Kysar, and Driesen, "Cost-Benefit Analysis," 54–57.

21. "The Issues—Cost-Benefit Analysis," Institute for Policy Integrity, accessed February 17, 2014, http://policyintegrity.org/issues/filter/cost-benefit-analysis/;

Michael A. Livermore and Richard A. Revesz, "Retaking Rationality Two Years Later," *Houston Law Review* 48, no. 1 (2011): 26–33.

22. Antonin Scalia, "Responsibilities of Regulatory Agencies under Environmental Laws," *Houston Law Review* 24, no. 1 (1987): 101 (describing a version of CBA not dependent on monetization); John D. Graham, "Saving Lives through Administrative Law and Economics," *University of Pennsylvania Law Review* 157, no. 2 (2008): 447–448 (describing this form of CBA as "intuitive balancing"); and Daniel A. Farber, *Eco-pragmatism: Making Sensible Environmental Decisions in an Uncertain World* (Chicago: University of Chicago Press, 1999), 114–123 (proposing a form of CBA to assure that costs of policies are not "patently disproportional to the potential benefits").

23. Clean Water Act, 33 U.S.C. §§ 1251–1387 (2012); Clean Air Act, 42 U.S.C. §§ 7401–7671q (2012); Endangered Species Act, 16 U.S.C. §§ 1531–1544 (2012); Comprehensive Environmental Response, Compensation, and Liability Act, 42 U.S.C. §§ 9601–9675 (2012); Resource Conservation and Recovery Act, Public Law No. 94–580, 90 Stat. 2795 (1976), 42 U.S.C. §§ 6901–6922k (2012); Emergency Planning and Community Right-to-Know Act, 42 U.S.C. §§ 11001–11005, 11021–11023, 11041–11050 (2012); and the Oil Pollution Act of 1990, 33 U.S.C. §§ 2701–2762. Exec. Order No. 12,291, 3 C.F.R. 127 (1982) (repealed 1993); Exec. Order No. 12,866, 3 C.F.R. 638 §6(a)(3)(C) (1993), reprinted as amended in 5 U.S.C. § 601 note (2012).

24. Compare Sunstein, *The Cost-Benefit State,* 59–60, and Cass R. Sunstein, *Risk and Reason: Safety, Law, and the Environment* (New York: Cambridge University Press, 2002), 202–205, with Amy Sinden, "Cass Sunstein's Cost-Benefit Lite: Economics for Liberals," *Columbia Journal of Environmental Law* 29, no. 2 (2011): 240. Farber, *Eco-pragmatism,* 114–123.

25. Citizens to Preserve Overton Park, Inc. v. Volpe, 401 U.S. 402, 413 (1971).

26. TVA v. Hill, 437 U.S. 153, 187 (1978).

27. Ibid. at 195–196, 202–206 (Powell, J., dissenting).

28. American Textile Manufacturers Institute, Inc. v. Donovan, 452 U.S. 490, 508–509 (1981); 29 U.S.C. § 655(b)(5) (2012).

29. American Textile, 452 U.S. at 509–510.

30. Robert V. Percival, "Environmental Law in the Supreme Court: Highlights from the Marshall Papers," *Environmental Law Reporter* 23, no. 1 (1993): 10, 606–10, 625.

31. American Textile, 452 U.S. at 544–545 (Rehnquist, J., dissenting); Entergy Corporation v. Riverkeeper, Inc., 556 U.S. 208, 223 (2009).

32. Cass R. Sunstein, "Interpreting Statutes in the Regulatory State, *Harvard Law Review* 103, no. 2 (1989): 492–493. To similar effect, see Cass R. Sunstein, "Paradoxes of the Regulatory State," *University of Chicago Law Review* 57, no. 2 (1990): 437; Industrial Union Department, AFL-CIO v. American Petroleum Institute, 448 U.S. 607 (1980).

33. Whitman v. American Trucking Associations (ATA), 531 U.S. 457, 468–471 (2001). Chief Justice Rehnquist and Justices Stevens, O'Connor, Kennedy, Souter, Thomas, and Ginsburg joined the Court's opinion on this issue; Justice

Breyer agreed with the result in a concurring opinion. Clean Air Act § 109(b)
(1), 42 U.S.C. § 7409(b)(1) (2012).

34. See, for example, discussion of Lucas v. South Carolina Coastal Council, 505
U.S. 1003 (1992), in Chapter 8.

35. City of Chicago v. Environmental Defense Fund, 511 U.S. 328 (1994).

36. Stephen Breyer, *Breaking the Vicious Circle* (Cambridge, MA: Harvard University Press, 1993) 11–19; Stephen Breyer, *Regulation and Its Reform* (Cambridge, MA: Harvard University Press, 1982), 264. See Lisa Heinzerling, "Justice Breyer's Hard Look," *Administrative Law Journal of the American University* 8, no. 4 (1995): 768–771.

37. ATA, 531 U.S. at 490, 494 (Breyer, J., concurring).

38. Michael A. Livermore and Richard L. Revesz, "Rethinking Health-Based Environmental Standards," *New York University Law Review* 89, no. 4 (2014): 1184–1267. EPA, "Regulatory Impact Analysis for the Particulate Matter and Ozone National Ambient Air Quality Standards and Proposed Regional Haze Rule," (July 16, 1997), 13–3, table 13.1, http://yosemite1.epa.gov/EE/EPA/ria.nsf/EIO/1445F033E6A81FAA852564E3004D9BD1.

39. Entergy Corp. v. Riverkeeper, Inc., 556 U.S. 208 (2009).

40. 33 U.S.C. § 1326(b) (2012); Phase II Final Cooling Water Rule, 69 Federal Register 41,576, 41,601 and n44 (July 9, 2004). 40 C.F.R. §§ 125.94(a)(5), 125.94(b)(4) (2013).

41. 69 Federal Register at 41,586, 41,601, 41,603, 41,605, 41666; U.S. Environmental Protection Agency, "Economic and Benefits Analysis for the Final Section 316(b) Phase II Existing Facilities Rule C3–1," (EPA-821-R-04-005, U.S. Environmental Protection Agency, Washington, DC, 2004), http://water.epa.gov/lawsregs/lawsguidance/cwa/316b/upload/Cooling-Water_Phase-2_Economics_2004.pdf.

42. 69 Federal Register at 41,660–41,662; EPA, "Economic and Benefits Analysis for the Final Section 316(b) Phase II Existing Facilities Rule."

43. 69 Federal Register at 41,605.

44. Riverkeeper, Inc. v. EPA, 475 F.3d 83, 98-99 (2d Cir. 2007); 33 U.S.C. §§ 1311(b), 1316(a) (2012). Compare 33 U.S.C. §§ 1314(b)(1)(B) ("consideration of the total cost . . . in relation to . . . benefits") and 1314(b)(4)(B) ("consideration of the reasonableness of the relationship between the costs . . . and the . . . benefits") with 33 U.S.C. §§ 1314(b)(2)(B) (including "cost" in factors to be taken into account but not mentioning "benefits") and 33 U.S.C. § 1316(b) (same).

45. Entergy, 556 U.S. at 217; Brief for Petitioners Entergy Corp., PSEG Fossil LLC, and PSEG Nuclear LLC at 28–29, Entergy Corporation v. Riverkeeper, Inc., 556 U.S. 208 (2009) (Nos. 07-588, 07-589, and 07-597) (emphasis in original); Brief for Federal Parties as Respondents Supporting Petitioners at 31, Entergy Corporation v. Riverkeeper, Inc., quoting Whitman v. American Trucking Association, Inc., 531 U.S. 457, 490 (2001) (Breyer, J., concurring in part and in the judgment).

46. Brief for Petitioners Entergy Corp. at 15–18, Entergy Corporation v. Riverkeeper, Inc.

47. Richard Lazarus, e-mail message to author, May 9, 2012.

48. Brief for Respondents Riverkeeper, Inc., et al. at 29, Entergy Corporation v. Riverkeeper, Inc.; Transcript of Oral Argument at 53, Entergy Corporation v. Riverkeeper, Inc.
49. Transcript of Oral Argument at 56, Entergy Corporation v. Riverkeeper, Inc.
50. Ibid. at 39, 49–52, 55.
51. Ibid. at 17–18, 20–25, 37, 61–63; Brief for Economists Frank Ackerman et al. as Amici Curiae Supporting Respondents at 11, Entergy Corporation v. Riverkeeper, Inc. (EPA used CBA "to identify allocatively efficient regulation."); Brief of Amicus Curiae OMB Watch in Support of Respondents at 4–5, Entergy Corporation v. Riverkeeper, Inc. (EPA used "formal" CBA to select among options); Entergy, 556 U.S. at 224 (Scalia, J.) (EPA used a form of CBA seeking to avoid "extreme disparities between costs and benefits."), 235 (Breyer, J.) (EPA used CBA to "prevent results that are absurd or unreasonable in light of extreme disparities between costs and benefits.").
52. Entergy, 556 U.S. at 226–227, 230–236 (Breyer, J., concurring in part, dissenting in part), 236–237 (Stevens, J., dissenting).
53. Ibid. at 231–232 (Breyer, J., concurring in part, dissenting in part).
54. Ibid. at 231–233 (Breyer, J., concurring in part, dissenting in part).
55. Ibid. at 231–232, 234–235 (Breyer, J., concurring in part, dissenting in part).
56. Ibid. at 235–237 (Breyer, J., concurring in part, dissenting in part).
57. Ibid. at 218, 220–221. See Massachusetts v. EPA, 549 U.S. 497, 549–554 (2007) (Scalia, J., dissenting) (making room for authority-limiting EPA interpretation).
58. Whitman v. American Trucking Association, Inc., 531 U.S. at 466–486; Entergy, 556 U.S. at 222.
59. Entergy, 556 U.S. at 223, 245n11 (Stevens, J., dissenting) (characterizing Justice Scalia's suggested limitation "as a concession that cost-benefit analysis, as typically performed, may be inconsistent with the BTA mandate").
60. Richard Lazarus, e-mail message to author, August 9, 2009.
61. Scalia, "Responsibilities of Regulatory Agencies," 101 (emphasis in original).
62. Riverkeeper, Inc. v. EPA, 475 F.3d at 99; Entergy, 556 U.S. at 238–239.
63. Entergy, 556 U.S. at 237, 246n13 (Stevens, J., dissenting).
64. Ibid. at 237, 245 (Stevens, J., dissenting).
65. Ibid. at 239–246 (Stevens, J., dissenting).
66. Richard Lazarus, e-mail message to author, August 9, 2009.
67. Kysar, *Regulating from Nowhere*, 208.
68. See Heinzerling, "Justice Breyer's Hard Look," 771–773 (critiquing Justice Breyer's use of a weak form of CBA as discouraging protective policies).
69. EME Homer, 134 S.Ct. at 1610–1621 (Scalia, J., dissenting).
70. Ibid. at 1611, 1612, 1615; Dan Farber, "Justice Scalia's Puzzling Dissent," *Legal Planet* (blog), May 5, 2014, http://legal-planet.org/2014/05/05/justice-scalias-puzzling-dissent-2/.http://legal-planet.org/2014/05/05/justice-scalias-puzzling-dissent2/.

Chapter 6: Standing

1. Aldo Leopold, *A Sand County Almanac, with Essays on Conservation from Round River* (New York: Ballantine Books, 1966), 190, 237–246.

2. See Jonathan Cannon and Jonathan Riehl, "Presidential Greenspeak: How Presidents Talk about Environment and What It Means," *Stanford Environmental Law Journal* 23, no. 2 (2004): 264–267.

3. Public Law No. 79–404, 60 Stat. 237, § 10(a), (e) (1946) (codified as amended in scattered sections of 5 U.S.C. and 28 U.S.C.). See, for example, 16 U.S.C. § 1540(g) (2012) (Endangered Species Act); 33 U.S.C. § 1365 (2012) (Clean Water Act); 42 U.S.C. § 7604 (2012) (Clean Air Act). See also, for example, Kenneth M. Murchison, "Learning from More than Five-and-a-Half Decades of Federal Water Pollution Control Legislation: Twenty Lessons for the Future," *Boston College Environmental Affairs Law Review* 32, no. 3 (2005): 549.

4. Lujan v. Defenders of Wildlife, 504 U.S. 555, 560–561 (1992).

5. Cass R. Sunstein, "What's Standing after *Lujan*? Of Citizen Suits, 'Injuries,' and Article III," *Michigan Law Review* 91, no. 2 (1992): 166–167; William A. Fletcher, "The Structure of Standing," *Yale Law Journal* 98, no. 2 (1988): 231–233.

6. Lujan, 504 U.S. 555, 581 (Kennedy, J., concurring), quoting Valley Forge Christian College v. Americans United for Separation of Church and State, Inc., 454 U.S. 464, 472 (1982).

7. Ibid. at 581 (1992). Flast v. Cohen, 392 U.S. 83 (1968).

8. *Valley Forge Christian College,* 454 U.S. 464, 471–474 (1982); Warth v. Seldin, 422 U.S. 490, 498 (1975).

9. Antonin Scalia, "The Doctrine of Standing as an Essential Element of the Separation of Powers," *Suffolk University Law Review* 17, no. 4 (1983): 881–886, 894.

10. Scalia, "Doctrine of Standing," 897 (emphasis omitted).

11. Sunstein, "What's Standing after *Lujan*," 218–220.

12. Michael Herz, "The Rehnquist Court and Administrative Law," *Northwestern University Law Review* 99, no. 1 (2004): 354.

13. Sunstein, "What's Standing after *Lujan*," 218.

14. See Lujan v. Defenders of Wildlife, 504 U.S. 555 (1992); Bennett v. Spear, 520 U.S. 154 (1997).

15. See Jedediah Purdy, "American Natures: The Shape of Conflict in Environmental Law," *Harvard Environmental Law Review* 36, no. 1 (2012): 221–223. Joseph L. Sax, "Standing to Sue: A Critical Review of the Mineral King Decision," *Natural Resources Journal* 13, no. 1 (1973): 88.

16. See, for example, Friends of the Earth, Inc. v. Laidlaw Environmental Services (TOC), Inc., 528 U.S. 167 (2000); *Lujan,* 504 U.S. 555 (1992); Sierra Club v. Morton, 405 U.S. 727 (1972).

17. Sierra Club v. Morton, 405 U.S. 727, 758, 760, n.2 (1972) (Blackmun, J., dissenting).

18. United States v. Students Challenging Regulatory Agency Procedures (SCRAP), 412 U.S. 669, 678 (1973).

19. SCRAP v. United States, 346 F. Supp. 189, 191, 195–196 (D.D.C. 1972).

20. Brief for the United States and the Interstate Commerce Commission at 19, United States v. SCRAP, 412 U.S. 669 (1973) (No. 72–535); Transcript of Oral Argument at 10, United States v. SCRAP. See Brief of the Aberdeen and Rock-

fish Railroad Company et al., at 84–85, United States v. SCRAP. Brief for the
United States and the Interstate Commerce Commission at 15–16, United States
v. SCRAP. See United States v. SCRAP, 412 U.S. at 686–690, 698. The Administrative Procedure Act § 10(a), 5 U.S.C. § 702 provides judicial review for "a
person . . . adversely affected or aggrieved by agency action."

21. *SCRAP,* 412 U.S. at 686–688.
22. Ibid. at 688–689, n14. See Daniel A. Farber, "Stretching the Margins: The Geographic Nexus in Environmental Law," *Stanford Law Review* 48, no. 5 (1996):
1250.
23. SCRAP, 412 U.S. at 722–723 (White, J., dissenting).
24. Scalia, "Doctrine of Standing," 890, 898.
25. Whitmore v. Arkansas, 495 U.S. 149, 158–159 (1990).
26. Lujan v. National Wildlife Federation, 497 U.S. 871, 888–889 (1990).
27. Lujan v. Defenders of Wildlife, 504 U.S. 555 (1992).
28. See ibid. at 557–559. The Secretary of Interior issued the rule jointly with the
Secretary of Commerce. Ibid. at 558.
29. 16 U.S.C. § 1540(g)(1)(A) (2012). 504 U.S. at 563.
30. Defenders of Wildlife v. Hodel, 707 F. Supp 1082 (D. Minn. 1989); Defenders
of Wildlife v. Lujan, 911 F.2d 117, 120 (8th Cir. 1990). The court of appeals
also declared that Defenders had "procedural injury" sufficient for standing by
virtue of the citizen suit provision of the Endangered Species Act, which
authorized "any person" to sue for violations of the act. Defenders did little to
defend this proposition on review, and the Court rejected it on separation-of-
powers grounds, echoing Justice Scalia's Suffolk article. 504 U.S. at 571–573.
31. Transcript of Oral Argument at 29, Lujan v. Defenders of Wildlife, 504 U.S. 555
(1992) (No. 90–1424). Brief for the Petitioner at 18–27, Lujan v. Defenders of
Wildlife.
32. Allen v. Wright, 468 U.S. 737 (1984); Sunstein, "What's Standing after *Lujan,*"
199.
33. Lujan v. Defenders of Wildlife, 504 U.S. 555, 560–561, 564 (1992) (quotations
and citations omitted).
34. Ibid. at 555, 565–566. Cass Sunstein characterizes the proffered "ecosystem
nexus" broadly as advancing "a nexus linking the affected habitats with all the
world's ecosystems." Sunstein, "What's Standing after *Lujan,*" 199.
35. *Lujan,* 504 U.S. 555, 566–567. See ibid. at 594 (Blackmun, J., dissenting).
36. Ibid. at 571.
37. Compare *SCRAP,* 412 U.S. 669, 680–681 (1973) with *Lujan II,* 504 U.S. 555,
566, 591 (1992).
38. Justice Souter, Memorandum to Justice Scalia (May 28, 1992), Box 591, Folder
11, Harry A. Blackmun Papers, 1913–2001, Library of Congress; Justice Kennedy, Memorandum to Justice Scalia (May 28, 1992), Box 591, Folder 11,
Blackmun Papers. Scalia, "Doctrine of Standing," 895–896. Justice Scalia,
Memorandum to Justice Souter (June 1, 1992), Box 591, Folder 11, Blackmun
Papers.
39. Peter Manus, "Wild Bill Douglas's Last Stand: A Retrospective on the First Supreme Court Environmentalist," *Temple Law Review* 72, no. 1 (1999): 131;

Christopher Warshaw and Gregory E. Wannier, "Business as Usual? Analyzing the Development of Environmental Standing Doctrine since 1976," *Harvard Law and Policy Review* 5, no. 2 (2011): 305; Herz, "Rehnquist Court," 354.

40. Jeff Meyer, Memorandum to Justice Blackmun (June 5, 1992), Box 592, Folder 3, Blackmun Papers. Lujan v. Defenders of Wildlife, 504 U.S. at 579 (Kennedy, J., concurring).

41. *Lujan,* 504 U.S. at 580, 582.

42. Ibid. at 594–596, 567 (Blackmun, J., dissenting).

43. Ibid. at 581, 584 n.2 (Stevens, J., concurring in the judgment).

44. Ibid. at 567 n3. Justice Stevens, Memorandum to Justice Scalia (June, 10, 1992), Box 591, File3, Blackmun Papers.

45. Bennett v. Spear, 520 U.S. 154, 166–167, 176–179 (1997).

46. Scalia, "Doctrine of Standing," 884. Purdy, "American Natures," 222.

47. Steel Company v. Citizens for a Better Environment, 523 U.S. 83, 106 (1998).

48. Federal Election Commission v. Akins, 524 U.S. 11 (1998). Friends of the Earth, Inc. v. Laidlaw Environmental Services (TOC), Inc., 528 U.S. 167 (2000).

49. Facts about the Laidlaw facility are taken from the Supreme Court's opinion, *Laidlaw,* 528 U.S. at 175–180, and the district court's findings of fact, conclusions of law, and order, 956 F. Supp. 588, 592–601 (D.S.C. 1996).

50. *Laidlaw,* 956 F. Supp. at 591–592. "About Our Firm," Terris Pravlik & Millian, LLP, accessed November 5, 2013, http://tpmlaw.com/lawyer/About-our -Firm_cp2206.htm. William W. Buzbee, "The Story of *Laidlaw*: Standing and Citizen Enforcement," in *Environmental Law Stories,* ed. Richard J. Lazarus and Oliver A. Houck (New York: Foundation Press, 2005), 207–208.

51. *Laidlaw,* 956 F. Supp. at 600, 611. This was less than half the amount that the district judge found Laidlaw had benefited by delaying its compliance, but he deemed it appropriate, taking into account the significant legal fees that Laidlaw would have to pay to the Terris firm as well as Laidlaw's own "significant legal expenses" and considering his finding of no "significant harm to the environment." Ibid. at 600, 610–611. *Laidlaw,* 528 U.S. at 177.

52. Friends of the Earth, Inc. v. Laidlaw Environmental Services (TOC), Inc., 149 F. 3d 303, 306–307 (4th Cir. 1998).

53. Buzbee, "The Story of *Laidlaw*," 213.

54. Brief for Respondent at 64a–65a, Friends of the Earth, Inc. v. Laidlaw Environmental Services (TOC), Inc., 528 U.S. 167 (2000) (No. 98–822).

55. *Laidlaw,* 528 U.S. at 180, 187. See Kelly D. Spragins, "Rekindling an Old Flame: The Supreme Court Revives Its 'Love Affair with Environmental Litigation' in *Friends of the Earth v. Laidlaw Environmental Services,*" *Houston Law Review* 37, no. 3 (2000): 955–978.

56. See *Laidlaw,* 528 U.S. at 173–176, 181, 198–199, quoting Friends of the Earth, Inc. v. Laidlaw Environmental Services (TOC), Inc., 956 F. Supp. 588, 602 (D.S.C. 1997). *Laidlaw,* 956 F. Supp. at 602–603.

57. See *Laidlaw,* 528 U.S. at 181–184.

58. See William W. Buzbee, "Standing and the Statutory Universe," *Duke Environmental Law and Policy Forum* 11, no. 2 (Spring 2001), 262–267 (concluding that *Laidlaw* reflects a recent pattern of "giving the statutory universe a prom-

inent, if not paramount role, in standing analysis" [264]). See also 33 U.S.C. § 1251(a) (2012); 33 U.S.C. § 1319 (2012). *Laidlaw,* 528 U.S. 167, 181 (2000).

59. See Daniel A. Farber, "Environmental Litigation after Laidlaw," *Environmental Law Reporter* 30, no. 7 (2000): 10,519.

60. *Laidlaw,* 528 U.S. at 199–200, quoting Los Angeles v. Lyons, 461 U.S. 95, 107 n8 (1983); ibid. at 201.

61. Massachusetts v. EPA, 415 F. 3d 50, 54.

62. Massachusetts v. EPA, 415 F.3d at 60, 64–67.

63. Transcript of Oral Argument at 5, 13, 14–15, Massachusetts v. EPA, 549 U.S. 497 (2007) (No. 05–1120).

64. Massachusetts v. EPA, 549 U.S. at 524.

65. Daniel A. Farber, "A Place-Based Theory of Standing," *UCLA Law Review* 55, no. 6 (2008): 1506, quoting Donne to same effect.

66. Linda Greenhouse, "For the Chief Justice, a Dissent and a Line in the Sand," *New York Times,* April 8, 2007, C12, quoted in Andrew Long, "Standing & Consensus: Globalism in *Massachusetts v. EPA,*" *Journal of Environmental Law and Litigation* 23, no. 1 (2008): 106. John G. Roberts Jr., "Article III Limits on Statutory Standing," *Duke Law Journal* 42, no. 6 (1993): 1224.

67. Long, "Standing & Consensus," 106.

68. Massachusetts v. EPA, 549 U.S. at 548 (Roberts, J., dissenting).

69. Ibid. at 518. Lisa Heinzerling, "Climate Change in the Supreme Court," *Environmental Law* 38, no. 1 (2008): 16; Transcript of Oral Argument at 17, Massachusetts v. EPA.

70. Compare Connecticut v. American Electric Power Company, Inc., 582 F.3d 309 (2d Cir. 2009) (granting standing in a climate change case to land trusts as well as states), *jurisdiction affirmed by equally divided Court* 131 S. Ct. 2527 (2011), with Washington Environmental Council v. Bellon, 732 F.3d 1131 (9th Cir. 2013). See Bradford C. Mank, "No Article III Standing for Private Plaintiffs Challenging State Greenhouse Gas Regulations: The Ninth Circuit's Decision in *Washington Environmental Council v. Bellon,*" *American University Law Review* 63, no. 5 (forthcoming), http://papers.ssrn.com/sol3/papers.cfm?abstract _id=2393436.

71. Summers v. Earth Island Institute, 555 U.S. 488 (2009). American Electric Power Company, Inc. v. Connecticut, 131 S. Ct. 2527, 2535 (2011).

72. Chief Justice Roberts cited the Court's opinion in *Lujan II* nine times in his *Massachusetts v. EPA* dissent (Massachusetts v. EPA, 549 U.S. 497 [2007]).

Chapter 7: Federalism

1. Erin Ryan, *Federalism and the Tug of War Within* (Oxford: Oxford University Press, 2011), 1, 38, reading Justice Stevens's dissent in Lorillard Tobacco Co. v. Reilly, 533 U.S. 525 (2001), as suggesting "that the new federalism cases harbor a partisan antiregulatory agenda"; United States v. Morrison, 529 U.S. 598, 617–618 (2000).

2. New York v. United States, 505 U.S. 144 (1992); Christopher H. Schroeder, "Environmental Law, Congress, and the Court's New Federalism Doctrine,"

Indiana Law Journal 78, no. 1 (2003): 414. See, for example, National Federal of Independent Business v. Sebelius, 132 S. Ct. 2566 (2012) (holding that Medicaid expansion provisions of the Affordable Care Act exceeded the spending power clause and violated the Tenth Amendment's anticommandeering principle and concluding that the act's individual mandate exceeded Congress's power under the commerce clause); Morrison, 529 U.S. 598 (holding that a federal statute could not be sustained under the commerce clause); Printz v. United States, 521 U.S. 898 (1997) (holding that a federal statute commandeered state officials, in violation of the Tenth Amendment); United States v. Lopez, 514 U.S. 549 (1995) (commerce clause); Pennhurst State School & Hospital v. Halderman, 465 U.S. 89 (1984) (finding a lack of federal jurisdiction due to Eleventh Amendment considerations).

3. U.S. Const. art. 1, § 8, cl. 3; Lopez, 514 U.S. at 558–559. James Madison, "Federalist No. 39: Conformity of the Plan to Republican Principles," in *The Federalist Papers,* ed. Lawrence Goldman, Oxford World's Classics (New York: Oxford University Press, 2008), 187–193.

4. Henry N. Butler and Jonathan R. Macey, "Externalities and the Matching Principle: The Case for Reallocating Environmental Regulatory Authority," symposium issue, *Yale Law & Policy Review* 14 (1996): 25; Michael W. McConnell, "Federalism: Evaluating the Founders' Design," review of *Federalism: The Founders' Design,* by Raoul Berger, *University of Chicago Law Review* 54, no. 4 (1987): 1495; Richard B. Stewart, "Controlling Environmental Risks through Economic Incentives," *Columbia Journal of Environmental Law* 13, no. 2 (1988): 154.

5. Richard L. Revesz, "Rehabilitating Interstate Competition: Rethinking the 'Race-to-the-Bottom' Rationale for Federal Environmental Regulation," *New York University Law Review* 67, no. 6 (1992): 1227.

6. For example, Neal D. Woods, "Interstate Competition and Environmental Regulations: A Test of the Race-to-the-Bottom Thesis," *Social Science Quarterly* 87, no. 1 (2006): 174–189.

7. Daniel C. Esty, "Revitalizing Environmental Federalism," *Michigan Law Review* 95, no. 3 (1996): 638–648.

8. Jonathan H. Adler, "Judicial Federalism and the Future of Federal Environmental Regulation," *Iowa Law Review* 90, no. 2 (2005): 413–414. National Association of Homebuilders v. Babbitt, 130 F.3d 1041, 1058–1059 (D.C. Cir. 1997) (Henderson, J., concurring).

9. Adler, "Judicial Federalism," 414; *National Association of Homebuilders,* 130 F.3d at 1065 (Sentelle, J., dissenting).

10. Ryan, *Federalism and the Tug of War Within,* 38–44. Ryan also lists among "good governance values" associated with federalism the "promotion of accountable and participatory democratic governance" (see discussion of *New York v. United States* and *National Federation of Independent Business v. Sebelius* in Chapter 3); the "benefits of local autonomy, especially diversity, innovation and jurisdictional competition" (see discussion of interstate competition in this chapter); and subsidiarity (see discussion of "matching principle" in this chapter). Ryan, *Federalism and the Tug of War Within,* 44–67. For similar accounts of values supporting federalism, see Erwin Chermerinsky, "The

Values of Federalism," *Florida Law Review* 47, no. 4 (1995): 535; Richard H. Fallon Jr., "The 'Conservative' Paths of the Rehnquist Court's Federalism Decisions," *University of Chicago Law Review* 69, no. 2 (2002): 440–441. New York v. United States, 505 U.S. 144, 181–182, quoting Coleman v. Thompson, 501 U.S. 722, 759 (1991) (Blackmun, J., dissenting).

11. Ryan, *Federalism and the Tug of War Within,* 5.

12. Hodel v. Virginia Surface Mining & Reclamation Ass'n, 452 U.S. 264 (1981). The Court also addressed commerce clause issues in *Hodel*'s companion case, Hodel v. Indiana, 452 U.S. 314 (1981), but its treatment of those issues in the second case was relatively limited.

13. *Hodel,* 452 U.S. at 268, 273, 280–281. The mining interests also claimed violation of the Fifth Amendment's takings provision, which the Court held was not ripe for decision. Brief for the Virginia Surface Mining and Reclamation Association, Inc., the Town of Wise, Virginia, and the Commonwealth of Virginia at 17–21, 25–28, Hodel v. Virginia Surface Mining and Reclamation Association, Inc., 452 U.S. 264 (1981) (Nos. 79–1538 and 79–1596). Virginia Surface Mining Association, Inc. v. Andrus, 483 F.Supp. 425, 435 (W.D. Va. 1980).

14. Justice Blackmun, Notes (1981), Box 328, Folder 1, Papers of Harry A. Blackmun, Library of Congress; Justice Lewis F. Powell, Memorandum to Chief Justice Burger (March 5, 1981), Box 328, Folder 1, Blackmun Papers. See Robert V. Percival, "Environmental Law in the Supreme Court: Highlights from the Blackmun Papers," *Environmental Law Reporter* 35 (2005): 10,646–10,647.

15. *Hodel,* 452 U.S. at 281–283.

16. Christine A. Klein, "The Environmental Commerce Clause: Disguising Pragmatism with Metaphor," in *The Jurisdynamics of Environmental Protection: Change and the Pragmatic Voice in Environmental Law,* ed. Jim Chen (Washington, DC: Environmental Law Institute, 2003), 231, citing Daniel A. Farber, "Stretching the Margins: The Geographic Nexus in Environmental Law," *Stanford Law Review* 48, no. 5 (1996): 1250.

17. *Hodel,* 452 U.S. 307, 311 (Rehnquist, J., concurring in judgment).

18. Ibid. at 309–311.

19. United States v. Riverside Bayview Homes, 474 U.S. 121, 131, 139 (1985); 33 U.S.C. §§ 1311, 1344, 1362(7) (2012).

20. *Riverside Bayview,* 474 U.S. at 132–134.

21. *Riverside Bayview,* 474 U.S. at 129–130, 131 n. 8, 133–135. The six new justices were Scalia, Kennedy, Thomas, Souter, Ginsburg, and Breyer. Rehnquist, O'Connor, and Stevens were common to both cases.

22. United States v. Lopez, 514 U.S. 549 (1995); United States v. Morrison, 529 U.S. 598 (2000).

23. *Lopez,* 514 U.S. at 552, 559–560; *Morrison,* 529 U.S. at 610–613, 617–618. See Schroeder, "Environmental Law," 416, (articulating the rationale for aggregating the effects of individual action to support regulation), quoting Wickard v. Filburn, 317 U.S. 111 (1942).

24. *Morrison,* 529 U.S. at 615–616, n. 6. In *Lopez,* "areas of traditional state concern" figured prominently in the concurrence by Justices Kennedy and O'Connor. 514 U.S. at 577.

25. Solid Waste Agency of Northern Cook County v. U.S. Army Corps of Engineers (SWANCC), 531 U.S. 159 (2001).
26. *SWANCC,* 531 U.S. at 162–163.
27. Ibid. at 159, 163–165; 33 C.F.R. § 328.3(a)(3) (2013); Final Rule for Regulatory Programs of the Corps of Engineers, 51 Federal Register 41,217 (Nov. 13, 1986).
28. Thomas W. Merrill, "The Story of SWANCC: Federalism and the Politics of Locally Unwanted Land Uses," in *Environmental Law Stories,* ed. Richard J. Lazarus and Oliver A. Houck (New York: Foundation Press, 2005), 290–291, 293–298. *SWANCC,* 531 U.S. at 165.
29. Solid Waste Agency of Northern Cook County v. U.S. Army Corps of Engineers, 998 F. Supp. 946 (N.D. Ill. 1998); Solid Waste Agency of Northern Cook County v. United States Army Corps of Engineers, 191 F.3d 845, 850 (7th Cir. 1999); *SWANCC,* 531 U.S. at 165.
30. Brief for Federal Respondents at 75, Solid Waste Agency of Northern Cook County v. United States Army Corps of Engineers, 531 U.S. 159 (2001) (No. 99–1178).
31. *SWANCC,* 531 U.S. at 166–167, 171–172, 174.
32. *SWANCC,* 531 U.S.at 159, 172–174. Section 404(a) reads: "Discharge into navigable waters at specified disposal sites. The Secretary may issue permits, after notice and opportunity for public hearings for the discharge of dredged or fill material into the navigable waters at specified disposal sites. Not later than the fifteenth day after the date an applicant submits all the information required to complete an application for a permit under this subsection, the Secretary shall publish the notice required by this subsection." 33 U.S.C. § 1344(a) (2012).
33. John F. Manning, "Clear Statement Rules and the Constitution," *Columbia Law Review* 110, no. 2 (2010): 407–408, 432–434; Ernest A. Young, "The Story of Gregory v. Ashcroft (1991): Clear Statement Rules and the Statutory Constitution of American Federalism," in *Statutory Interpretation Stories,* ed. William N. Eskridge Jr., Philip P. Frickey, and Elizabeth Garret (New York: Thomson Reuters/Foundation Press, 2011), 196–225.
34. *SWANCC,* 531 U.S. at 167, 174.
35. Ibid. at 176 n.2, 181–182 (Stevens, J., dissenting).
36. Ibid. at 173, 194–195, quoting United States v. Morrison, 529 U.S. 598, 617 (2000).
37. Merrill, "Story of SWANCC," 313–317.
38. Rapanos v. United States, 547 U.S. 715 (2006).
39. These facts about Rapanos are assembled from the Sixth Circuit's opinion in United States v. Rapanos, 376 F.3d 629, 632–634 (6th Cir. 2004) and from Justice Kennedy's concurrence and Justice Stevens's dissent in Rapanos v. United States, 547 U.S. at 762–765 (Kennedy, J., concurring), 788–792 (Stevens, J., dissenting). The Supreme Court denied Rapanos's petition for writ of certiorari in the criminal case, 541 U.S. 972 (2004). Compare Nolan Finley, "Feds Destroy Lives and Property Rights," *Detroit News,* May 9, 2004, with Jay Taylor, "There Is No Excuse for Destroying Wetlands," Chesapeake Bay

Group Sierra Club, accessed November 7, 2013, http://virginia.sierraclub.org/cbg/jtaylor.html.

40. Brief for Petitioners at 9, Rapanos v. United States, 547 U.S. 715 (2006) (No. 04-1034). Brief for Petitioners at 5, Carabell v. United States (No. 04-1384) (Consolidated and reported under Rapanos v. United States, 547 U.S. 715 (2006)(No. 1034); Brief for the United States at 8, Rapanos v. United States, 547 U.S. 715 (2006) (Nos. 04-1034 and 04-1384); Transcript of Oral Argument at 4–5, 16–17, 43–45, 47–49, Rapanos v. United States, 547 U.S. 715 (2006) (Nos. 04-1034 and 04-1384).

41. *Rapanos,* 547 U.S. 715.

42. *Rapanos,* 547 U.S. at 721; Scalia has storied their counterparts elsewhere, for example, in his opinion for the Court in *Lucas v. South Carolina Coastal Council,* 505 U.S. 1003 (1992) (enterprising property owner prevented by state environmental rules from building houses on two beach front lots), and in his dissent in *Babbitt v. Sweet Home Chapter of Communities for a Great Oregon,* 515 U.S. 687, 714 (1995) ("the simplest farmer who finds his land conscripted [by Endangered Species Act regulation] to national zoological use").

43. *Rapanos,* 547 U.S. at 721–722; 547 U.S. at 777 (Kennedy, J., concurring in judgment).

44. 33 U.S.C. §1251(b) (2012).

45. *Rapanos,* 547 U.S. at 732, quoting from *Webster's New International Dictionary,* 2nd ed. (1954), 732n4, 734.

46. Ibid. at 739, 752.

47. *SWANCC,* 531 U.S. at 167.

48. Massachusetts v. EPA, 549 U.S. 497, 559–560 (Scalia, J., dissenting) (2007); *Sweet Home,* 515 U.S. 687.

49. *Rapanos,* 547 U.S. at 748–749; Lujan v. Defenders of Wildlife (Lujan II), 504 U.S. 555, 595 (1992).

50. *Rapanos,* 547 U.S. at 798n8 (Stevens, J., dissenting). See also 547 U.S. at 777 (Kennedy, J., concurring) (arguing that the plurality opinion is "unduly dismissive" of environmental interests).

51. PUD No. 1 v. Washington Department of Ecology, 511 U.S. 700, 719–720(1994); 511 U.S. at 735–736 (Thomas, J., dissenting) (emphasis in original).

52. 33 U.S.C. § 1251.

53. *Rapanos,* 547 U.S. at 794, 792–793 (Stevens, J., dissenting, quoting Riverside Bayview, 424 U.S. 121, 123, emphasis added; "Our unanimous opinion in Riverside Bayview squarely controls these cases").

54. Ibid. at 801.

55. Ibid. at 803–805.

56. Thomas W. Merrill, "Textualism and the Future of the *Chevron* Doctrine," *Washington University Law Quarterly* 72, no. 1 (1994): 357.

57. *Rapanos,* 547 U.S. at 776, 782 ("This interpretation of the Act does not raise federalism or Commerce Clause concerns sufficient to support a presumption against its adoption").

58. Ibid. at 781–782, 786.

59. *SWANCC,* 531 U.S. at 167; *Rapanos,* 547 U.S. at 786.

60. *Rapanos,* 547 U.S. at 758 (Roberts, C.J., concurring); United States v. Gerke Excavating, Inc., 464 F.3d 723 (7th Cir. 2006); United States v. Robison, 505 F.3d 1208 (11th Cir. 2007) (applying Justice Kennedy's "significant nexus" test); United States v. Johnson, 467 F.3d 56 (1st Cir. 2006), United States v. Donovan, 661 F.3d 174 (3d Cir. 2011), cert. denied, 132 S. Ct. 2409 (2012), and United States v. Bailey, 571 F.3d 791 (8th Cir. 2009) (applying the "significant nexus" test or the plurality test or both); Northern California River Watch v. Wilcox, 633 F.3d 766 (9th Cir. 2011), Precon Development Corporation, Inc. v. U.S. Army Corps of Engineers, 633 F.3d 278 (4th Cir. 2011), United States v. Cundiff, 555 F.3d 200 (6th Cir. 2009), United States v. Lucas, 516 F.3d 316 (5th Cir. 2008), and Northern California River Watch v. City of Healdsburg, 496 F.3d 993 (9th Cir. 2006) (reserving the question of which test should govern and deferring to the agency's interpretation).

61. United States Environmental Protection Agency and U.S. Army Corps of Engineers, *Draft Guidance on Identifying Waters Protected by the Clean Water Act* (Washington, DC: U.S. Environmental Protection Agency, 2011), http://www.epa.gov/tp/pdf/wous_guidance_4-2011.pdf; "Definition of 'Waters of the United States' under the Clean Air Act," 79 *Federal Register* 22,188–22,274 (Apr. 21, 2014).

62. National Federation of Independent Businesses v. Sebelius, 132 S.Ct. 2566, 2589 (2012).

63. Rancho Viejo, LLC v. Norton, 323 F.3d 1062 (D.C. Cir. 2003); GDF Realty Investments, Ltd. v. Norton, 326 F.3d 622 (5th Cir. 2003); Gibbs v. Babbitt, 214 F.3d 483 (4th Cir. 2000); National Association of Home Builders v. Babbitt, 130 F.3d 1041 (D.C. Cir. 1997); Ranch Viejo, LLC v. Norton, 334 F.3d 1158, 1162 (D.C. Cir. 2003), rehearing en banc denied, 323 F.3d 1062 (D.C. Cir. 2003) (Sentelle, J., and Roberts, J., dissenting).

Chapter 8: Private Property

1. Robert C. Ellickson, "Property in Land," *Yale Law Journal* 102, no. 6 (1993): 1317.

2. See, for example, John R. Nolon, "Introduction: Discovering and Evaluating Local Environmental Law," in *New Ground: The Advent of Local Environmental Law,* ed. John R. Nolon (Washington, DC: Environmental Law Institute, 2003), xxii–xxiii.

3. See generally Philip Shabecoff, *A Fierce Green Fire: The American Environmental Movement,* rev. ed. (Washington, DC: Island Press, 2003), 84.

4. See Michael S. Greve, *The Demise of Environmentalism in American Law* (Washington, DC: AEI Press, 1996), 4–5.

5. Thomas E. Merrill, "Property and the Right to Exclude," *Nebraska Law Review* 77, no. 4 (1998): 734–739.

6. Loretto v. Teleprompter Manhattan CATV Corp., 458 U.S. 419, 435 (1982). See also Andrus v. Allard, 444 U.S. 51, 65–66 (1979) (framing property as a "bundle of property rights"); Merrill, "Property and the Right to Exclude," 737–739.

7. Richard A. Epstein, "The Harm Principle and How It Grew," *University of Toronto Law Journal* 45, no. 4 (1995): 369–417.

8. Eric T. Freyfogle, "Property and Liberty," *Harvard Environmental Law Review* 34, no. 1 (2010): 95; Eric T. Freyfogle, "The Owning and Taking of Sensitive Lands," *UCLA Law Review* 43, no. 1 (1995): 104–105.

9. Ellickson, "Property in Land," 1344–1345, 1353.

10. Eric T. Freyfogle, *On Private Property* (Boston: Beacon Press, 2007), 74, 137.

11. Freyfogle, "Owning and Taking," 96–97. Aldo Leopold, *A Sand County Almanac, with Essays on Conservation from Round River* (New York: Ballantine Books, 1966), 239.

12. Lucas v. South Carolina Coastal Council, 505 U.S. 1003, 1015 (1992). Richard A. Epstein, "Lucas v. South Carolina Coastal Council: A Tangled Web of Expectations," *Stanford Law Review* 45, no. 5 (1993): 1369–1392. Justice Souter wrote a "statement" arguing that the case should be dismissed because of an unresolved question of fact: the residual value of Lucas's property. 505 U.S. 1076–1077 (statement of Souter, J.).

13. U.S. Const. amend. V. Compare Michael Treanor, "The Original Understanding of the Takings Clause and the Political Process," *Columbia Law Review* 95, no. 4 (1995): 782–887, with Andrew S. Gold, "Regulatory Takings and Original Intent: The Direct Physical Takings Thesis Goes Too Far," *American University Law Review* 49, no. 1 (1999): 181–242. Mugler v. Kansas, 123 U.S. 623, 669 (1887); Hadecheck v. Sebastian, 239 U.S. 394 (1915); Goldblatt v. Town of Hempstead, 369 U.S. 590 (1962). *Lucas,* 505 U.S. 1003, 1040 (Blackmun, J., dissenting). Compare the majority's acknowledgment in *Lucas* that the *Mugler* line of cases had "suggested that 'harmful or noxious uses' of property may be proscribed by government regulation without the requirement of compensation." *Lucas,* 505 U.S. at 1022.

14. Pennsylvania Coal Company v. Mahon, 260 U.S. 393, 415, 417 (1922).

15. Penn Central Transportation Co. v. New York City, 438 U.S. 104, 124 (1978).

16. Keystone Bituminous Coal Association v. DeBenedictis, 480 U.S. 470, 488 (1987). Richard J. Lazarus, "The Measure of a Justice: Justice Scalia and the Faltering of the Property Rights Movement within the U.S. Supreme Court," *Hastings Law Journal* 57, no. 4 (2006): 789.

17. Richard A. Epstein, *Takings: Private Property and the Power of Eminent Domain* (Cambridge, MA: Harvard University Press, 1985), 138.

18. Joseph L. Sax, "Takings, Private Property and Public Rights," *Yale Law Journal* 81, no. 2 (1971): 149–187.

19. The period from *Keystone* (1987) to *Lucas* (1992) saw Justices Kennedy, Thomas, and Souter join the Court, while Justices Powell, Brennan, and Marshall departed. Later, Justice Ginsburg joined the Court after Justice White departed, and Justice Breyer joined after Justice Blackmun departed. "Members of the Supreme Court of the United States," United States Supreme Court, accessed July 22, 2014, www.supremecourt.gov/about/members.aspx.

20. *Lucas,* 505 U.S. at 1008–1009. "About Us: Island History," City of Isle of Palms, accessed November 5, 2013, http://www.iop.net/aboutus/islandhistory.aspx.

21. Beachfront Management Act, §§ 1(1), 1(4), 2(2), 1988 Acts and Joint Resolutions, South Carolina 5130–5136.

22. David Lucas, *Lucas vs. the Green Machine* (Alexander, NC: Alexander Books, 1995), 6, 23, 260–261.

23. Lucas v. South Carolina Coastal Council, 404 S.E.2d 895, 902 (1991). For discussion of Justice Toal's prior involvement with the BMA, see Lucas, *Lucas vs. the Green Machine,* 142–145.

24. Petitioner's Brief on the Merits at 19–45, Lucas v. South Carolina Coastal Council, 505 U.S. 1003 (1992) (No. 91–453). Petitioner's Reply Brief on the Merits 13–19, Lucas v. South Carolina Coastal Council; Transcript of Oral Argument before the Supreme Court at 26, Lucas v. South Carolina Coastal Council.

25. Lucas, *Lucas vs. the Green Machine,* 185–186. Brief of the Institute for Justice as Amicus Curiae in Support of Petitioner 13–14, Lucas v. South Carolina Coastal Council.

26. Oral Argument Transcript at 16, 30, 34–46, Lucas v. South Carolina Coastal Council; Respondent's Brief on the Merits at 37, 44–49, Lucas v. South Carolina Coastal Council. *Lucas,* 505 U.S. at 1033–1034 (Kennedy, J., concurring in judgment), 1043–1045 (Blackmun, J., dissenting), 1065n3 (Stevens, J., dissenting), 1076–1078 (statement of Souter, J.).

27. Respondent's Brief at 8–12, Lucas v. South Carolina Coastal Council. *Lucas,* 505 U.S. at 1013, 1045, 1062–1063. Richard J. Lazarus, "Putting the Correct Spin on Lucas," *Stanford Law Review* 45, no. 5 (1993): 1420–1421.

28. Oral Argument Transcript at 29–30, 32, 42, Lucas v. South Carolina Coastal Council. Lucas, *Lucas,* 210.

29. Richard J. Lazarus, "Measure of a Justice," *Hastings Law Journal* 5, no. 4 (2006): 803.

30. *Lucas,* 505 U.S. at 1015, 1023–1025, 1026.

31. Ibid. at 1018–1019.

32. Joseph L. Sax, "Property Rights and the Economy of Nature: Understanding Lucas v. South Carolina Coastal Council," *Stanford Law Review* 45, no. 5 (1993): 1438–1439.

33. See Oliver A. Houck, "More Unfinished Stories: Lucas, Atlanta Coalition, and Palilia/Sweet Home," *University of Colorado Law Review* 75, no. 2 (2004): 355.

34. *Lucas,* 505 U.S. at 1007, 1024–1025, n. 11.

35. Sax, "Property Rights," 1438.

36. *Lucas,* 505 U.S. at 1027–1028. See *Oxford English Dictionary,* 2nd ed., s.v. "confiscatory."

37. Antonin Scalia and Bryan Garner, *Reading Law: The Interpretation of Legal Texts* (St. Paul, MN: Thompson/West, 2012), 56.

38. *Lucas,* 505 U.S. at 1060.

39. Ibid. at 1030–1032. The background principles are provided by the state law of private nuisance, by the state power to abate public nuisances, and by other principles, including decisions that absolve parties of responsibility when responding to fire or other grave threats. Ibid. at 1029 and n.16. Richard J. Lazarus, "Lucas Unspun," *Southeastern Environmental Law Journal* 16, no. 1 (2007): 23–25.

40. See Freyfogle, "Owning and Taking," 103–104 ("As courts stood by watching, the wisdom of ecology permeated the popular consciousness through books like *Silent Spring*."); Richard J. Lazarus, *The Making of Environmental Law* (Chicago: University of Chicago Press, 2004), 121 ("The essential premise of much environmental law is . . . that the physical characteristics of the eco-system generate spatial and temporal spillovers that require restrictions on the private use of natural resources far beyond those contemplated by centuries-old common law tort rules.").

41. Lucas v. South Carolina Coastal Council, 505 U.S. 1003, 1031 (1992).

42. See Leopold, *Sand County Almanac,* 197 (asserting that a "penalt[y] of an eco-logical education is [to live] alone in a world of wounds").

43. *Lucas,* 505 U.S. at 1031.

44. See Epstein, "Lucas v. South Carolina Coastal Council," 1385–1387. Palazzolo v. Rhode Island, 533 U.S. 606 (2001). While not ruling out entirely that legis-lative enactments could render a change in "background principles," the Court observed that "a regulation that otherwise would be unconstitutional absent compensation is not transformed into a background principle of the State's law by mere virtue of the passage of title." Ibid. at 629–630.

45. Lucas, *Lucas,* 221 (stating that the chilling effect on state regulation "was one of the main reasons that I had pressed the case"); Houck, "More Unfinished Sto-ries," 344, quoting Jim Burling (an attorney for Pacific Legal Foundation, which filed an amicus brief supporting Lucas) that the goal was "to 'get rid of the regu-latory state.'" The Court remanded *Lucas* to the South Carolina Supreme Court to determine whether common law principles would have prevented construc-tion on Lucas's land. The state court held that the BMA was not a public nui-sance statute. Lucas v. South Carolina Coastal Council, 309 S.C. 424, 427 (1992).

46. *Lucas,* 505 U.S. 1003, 1035 (1992) (Kennedy, J., concurring in judgment).

47. Ibid. at 1063, 1068–1070 (Stevens, J., dissenting). Leopold, *Sand County Al-manac,* 263.

48. *Lucas,* 505 U.S. at 1036, 1050, 1053 (Blackmun, J., dissenting).

49. Molly McUsic, Memorandum to Justice Blackmun (June 25, 1992), Box 599, Folder 5, Harry A. Blackmun Papers, 1913–2001, Library of Congress.

50. Sax, "Property Rights," 1442, 1445.

51. Ibid., 1446. Sax goes on in his article to propose a version of property law that would "accommodate ecological needs without impairing the necessary func-tions of the transformational economy," Sax, "Property Rights," 1446; Albert Gidari, "The Economy of Nature, Private Property and the Endangered Spe-cies Act," *Fordham Environmental Law Journal* 6, no. 3 (1995): 661–688.

52. Epstein, "Lucas v. South Carolina Coastal Council," 1369–1392.

53. Soon after *Lucas* came down, the lawyer for council, Richard Lazarus, predicted that the Court's per se rule would discourage lower courts from finding a taking in the vast majority of cases in which landowners could not establish complete loss of value. Epstein himself suggested the same. Fifteen years later, Lazarus reported that in the hundreds of cases in which state and federal courts had entertained *Lucas* takings claims, courts relied on *Lucas* to find a taking in fewer than ten. Lazarus, "Lucas Unspun," 28 and n102. Carol M. Rose, "The Story of Lucas: Environmental Land Use Regulation between

Developers and the Deep Blue Sea," in *Environmental Law Stories,* ed. Richard J. Lazarus and Oliver A. Houck (New York: Foundation Press, 2005), 269.

54. Vicki Been, "Lucas v. the Green Machine: Using the Takings Clause to Promote More Efficient Regulation?" in *Property Stories,* ed. Gerald Korngold and Andrew P. Morriss (New York: Foundation Press, 2004), 239, 245–249.

55. Palazzolo v. Rhode Island, 533 U.S. 606 (2001). Tahoe-Sierra Preservation Council, Inc. v. Tahoe Regional Planning Agency, 535 U.S. 302, 307 (2002).

56. In another progovernment takings decision, *Kelo v. City of New London, Connecticut,* 545 U.S. 469 (2005), the Court upheld the city's taking of private property for economic redevelopment. In this case, the government had paid compensation, and the question was whether the taking was permissible under the public use clause of the Fifth Amendment.

57. Babbitt v. Sweet Home Chapter of Communities for a Great Oregon, 515 U.S. 687 (1995); Richard A. Epstein, "Babbitt v. Sweet Home Chapters of Oregon: The Law and Economics of Habitat Preservation," *Supreme Court Economic Review* 5 (1997): 48–57.

58. 16 U.S.C. §§ 1538(a)(1)(B), 1532(19) (2012).

59. See 50 C.F.R. § 17.3 (2013).

60. Sweet Home Chapter of Communities for a Great Oregon v. Lujan, 806 F. Supp. 279, 281–282 (1992). Sweet Home Chapter of Communities for a Great Oregon v. Babbitt, 17 F.3d 1465 (D.C. Cir. 1994).

61. Transcript of Oral Argument at 5–8, Babbitt v. Sweet Home Chapter of Communities for a Great Oregon, 515 U.S. 687 (1995) (No. 94–859).

62. *Babbitt,* 515 U.S. 687, 697–702 (1995), quoting 16 U.S.C. § 1531(b) (2006). The Court's analysis also relied on section 10(a)(1)(B) of the act, which authorizes the Department of the Interior to permit certain actions that "take" endangered species "if such taking is incidental to, and not the purpose of" the action. The Court reasoned that if "take" contemplated only direct harm to endangered species, the provision for incidental take permits would be of no use. Ibid. at 691.

63. Ibid. at 714 (Scalia, J., dissenting). Sax, "Property Rights," 1442.

64. *Babbitt,* 515 U.S. 687, 715–718 (1995) (Scalia, J., dissenting).

65. See ibid. at 726–728, 714 (Scalia, J., dissenting).

66. Ibid. at 721 (Scalia, J., dissenting).

67. Ibid.

68. Ibid. at 708–709, 712, 696n9 (O'Connor, J., concurring).

69. Ibid. at 713 (O'Connor, J., concurring).

70. J. B. Ruhl, "The Endangered Species Act's Fall from Grace in the Supreme Court," *Harvard Environmental Law Review* 36, no. 2 (2012): 502–503. TVA v. Hill, 437 U.S. 153, 179 (1978).

71. Richard J. Lazarus, "Measure of a Justice," *Hastings Law Journal* 57, no. 4 (March 2006): 783–808; Nollan v. California Coastal Commission, 483 U.S. 825 (1987); Dolan v. City of Tigard, 512 U.S. 374 (1994).

72. Koontz v. St. Johns River Water Management District, 133 S.Ct. 2586, 2607 (Kagan, J., dissenting).

73. Ibid. at 2592, 2611.

74. Ibid. at 2590, 2611.
75. Ibid. at 2595, 2589, 2591. Nollan v. California Coastal Commission, 483 U.S. 825, 837, quoting J.E.D. Associates, Inc. v. Atkinson, 432 A.2d 12 (New Hampshire, 1981).
76. *Koontz,* 133 S.Ct. at 2608–2609 (Kagan, J., dissenting).
77. Compare John D. Echeverria, "Koontz: The Very Worst Takings Decision Ever?" (working paper, Vermont Law School, 2014): 2, 33–44, http://papers.ssrn.com /sol3/papers.cfm?abstract_id=2316406##, with Robert C. Ellickson et al., *Land Use Controls: Cases and Materials,* 4th ed. (New York: Walters Kluwer Law & Business, 2013), 707. See also Sackett v. EPA, 132 S. Ct. 1367 (2012) (unanimous ruling with property rights overtones establishing landowner's entitlement to judicial review of EPA notice of violation).
78. Lujan v. Defenders of Wildlife, 504 U.S. 555 (1992).
79. Babbit v. Sweet Home Chapter of Communities for a Great Oregon, 515 U.S. at 721.
80. *Lujan,* 504 U.S. 555, 579 (Kennedy, J., concurring). Lucas v. South Carolina Coastal Council, 505 U.S. 1003, 1035 (Kennedy, J., concurring).
81. Rapanos v. United States, 547 U.S. 715, 776 (Kennedy, J., concurring, discussing holding in *SWANCC*).

Chapter 9: The Eclipse of NEPA

1. "New Federal Law May Be Giant Step on Road to Environmental Quality," *Conservation Foundation Letter,* April 1970, 10–11, quoting Congressman Reuss; R. Frederic Fisher, "Environmental Lawyer in the Lion's Mouth: Litigation before and against Administrative Agencies," in *National Conference on Environmental Law, Transcripts of the Speeches, November 1970* (1971), 102.
2. For example, John D. Echeverria, "No Success Like Failure: The Platte River Collaborative Watershed Planning Process," *William & Mary Environmental Law & Policy Review* 25, no. 3 (2001): 582; Daniel R. Mandelker, *NEPA Law and Litigation,* 2nd ed. (Eagan, MN: Thomson Reuters, 2013), § 1.1; Michael C. Blumm and Marla Nelson, "Pluralism and the Environment Revisited: The Role of Comment Agencies in NEPA Litigation," *Vermont Law Review* 37, no. 5 (2012): 5; Sam Kalen, "Ecology Comes of Age: NEPA's Lost Mandate," *Duke Environmental Law & Policy Forum* 21, no. 1 (2010): 118; Matthew J. Lindstrom and Zachary A. Smith, *The National Environmental Policy Act: Judicial Misconstruction, Legislative Indifference, and Executive Neglect* (College Station: Texas A&M University Press, 2001), 4; Arthur W. Murphy, "The National Environmental Policy Act and the Licensing Process: Environmentalist Magna Carta or Agency Coup de Grace?" *Columbia Law Review* 72, no. 6 (1972): 983.
3. Lynton Keith Caldwell, *The National Environmental Policy Act: An Agenda for the Future* (Bloomington: Indiana University Press, 1998), xvi.
4. Kleppe v. Sierra Club, 427 U.S. 390, 421 (1976) (Marshall, J., concurring in part and dissenting in part). Andrus v. Sierra Club, 442 U.S. 347, 358 (1979); Robertson v. Methow Valley Citizens Council, Inc., 490 U.S. 332, 355 (1989).

5. Richard Lazarus, "The National Environmental Policy Act in the U.S. Supreme Court: A Reappraisal and a Peek behind the Curtains," *Georgetown Law Journal* 100, no. 5 (2012): 1510–1511, 1523–1524.

6. Lazarus, "National Environmental Policy Act," 1529–1534.

7. Ibid. at 1565.

8. For example, Solid Waste Agency of Northern Cook County v. U.S. Army Corps of Engineers, 531 U.S. 159 (2001) ("SWANCC").

9. Winter v. Natural Resources Defense Council, Inc., 555 U.S. 7 (2008).

10. I am indebted for this insight to Michael Vandenbergh.

11. 42 U.S.C. § 4331(a)–(b) (2012).

12. Senate Committee on Interior and Insular Affairs, 90th Congress, National Policy for the Environment: A Report on the Need for a National Policy for the Environment: An Explanation of Its Purpose and Content; An Exploration of Means to Make It Effective; and a Listing of Questions Implicit in Its Establishment (Washington, DC: U.S. Government Printing Office, 1968) ("National Policy for the Environment Report").

13. National Policy for the Environment Report at 3, 6, 16, 17, 23.

14. Lindstrom and Smith, *National Environmental Policy Act,* 7.

15. National Environmental Policy: Hearing Before the Senate Committee on Interior and Insular Affairs on S. 1075, S. 237, and S. 1752, 91st Congress (1969). 42 U.S.C. § 4332(1), (2)(C), (2)(E), (2012).

16. Caldwell, *National Environmental Policy Act,* 21, 78, 170.

17. Calvert Cliffs' Coordinating Committee, Inc. v. United States Atomic Energy Commission, 449 F.2d 1109 (D.C. Cir. 1971); San Antonio Conservation Society v. Texas Highway Department, 400 U.S. 968 (1970).

18. *San Antonio Conservation Society,* 400 U.S. at 968–969, 977–978.

19. A. Dan Tarlock, "The Story of Calvert Cliffs: A Court Construes the National Environmental Policy Act to Create a Powerful Cause of Action," in *Environmental Law Stories,* ed. Richard J. Lazarus and Oliver A. Houck (New York: Foundation Press, 2005), 77, 95, citing Jack Bass, *Unlikely Heroes: The Dramatic Story of the Southern Judges of the Fifth Circuit Who Translated the Supreme Court's Brown Decision into a Revolution of Equality* (New York: Simon and Schuster, 1981).

20. *Calvert Cliffs',* 449 F.2d 1109, 1111 (D.C. Cir. 1971).

21. Tarlock, "Story of Calvert Cliffs," 97.

22. *Calvert Cliffs',* 449 F.2d at 1117–1118, quoting from 10 C.F.R. pt. 50 App. D as then in effect.

23. Ibid. at 1115. Environmental Defense Fund, Inc. v. Corps of Engineers of United States Army, 470 F.2d 289, 297 (8th Cir. 1972); Sierra Club v. Froehlke, 486 F.2d 946, 952 (7th Cir. 1973); Conservation Council of North Carolina v. Froehlke, 473 F.2d 664, 665 (4th Cir. 1973). Justice Douglas added his voice to the view that NEPA imposes "substantive duties" and that "environmental considerations are, so far as possible, to shape all agency policies and decisions." U.S. v Students Challenging Regulatory Agency Procedures (SCRAP), 412 U.S. 669, 712, 714 (1973) (Douglas, J., dissenting in part).

24. 42 U.S.C. § 4332(1) (2012). House of Representatives, Report 91–765, at 9–10 (1969) (Conference Report). Caldwell, *National Environmental Policy Act*, 12.

25. See 5 U.S.C. § 706(2)(A) (2012). Council on Environmental Quality, Environmental Quality—1977: The Eighth Annual Report of the Council on Environmental Quality (Washington, DC: Executive Office of the President and Council on Environmental Quality, 1977), 121. See Nicholas C. Yost, "NEPA's Promise—Partially Fulfilled," *Environmental Law* 20, no. 3 (1990): 546–547.

26. Kleppe v. Sierra Club, 427 U.S. 390, 410n21 (1976); Vermont Yankee Nuclear Power Corp. v. Natural Resources Defense Council, Inc., 435 U.S. 519, 557–558 (1978); Strycker's Bay Neighborhood Council, Inc. v. Karlen, 444 U.S. 223, 227–228 (1980); Robertson v. Methow Valley Citizens Council, Inc., 490 U.S. 332, 351 (1989).

27. *Kleppe*, 427 U.S. 390 (1976).

28. Ibid. at 398; Sierra Club v. Morton, 514 F.2d 856, 867 (D.C. Cir. 1975); Sierra Club v. Morton, 421 F. Supp. 638, 643 (D.D.C. 1974).

29. *Sierra Club*, 421 F. Supp. at 646. Sierra Club, 514 F.2d at 877–878, 880.

30. Transcript of Oral Argument 9, Kleppe v. Sierra Club, 427 U.S. 390 (1976) (Nos. 75–552 & 75–561); Brief for the Petitioners at 8–9, 29, 47, Kleppe v. Sierra Club; Reply Brief for the Petitioners at n.3, Kleppe v. Sierra Club. Brief for the Respondents at 2, Kleppe v. Sierra Club. *Kleppe*, 427 U.S. at 406 and n.15 (emphasis in original).

31. *Kleppe*, 427 U.S. at 409, 414.

32. Ibid. at 416–419. Compare 427 U.S. at 409 with 427 U.S. at 417–418 (Marshall, J., dissenting).

33. Justice Blackmun, Notes on Conference (Apr. 27, 1976), Box 232, Folder 5, Harry A. Blackmun Papers, 1913–2001, The Library of Congress; Justice Harry A. Blackmun, Memorandum (Apr. 27, 1976), Box 232, Folder 5, Blackmun Papers.

34. *Kleppe*, 427 U.S. at 410 n.21.

35. Lindstrom and Smith, *National Environmental Policy Act*, 118.

36. Vermont Yankee Nuclear Power Corporation v. Natural Resources Defense Council, Inc., 435 U.S. 519 (1977). Lazarus, "National Environmental Policy," 1580.

37. 42 U.S.C. § 5801 (2012).

38. See Natural Resources Defense Council, Inc. v. Nuclear Regulatory Commission, 547 F.2d 633, 645, 654 (internal quotes omitted), 655 (D.C. Cir. 1976). Aeschliman v. U.S. Nuclear Regulatory Commission, 547 F.2d 622 at 631–632 (D.C. Cir. 1976).

39. *Vermont Yankee*, 435 U.S. 519, 538, quoting 41 Federal Register 45,849 (1976). (1978). Justices Blackmun and Powell did not participate in the case. Brief for the Federal Respondents 30–31, Vermont Yankee Nuclear Power Corporation v. Natural Resources Defense Council, Inc., 435 U.S. 519 (1978) (Nos. 76–619 and 76–528); Transcript of Oral Argument 19–20, Vermont Yankee Nuclear Power Corp. v. Natural Resources Defense Council, Inc.

40. Justice William J. Brennan, Memorandum to the Conference, Vermont Yankee Power Corporation v. Natural Resources Defense Council, Inc. (Jan. 12, 1978), Box 258, Folder 5, Blackmun Papers. Justice Rehnquist, Memorandum (1st Draft), 3–4 n. 1a, Vermont Yankee Power Corporation v. Natural Resources Defense Council, Inc. (Feb. 24, 1978), Box 258, Folder 5, Blackmun Papers. Justice William Rehnquist, Memorandum to Justice William Brennan, Vermont Nuclear Power Corp. v. NRDC (Feb. 27, 1978), responding to Memorandum from Justice William A. Brennan Jr., to Justice William Rehnquist, Vermont Nuclear Power Corp. v. NRDC, Consumers Power Corp. v. Aeschliman (Feb. 27, 1978), Box 258, Folder 5, Blackmun Papers; Justice William Rehnquist, Memorandum to Justice Thurgood Marshall, Vermont Nuclear Power Corp v. NRDC (Mar. 6, 1978), responding to Memorandum from Justice Thurgood Marshall to Justice William Rehnquist, Vermont Nuclear Power Corp. v. NRDC (Mar. 3. 1978), Box 258, Folder 5, Blackmun Papers. Justice William J. Brennan Jr., Memorandum to Justice William Rehnquist, Vermont Yankee v. NRDC (Mar. 20, 1976), Box 258, Folder 5, Blackmun Papers.
41. *Vermont Yankee*, 435 U.S. at 525, 542, 548.
42. Ibid. at 557–558.
43. "Kafkaesque" first appeared in the *New York Times* in April 1947 but was uncommon until the 1970s. The distribution of its use in the *Times* is as follows: 1940s: 2; 1950s: 10; 1960s: 69; 1970s: 186; 1980s: 204; 1990s: 243; 2000s: 214. ProQuest Historical Newspapers search (Aug. 20, 2013). Subsequent uses are Dobbert v. Wainwright, 468 U.S. 1231, 1242 n.* (1984) (Marshall, J., dissenting) ("The frenzied rush to execution that characterizes this case has become a common, if Kafkaesque, feature of the Court's capital cases."); Gardebring v. Jenkins, 485 U.S. 415, 422 (1988) ("In explaining its basic holding, the Court of Appeals pointed out that advance notice to lump-sum recipients was necessary to achieve the purposes of the 1981 amendment, and that to impose the new rule on a family that assumed that the old rule was still in effect 'would be truly Kafkaesque.' ") (footnotes omitted); Commissioner, I.N.S. v. Jean, 496 U.S. 154, 163 (1990) ("As petitioners admit, allowing a 'substantial justification' exception to fee litigation theoretically can spawn a 'Kafkaesque judicial nightmare' of infinite litigation to recover fees for the last round of litigation over fees."); PGA Tour, Inc. v. Martin, 532 U.S. 661, 705 (2001) (Scalia, J., dissenting) ("Complaints about this case are not 'properly directed to Congress,' . . . They are properly directed to this Court's Kafkaesque determination that professional sports organizations, and the fields they rent for their exhibitions, are 'places of public accommodation' to the competing athletes, and the athletes themselves 'customers' of the organization that pays them").
44. Memorandum from William J. Brennan Jr. to Justice William Rehnquist, Re: Vermont Yankee Nuclear Power Corp. v. NRDC, Consumers Power Corp. v. Aeschliman (Feb. 27, 1978), Box 258, Folder 5, Blackmun Papers (internal quotes removed).
45. Lazarus, "National Environmental Policy Act," 1583.
46. Trinity Episcopal School Corp. and Trinity Housing Co., Inc. v. Romney, 523 F.2d 88, 95 (2d Cir. 1975).

47. Karlen v. Harris, 590 F.2d 39, 42 (2d Cir. 1978), quoting Special Environmental Clearance Report.

48. Ibid. at 43–44.

49. Ibid. at 43.

50. Brief for the United States for Petition for a Writ of Certiorari to the United States Court of Appeals for the Second Circuit at 14–15, 15n16, Harris v. Karlen, rev'd sub nom. Strycker's Bay Neighborhood Council, Inc. v. Karlen, 444 U.S. 223 (1980) (No. 79–184).

51. Brief in Opposition to Petition for Writ of Certiorari to the United States Court of Appeals for the Second Circuit at 18, 33–36, Harris v. Karlen.

52. Lazarus, "National Environmental Policy Act," 1546. Strycker's Bay Neighborhood Council, Inc. v. Karlan, 444 U.S. 223, 227–228 and n.2.

53. Lazarus, "National Environmental Policy Act," 1524.

54. *Strycker's Bay,* 444 U.S. at 229 (emphasis in Justice Marshall's quote from *Vermont Yankee*) (internal quotes omitted), 230–231 and n.2.

55. Ibid. at 227 (emphasis supplied).

56. Richard I. Goldsmith and William C. Banks, "Environmental Values: Institutional Responsibility and the Supreme Court," *Harvard Environmental Law Review* 7, no. 1 (1983): 5–6 (footnotes omitted).

57. Robertson v. Methow Valley Citizens Council, Inc., 490 U.S. 332 (1989).

58. Methow Valley Citizens Council, Inc. v. Regional Forester, 16 Environmental Law Reporter 20,935–20,938 (D. Or. 1986).

59. Ibid. at 20,932, 20,938; Methow Valley Citizens Council v. Regional Forester, 833 F.2d 810, 817–820 (9th Cir. 1987).

60. The case was argued together with *Marsh v. Oregon Natural Resources Council,* 490 U.S. 360 (1989), a NEPA case on the question of whether an EIS must be supplemented with new information. Transcript of Oral Argument at 22, Robertson v. Methow Valley Citizens Council, Inc., 490 U.S. 332 (1989) and Marsh v. Oregon Natural Resources Council, 490 U.S. 360 (1989) (Nos. 87–1703 & 87–1704).

61. *Robertson,* 490 U.S. at 339, 351, 359. Lazarus, "National Environmental Policy Act," 1555.

62. *Robertson,* 490 U.S. at 349–351.

63. Ibid. at 342–343; Yost, "NEPA's Promise," 547. See also Tarlock, "Story of Calvert Cliffs," 103–105 (*Strycker's Bay* and *Methow* together produced for NEPA the "truthful teenager rule").

64. *Robertson,* 490 U.S. at 332, 349–350.

65. For example, Joseph L. Sax, "The (Unhappy) Truth about NEPA," *Oklahoma Law Review* 26, no. 2 (1973): 245–248; Oliver A. Houck, "Is That All? A Review of *The National Environmental Policy Act, an Agenda for the Future,* by Lynton Keith Caldwell," *Duke Environmental Law & Policy Forum* 11, no. 1 (2000): 173–177, 179; R. N. L. Andrews, "The Unfinished Business of National Environmental Policy," in *Environmental Policy and NEPA: Past, Present, and Future,* ed. Ray Clark and Larry Canter (Boca Raton, FL: St. Lucie Press, 1997), 85–98. Brief for Petitioner United States, Petition for Writ of Certiorari to the United States Court of Appeals for the Second Circuit 14–15 (Aug. 3,

1979), Harris v. Karlen, decided *sub nom.* Strycker's Bay Neighborhood Council, Inc. v. Karlen, 444 U.S. 223 (1980).

66. See Eric Pearson, "Section 102(1) of the National Environmental Policy Act," *Creighton Law Review* 41, no. 3 (2008): 369–384.

67. Gerald N. Rosenberg, *The Hollow Hope: Can Courts Bring About Social Change?* 2nd ed. (Chicago: University of Chicago Press, 2008), 282.

68. Citizens to Pres. Overton Park, Inc. v. Volpe, 401 U.S. at 416.

69. Patrick M. Garry, "Judicial Review and the 'Hard Look' Doctrine," *Nevada Law Journal* 7, no. 1 (2006): 157n42; Gillian E. Metzger, "The Story of Vermont Yankee," in *Administrative Law Stories,* ed. Peter L. Strauss (New York: Foundation Press, 2006), 146. Greater Boston Television Corp. v. F.C.C., 444 F.2d 841, 851, 853 (D.C. Cir. 1970).

70. Harold Leventhal, "Environmental Decisionmaking and the Role of the Courts," *University of Pennsylvania Law Review* 122, no. 3 (1974): 523–524.

71. Kleppe v. Sierra Club, 427 U.S.390, 409–410, 414. For example, Marsh v. Oregon Natural Resources Council, 490 U.S. 360, 378 (1989) (according agency "discretion to rely on the reasonable opinions of its own qualified experts" in deciding the significance of new information on effects of dam); Baltimore Gas & Electric Co. v. Natural Resources Defense Council, Inc., 462 U.S. 87, 103 (1983) (in reviewing NRC's assumption of "zero release" from disposal of nuclear waste, a prediction within NRC's "special expertise, at the frontiers of science . . . a reviewing court must generally be at its most deferential").

72. *Kleppe,* 427 U.S. at 414; Calvert Cliffs' Coordinating Committee, Inc. v. U.S. Atomic Energy Commission, 449 F.2d at 1114. Flint Ridge Development Co. v. Scenic Rivers Association of Oklahoma, 426 U.S. 776 (1976); Lazarus, "National Environmental Policy Act," 1539–1540 and n.165.

73. See Lazarus, "National Environmental Policy Act," 1578–1580 (Justice Rehnquist successfully arguing for deletion of quotation of Calvert Cliffs from Justice Marshall's draft opinion in Flint Ridge, 426 U.S. 776 [1976]).

74. Aeschilman v. U.S. Nuclear Regulatory Commission, 547 F.2d 622, 628 and n. 13 (D.C. Cir. 1976).

75. Vermont Yankee Nuclear Power Corporation v. Natural Resources Defense Council, Inc., 435 U.S. 519, 532, 551–554 (1978). See Metzger, "Story of Vermont Yankee," 142n65, 143.

76. *Vermont Yankee,* 435 U.S. at 553–554.

77. Department of Transportation v. Public Citizen, 541 U. S. 752 (2004); Calvert Cliffs' Coordinating Committee, 449 F.2d at 1112; Flint Ridge, 426 U.S. 776 (1976); Lazarus, "National Environmental Policy Act," 1540, 1558.

78. *Department of Transportation,* 541 U.S. at 759–761.

79. Ibid. at 761–762. Public Citizen v. Department of Transportation, 316 F.3d 1002, 1022 (2003). See 40 C.F.R. § 1508.8.

80. *Department of Transportation,* 541 U.S. at 766.

81. Ibid. at 768, 770.

82. Brief for the Respondents at 38–42, Department of Transportation v. Public Citizen, 541 U.S. 752 (2004) (03–358).

83. *Department of Transportation,* 541 U.S. at 769n.2.

84. Ibid at 767.

85. For example, Andrus v. Sierra Club, 442 U.S. 347, 350–351 (1979).
86. Winter v. Natural Resources Defense Council, Inc., 555 U.S. at 20–21, 33; Monsanto Co. v. Geertson Seed Farms, 561 U.S. 139, 156–157 (2010).
87. Weinberger v. Romero-Barcelo, 456 U.S. 305, 306 (1982). For another example of this approach, see Amoco Production Co. v. Village of Gambell, 480 U.S. 531(1987) (declining injunction against oil exploration leasing in violation of Alaska National Interest Lands Conservation Act).
88. Natural Resources Defense Council, Inc. v. Winter, 530 F. Supp. 2d 1110, 1114–1115, 1118 (C.D. Cal. 2008), *aff'd*, 518 F.3d 658 (9th Cir. 2008).
89. *Winter*, 555 U.S. at 12, 24–25, 33.
90. Ibid. at 12, 14, 21, 23, 33.
91. Ibid. at 26, 33.
92. Natural Resources Defense Council, Inc. v. Winter, 518 F.3d at 703; *Winter*, 555 U.S. at 31, 33.
93. In his partial concurrence, Justice Breyer agreed with the majority that the lower courts had not justified their assessment of the public interest and would have vacated the portions of the district court's preliminary injunction challenged by the Navy, but he would have kept in effect the terms of a stay order issued by the Ninth Circuit "pending completion of an acceptable EIS." *Winter*, 555 U.S. at 41–43, 52–53.
94. Transcript of Oral Argument at 44, Winter v. Natural Resources Defense Council, Inc., 555 U.S. 7 (2008) (No. 07–1239). *Winter*, 555 U.S. at 9.
95. Monsanto Co. v. Geertson Seed Farms, 561 U.S. at 184.
96. Andrews, "Unfinished Business," 86–87.
97. Sax, "(Unhappy) Truth," 248. Joseph L. Sax, "Introduction," *University of Michigan Journal of Law Reform* 19, no. 4 (1986): 804.
98. San Antonio Conservation Society v. Texas Highway Department, 400 U.S. 968, 977–978.
99. Lazarus, "National Environmental Policy Act," 1574.

Chapter 10: Environmentalist Futures

1. Transcript of Oral Argument at 34, Department of Transportation v. Public Citizen, 541 U.S. 752 (2004) (No. 03-358).
2. Richard E. Levy and Robert L. Glicksman, "Judicial Activism and Restraint in the Supreme Court's Environmental Law Decisions," *Vanderbilt Law Review* 42, no. 2 (1989): 346; Richard J. Lazarus, "Restoring What's Environmental about Environmental Law in the Supreme Court," *UCLA Law Review* 47, no. 3 (2000): 735–736; *Environmental Cases Decided by the United States Supreme Court, October Term 1969–October Term 2013* (spreadsheet with updates by author of Richard Lazarus's compilation through October Term 2013) (on file with author).
3. Thomas M. Keck, *The Most Activist Supreme Court in History: The Road to Modern Judicial Conservatism* (Chicago: University of Chicago Press, 2004), 134, 143–151, 199. Thomas R. Hensley, *The Rehnquist Court: Justices, Rulings and Legacy* (Santa Barbara, CA: ABC-CLIO, 2006), 24; Barry Friedman, *The Will of the People* (New York: Farrar, Straus and Giroux, 2009), 358–364.

4. Lee Epstein, William M. Landes, and Richard A. Posner, "Is the Roberts Court Pro-business?" 2007, 2, http://epstein.usc.edu/research/RobertsBusiness.pdf (published in support of *New York Times* article). But see Jonathan H. Adler, "Business, the Environment, and the Roberts Court: A Preliminary Assessment," *Santa Clara Law Review* 49, no. 4 (2009): 953 (concluding on the basis of a review of environmental decisions that the Roberts Court has not shown a pro-business bias). Andrew Dugan, "Americans Still Divided on Approval of U.S. Supreme Court," Gallup Politics, October 4, 2013, http://www.gallup.com /poll/165248/americans-still-divided-approval-supreme-court.aspx.

5. Cary Coglianese, "Social Movements, Law, and Society: The Institutionalization of the Environmental Movement," *University of Pennsylvania Law Review* 150, no. 1 (2001): 102–105, 118; Michael Shellenberger and Ted Nordhaus, *The Death of Environmentalism: Global Warming Politics in a Post-environmental World,* 2004, 8, http://www.thebreakthrough.org/images /Death_of_Environmentalism.pdf; James Gustave Speth, "The Case for New American Environmentalism," *Environmental Law Reporter News & Analysis* 39 (2009): 10,066 ("Our environmental organizations have grown in strength and sophistication, but the environment has continued to go downhill."); Lorna Salzman, "A Critique of the Shellenberger-Nordhaus Report, *The Death of Environmentalism,*" accessed December 18, 2013, http://www.lorna salzman.com/collectedwritings/Shellenberger-Nordhaus.html ("It is undeniable that environmentalism has faded into the background since Earth Day 1970, at least relative to other pressing concerns like the Iraq war, health care, corporate corruption, and the loss of jobs.").

6. Riley E. Dunlap, "At 40, Environmental Movement Endures, with Less Consensus," Gallup, April 22, 2010, www.gallup.com/poll/127487/Environmental -Movement-Endures-With-Less-Consensus.aspx.

7. Lydia Saad, "More Americans Still Prioritize Economy over the Environment," Gallup, April 3, 2013, http://www.gallup.com/poll/161594/americans-prioritize -economy-environment.aspx (internal quotations omitted); Jeffrey M. Jones, "Worry about U.S. Water, Air Pollution at Historical Lows," Gallup, April 13, 2012, http://www.gallup.com/poll/153875/Worry-Water-Air-Pollution-Historical -Lows.aspx; "Most Important Problem," Gallup, 2013, http://www.gallup .com/poll/1675/most-important-problem.aspx. But see The Pew Research Center for the People & the Press, *Deficit Reduction Rises on Public's Agenda for Obama's Second Term* (Pew Research Center, Washington, DC, 2013), http://www.people-press.org/2013/01/24/deficit-reduction-rises-on-publics -agenda-for-obamas-second-term/ (percentage of respondents in 2013 poll identifying the environment as a top priority increased by 11 percent from 2012 although it was lower by ten points or more than percentages for jobs, health care, and education).

8. Coglianese, "Social Movements," 110.

9. GOP, "We Believe in America: 2012 Republican Platform," 19, accessed July 16, 2014, http://www.presidency.ucsb.edu/papers_pdf/101961.pdf.

10. Coglianese, "Social Movements," 99–101.

11. Ibid., 102.

12. Shellenberger and Nordhaus, *Death of Environmentalism*, 8, 23; Speth, "Case for New American Environmentalism," 10,067–10,068.

13. Coglianese, "Social Movements," 113–114.

14. Ibid., 102–105, 113–114. See Jedediah Purdy, "Our Place in the World: A New Relationship for Environmental Ethics and Law," *Duke Law Journal* 62, no. 4 (2013): 880.

15. E. Donald Elliott, Bruce A. Ackerman, and John C. Millian, "Toward a Theory of Statutory Evolution: The Federalization of Environmental Law," *Journal of Law, Economics, & Organization* 1, no. 2 (1985): 313–340; Purdy, "Our Place in the World," 880.

16. "Moving America Forward: 2012 Democratic National Platform," 20–21, accessed July 16, 2014, http://www.presidency.ucsb.edu/papers_pdf/101962 .pdf. GOP, "We Believe in American: 2012 Republican Platform," 15–18, accessed 2014, http://www.presidency.ucsb.edu/papers_pdf/101961.pdf. Dunlap, "At 40, Environmental Movement Endures," (showing an approximate 25 percent disparity between Republicans and Democrats with favorable views of the movement and substantial decline among Republicans with favorable views between 2000 and 2010).

17. See also Norfolk and Western Railway Co. v. Ayers, 538 U.S. 135 (2003) (Justice Scalia joined the opinion for the Court by Justice Ginsburg upholding mental anguish damages in cases of asbestosis caused by work-related asbestos exposures under the Federal Employers' Liability Act.); Decker v. Northwest Environmental Defense Center, 133 S. Ct. 1326 (2013) (Scalia, J., concurring and dissenting) (arguing in dissent for an interpretation of EPA regulations requiring that stormwater discharges from forest roads through man-made ditches to navigable waters be regulated under the CWA).

18. Coglianese, "Social Movements," 108.

19. "Our Values," Defenders of Wildlife, accessed January 9, 2014, http://www .defenders.org/our-values; The Nature Conservancy, *Nature Protects Nourishes Strengthens Inspires Empowers Quenches Matters: 2012 Annual Report* (Arlington, VA: Nature Conservancy, 2012), http://www.nature.org/media /annualreport/annualreport2012_global.pdf; Greenpeace, accessed January 9, 2014, http://www.greenpeace.org/usa/en/about/; Center for Biological Diversity, accessed January 9, 2014, http://www.biologicaldiversity.org/; Natural Resources Defense Council, *2011 Annual Report* (New York: NRDC, 2011), 2, http://www.nrdc.org/about/annual/nrdc_annual_report2011.pdf; "Commitments," Cloud of Commitments, accessed February 14, 2014, http://www. cloudofcommitments.org/commitments/ (NRDC initiative to "encourage and hold accountable the hundreds of sustainability initiatives undertaken at Rio+20 and elsewhere by governments at all levels, business, and civil society").

20. Purdy, "Politics of Nature," 1196.

21. Speth, "The Case for New American Environmentalism," 10,068.

22. Wen Stephenson, "Gus Speth: 'Ultimate Insider' Goes Radical," *Grist*, September 17, 2012, http://grist.org/climate-energy/gus-speth-ultimate-insider-goes-radical /#disqus_thread. James Gustave Speth, *America the Possible: Manifesto for a New Economy*, 189 (New Haven: Yale University Press, 2012).

23. Ted Nordhaus and Michael Shellenberger, *Break Through: From the Death of Environmentalism to the Politics of Possibility* (Boston: Houghton Mifflin Co., 2007), 5, 153 (emphasis in original).

24. Speth, *America the Possible,* 11; Douglas A. Kysar, "The Consultants' Republic," review of *Break Through: From the Death of Environmentalism to the Politics of Possibility,* by Ted Nordhaus and Michael Shellenberger, *Harvard Law Review* 121, no. 8 (2008): 2070.

25. Speth, "Case for New American Environmentalism," 10,067.

26. John Gastil, Dan M. Kahan, and Donald Braman, "Ending Polarization: The Good News about the Culture Wars," *Boston Review* 31, no. 2 (March/April 2006): 18; Dan M. Kahan, "Two Conceptions of Emotion in Risk Regulation," *University of Pennsylvania Law Review* 156, no. 3 (2008): 765.

27. Stephen M. Gardner, "A Perfect Moral Storm: Climate Change, Intergenerational Ethics and the Problem of Moral Corruption," *Environmental Values* 15, no. 3 (2006): 397; Richard J. Lazarus, "Super Wicked Problems and Climate Change: Restraining the Present to Liberate the Future," *Cornell Law Review* 94, no. 5 (2009): 1153; Dan M. Kahan et al., "The Tragedy of the Risk-Perception Commons: Culture Conflict, Rationality Conflict, and Climate Change" (Working Paper No. 89, Cultural Cognition Project, Yale University Law School, 2011), 6; Daniel Sarewitz, "Does Climate Change Knowledge Really Matter?," *WIREs Climate Change* 2, no. 4 (2011): 475.

28. See Jedediah Purdy, "The Politics of Nature: Climate Change, Environmental Law, and Democracy," *Yale Law Journal* 119, no. 6 (2010): 1206.

29. Tommy Millsaps, "A Look Back: Closing the Tellico Dam Gates," *The Advocate and Democrat (Sweetwater, TN),* November 30, 2009, accessed January 9, 2014, http://www.advocateanddemocrat.com/news/article_1d2oabdc-a6e6-5006-9931-389bbe40538e.html.

30. GOP, "We Believe in America: 2012 Republican Platform," 18, accessed July 16, 2014, http://www.presidency.ucsb.edu/papers_pdf/101961.pdf.

31. George W. Bush, "Remarks to the Cattle Industry Annual Convention and Trade Show in Denver, Colorado" (Feb. 8, 2002), in *Weekly Compilation of Presidential Documents* 38 (2002), 201; Wolf Creek Farm, accessed July 17, 2014, http://www.wolfcreekfarm.com; Telephone interview with John Whiteside (July 10, 2014); American Grassfed, accessed July 23, 2014, http://www.americangrassfed.org/; Michael P. Vandenbergh, "Private Environmental Governance," *Cornell Law Review* 99, no. 1 (2013): 133–134. See Anthony Leiserowitz et al., "Public Support for Climate and Energy Policies in April 2013," (Yale University and George Mason University, Yale Project on Climate Change Communication, New Haven, Apr. 2013), 11 (showing that larger percentages of Americans say corporations and individuals should be doing more to address climate change than say Congress or the president should be doing more).

32. Vandenbergh, "Private Environmental Governance," 149.

33. Ibid. at 157–158.

34. U.S. Environmental Protection Agency, "EPA Green Buildings," accessed October 20, 2014, http://www.epa.gov/oaintrnt/projects/.

35. Vandenbergh, "Private Environmental Governance," 188–190.

36. Paul L. Joskow and Richard Schmalensee, "The Political Economy of Market-Based Environmental Policy: The U.S. Acid Rain Program," *Journal of Law and Economics* 41, no. 1 (1998): 48; Gastil, Kahan, and Braman, "Ending Polarization," 19.

37. Policy Options for Reducing Greenhouse Gas Emissions: Hearing Before the Senate Committee on Energy and Natural Resources, 111th Congress, 16 (2009) (Testimony of David G. Hawkins, Director of Climate Programs, Natural Resources Defense Council), http://www.gpo.gov/fdsys/browse/committee cong.action?collection=CHRG&committee=energy&chamber=senate&congr essplus=111&ycord=0 (quoting from the January 2009 Blueprint for Legislative Action of U.S. Climate Action Partnership (USCAP), a business-environmental coalition of which NRDC was a member); Michael Bastasch, "Environmentalists Cheer on Another Carbon Tax Push," *The Daily Caller,* March 4, 2013, http://dailycaller.com/2013/03/14/environmentalists-cheer-on -another-carbon-tax-push/.

38. Jonathan H. Adler, "Conservative Principles for Environmental Reform," *Duke Environmental Law & Policy Forum* 23, no. 2 (2013): 253. See also William D. Ruckelshaus et al., "A Republican Case for Climate Action," *New York Times,* August 2, 2013 (offering carbon tax as "best path to reducing greenhouse gas emissions").

39. Rachel Cleetus et al., Letter to Senior U.S. Government Officials (Feb. 8, 2011), available at http://policyintegrity.org/documents/SCC_Senior_Gov_Official _Letter_2_28_11.pdf.

40. Sierra Club v. Morton, 405 U.S. 727, 741, 750–751 (1972) (Douglas, J., dissenting).

41. Nordhaus and Shellenberger, *Break Through,* 130–135.

42. I am indebted to Jedediah Purdy for this insight into Carson's work.

43. Bill McKibben, *The End of Nature* (New York: Random House Trade Paperbacks, 2006), 47–48; Peter Kareiva et al., "Domesticated Nature: Shaping Landscapes and Ecosystems for Human Welfare," *Science,* June 29, 2007, 1866–1869.

44. Robert F. Kennedy Jr., "An Ill Wind off Cape Cod," *New York Times,* December 16, 2005.

45. Nordhaus and Shellenberger, *Break Through,* 89–95; Lisa Hymans, "Over 150 activists send letter asking Kennedy to reconsider position," *Grist,* January 7, 2006, http://grist.org/article/enviros-call-on-rfk-jr-to-support-cape-wind-project/; U.S. Department of the Interior, "Secretary Salazar Announces Approval of Cape Wind Energy Project on Outer Continental Shelf off Massachusetts," DOI News, April 28, 2010, http://www.doi.gov/news/doinews/Secretary-Salazar-Ann ounces-Approval-of-Cape-Wind-Energy-Project-on-Outer-Continental-Shelf -off-Massachusetts.cfm.

46. Kenneth Caldeira et al., "To Those Influencing Environmental Policy but Opposed to Nuclear Power" (November 3, 2013) (letter on file with author); Environmentalists for Nuclear Energy, accessed January 9, 2014, http://www.ecolo .org/base/baseen.htm; Joe Garofoli, "Some Environmentalists Back Nuclear Power," *San Francisco Chronicle,* June 12, 2013, http://www.sfgate.com/politics /joegarofoli/article/Some-environmentalists-back-nuclear-power-4597572.php. See also "Carbon Capture & Storage: A Critical Part of the Climate Change

Solutions Portfolio," ENGOnetworks on CCS, accessed January 9, 2014, http://www.engonetwork.org (endorsing an industrial level end-of-pipe technology for reducing greenhouse gas emission). Dan M. Kahan et al., "The Second National Risk and Culture Study: Making Sense of—and Making Progress In—the American Culture War of Fact" (working paper, George Washington University Legal Research Paper No. 370, Washington, DC, 2007), 4–5.

47. "About Us," BlueGreen Alliance, accessed January 9, 2014, http://www.bluegreenalliance.org/about. Richard L. Trumka, "Remarks by AFL-CIO President Richard L. Trumka" (speech, 2013 BlueGreen Alliance: Good Jobs, Green Jobs Conference, Washington, DC, April 17, 2013), http://www.aflcio.org/Press-Room/Speeches/Remarks-by-AFL-CIO-President-Richard-L.-Trumka-2013-Immigration-Campaign-Launch-Event-Chicago-Illinois/Remarks-by-AFL-CIO-President-Richard-L.-Trumka-2013-BlueGreen-Alliance-Good-Jobs-Green-Jobs-Conference-Washington-Hilton-Washington-DC.

48. Mark Lynas, *The God Species: Saving the Planet in the Age of Humans* (Washington, DC: National Geographic, 2011), 10.

49. Peter Kareiva, "Failed Metaphors and a New Environmentalism for the 21st Century," (speech, Distinctive Voices @ The Beckman Center, Irvine, CA, Nov. 16, 2011), https://www.youtube.com/watch?v=4BOEQkvCook. See Stephen Cushman, "Lumber Trucks Lumber," DrunkenBoat.com (forthcoming). Peter Kareiva, Michelle Marvier, and Robert Lalaz, "Conservation in the Anthropocene: Beyond Solitude and Fragility," in *Love Your Monsters: Postenvironmentalism and the Anthropocene,* ed. Michael Shellenberger and Ted Nordhaus (Oakland, CA: The Breakthrough Institute, 2011), 26.

50. "'Old Greens Versus New'—E. O. Wilson & APR President Sean Gerrity at the Aspen Environment Forum," American Prairie Reserve, June 22, 2012, http://www.americanprairie.org/news/sean-gerrity-a-aspen-environmental-forum/. Andrew Revkin, "Emma Marris: In Defense of Everglades Pythons," Dot Earth (blog), *New York Times,* August 17, 2012, http://dotearth.blogs.nytimes.com/2012/08/17/emma-marris-in-defense-of-everglades-pythons/?_r=0. Emma Marris, *Rambunctious Garden: Saving Nature in a Post-Wild World* (New York: Bloomsbury, 2011).

51. Purdy, "Our Place in the World," 860; Purdy, "Politics of Nature," 1196.

52. Bill McKibben, *Wandering Home* (New York: Crown Journeys, 2005), 100.

53. "Benign mastery" is Jedediah Purdy's phrase, growing from a conversation that we had on this issue at the Colorado/Duke Climate Change, Energy, and Environment Works-in-Progress Symposium on August 7, 2014, in Boulder, CO.

54. Purdy, "Politics of Nature," 1199–1200.

55. McPhee, *Encounters with the Archdruid,* 241.

56. Paul Shepard, "Introduction: Ecology and Man—A Viewpoint," in *The Subversive Science: Essays Toward an Ecology of Man,* ed. Paul Shepard and Daniel McKinley (Boston: Houghton Mifflin Co., 1969), 5.

57. Kysar, "Consultants' Republic," 2079, quoting A. Dan Tarlock, "Is There a There There in Environmental Law?" *Journal of Land Use* 19, no. 2 (2004), 223.

58. See Richard J. Lazarus, "Environmental Law at the Crossroads: Looking Back 25, Looking Forward 25," *Michigan Journal of Environmental and Administrative Law* 2, no. 2 (2013): 267.

Index

Marx, Karl, 140

Massachusetts v. EPA: affirmation of in
other cases, 68–71; appeals court ruling
in, 62, 164; atomistic model and,
226–227; decision in, chipped away at,
69–70; deference to agencies' legal
interpretations and, 64–65; dissents in,
67–68, 166–167, 168, 226, 227;
ecological model and, 228; environmentalism versus dominant culture and, 78;
environmentalist poles and center and,
281–282; environmental urgency and,
278; events leading to, 60; factors
influencing Supreme Court in, 65–66;
as first Supreme Court case on climate
change, 59; interdependence and,
164–169; IPCC reports and, 59; judicial
reviewability and, 65–66; judiciary versus
legislature in public policy, 77; legacy of,
70–71; legal principles versus justices'
values and, 66; meaning of pollution and,
125–126; origins of case and, 61–63;
petitioners' strategy in, 62; plaintiff in,
167; precautionary approach and, 25;
public opinion on climate change and,
59–60; revival of Court's enthusiasm for
environmentalism, 164; science, opinion,
and law in, 59–61; *SCRAP* case and, 164,
167, 169; separation of powers and,
65–66; standing in, 63–64, 164–169; state
exceptionalism and, 167; Supreme Court's
decision in, 63–67, 165–166; Supreme
Court's response to environmentalist
tenets and, 58, 158, 167, 169; as
transformative case, 277; as victory for
environmentalists, 167, 270–272

mastery: atomistic model and, 269;
autonomy and, 142; benign, 297; Cape
Wind project and, 293–294; ecological
model versus, 192; *Entergy* case and, 138;
federalism and, 174, 180; versus
interdependence, 168, 226; in interpretive
guide to cases, 48; limitation of jurisdictional landscape and, 194; *Lyng* case and,
101; mastery-harmony value dimension
and, 13–15, 101, 138; material progress
and, 238; *Overton Park* case and, 52;
private property and, 200, 202, 215;
Rapanos case and, 188; reconsideration
of, 292–295; *SWANCC* case and,
181–182, 188; upending of narrative of,
22

MA v. EPA. See Massachusetts v. EPA

McCall, Nellie, 288

McCloskey, Michael, 5, 82–84
McConnell, Michael, 172
McCright, Aaron, 6–7
McKibben, Bill, 10, 17, 20, 293–294, 297
McPhee, John, 15, 23
Merrill, Thomas, 113, 185
Methow case. See *Robertson v. Methow
Valley Citizens Council*
Meyer, Jeff, 155
Midland case, 244, 245
Migratory Bird Rule, 181–185
Milbrath, Lester, 7, 10
Milkey, James, 62, 165, 167
Millian, John, 279
Monsanto case. See *Monsanto v. Geertson
Seed Farms*
Monsanto v. Geertson Seed Farms, 264–265
moral foundations theory, 9, 67
More, Thomas, 97, 99
Morrison case. See *United States v. Morrison*
Moynihan, Daniel, 74
Mugler case. See *Mugler v. Kansas*
Mugler v. Kansas, 203, 204–205, 207–208,
210, 212, 214
Muir, John, 4, 11, 22, 82, 119–120, 173
Muskie, Edmund, 28, 134

NAAQS (national ambient air quality
standards). *See* air quality standards
NAHB case. See *National Association of
Homebuilders v. Defenders of Wildlife*
*Named Members of San Antonio Conserva-
tion Society v. Texas Highway Depart-
ment*, 237, 242, 266
NAS. *See* National Academy of Sciences
(NAS)
National Academy of Sciences (NAS), 61,
62, 64
*National Association of Homebuilders
v. Babbitt*, 173–174, 175
*National Association of Homebuilders
v. Defenders of Wildlife*, 98–99, 108, 269
National Audubon Society. *See* Audubon
Society
National Environmental Policy Act (NEPA):
achievements and shortcomings of,
265; *Calvert Cliffs* case and, 236–239,
255–257, 260–261, 265–266; cautionary
thrust of, 264–265; deference to agencies
and, 260–261; *DOT* case and, 257–260;
eclipse of in Supreme Court, 232–234,
236, 243, 249, 265–266, 270; in environmental canon, 31; *Flint Ridge* case and,
256, 258; futility of, 254; hard look